SPIRITUAL GRAMMAR

Comparative Theology: Thinking Across Traditions / *Loye Ashton and John Thatamanil, series editors*

This series invites books that engage in constructive comparative theological reflection that draws from the resources of more than one religious tradition. It offers a venue for constructive thinkers, from a variety of religious traditions (or thinkers belonging to more than one), who seek to advance theology understood as "deep learning" across religious traditions.

SPIRITUAL GRAMMAR

Genre and the Saintly Subject in Islam and Christianity

F. DOMINIC LONGO

Fordham University Press NEW YORK 2017

Fordham University Press also publishes its books in a variety of electronic formats. Some content that appears in print may not be available in electronic books.

Visit us online at www.fordhampress.com.

Library of Congress Cataloging-in-Publication
Data available online at http://catalog.loc.gov.

Printed in the United States of America
19 18 17 5 4 3 2 1

First edition

For Kathleen M. Quinn,
who more than anyone
taught me the grammar of hearts

CONTENTS

ABBREVIATIONS

Du Pin	Jean Gerson, *Opera omnia*, ed. Louis Ellis du Pin (Hildesheim and New York: Olms, 1987).
DM	*Moralized Grammar*, in Jean Gerson, *Opera omnia*, vol. 4, ed. Louis Ellis Du Pin (Antwerp: 1706; repr. Hildesheim and New York: Olms, 1987).
NQ	*Naḥw al-qulūb al-kabīr* [The Grammar of Hearts], by ʿAbd al-Karīm al-Qushayrī, ed. Ibrāhīm Basyūnī and Aḥmad ʿAlam al-Dīn al-Jundī (al-Qāhirah [Cairo]: Maktabat ʿAlam al-Fikr, 1994).
Risāla	*Al-Risāla al-Qushayrīyah fī ʿilm al-taṣawwuf*, by ʿAbd al-Karīm al-Qushayrī, ed. Muḥammad ʿAbd al-Raḥmān al-Marʿashlī (Beirut: Dār Iḥyā al-Turāth al-ʿArabī: Muʿassasat al-Tarīkh al-ʿArabī, 1998).

PREFACE

The structure of this book is designed to give readers what they need in order to make sense of two strange and intriguing texts composed by creative writers who were great scholars, devoted teachers, and spiritual guides eager to help seekers as they journeyed toward God. Hoping to reach readers who are keenly interested in the practice of comparative theology, language and its ultimate significance, spirituality and its history, medieval religious culture and its texts, plus literary theory and its applicability to theology, I have assumed no particular expertise or background. I hope equally to entice students of Islamic thought to read about Gerson and enter his world as to entice students of Christian thought to read about Qushayrī and enter his world.

The introductory chapter poses the question at the heart of this inquiry, namely, the theological significance of the queer literary genre of Qushayrī's *Grammar of Hearts* and Gerson's *Moralized Grammar*. Thematizing "spiritual grammar," the Introduction contrasts this hybrid genre with other writings that intermix the spiritual and the grammatical or the religious and the linguistic. It is here that I first begin developing a description of spiritual grammar as a genre based on the metaphor of the self embedded in the grammatical structures of spiritual reality. Through their distinctive *mélange* of grammatical and religious genres, spiritual grammar blatantly violates what Derrida calls "the law of genre." The non-invisibility of the genre of such texts makes their stage unmissable, their performance unmistakable, and calls into question the genres of theology and the genders of Christian and Muslim believers—frames of knowledge and being that are commonly transparent and invisible. In this way, the genre of "spiritual grammar" creates a space for the reader to become a certain kind of person, in a certain kind of world.

Chapter 1 offers the most detailed comparison to date of the medieval Arab Islamic and Latin Christian diglossic sociolinguistic situations, where grammar was inextricable from education and religion, and where Arabic *fuṣḥā* and Latin were both "father tongues" holding considerable prestige and power. In both Qushayrī's eleventh-century Persia and Gerson's fifteenth-century France, a vernacular mother tongue was on the historical verge of challenging the societal "father tongue" for dominance in literary and intellectual realms. The two medieval masters both used the power of the "father languages" of Arabic and Latin to give force to their spiritual grammars as part of a pedagogical project akin to what Michel Foucault would call forming the self and constructing the subject.

Chapter 2 demonstrates how Jean Gerson used a number of genres to engender saintly subjectivities. His texts are different kinds of genre performances coming out of his various positions as university professor, master of theology, preacher, and speaker in the public sphere. The sermon, which was the central genre of religious literature in the medieval West, and the tract, a new genre in early-fifteenth-century French society, provide specific examples of Gerson's adaptive versatility as a writer and theologian. In his *Sermon Against Gluttony*, Gerson donned the illustrious gown of the University master and preached in the "father tongue." In his French sermon, *Videmus nunc*, Gerson put on the robe of the parish priest and evangelized in the mother tongue. In his tract *De pollutione nocturna*, Gerson used an innovative, streamlined genre to write in the voice of a "sexual theologian," addressing a pressing moral question for clerics of his day.

Chapter 3 is a primer in "spiritual grammar." Here I perform a close reading of Gerson's *Moralized Grammar (Donatus moralizatus)*. This theological and literary exposition initiates the reader into how this unusual text's hybrid genre works. With appreciation of the author's pastoral agenda and the theological content of the text, this interpretation of *Moralized Grammar* illuminates the considerable skill involved in transforming into a sermonic moral catechism the grammatical primer written by Aelius Donatus (fl. 350 C.E.), which was foundational to education for 1,000 years in the West. This chapter argues that in *Moralized Grammar* Gerson accomplished a feat of literary creativity for the purpose of crafting a synopsis of the Christian moral and spiritual life that would have been extraordinarily memorable for the growing class of literate Christians of his time.

As chapter 2 did for Gerson, chapter 4 examines the use of literary genre by Qushayrī. The theme of *dhikr*—that is, the ritual recitation of the names of God—provides a red thread to trace throughout a range of genres where the intersection of spiritual and linguistic concerns is particularly evident in Qushayrī's thought. This chapter examines his *Risāla*, which is Qushayrī's most well-known work and the handbook used for centuries to introduce students to Sufism; *Laṭā'if al-ishārāt*, his work of Qur'anic exegesis; *Sharḥ asmā' Allāh al-ḥusnā*, his commentary on the names of God; and a work of Qushayrī's on spiritual direction, *Tartīb al-sulūk fī ṭarīq Allāh*. Besides analyzing how Qushayrī made use of genre in the Sufi literature he produced, this chapter provides familiarity with Qushayrī's scholarly concerns, historical milieu, and authorial character so as to prepare for a close reading of *The Grammar of Hearts*.

Chapter 5 explains how to read Qushayrī's *Naḥw al-qulūb (Grammar of Hearts)* through providing a textual analysis of 20 of the 60 sections in the text, including background ideas necessary for understanding this "spiritual grammar." Qushayrī, like Gerson, takes as his starting point an assumption of his reader's familiarity with the discipline of grammar. As such, he does not dwell on linguistic niceties or details, for they are not his concern. He rather invokes grammatical terms, concepts, and phenomena familiar to his reader in order to proceed to spiritual matters. Like the foundational grammatical text of the Arabic linguistic tradition, Sībawayhi's famous *Kitāb*, Qushayrī's *Grammar of Hearts* combines prescriptive and descriptive grammar for the purpose of developing Sufi "grammatical competence" among his readers. Ever the *shaykh* in both pedagogical and spiritual senses of the term, Qushayrī is "spiritually *faṣīḥ*" and wants his students to become similarly adept in the grammar of ultimate reality.

The final chapter undertakes a comparative literary and theological analysis of Qushayrī's and Gerson's text to make possible a fuller description of spiritual grammar as a genre, which in turn begins the construction of a theology of grammar. Like actual grammar instructors, Qushayrī and Gerson hoped to teach students about the spiritual realities in which they were already deeply and inescapably situated. Grammar enables us to see, understand, and operate in the reality in which we live. In adopting an ontological frame that depicts the subject as embedded in a reality that is linguistic and structured by grammar, spiritual grammars model what Paul Ricoeur describes as the relationship between textuality and subjectivity that holds for all texts. The Islamic and Christian spiritual grammars of Qushayrī and Gerson can help contemporary readers who are trying to find their own way to becoming spiritually adept in the structures of ultimate reality.

While this sequence of chapters constructs a path for comparative theological back-and-forth reading of *Moralized Grammar* and *The Grammar of Hearts*, readers might usefully pick and choose among the chapters for specific purposes. Readers who are interested most of all in learning about Gerson and in finding a survey of some of his writings may like to go straight to chapter 2. Others whose interest focuses on Qushayrī and his writings might start with chapter 4. Those who are most of all interested in the Latin and Arabic languages and the history of grammar as a subject of study in medieval Christian and Islamic cultures can read chapter 1 on its own. Readers of Latin or of Arabic will find chapters 3 and 5, respectively, to be helpful guides to studying the actual untranslated versions of Gerson's and Qushayrī's spiritual grammars. Readers studying religion or theology could read the Introduction and chapter 6 to gain an understanding of the genre of spiritual grammar without delving into the particularities specific to Gerson, Qushayrī, and their texts. Indeed, one could profitably read chapter 6 on its own for a taste of the two primary sources, an illustration of how these two texts operate, an explication of their significance, and the beginning of a constructive theological interpretation of spiritual grammar for today.

Writing *Spiritual Grammar* has been a journey of learning, exploring, and growing for me. My gratitude to those who have helped and accompanied me along this path continues to grow.

Since I embarked on this journey, many of my principal guides have themselves passed beyond—my beloved parents and grandparents, several wise avuncular friends, and my greatly admired *Doktorvater.* As these wayfarers have reached the great beyond and passed out of my life, I have often reflected on the saying *When the student is ready, the teacher appears.* Of late, I have far too often had the occasion to wonder, *What happens when the teachers disappear?*

T. Frank Kennedy, SJ, and Art Shirk in particular have in the last year taught me what it looks like to die well—the last, but not the least, of the wisdom they modeled for me and many others.

This comparative theological study is the fruit of a great deal of mentoring. In particular, the intellectual communities of Boston College and Harvard University formed and nourished and refreshed me along the journey of reading Qushayrī and Gerson. In those two academic villages, I found both friends and guides.

Those who taught me to read in new languages and new ways have played an especially significant role in my development and for that deserve my heartfelt thanks: Wolfhart Heinrichs in classical Arabic and Islamic thought; Frank Clooney, SJ, in comparative theology; Francis Schüssler-Fiorenza in hermeneutics; Ahmad Mahdavi Damghani in Sufi literature; Beverly Kienzle in medieval Latin and especially sermons; Kevin Newmark in literary theory and French literature; Leila Ahmed in gender studies; Lisa Cahill in classics of Christian theology; Michael Connolly and Stephen Pinker in the structures of language; James Bernauer, SJ, in Foucault; Mark Jordan in queer theology; Sarah Coakley in Christian mystical theology; Amy Hollywood in Derrida; Mark Haynes, Mark Niemann, SJ, and Ted Ahern in Latin language and Roman literature; Khaled El-Rouayheb in Islamic theology; Mark O'Connor, and Dayton Haskin in the "great books"; Joe Appleyard, SJ, in postmodern thought; Sue Stein in British literature (and writing and so much more); T. Frank Kennedy, SJ, and Jeremiah McGrann in Western music; Michael Resler in German; Chas Kestermeier, SJ, Lynne Bacon, Terry Brennan, SJ, and Stephen Bold in French; Hakan Karateke and Selim Kuru in Turkish; David Gill, SJ, in ancient Greek; Zahava Carpenter in Hebrew and kindness; David Neuhaus, SJ, and Ray Helmick, SJ, in interreligious dialogue and the ways of Jerusalem; John Heineman in European history; Patrizia Rodomonti and Chiara Curtoni in Italian; Mona Mourshed in educational systems; David Hollenbach, SJ, in the impact of theology in the world; and Cecilia Sierra, William Sidhom, SJ, Ryszard Wtorek, SJ, Paul Heck, and Magdi Seif Aziz, SJ, in living as Christians in solidarity and love with Muslims.

Teachers at Dar Comboni and the American University in Cairo skillfully initiated me into the worlds of Arabic as I fell in love with the worlds of Egypt. I am especially grateful to Ashgan, Abbas al-Tonsi, Nadia Harb, and Heba Salem. Mahmoud Abdalla at Middlebury's Arabic School also made an especially significant contribution to my Arabic proficiency.

My teachers of spiritual grammar over the years have included Larry Gillick, SJ, Howard Gray, SJ, Dick Tomasek, SJ, Michael Buckley, SJ, Ted Bohr, SJ, Jim Keenan, SJ, and Rose Allocca, all in the Ignatian tradition, as well as Art Shirk, Sam House, Pat Carrington-House, Amy Elizabeth

Fox, Alexander Kuilman, Joanna Barsh, Johanne Lavoie, and many others from the worlds of coaching and leadership development.

Besides these many teachers and mentors, Bill Graham and Juan Miguel Marin have been exceedingly supportive of this project over many years—Bill by sharing generously of his encouragment, counsel, and advice, Juan by reading more iterations of this manuscript than anyone besides me (!) and always giving helpful suggestions. Michael Carter was exceedingly generous in sharing his expertise and erudition, especially when Wolfhart Heinrichs was no longer in this world to offer his guidance. Jan Ziolkowski and Ali Asani gave much-needed support and several surgical suggestions for improvement. Louis Pascoe, SJ, read the manuscript and gave both erudite comments and hearty affirmation. Francesco Chiabotti and Martin Nguyen have been companions in Qushayrī studies for many years now. Rebecca Manring was unstinting in sharing her knowledge of Sanskrit religious grammars. Cynthia Verba provided incisive criticism and crucial guidance at several critical moments of the gestation of this book. I am extremely grateful for all of this!

I am also very grateful for the inestimable friendship, companionship, care, and advice of Justin Goldblatt, Sarah Eltantawi, Omar Farahat, Karim Tartoussieh, Graeme Reid, Danny Bowles, Patrick Nolan and Clément Gaujal, Neil MacFarquhar, Ryan Millikan, Yaron Klein, Naseem Surhio, Ahmed Ragab, Soha Bayoumi, Khaled Fahmy, Hossam Bahgat, Amr Shalakany, Martin Nguyen, Nuri Friedlander, Charles Stang, Avigail Noy, Ramy Zaki, Hany Rizkallah, Leonard Wood, Michael Pettinger, Fenton Whelan, Luke Leafgren, Kelly Raths, Roxanne Brame, Eric Calderwood, Henning Kober, Bill Laird, Tricia Kult, David Loftus, Can Icöz, Ferhat Jak Icoz, Emre Hakgüder, Dan Finkbeiner, Ted Warin, Hicham Naimy, Kristin Fabbe, Namira Negm, Alexandre Stutzmann and Silvio Gonzato, Stephan van Erp, the "Magpies," and my most loving extended family, especially Carrie Palmesano, Mark McMillan, Marilyn Longo, and the entire Longo, Quinn, and McMillan clans.

Thanks go also to the Theology Department at the University of St. Thomas in Minnesota for giving me the opportunity to teach comparative theology and promote Muslim–Christian dialogue. The warm collegiality of this department has been a blessing.

The institutions that generously supported this project with funding and other resources include the Graduate School of Arts & Sciences, Divinity School, Widener Library, and Houghton Library at Harvard University; Butler Library at Columbia University and Bobst Library at

New York University, which were accessible to me through the New York Public Library Scholars program; O'Neill Library at Boston College; and the Staatsbibliothek zu Berlin. Without the Center for Arabic Study Abroad, funded by the U.S. Department of Education, and the Ford and Mellon foundations, my Arabic education would have been greatly impoverished. I am also particularly grateful to McKinsey and Company for its "Take Time" program, which allowed me to take a month off on several occasions to continue my work on this book.

I am very grateful for opportunities to speak about *Spiritual Grammar*, especially the invitations of the Prince Alwaleed Bin Talal Islamic Studies Program at Harvard University, the Philosophy Club at the University of St. Thomas, the Faculty of Theology and Religious Studies at KU Leuven, and the Heinz Bluhm lecture series at Boston College.

I thank Ethné Clarke for preparing the index, and Aldene Fredenburg for copy editing the manuscript. Both contributed to the precision and accuracy of this book on many counts.

Special thanks to Jim Keenan, SJ, who has been extraordinarily generous with his warm friendship, sage advice, admirable example, and scholarly encouragement, especially after reading this manuscript.

I further extend my warm gratitude to series editors Loye Ashton and John Thatamanil, and to Richard Morrison, Eric Newman, John Garza, and everyone at Fordham University Press who worked to bring this book into the world. Many thanks also to Catherine Cornille for her kindness, her mentoring, and for pointing me in the direction of Fordham University Press.

SPIRITUAL GRAMMAR

Introduction: Genre Trouble

QUEERING GRAMMAR FOR SPIRITUAL PURPOSES

Grammar is *al-naḥw*, "the way." We journey along "the way" today as wayfarers before us have done. "The way" gives us direction, even if we sometimes stray from it with missteps and slipups of various magnitudes. The two texts that are the focus of the present study are works that school readers in "the way." Their authors, both master wayfarers, hoped to make "the way" easier and clearer for those who followed. My study of their texts has led to the discovery of "spiritual grammar," a genre of religious literature that until now has not been recognized as such.

"Spiritual grammar" evokes the transcendent and the linguistic, the pedagogical and the divine, the depths of human being and our means of mundane communication. The theology of grammar may not seem pressing or urgent today, especially when the starting points are religious texts written hundreds of years ago. Yet, in what I am calling "spiritual grammar," the present study finds insights and wisdom about gender, the postmodern self, and Muslim-Christian understanding—issues that preoccupy many today. Spiritual grammar and the theology of grammar that is made possible through understanding it also offer teachings about texts, hermeneutics, literary genre, linguistic theory, the path to the divine, and other spiritual realities—issues no less important, though perhaps less common, preoccupations. The "way" opened up by this book into these various issues is both scholarly and spiritual, analytic and speculative, comparative and constructive, literary and theological. Like "spiritual grammar" itself, this study of it is hybrid on several levels.

The Grammar of Hearts, by the famous Sufi apologist ʿAbd al-Karīm al-Qushayrī (d. 1072), bears the trappings of a grammar manual. Called in Arabic *Naḥw al-qulūb*, it begins, "Grammar [*al-naḥw*] in language is the pursuit of correct speech. It is said, '*naḥawtu naḥwahu*' 'I went in his direction,' meaning, in other words, 'I pursued his way.' This sort of thing in Arabic is called grammar [a 'way'] because it is the pursuit of correct speech."[1] Students of traditional Arabic textbooks would have heard explanations like this one for why "grammar" in Arabic is called "*naḥw*," meaning "way."[2] However, our author, Qushayrī, is well-known in the Islamic tradition as author of another kind of manual or textbook.[3] His famous *Treatise*, called *al-Risāla al-qushayriyya* in Arabic, has been used for centuries to teach students the basics of Sufism, the Islamic mystical tradition.[4]

To begin reading a text by this famous religious expert and discover in it grammatical lessons is puzzling, provoking immediate questions as to his aims.

A polymath without doubt, Qushayrī is known to have worked in the Islamic science of discursive theology (*kalām*) and in *ḥadīth*, the study of traditions and sayings by and about the Prophet Muhammad and his companions. Teaching the intricacies of Arabic words and structures was not, however, one of Qushayrī's many scholarly activities, nor is it the purpose of *The Grammar of Hearts*, as becomes evident in the sentences that immediately follow those quoted previously. There Qushayrī uses the phrase for which this puzzling text is named: "But the grammar of the heart [*naḥw al-qalb*] is the pursuit of praiseworthy speech with the heart. Praiseworthy speech is talking to God with the tongue of the heart. Such talk is divided into calling out [*al-munādā*] and secret whisperings [*al-munājā*]." By so swiftly shifting to the subject of God and human intercourse with God and by using technical Sufi terminology ("*al-munādā*" and "*al-munājā*"), Qushayrī signals that *The Grammar of Hearts* is a Sufi text. Even so, the text remains puzzling and indeed very difficult to read. The correlation between the grammatical and the Sufi aspects of the book is not at all obvious, and none of the very few scholarly treatments of the text has offered an interpretation that resolves this enigma.

A certain Latin text, titled *Moralized Grammar*,[5] was written by another polymath, a Christian religious scholar.[6] Its author, Jean Gerson (d. 1429), specialized in the mystical life, like his Muslim predecessor Qushayrī had.[7] Chancellor of the University of Paris, renowned Catholic theologian, influential preacher to church councils, popes, kings, professors, students, and the laity, Gerson, like Qushayrī, was a versatile and gifted writer.[8] Though learned in Latin, even perhaps the greatest Latin stylist of his time, Gerson did not teach Latin grammar. Nonetheless, his *Moralized Grammar*, whose original Latin title was *Donatus moralizatus*, "moralizes" a well-known schoolbook commonly referred to for centuries as "Donatus," which is simply the name of the author of that schoolbook. The basic grammar handbook used for more than a thousand years to teach pupils Latin, the *Ars minor* made "Donatus" synonymous with "grammar."[9]

Gerson's text cites verbatim the fundamental questions and answers that structured this famous Latin primer by Aelius Donatus, who flourished around 350 C.E.[10] Exactly like Aelius Donatus's *Ars minor*, Gerson's *Moralized Grammar* begins with these words: "How many parts of speech are there? Eight. What are they?"[11] Like Qushayrī's *Grammar of Hearts*, Gerson's *Moralized Grammar* swiftly shifts from grammatical into religious discourse. Instead of answering this question with Donatus's expected answer listing noun, verb, preposition, and the other parts of speech, Gerson substitutes a different kind of response:

> Knowledge of substance, knowledge of the precepts of God, performance of the same, knowledge of the human being with regard to God and with regard to nature, consideration of the Judgment which is to be, consideration of the joys of the elect, and consideration of the sorrows of the damned.[12]

The swift shifts from the grammatical to the religious in Qushayrī's and Gerson's texts are strikingly similar indeed.

Within the contexts of the eleventh-century Islamic and the late fourteenth- or early fifteenth-century Christian worlds from which they respectively come, these two texts are unmistakably odd. For readers today they are disorienting. Engendered of the grammatical and the religious, these hybrids mix two kinds of discourse that we do not expect to commingle. Besides strange, the literary form of these religious texts is also profoundly suggestive. In both cases, the hybrid literary form chosen by the authors shapes the theological content. The genre highlights the possibility that, in the religious visions of the two authors, the structure of language has some special significance.

Illuminating the significance of the interplay between the grammatical and the religious in these two texts is the occasion for the present study. Put another way, the question at the heart of this inquiry regards the theological significance of the queer literary genre of these two texts.

By naming these medieval texts "queer," I begin to suggest that the two spiritual grammars are especially conducive to a queer theological approach. I think as much first of all because in crafting these texts,

Qushayrī and Gerson so courageously transgress boundaries and norms. Like queer theologians today, the two medieval authors incite, with these spiritual grammars, reflection on the construction and the performance of the self.[13] They traverse categories. In multiple ways, these spiritual grammars are in line with David Halperin's definition of queer as "by definition, whatever is at odds with the normal, the legitimate, the dominant. . . . [Queer] demarcates not a positivity but a positionality vis-à-vis the normative."[14] Moreover, like theology generally, the spiritual grammar of Qushayrī and Gerson "lives at the boundary between theory and practice, speculation and advocacy."[15]

The mere snippets from the two texts presented in the foregoing pages already make evident the disruption instigated by spiritual grammar from within the regulatory discipline of school grammar. This hybrid ruptures the standard package of the pedagogical handbook. It also interrupts "serious" speech, whether about religion or language.[16] Spiritual grammar is ironic. It twists unexpectedly from the grammatical to the spiritual and then back again.

Moreover, spiritual grammar casts as provisional the standard ways of human being. Desiring God, the spiritual aspirant transgresses normative boundaries for how to operate. Indeed, each in its own way, the queer and the Christian and the Muslim all hold "hope for a new creation and a life-beyond death" and "an obsolescence and a provisionality for existing regulatory identities."[17] Spiritual grammar reveals the obsolescence of familiar, "generic" molds for Muslim and Christian subjects. Breaking in a single blow the standard molds for literary genre and the staid shapes for the religious self, spiritual grammar brings forth transcendent possibilities, elevated paths, and "ways" that lead to the divine.

While neither Qushayrī nor Gerson thematizes femininity or masculinity in *The Grammar of Hearts* or *Moralized Grammar*, these spiritual masters do explore in these texts the molds and masks, paths and possibilities for being human in the world. Through this exploration, the spiritual grammars create for us opportunities to transform our understanding of gender. The genre performances of spiritual grammar call into question the often unquestioned frames of knowledge and being that are commonly transparent and invisible—namely, the genres of theology and the genders of Christian and Muslim believers.

Spiritual grammar interrupts typical religious discourse and subverts grammatical discipline. Queering grammar for religious purposes, spiritual grammar ruptures the identities of stable literary genres and generic human genders produced by regulatory regimes.[18] It crosses the limits of the *genus*, the generic mold and mask.[19] Spiritual grammar thus elicits a "hope for a new creation," a mystical self that traverses boundaries to God.

Queer theology and queer theory will thus be among the resources we use in interpreting *The Grammar of Hearts*, *Moralized Grammar*, and their nonconforming genre. This risks anachronism, as many others have noted of approaching medieval texts with consciousness of queer theory or gender theory.[20] Simon Gaunt, in his *Gender and Genre in Medieval French Literature*, found that, contrary to perceptions today that belie our own heteronormativity, the medieval texts he studied "do not in practice treat gender as a rigid, immutable, or 'natural' phenomenon."[21] Indeed, "Without having a theory of gender, the texts themselves theorize gender through their own practice."[22]

Qushayrī's *Grammar of Hearts* and Gerson's *Moralized Grammar* are not theoretical works, much less contributions, on their own, to gender theory or queer theory. They are, however, queer texts, running askew and athwart standard religious categories and normative literary models.

The Genre of "Spiritual Grammar"

There is no evidence that Gerson had any knowledge of Qushayrī or his writings. Gerson was Catholic Christian, a French speaker writing in Latin, a professor of theology, a renowned preacher, and the chancellor of the University of Paris. Qushayrī was Sunni Muslim, a Persian speaker writing in Arabic, an Ashʿarī theologian, and a Sufi spiritual master in the city of Nishapur.[23] Despite all their differences, the two religious experts were both schooled in grammar, though were not by any means specialists in this intellectual discipline that enjoyed such enormous intellectual centrality in the authors' respective contexts. In composing *The Grammar of Hearts* and *Moralized Grammar*, the religious scholars drew on the science of grammar for technical terminology and linguistic phenomena familiar to their literate contemporaries. This turn to grammar served them equally well. In these two texts, Qushayrī and Gerson both used grammatical terms and concepts to express deep religious truths in a fresh and accessible way. They composed creative texts based on the possibility that spiritual truths in grammatical language and form could somehow be worth engendering. This commonality is the grounds for studying the two texts together.

Qushayrī's *Grammar of Hearts* and Gerson's *Moralized Grammar* are so similar in such distinctive ways that we must recognize them as two instances of the same genre of cross-breeding. The authors both bred texts that show the marks of miscegenation between a kind of grammar schoolbook and religious instruction. I call this genre of literary production "spiritual grammar." Indeed, central to this study is the claim that the best way to understand these two texts is to recognize them as belonging to this genre of religious writing.

Since I am coining a term and claiming to discover spiritual grammar as a genre of religious literature, let me state plainly how I mean these two words. "Spiritual" I mean in the following sense: "Of or pertaining to, affecting or concerning the spirit or higher moral qualities, esp. as regarded in a religious aspect."[24] "Spiritual" regards the states of the soul and its moral development on a horizon beyond the space-time universe here and now. I emphasize the distinction between the temporal and the spiritual. By "grammar" I mean both the structures of a language and the scholarly discourse that aims to describe those structures. Such discourse is familiar to schoolchildren and other beginners who learn the so-called "proper" usage of a "standard" language. At the same time grammatical discourse encompasses the scholarly work of highly specialized experts who conduct field research, formulate descriptive rules, and inquire into the intricacies of language. Today this kind of scholarly work makes part of the discipline called "linguistics."

The primary mark of the genre of spiritual grammar is the metaphor of the self embedded in the grammatical structures of spiritual reality. In this genre of religious literature, the metaphor of grammar encompasses two senses of grammar—namely, the actual structures of spiritual reality and the descriptions of those realities.

In the grammar of language, teachers formulate grammatical rules (for example, "To make a noun plural, add an /s/ sound") and paradigms (like "I run, you run, he runs . . .") for the purposes of describing to students the structures of a specific language and instructing them how to conduct themselves appropriately in that language. The discipline of grammar thus consists of more or less expert descriptions of how language works plus prescriptions for how we are to use language felicitously. Again, "grammar" refers not only to descriptions and prescriptions, but also to the actual structure of language apart from any scholarly endeavor. Human languages have grammar—in other words, they have structures—whether or not any scholar consciously notices or adequately describes them.

Likewise, religious teachings are constructs made by religious experts and authorities for the purposes of describing the structures of spiritual reality (for instance, "Muhammad is the messenger of God"; "Jesus Christ is the Son of God") and teaching people to conduct themselves appropriately in that reality (as in "Thou shall not commit adultery"). In the cases of both language and spiritual reality, the actual structures of the realities in question can be mysterious and difficult to grasp, and thus scholarly descriptions and prescriptions are typically imperfect.

In spiritual grammar, the fundamental metaphorical scheme, which likens grammar to the structures of the spiritual reality in which we are embedded, creates a complementary scheme of metaphors that liken language to spiritual reality itself. The linguistic metaphors for spiritual reality pertain to the ultimate reality of God, the really real, and they also pertain to all else in relation to God. What we are calling "spiritual reality," which Qushayrī and Gerson describe, encompasses the created world but is not limited to it. It is the here and the hereafter, the human and the divine, the created and the uncreated, the finite and the infinite. The "grammar" of this spiritual reality is the structure of how all these elements fit together.

Beyond these metaphorical schemes around language, grammar, spiritual reality, and its structure, a second defining mark of the genre of spiritual grammar is that its purpose is the religious advancement and spiritual development of its readers. Defined by the mark of this metaphor of the self embedded in the structure of spiritual reality, the genre of spiritual grammar aims primarily to engender saintly subjects. Spiritual grammars mean to achieve spiritual effects.

Consider this evocative sentence written by twentieth-century Catholic theologian Karl Rahner: "God establishes creatures by his creative power insofar as he establishes them from out of nothing in their own non-divine reality as the *grammar of God's possible self-expression*."[25] This is not an attempt on Rahner's part to say anything serious about grammar. His focus is rather on the relationship between God and creation. The word "grammar" appears in the sentence as part of a brilliant metaphor that corresponds to multiple elements of the theology that Rahner develops, including the central importance of his understanding of God's self-expression and the Word of God, Jesus Christ, as the highpoint of that divine revelation in and through human nature. The pedagogical effect of this momentary appearance of "spiritual grammar" in Rahner is that readers consider themselves as integral to the reality wherein God's self-expression is possible.

Other philosophers and theologians, from Augustine and Bhartṛhari to Derrida and Ricoeur, take up explicit discussions of actual linguistic and grammatical issues and integrate these issues with discussion of religion or ultimate reality. *Moralized Grammar* and *The Grammar of Hearts*, on the other hand, are like Rahner's trope. Neither Gerson nor Qushayrī means to teach anything about Latin or Arabic or the grammar of these languages. Instead, they spin metaphors. They trope grammar and language for religious purposes. Gerson and Qushayrī use grammar and the literary form of the grammar book as an extended trope. In that sense, their spiritual grammars are built around a specific type of wordplay, a grammatical ruse with serious religious purposes. There is a tongue-in-cheek aspect to both of their texts. Tropes, too, however, have their meanings. Though the authors were not "serious" about saying anything about language or grammar, the meanings of the extended trope need exploration and serious inquiry.[26] In interpreting their metaphors, we as readers must reflect on the theological implications of their irony, their puns and play, their "troping."[27]

Situating Spiritual Grammar

In order to situate the genre of spiritual grammar more clearly within the context of religious literature, a brief consideration of other writings that intermix the spiritual and the grammatical or the religious and the linguistic will be helpful. Though the two examples of spiritual grammar that are our focus strike us as strange, in fact over the ages philosophers and theologians and intellectuals of many kinds have turned to grammar and other sorts of discourse about language as they searched for meaning and contemplated questions of ultimate reality. Surveying the religious, theological, and philosophical writings that thematize language or grammar, we cast our eyes at an extremely wide range of discourse, which we might associate with spiritual grammar. The very term "spiritual grammar" might be modified to "religious grammar" or "mystical grammar." Religious, spiritual, mystical, and theological discourse on grammar and grammatical discourse on religious, spiritual, mystical, or theological topics are all not so far afield from each other. Philosophical discourse on language and grammar similarly overlaps with these areas of discourse. Thematizations of religious language itself, of mystic speech, and of the language of theology likewise cannot be set aside as unrelated to spiritual grammar. Grammatical metaphors and linguistic illustrations in the service of religious and theological goals are also closely related to our main topic. The potential bibliography of these interrelated and overlapping themes, fields, and discourses is vast, especially as we expand our inquiry across boundaries of religious tradition, language, culture, and historical era. Even a provisional sketch of the contours and interrelations of these fields where grammar and language meet theology and religion is beyond the scope of this study.

Just a few examples will lay a groundwork and at least intimate how far and wide such a sketch could go. Within Christian discourse an obvious starting point is the very beginning of John's Gospel: "In the beginning was the Word." For Western thought, the philosophical and theological influence of these few words has been extraordinary. Besides any exegetical exploration into the Prologue of John's Gospel, Christian reflection on creation, revelation, Christology, trinitarian theology, preaching and evangelization cannot pass over Jesus Christ as Word of God. Moreover, since the original Greek term translated here as "Word" is "*logos*," which also means "discourse" and "reason," these theological topics are profoundly correlated to ancient Greek philosophy, where *logos* is a key concept for Plato and others. To name just three major theologians whose reflection on "the Word" has been extremely significant, Augustine of Hippo (in proposing the different senses of Scripture in *De doctrina christiana*), Karl Barth (in his theology of the Word encompassing, among other aspects of Christian thought and life, evangelization and Christology), and Bonaventure (with his theology of the threefold Word) have all written classic works derived in some part from reflection on this theme.

Indian traditions are particularly rich in treating religious and grammatical or linguistic issues together. Bhartṛhari (fl. c. 450–500 C.E.) is one particularly important figure in Indian thought where these issues are profoundly interrelated.[28] The first few verses of the *Brahmakāṇḍa* or "section on Brahman" of his major work on grammar and language, the *Vākyapadīya*, which in English could be called "a treatise on the sentence and the word,"[29] illustrate this profound interrelation:

> Brahman, the True Word, which is without beginning or end, which is the imperishable Syllable, manifests itself in the form of objects; from it the production of the world [proceeds]. (1) Although it is proclaimed to be one, it is divided through having recourse to its powers. Although it is not different from its powers, it exists as if it were different from them. (2) The six transformations of beings, beginning with birth, which are the source of the differentiation of beings, are dependent upon its power of time, to which parts have been attributed. (3) Of that One, which is the seed of all things, there is this state of multiplicity, having the form of the enjoyer, the object to be enjoyed, and the enjoyment. (4)[30]

David Carpenter's comparative study of St. Bonaventure and Bhartṛhari and their theories of revelation provides in-depth and sophisticated considerations of both authors' writings as well as a sensitive comparison that is a model for the present study. A specialist in Sanskrit grammar himself, "Bhartṛhari was to examine the problem of revelation from the point of view of the language of revelation *as language*, which was for him both a form of *dharma*, the socio-cosmic order of the Brahmanical universe, and a self-manifestation of ultimate Reality that underlay that universe, Brahman."[31] Bhartṛhari's expertise in grammar and his profoundly religious concerns make for a detailed and explicit inquiry into issues of Ultimate Reality by means of grammar.

> There is, therefore, an impressive fit between Bhartṛhari's general ontology and his analysis of language. This should not be surprising, in the light of his avowal, along with his tradition, that the manifest universe is a transformation of the Word. But what is impressive is that Bhartṛhari does not leave this traditional belief at the level of a mere assertion but explicates it through the minutiae of his grammatical analysis, which shows at the level of specific morphology and syntax that language and action are two sides of a single reality, or, more precisely, that they together make manifest the dynamic potential of that Reality.[32]

Carpenter's study of Bhartṛhari's profoundly grammatical discourse on metaphysical and religious issues makes evident and accessible an example in religious literature of explicit integration of grammar and theology in one discourse.[33]

A different kind of Indian religious grammar is exemplified by *Harināmāmṛta-vyākaraṇam*, called in English *The Grammar of the Nectar of the Names of Hari*, of Jīva Gosvāmī (d. 1608). Rebecca J. Manring explains that Jīva Gosvāmī wrote this *Grammar of the Nectar of the Names of Hari* in order to teach the Sanskrit language to his fellow Gauḍīya Vaiṣṇavas, while not diverting them from their practice of praising Lord Kṛṣṇa.[34]

> [Jīva] realized that in order to understand the theological texts that he and his uncles had written, in Sanskrit, Gauḍīyas needed to know how Sanskrit works. But Jīva did not want them to have to give up their primary practices while suffering through memorizing endless paradigms. . . . So he produced his own pedagogical grammar. Since Vaiṣṇavas are enjoined to keep Kṛṣṇa's name on their lips, he needed a dual purpose grammar: one that would (i) teach Sanskrit, while allowing devotees to (ii) constantly recite the Name.[35]

In the universe of writings where religion and grammar intersect, Bhartṛhari's *Vākyapadīya* is a paradigm for complete integration of theological and grammatical discourse, while Jīva's sectarian grammar illustrates another extreme, where actually teaching grammar is the central purpose. His *Hari-nāmāmṛta-vyākaraṇam* is in that sense much closer to nonreligious pedagogical grammar books. As we shall see, Gerson's *Moralized Grammar* and Qushayrī's *The Grammar of Hearts* are at the opposite extreme in that they have no grammatical goal *per se*. Neither text aims at teaching the student anything grammatical about Latin or Arabic. The goals of these texts are rather almost completely religious.

In Islamic thought, this field encompasses many areas within medieval Arabic grammatical theory and Qu'ran studies. Two topics in which religious and linguistic material are especially profoundly interwoven are the institution or origin of language (*waḍʿ al-lugha*) and the inimitability of the Qur'an (*iʿjāz al-qurʾān*). The science of *uṣūl al-fiqh*, Islamic jurisprudence, is particularly linguistic in its concerns and treats such issues. For example, Fakhr al-Dīn al-Rāzī discusses the institution of language in his *Al-Maḥṣūl fī ʿilm uṣūl al-fiqh*.[36] As another example, in the *Comprehensive Treatise* ascribed to al-Ḥakīm al-Majrīṭī, the existence of different languages is treated.[37] The influence of Qushayrī's *Grammar of Hearts* on Sufis after him is apparently considerable and could be linked to a number of spiritual grammatical writings down to the twentieth century. For example, several Sufi commentaries on an elementary pedagogical grammatical text known as the *Ājurrūmiyya* are known.[38] This extremely concise treatise by Ibn Ājurrūm (d. 723/1323) treating the Arabic system of *iʿrāb* or inflection has been a very popular text, one memorized by students across the Arab world for centuries.[39] By one account, some sixty commentaries on *Al-Muqaddima al-Ājurrūmiyya* exist, several of them by Sufis. Michael Carter has studied one of these,[40] that by the well-known Sufi Ibn Maymūn (d. 917/1511), entitled *Al-Risāla al-Maymūniyya fī Tawḥīd al-ʾĀğurrūmiyya.*[41] Carter's article also mentions a text called *The Grammar of Hearts* by Ibn ʿArrāq (Syrian, d. 1526).[42] Francesco Chiabotti points to evidence of Qushayrī's influence on the Algerian Sufi master Aḥmad b. ʿAlāwa, who speaks of "the reform of language" (*iṣlāḥ al-lisān*) and "the reform of hearts" (*iṣlāh al-qulūb*), at the beginning of the twentieth century.[43]

This very brief illustration of where discourse on grammar and language meets theology and religion might seem a tour of the exotic. Spiritual grammar, after all, had not before now been recognized as a genre of writing. For our purposes, it bears noting that theology is a mode of inquiry that always needs some other academic discipline to mediate its theoretical exploration and explication of revelation. Contemporary theologian Graham Ward's illustration of this point cites Thomas Aquinas's justification for why theology is dependent on other disciplines:

> Theology's business has always been the transgression of boundaries. It is a discourse which requires other discourses for its very possibility. In article five of the opening *quaestio* of the *Summa Theologiae*, Aquinas observes the way the science of theology has to make use of the other sciences: "That it uses them is not due to its own defect or insufficiency, but to the defect of our intelligence, which is more easily led by what is known through natural reason (from which proceed the other sciences), to that which is above reason."[44]

The discipline that mainstream, orthodox Western Christian theology has most often used for this mediating purpose is philosophy and, more specifically, metaphysics. "Traditionally in the West, philosophy has provided theology not only with a theoretical framework of interpretation but also with a particular kind of questioning."[45] In a Catholic context, the normative position of Aquinas's theology using Aristotelian philosophy epitomizes the hegemony of this disciplinary alliance. More broadly, many Christian and Muslim theologians over the ages have made much of Plato's and Aristotle's attempts at wrestling with the meaning of being.

Recently, more subversive theologians have used disciplines besides philosophy as a mediating discipline. Drawing attention to the monocular effects of relying solely on the philosophy of white European men and their models of rationality, contemporary theologians concerned with issues of justice have challenged the monopoly of philosophy in mediating theological discourse. Gustavo Gutiérrez, for example, used economics and politics as mediating sciences in initiating liberation theology from a particularly Latino perspective.[46] Queer theologians, such as Marcella Althaus-Reid, use queer theory as a mediating science in theologizing from the margins of heteronormativity.[47] Like these contemporary examples, the religious writings surveyed in the preceding pages do not use philosophy as their mediating discipline. Instead they transgress standard disciplinary boundaries and use grammar and other language sciences as mediating disciplines for theologizing.

The "Genre" of Spiritual Grammar

Whether or not considered within the broader context of religious literature that deals with language or grammar, the genre of *Moralized Grammar* and *The Grammar of Hearts* is problematic. Passages such as this one from *The Grammar of Hearts* are difficult to construe—even destabilizing and troubling.

> The noun in the grammar of the heart is what the predicate is about in the speech of God. The verb is what the predicate is in a person's talk with God. Particles are the linkages by means of which the meaningful messages [*fawāʾid*] of the speech of the heart are completed.[48]

Indeed, interpreting the genre of such passages in *Moralized Grammar* and *The Grammar of Hearts* is the core problematic at the heart of understanding them. In these texts, the mixing of disparate marks and traits is so transgressive that their genre becomes unrecognizable and consequently their meaning verges on the unintelligible. Not bearing familiar trappings or wearing the authorized uniform of an official or sanctioned genre, *Moralized Grammar* and *The Grammar of Hearts* display their "queer" genre.[49] Whereas sanctioned and official genres of religious literature such as sermons and creeds pose as transparent categories that are at once recognizable and yet overlooked, *Moralized Grammar* and *The Grammar of Hearts* show off their own literariness—that is, their artifice.

These two texts are examples of religious discourse; yet, unlike so much religious and theological writing, they do not pretend to be immediate or unmediated in their conveyance of truth. The noninvisibility of their genre makes their stage unmissable, their performance unmistakable.

With these texts, the reader is not subject to any illusion of "genre-less" discourse. Religious in intention, these texts trope grammar. Like drag queens on stage transgressing gender norms by mixing marks of categories normally assumed to be natural and inviolable, *Moralized Grammar* and *The Grammar of Hearts* violate what Derrida calls "the law of genre."[50] They make visible their genre and draw attention to their artfully queer performances, which transgress categories.

The identity of these two texts in the systems of genre operative in their respective worlds is in question. In fact, the queerness of *Moralized Grammar* and *The Grammar of Hearts* calls into question the fixed stability of our familiar discursive realms and the bodies of texts that comprise them. In sum, we must ask *Moralized Grammar* and *The Grammar of Hearts* about their genre. To interpret them, we must come to an understanding of the meaning of their mixed nature. For this interrogation and interpretation to be possible, a challenge to our own preconceptions about genre as category is in order.

The common concept of genre traces its august genealogy, rightly or wrongly,[51] back to Aristotle's taxonomic model of genre (in his *Poetics*), which repeats distinctions made by Socrates in Plato's *Republic* (Book III) and continues in neo-classical theories of genre that dominated Western thought, especially in the seventeenth and eighteenth centuries.[52] The Aristotelian model of taxonomy assumes the possibility of an exhaustive classification that can sort any item into one and only one category.[53] The tried and true taxonomic model supposes "a logical relationship that allows for no slippage, no lack of fit, between one level and the other."[54] In static and essentialized notions of genre, "membership of a text in a genre is taken to be a relationship between a general type and a particular instance or 'token' of that type." Two assumptions are implicit in such classical taxonomic theories of genre:

1. "that a text is 'in' a genre, i.e., that it is primarily, or solely, describable in terms of the rules of one genre," and
2. "that genre is 'in' a text, i.e., that the features of a text will correspond to the rules of the genre."[55]

The standard triad of literary genres that theorists attributed to Aristotle is the epic, the dramatic, and the lyric.[56] All imaginative literature is meant to belong to one and only one of these three categories, which supposedly possess a natural epistemological status, like one and zero or north, south, east, and west. Classical literary theory thus substantialized genres by giving them an "essence" with "timeless validity"[57] that was epitomized by masterworks with a "seemingly unquestionable 'eternal meaning.'"[58] Traditional philologists developed their theory of genre using examples from the classical Greco-Roman literary periods and systematizing it "according to canonized rules."[59]

In his fertile problematization of what he calls "the law of genre," Jacques Derrida at certain points takes on the voice of a proponent of classical literary theory and characterizes the traditional generic schema as based on a defining mark:

> There should be a trait upon which one could rely in order to decide that a given textual event, a given "work," corresponds to a given class (genre, type, mode, form, etc.). And there should be a code enabling one to decide questions of class-membership on the basis of this trait.[60]

Once decreed, this classical limit-defining law of generic classification is soon followed by interdictory rules like that with which Derrida begins his work: "Genres are not to be mixed," "*Ne pas mêler les genres.*"[61] It is precisely this law that *Moralized Grammar* and *The Grammar of Hearts* so blatantly violate through their distinctive *mélange* of grammatical and religious genres.

Proceeding to read this interdiction of miscegenation through several generic lenses, Derrida proposes a possibility engendered by "the law of genre":

> And suppose for a moment that it were impossible not to mix genres. What if there were, lodged within the heart of the law itself, a law of impurity or a principle of contamination? And suppose the condition for the possibility of the law were the *a priori* of a counter-law, an axiom of impossibility that would confound its sense, order, and reason?[62]

Following the folds—invaginations, he calls them—of the inside and outside of the bodies of texts that make up genres, Derrida points to citation or intertextuality as a source of instability to the corporal integrity of the notion of closed-off genres. He thus highlights the generative and iterative possibility of mixing genres. The problem that this fertile instability raises is, "how can there be new text, original text, which nevertheless is recognizable as text, which is formally intelligible?"[63]

John Frow illuminates—with less performative intensity than Derrida—the significance of intertextuality for understanding genre:

> What I mean by [intertextuality] is the range of processes by which a text invokes another, but also the way texts are constituted as such by their relationships with other texts. No text is unique; we could not recognise it if it were. All texts are relevantly similar to some texts and relevantly dissimilar to others. . . . All texts are shaped by the repetition and the transformation of other textual structures.[64]

The necessarily intertextual character of all texts is, then, following Derrida and Frow, both the generative source of fertile instability and simultaneously what makes any text recognizable and intelligible. Gerson's *Moralized Grammar*, for example, conspicuously invokes Aelius Donatus's *Ars minor*. It is a repetition and a transformation of this grammar textbook that was familiar to virtually any literate person in the Latin world of Gerson's time.[65] *Moralized Grammar* also cross-breeds the grammar manual with the catechism and other religious genres.[66] It is "relevantly similar" and "relevantly dissimilar" to such texts.

The elements of genre are multiple, and each is a dimension of possible interrelationships among texts. Frow identifies the following structural dimensions: "a set of formal features"; "a thematic structure which draws upon a set of highly conventional topics or *topoi* . . . and projects a schematic but coherent and plausible world from these materials"; "a situation of address"—"This speaking position brings with it a certain kind of authority and moral force," "tone"; "structure of implication, which both invokes and presupposes a range of relevant background knowledges, and in so doing sets up a certain complicity with the reader"; "a rhetorical function . . . to achieve certain pragmatic effects"; "a physical setting . . . a regulative frame."[67] In our close reading of *Moralized Grammar* and *The Grammar of Hearts*, we will examine these dimensions of formal organization, rhetorical structure, and thematic content.[68]

By claiming the genre of *Moralized Grammar* and *The Grammar of Hearts* to be the core problematic of these texts, I am arguing that their genre is constitutive of their meaning.

> Genre . . . is a set of conventional and highly organised constraints on the production and interpretation of meaning. . . . Its structuring effects are productive of meaning; they shape and guide, in the way that a builder's form gives shape to a pour of concrete, or a sculptor's mould shapes and gives structure to its materials.[69]

Genre is the place where meaning-making happens. For this reason, the metaphors of genre as stage for performance and frame for artistic creation are also apt. Indeed, the "meaning-making" of genre is "deeper and more forceful than that of the explicit 'content' of the text."[70]

Certain genres of writing project the pretense or illusion of making meaning outside of any stage or frame. Authoritative modes of philosophy, science, and theology are especially prone to the pretense of this kind of immediacy:

> The force of genre is felt more thoroughly in those genres whose trait is a constitutional *naïveté*, the trait of the transparency of their own means of representation. In this category can be found genres aimed at truth-telling (like some philosophy); the revealing of reality "as it is" (empirical sciences of physical or social types); and, in general, genres of writing aimed at representing something without reference to the possibility of its representation.[71]

Representing the presence of true reality, religious discourse then often aims to be like truth-telling philosophy and empirical science in concealing the stage on which it is performed. These genres intend to reveal reality "as it is." In other words, these kinds of discourse downplay their framing devices in order not to dispel their theatrical illusion. Truth-telling philosophy, empirical science, and religious discourse tend to aim for the ontological effect of presenting their truths as reality rather than as representations. The invisible transparence of genre serves this end.

As we shall see throughout this study, the genre of *Moralized Grammar* and *The Grammar of Hearts* is reality-forming, but not at all transparent. Through a mixing of genres that is based on a set of metaphors, *Moralized Grammar* and *The Grammar of Hearts* disclose realities while constantly reminding the reader of the stage or frame on which this creative meaning-making is being performed.

The Grammar of Genre

Another way of framing genre that contributes to our study of *The Grammar of Hearts* and *Moralized Grammar* applies modern linguistic theory to literary systems and the texts that comprise them. Developed by Hans Robert Jauss (d. 1997), this conception of genre likens texts to speech events—that is, what happens when a speaker of a language says something meaningful to other speakers of that language. Jauss's theory is based on an extended metaphor relating a corpus or body of literature to a language with a grammar.[72] Applying Jauss to the troubling genre of *Moralized Grammar* and *The Grammar of Hearts* thus entails conceiving of these texts as unique "utterances" in specific literary systems at particular moments in time.

In creating this linguistic metaphor for relating genres to one another, Jauss makes use of key concepts from Ferdinand de Saussure's theory of language. Saussure (d. 1913) revolutionized linguistic theory by recognizing the static system of relations among linguistic elements at a single historical moment, for which he used the term "synchronic"—literally, "together in time." Saussure contrasts his own "synchronic" approach to what he calls the "diachronic" approach (meaning "over the course of time") of nineteenth-century philologists, who had applied the new historical consciousness of that epoch to the development of language. Saussure's approach thus opened the way for twentieth-century linguistics to examine the linguistic system of signs not through its historical evolution but rather as a living organism cryogenically preserved, frozen in time so as to be analyzed as it functioned at a particular moment in history.

Jauss, in turn, took the concept of a "synchronic system" and located it in the relationships among the literary genres of any particular time period and culture. "For literature as well is a kind of grammar or syntax, with relatively fixed relations of its own: the arrangement of the traditional and the uncanonized genres; modes of experience, kinds of style, and rhetorical figures."[73]

For Saussure, linguistic utterances, which he calls *la parole*, only happen and only make sense within the arbitrary conventions of a linguistic system, *la langue*, which he famously compares to chess.[74] A language has items and rules, just as the game of chess does. For Jauss, no item of literature occurs or makes sense except within a literary system of genres, which likewise has its own conventions and rules:

> Just as there is no act of verbal communication that is not related to a general, socially or situationally conditioned norm or convention, it is also unimaginable that a literary work set itself into an informational vacuum, without indicating a specific situation of understanding. To this extent, every work belongs to a genre—whereby I mean neither more nor less than that for each work a preconstituted horizon of expectations must

> be ready at hand (this can also be understood as a relationship of "rules of the game" [*Zusammenhang von Spielregeln*] to orient the reader's (public's) understanding and to enable a qualifying reception.[75]

These norms and conventions, and the meta-language used to describe them, are grammar—the grammar of genre.

A single piece of literature, with its specific generic character, Jauss likened to a linguistic utterance (*la parole*). The entire literary system of genres in which that piece of literature is produced Jauss likened to language (*la langue*). The collection of rules, norms, or conventions that describe the elements of this literary system and the relationships among those elements is grammar, like the grammar of a language. "Grammar," here as elsewhere, refers both to the structures of the system themselves and to the scholarly discourse or meta-language used to describe those structures. Or, using Saussure's famous metaphor, each text, like each linguistic utterance, is a specific move by a chess player. The literary system, like a language at a particular historical moment, is the game of chess. The norms and conventions characterizing both the genres at play in that literary system and their relationships with each other, like the grammar of the language, comprise the rules of the game.

The reception of any one text, then, like the comprehension of *la parole* in Saussure, can only be grasped in light of its place within the grammar of genres in which its readers read it. The reception by different readers, at various points throughout history, is thus at no point separable from the meaning of the text. "In the triangle of author, work, and public the last is no passive part, no chain of mere reactions, but rather itself an energy formative of history. The historical life of a literary work is unthinkable without the active participation of its addressees."[76] Reading, too, is a performance art. The interaction between *The Grammar of Hearts* or *Moralized Grammar* and a reader is dialogical, a two-way conversation. "The historicity of literature as well as its communicative character presupposes a dialogical and at once process-like relationship between work, audience, and new work that can be conceived in the relations between message and receiver as well as between question and answer, problem and solution."[77] Different readers, with different expectations, find different meanings in what is apparently the same text. Indeed, genre for Jauss is all about expectations.

> A literary work, even when it appears to be new, does not present itself as something absolutely new in an informational vacuum, but

> predisposes its audience to a very specific kind of reception by announcements, overt and covert signals, familiar characteristics, or implicit allusions. It awakens memories of that which was already read, brings the reader to a specific emotional attitude, and with its beginning arouses expectations from the "middle and end," which can then be maintained intact or altered, reoriented, or even fulfilled ironically in the course of the reading according to specific rules of the genre or type of text.[78]

The reality of genre is thus communal and cultural. Readers' expectations come out of a common consciousness, cultural memory, and understanding of signs and signals. For this reason, Jauss's conceptual model for genres is language itself, that definitive element of community and culture.

Though he forswears the applicability of "organic growth" or "Darwinian selection," Jauss understands genres to coexist in a nonteleological "sequence of rivalries" whereby authors' experimentation and variation lead to the emergence of certain "dominant" genres.[79] Rejecting the neoclassical categories of epic, lyric, and dramatic literature as insufficient and inapplicable to medieval Romance literature, Jauss instead constructs his theory from a dizzying array of genres, which he sees as the product of mutations.[80] The idea of mutation is crucial in a literary landscape where rivalries and struggle determine which genres win out and become dominant for any period of time. Jauss expresses this idea of literary change and experimentation by referring back to his idea of a horizon of expectations: "the relationship between the individual text and the series of texts formative of a genre presents itself as a process of the continual founding and altering of horizons."[81] Drawing on common consciousness and cultural memory, "The new text evokes for the reader (listener) the horizon of expectations and 'rules of the game' familiar to him from earlier texts, which as such can then be varied, extended, corrected, but also transformed, crossed out, or simply reproduced."[82] As hybrids and cross-fertilization can be extraordinarily productive in a biological setting, so do so-called "mixed genres" play a highly significant role in medieval European literature.[83] In order to make sense of the "mixed genre" of *Moralized Grammar* and *The Grammar of Hearts*, we will need to collect some literary points of reference from which to extrapolate an approximation of the horizon of expectations within which Gerson and Qushayrī were writing. As in an archaeological analysis of excavated artifacts found in a cross-section of a single stratum, we make sense of texts within the literary system of genres of their day.

Because classical genre theory still today dominates so much discourse on genre, it is worth emphasizing the point that canonized rules about language (or genre) are not as important as the relatively stable yet dynamic existence of language (or genre) in the minds and interactions of people in a community. Prescriptive grammar lessons undoubtedly have some effect on pupils who endure inane instruction on split infinitives and the like.[84] The grammar that linguists study—at least since Saussure—exists, however, not in handbooks, but in native speakers' minds. Analogously, while canonized rules and handbooks about how to write in a certain genre sometimes develop to police propriety, these external influences come only at a particular historical moment in the maturation of literary genres. For some genres, such policing never comes at all.

Religious genres are no different from other genres in these respects. Expectations of a minister's homily or an imam's *khutba* are established as congregants attend religious services over time and listen to such discourse. Though sermon handbooks in Europe after about 1200 became enormously influential aids to sermonizers, few in the congregation would have ever read such guides—much less let such guides determine their understanding of what a sermon meant. Students of religion in the Christian and Islamic traditions similarly learn what to expect from books of systematic theology or biblical commentary or Qur'anic *tafsīr* (exegesis) not from reading theory about the rules of such genres, but rather from reading individual texts that enact these genres. As readers become more expert in one or another genre, their expectations become more elaborate and more refined. Readers' collective expectations also change and develop.

> A literary work is not an object that stands by itself and that offers the same view to each reader in each period. It is not a monument that monologically reveals its timeless essence. It is much more like an orchestration that strikes ever new resonances among its readers and that frees the text from the material of the words and brings it to a contemporary existence.[85]

While the horizons of expectations in the face of which *Moralized Grammar* and *The Grammar of Hearts* were originally created possess a special significance, so too do my own expectations and reception of these works. I am after all the reader who is retrieving these texts and endeavoring to make sense of them for other readers today. Moreover, by juxtaposing these texts and studying them from the disciplinary perspective of comparative theology, I am disruptively creating a new context in which to read them. As a result, my interpretation of the meaning of these two texts does not stop with cultural contextualization or textual analysis. My reception of these two retrieved texts sets them against the cultural, philosophical, and theological discourses of the contemporary world that my own perceived readers and I myself inhabit.

Jauss's aesthetics of reception provides some sound guidance for how to make sense of the two strange grammatical religious texts that are the focus of our present study. We will pay special attention to the expectations with which our two authors interacted in crafting these texts. In undertaking a close reading of *Moralized Grammar* and *The Grammar of Hearts*, I will explain the cultural, religious, and literary background that is most important to the horizons of expectations in which each was respectively written and first read. I will also present a few texts by each author in other genres as a kind of synchronic Jaussian cross-section of the system of genres in which the two "spiritual grammars" occurred.[86] Though no comprehensive investigation of all the works that Qushayrī and Gerson presupposed their readers to know will be undertaken here, these other texts are meant to offer especially helpful indications of what *Moralized Grammar* and *The Grammar of Hearts* were doing in their own respective eras and for their respective audiences.

Genres to Genders, Texts to Subjects

The genre of *The Grammar of Hearts* and *Moralized Grammar* constitutes their meaning, significance, and relevance for us today. Recognizing their ironic and playful genre performance as "queer" raises for us a number of pressing literary and theological questions all at once. Among these questions are the connections between genre and gender, literary text and human subject.

In her investigations of philosophy as writing, Robyn Ferrell connects the reality-forming and the generative qualities of genre. As we consider Gerson's and Qushayrī's generation of their "queer" texts, we also will see cause for connecting their cross-breeding of genres with the disclosure of realities.

> As it turns out, the observance of "begetting" is what is at stake in genre: *Genre emerges for philosophy as an ontological question.* Genre is the concept which seeks to capture the generative in thought. One might articulate this process of a reproduction of thought as one in which new thinking is produced but not immaculately. It is the process whereby new thinking can represent something of the old while being an original departure, *reiterating* something *as* new.[87]

She is not the only one who connects genre to ontology. Frow, too, points out how "the semiotic frames within which genres are embedded implicate and specify layered ontological domains—implicit realities which genres form as a pre-given reference."[88] Beyond ontology generally, Ferrell also specifically conceives of genre as a space for a certain way of acting or living.

> Perhaps it could also be said that the genre, conceived of in this way, produces the "zone" of possibility for an activity, or at least produces the conditions of its possibility. The desire to speak a certain way is a desire to enter into life in a certain way.[89]

The space created by the genre of *Moralized Grammar* and *The Grammar of Hearts* is a place for the reader to become a certain kind of person, in a certain kind of world. Indeed, looking at genres of writing across time, Ferrell argues that "[t]he history of genre can be seen to parallel the history of the subject and the individual."[90] Precisely here, in the linkage between genre and the subject, we can finally state plainly that the metaphor of sex developed in this section has not been mere play. Genre and subjectivity are not givens. They have a history. They are produced. Allow me to enact this understanding of genre by reframing and re-sexing a citation (by Graham Ward) from Judith Butler's *Gender Trouble.* Where Butler had "gender," I substitute "genre":

> [genre] is not a noun . . . [genre] is performatively produced and compelled by the regulatory practices of [genre] coherence . . . [genre] is always a doing. . . . There is no [genre] identity behind the expressions of [genre]; that identity is performatively constituted by the very "expressions" that are said to be its results.[91]

Just as Butler and other queer theorists today challenge the essentialist views of gender as natural and static categories, so do the genre theories of Jauss, Derrida, Frow, and others suggest that a more accurate understanding of genre starts with its performative nature, a "doing" that is produced by the regulatory practices of genre coherence and the transgression of those practices through mixing marks and traits. Genres, like genders, are better understood as dynamic, contextual performances than as static, natural categories.[92]

The Grammar of Hearts and *Moralized Grammar* are strikingly similar "queer" religious performances of the hybrid genre of spiritual grammar. Their common creative aim, moreover, is to engender saintly subjectivities. These transgressive performances also constitute interpretations of spiritual realities—realities that through any other genre could not be the same. At the same time, their ironic play performatively intensifies the problematic of how genres and genders relate to these spiritual realities. Retrieval of these two texts whose content and form face head-on the interplay between ultimate reality, the self, and the nature of language, thus contributes to the search for a postmodern self. After all, it is in this same interplay that postmoderns have shown the modern self-grounding self to be ultimately groundless and self-deconstructing.

> As the postmoderns make clear, however, the modern self, unfortunately for its foundationalist pretensions, must also use language. And the very self-deconstructing, nongrounding play of the signifiers in all language will assure that no signified—especially the great modern signified, the modern subject—will ever find the pure identity, the clear and distinct self-presence it seeks or the totality it grasps at. That self-grounding, self-present modern subject is dead: killed by its own pretensions to grounding all reality in itself.[93]

Qushayrī's and Gerson's experimental performances of spiritual grammar are spiritual and literary investigations into the embeddedness of the self within the grammatical structures of ultimate reality. Their "play" with this genre of tropes looks from our postmodern perspective like a medieval rebuke to Cartesian pretensions of "clear and distinct self-presence." The genre of spiritual grammar is newly important to us today, since it offers a way of conceiving a postmodern self that is neither illusory nor naïve nor egocentric.

Yet, the metaphor of the self mired in the grammatical structures of ultimate reality, spiritual reality, is not just a metaphor. Gerson's and Qushayrī's irony is not mere play, their performances not merely a ruse. Their texts offer nonfigurative truth about the signifying practices of language being precisely where and how the self is constituted and constitutes itself. Gerson and Qushayrī created spiritual grammars to signify possibilities through their texts for how readers could evolve their subjectivities beyond conventional, "generic" modes of being. Themselves spiritual masters, they hoped to convey some of their deep heart knowledge to the benefit of the spiritual advancement of their readers. They performed new genres so that their readers could find new "genders" or ontological frames for their own performances as subjects. Their subversion of standard genres is an "act" of parody that elicits laughter and delight. Their acts stage the production of new religious "genders" that go beyond conventional frames of being Christian or Muslim. They repeat with critical differences standard performances and thus make possible the proliferation of ways of being that move from the standard to the saintly, from the mundane to the holy.[94] They engender new forms for Christian and Islamic subjects.

1 Arabic, Latin, and the Discipline of Grammar in the Worlds of Qushayrī and Gerson

She holds a rod and a switch in her right hand and a book in her left. These pedagogical implements make Grammar recognizable, as do the two children below her, one kneeling and the other with head bowed. The southern Portail Royal of the western façade of Chartres Cathedral (ca. 1145–50) thus personifies Grammar as a disciplinarian and schoolteacher. Indeed, the discipline of grammar was largely about rectitude,[1] enforced by violence, as symbolized by the rod and the switch. None of the other Seven Liberal Arts of medieval European learning was represented in twelfth-century iconography as a teacher.[2] Grammar, the first of the arts taught to pupils, epitomized the pedagogue.

Students of this pedagogue in the medieval Islamic and European dominions learned what we now call the "standard" or "classical" Arabic or Latin languages through canons of grammatical, literary, and religious texts in elementary, secondary, and advanced stages of education. These students were mainly boys, and the pedagogues were men. Through their mastery of the prestige language of their cultural and religious tradition, the learned enjoyed not only geographic and temporal intercourse across vast territories and ages, but also political and social privilege in their present world. As such, grammar in the Islamic and European traditions was both a foundational and pivotal discipline of knowledge. Grammar was not only the stuff of schoolboys—though it was certainly that—but it was also an avenue for profound and erudite intellectual efforts to discover truth and meaning.

Prestige and power thus characterized the positions of the Latin and Arabic languages in their medieval milieus. Neither in Gerson's Paris nor in Qushayrī's Nishapur, nor anywhere else, was Latin or the Arabic called *al-ʿarabiyya al-fuṣḥā* anybody's native language. They were rather the languages of literature, of intellectual discourse, and of religion, in both instances harkening back to an ideal from centuries past. In other words, they were languages whose written rather than spoken forms had become primary and whose very use cited and nostalgically referred to a mythical past.

Diglossia is the sociolinguistic technical term to describe this phenomenon in which a society uses a privileged standard language for certain prestigious functions and a native vernacular language for other everyday purposes. Jan Ziolkowski, a scholar of medieval Latin, describes diglossia as "a circumstance in which a mother tongue coexists with a father tongue (usually a scriptural language is used by an educated elite)."[3] Calling Latin and Arabic "father tongues" matches the nature of their power in their respective medieval diglossic contexts. Indeed, Ziolkowski observes elsewhere that the term "*lingua paterna*" or "father tongue" is "particularly appropriate since medieval Latin was used predominantly by males to uphold a male-dominated or patriarchal society. It was a tongue that boys were forced to learn en route to positions in the Church, university, and state."[4]

The Power of Spiritual Grammar

By writing *Moralized Grammar* and *The Grammar of Hearts* in the form of grammar textbooks of Latin and Arabic, Jean Gerson and ʿAbd al-Karīm al-Qushayrī made a trope out of the grammar of these "father languages" for religious purposes. The power dynamics involved in this trope are not incidental or insignificant. Specifically, the operations of patriarchal power in the diglossic sociolinguistic situations of education and religious instruction are part of *Moralized Grammar* and *The Grammar of Hearts*. Texts are, after all, the product of specific social practices and circumstances. Moreover, genre "mediate[s] between a social situation and the text which realises certain features of this situation, or which responds strategically to its demands."[5] Genres link texts back to the social practices and contexts in which they are produced.

Contemporary critical theory, initiated in important ways by Nietzsche and further developed by Derrida and Foucault, offers a "hermeneutics of suspicion" that can be an incisive tool and revealing lens for excavating and examining power dynamics that easily remain concealed.[6] Indeed, a hermeneutics of suspicion can raise vital questions and perhaps impertinent objections to religious and theological studies, including our comparative study of *Moralized Grammar* and *The Grammar of Hearts*.

Regarding Gerson's and Qushayrī's spiritual grammars from the perspective of critical theory, we see traces of what Derrida called "phallogocentrism," a patriarchal insistence on the presence in language of transcendent meaning. In their trope of spiritual grammar, both Gerson and Qushayrī use their privileged positions as patriarchs to imbue the structures of the "father languages" of their respective societies with the metaphorical significance of the structures of spiritual reality. In their patriarchal insistence on the presence of meaning in language, Gerson and Qushayrī strive to bring about distinct changes in their readers. They have pastoral objectives for the spiritual formation of their readers' souls.

Precisely such techniques of formation of the self and the construction of the subject are at the core of Foucault's lifelong project of tracing the "genealogy of the subject."[7] Though nuanced, Foucault was unabashedly suspicious in his excavations of buried traces of insidious power.

Focusing single-mindedly on the patriarchal power dynamics in Gerson's and Qushayrī's texts and their marshaling of both pedagogical and religious discourse for specific pastoral goals related to what Foucault would call "the formation of subjects," we could handily cast aspersions on these spiritual grammars. From such a perspective we could fantasize a scene of Derrida's "phallogocentrism" and see that in writing these texts, Gerson and Qushayrī—both consummate patriarchs—took up the grammatical rod of the forcefully fatherly schoolmaster. Wielding that phallic instrument of pedagogic discipline in an aura of sanctity, the spiritual grammarians forcefully instruct their puerile pupils by pouring out onto their submissive tongues the sacred "logos" of religious meaning. These medieval masters and religious authorities thus call forth in the service of spiritual direction or pastoral care the scholarly powers of grammar, by which pupils are normally trained merely in linguistic correctness.

Such a view of the possibilities inherent in spiritual grammar is not without merit or insight. Power dynamics of domination and submission were at play in educational and religious relationships of authority in Qushayrī's and Gerson's world, as they are in different ways in our world today.[8] However, the violent fantasy that religious teachers like Qushayrī and Gerson are simply exploiting their paternal position to force a kind of moral or spiritual knowledge onto or into their pupils is reductive and cynical. At the same time, ignoring the power dynamics of domination and submission in Christian and Islamic education and spiritual formation is naively optimistic.

The spiritual grammars of Qushayrī and Gerson are especially well suited to a Foucauldian investigation of the genealogy of the subject—that is, an analysis of how techniques of domination interacted in the Western and Islamic traditions with techniques of the self.[9] In these texts of spiritual grammar, the patriarchal authors wielded the pedagogic power of grammar to impart to their pupils training in the formation of the self. As James Bernauer has argued, it is possible to find in Foucault's work a kind of negative theology.[10] A full-fledged analysis of the power dynamics at work in Gerson's and Qushayrī's world could thus bring to light the aspects of *The Grammar of Hearts* and *Moralized Grammar* and the authors' other writings that were and perhaps still are liberative rather than oppressive.[11]

In the present study, what Paul Ricoeur called a "hermeneutics of retrieval" or "hermeneutics of faith" rather than a "hermeneutics of suspicion" will predominate.[12] This interpretive approach reflects my intention of making these texts available and accessible to intellectual and religious readers today. I find them to be of value, and I hope that other readers will, as well. Emphasizing a "hermeneutics of faith" more than a "hermeneutics of suspicion" also fits my position as a theologian who risks still believing and still remaining a member of the Catholic faith community.

This chapter aims to uncover the linguistic politics and cultural significance of the intertextuality of *The Grammar of Hearts* and *Moralized Grammar* by which the authors interwove religious discourse with the grammatical discipline of the two "father languages" in question. This exploration of intellectual history in the contextual worlds of the two authors is worthwhile not because Schleiermacher was right that the way to determine the real meaning of a text is through recreating the mind of the author, but rather because a historically conscious reading of the texts will set some reasonable boundaries in our own interpretive efforts to find meaning in the texts for us today.

The Diglossia of the Latin and Arabic Worlds

A first step toward analyzing the linguistic politics and cultural significance of these spiritual grammars is to deepen our understanding of the place of standard Arabic and Latin in the worlds of Qushayrī and Gerson. One way to think about the language situation of the Arab world with its standard *fuṣḥā* "father language" and its many national and local *lahjāt* (Arabic dialects) is to compare it to an imaginary Europe where the French, the Portuguese, the Spaniards, the Italians, and the Romanians speak as they do today but write their texts, deliver their speeches, and undertake classroom conversation in classical Latin. Though Europeans today do not use Latin (much!), their medieval predecessors did indeed.

In fact, both Romance language scholars and Arabic scholars have noted the striking similarities between the Arabophone world today and medieval Europe. One Romance language professor, for example, asks suggestively:

> Is it not conceivable that the situation in early medieval Romance Europe was very similar to that of Modern Arabic, with a complex variety of realizations in speaking, of partly "Latin," i.e., written language, and spoken "Romance" in a dynamic and constantly shifting fashion, in which "the receptive awareness of speakers is much greater than their productive performances suggest?"[13]

Scholars of Arabic have drawn similar comparisons.[14] These comparisons come as scholars trace the history of these standard languages and their standing in language communities of various vernacular mother languages. Romance specialists agree that "the inhabitants of the Roman Empire spoke Latin, that spoken Latin developed eventually into the Romance vernaculars, and that in the Late Middle Ages Latin and the Romance languages were both used separately and kept conceptually distinct."[15] Scholars of Arabic generally agree that Arabicization occurred in a short time over a wide expanse of territory and that the colloquial varieties of Arabic spoken in the expanding Islamic Empire after the conquests developed into the Arabic dialects of today.[16]

For our purposes of comparing the histories of Arabic and Latin-Romance languages and the study of their respective grammars in order to understand better the meaning of Qushayrī's and Gerson's religious-grammatical texts, we can emphasize from the outset that Qushayrī's Nishapur and Gerson's Paris both were characterized by diglossic sociolinguistic situations. As educated men, both had full access to the so-called "high-register" languages used in their respective societies for the prestige roles of religious, literary, and scholarly discourse, though they were native speakers of other, vernacular, "low-register" languages. In other words, both men were bilingual.

The term "diglossia" pertains to a society and a social situation, while "bilingualism" pertains to an individual and his or her own internal negotiation of two languages that he or she knows. Bilingualism is thus individual and psychological in nature while diglossia is communal and sociological.[17] In Paris around 1400 and Nishapur around the mid-eleventh century, as for example among Hebrew and Yiddish speakers in pre–World War I Eastern Europe, there was a "fairly large and complex speech community in which the members have available to them both a range of *compartmentalized* roles [that is, roles for languages in society] as well as ready *access* to these roles." The language roles for "father languages" are compartmentalized in that people in diglossic societies use these high-register languages only in certain prestigious societal domains. Such domains typically include such areas as religious worship, high-brow literature, and scholarly debate.

The Paris of Gerson around 1400 and the Nishapur of Qushayrī in the mid-eleventh century were thus both diglossic, multilingual language communities. The cases are different in that Qushayrī was a native-Persian speaker, and thus his vernacular was not genetically related to his standard Arabic, while Gerson's native French vernacular was indeed related to his standard Latin. Just as medieval Arabic diglossia spread over some regions where both the high and low languages were varieties of Arabic and other regions, where the low language was, for example, a variety of Persian, so did medieval Latin spread over Romance-speaking and non-Romance-speaking regions. In any case, both Qushayrī and Gerson lived in societies where boys (and, less frequently, girls) studied the grammar of a "father language" as the very foundation of their education.

The elites who gained access to these standard languages were certainly privileged, and the bilingual speech communities in both cases were quite large and complex. The communities of *fuṣḥā* Arabic speakers and of Latin speakers during the lives of Qushayrī and Gerson respectively were transnational, spread over large geographic areas spanning multiple polities. These communities were also dominated by religious scholars. Designated men holding positions of religious power controlled much of the discourse in these high-register languages.

Among these religious scholars in Europe, writers such as Augustine (d. 430), Gregory the Great (d. 604), Isidore of Seville (d. 636), and the hagiographers of the eighth century may have expected their Latin works to be intelligible to illiterate people when read aloud.[18] Meanwhile, across the Channel, inhabitants of England and Ireland, whose first encounter with Latin was with its written rather than spoken form, developed a phonetic system of one-to-one correspondence between sound and letter (more or less how Latin readers today in the Anglo-world pronounce Latin).

> This strange and unnatural practice led to great differences between the way they pronounced Latin, in effect reading texts aloud as if they were in phonetic script, and the pronunciations that had become normal in the native Romance-speaking world, where many spellings were learnt and taught logographically rather than phonographically.[19]

In a perverse instance of imperial language control, this artificial but uniform pronunciation was then imposed on the Latin-Romance-speaking world through the educational reforms ordered by Charlemagne, who appointed Alcuin of York (England) for the task.

One of Alcuin's reforms was to have everyone pronounce Latin in the stilted way devised on the British Isles. Foreigners thus instructed the native-speakers how to pronounce their own language![20] Rabanus Maurus (d. 856 C.E.) promoted Alcuin's reforms throughout the clerical educational system,[21] and it spread to Romance-speaking locales even outside of the Carolingian realm, such as Iberia and southern Italy. Alcuin and Rabanus Maurus thus created and instituted a "newly standardized *grammatica*, conceptually separate from Romance."[22] One part of the reaction to this catalytic reform of "Latin" was the invention of new orthographic systems to represent the natural Romance language forms "because the educational reform meant that texts written in the old style could no longer necessarily, as before, be read aloud easily in the vernacular intelligible manner." This moment—when a new writing system was developed for the Romance vernaculars and concomitantly a new name arose for each vernacular as now its own language—happened in very different times in different areas, but for all of the Romance-speaking areas this transition occurred generally between 1000 and 1300.[23]

After this transition, students would still first have been taught to read Latin before learning to read their native Romance in the new writing system. However, at some point the balance between the two kinds of literacy shifted: "once there was a sizable group of people literate in their new local written Romance form but not in Latin—which happened in the thirteenth century—old-style written Latin forms could start to seem foreign even to the literate, and the change was for practical purposes complete."[24]

To avoid giving the impression here that schooling and literacy were synonymous, we must note how intensely oral the literary culture of medieval Europe was. Like Muslim pupils memorizing Qur'an in Islamic contexts, in Christian contexts "most little pupils memorized the entire Latin psalter either before or while learning to read."[25] The orality of medieval Western Christian culture meant that "a person could be educated and proficient in speaking Latin without being able to write it comfortably."[26]

The history of Arabic had a few different twists and turns. First, local vernacular dialects did not determine the oral realization of *fuṣḥā* Arabic texts so much as they did of Latin texts in the late classical and early medieval Romance-speaking world. The more important shift in pronunciation of the classical Arabic language—at some point well before Qushayrī's eleventh century—was the omission of declension endings rather than the development of regional pronunciations of *fuṣḥā*. The elite Persians who became Arabic *literati*, on the other hand, retained in their spoken *fuṣḥā* these *iʿrāb*, as declensional endings are called in Arabic, and thus sounded either "pure" or "stilted" to the native Arabic speaker, depending on the listener's meta-linguistic attitude.[27] To impose a uniform style of pronunciation—artificial or otherwise—on the community of Arabic speakers, no language reform like Alcuin's was necessary. The sacredness of the oral realization of the Qur'an ensured that full pronunciation of declensional features was retained throughout the Islamic community and by extension among non-Muslim Arabs as well.

A key difference between the history of Latin-Romance and the history of Arabic is thus that the language experts who standardized the Arabic writing system in the first and second Islamic centuries were native speakers whose measure, as mentioned previously, was not any artificial or academic pronunciation system of non-Arabic speakers (as the Insular pronunciation of Latin) but rather the Qur'an, which had its own linguistic peculiarities, demonstrating especially features of Hijazi Arabic, the kind of Arabic spoken in Mecca and Medina, where the Prophet had lived and died. This background to the position and status of Latin and Arabic as strong standard languages whose power and prestige possessed both scientific and religious dimensions begins to clarify certain aspects of the meaning of Latin grammar to Gerson and his first readers and of Arabic grammar to Qushayrī and his. Arabic and Latin were in both cases the language of conquerors who some centuries before our authors' times had brought with them their religion.

A closer look at the linguistic situation of Arabic in Persia from the time of the Islamic conquest to Qushayrī's mid-eleventh century will fill out this picture. Ibn al-Muqaffaʿ[28] in Ibn al-Nadīm's *Fihrist*[29] describes mid-seventh-century Iran as having five languages: "*pahlavī*, the language of the Fahla country . . . , *darī*, the language of the capital (Ctesiphon or al-Madāʾin), *pārsī*, language of the *mōbads* and scholars, *suryānī*, spoken in Sawād, and *khūzī*, used in Khūzistān."[30] By the third century A.H. / ninth century C.E., Darī (a variety of Persian) became the vernacular of Iran generally.[31] Though at first Arabic was the predominant language of the Arab immigrants in Nishapur and elsewhere, by the second/eighth century these Arabs spoke Darī as their daily language. Nonetheless, from this same period, Arabic was "the principal cultural language of Iran . . . not merely the administrative language . . . but also the medium of science and literature."[32] Eminent scholar of Iran Gilbert Lazard has explicitly compared the diglossia of ninth- to tenth-century C.E. Persia with the language situation of medieval Europe:

> Linguistic usage in Iran in about the 3rd/9th century may be summed up as follows: there were two languages in use all over Iran at the same time on different levels. One of them, dārī, was used, but only in speech, by the bulk of the population; the other, Arabic, was the medium of religion and the administration, of science and of literature, being written and spoken only by educated people. This situation was to continue in some degree even after the emergence of Persian literature: in the 4th/10th century Persian and Arabic poetry flourished side by side at the courts of Khurāsān and for a long time afterward Arabic remained the chief instrument of science and of philosophy. There was nothing exceptional about such a state of affairs in the Middle Ages—similar conditions prevailed in the countries of western Europe, where Latin, the educated language, was superimposed on the common speech, which was only gradually promoted to nobler usage.[33]

Qushayrī's eleventh-century Persia was approximately like Gerson's fourteenth-century France in terms of their respective diglossic language situations. There existed in both cases a standard language that carried great prestige and that fulfilled designated roles in society. At the same time, in both cases the "father language" was on the verge of being dethroned and usurped by the vernacular "mother languages" in many of the prestige domains.

Varieties of vernacular Persian and French were to become new standards. Intellectuals such as Ibn Sīnā (also known as Avicenna, d. 1037) already occasionally used Persian for scholarly works,[34] indicating that "there existed in Iran a wide public sufficiently interested in intellectual matters to wish to be informed but not very familiar with the Arabic language."[35] Similarly, Gerson and some of his predecessors had begun using French for some of their writings in order to bring their knowledge to the French-reading public who did not read Latin. Moreover, although for the most part the preeminence of Latin in France and Arabic in Persia would continue in the realm of religion, outside of that realm the high languages of our authors' respective societies were on the cusp of losing their special place. Thus, as French came into its own in the fifteenth century and Persian after the fifth century A.H. / eleventh century C.E., the medieval diglossia of France and Persia drew to a close. While the story of the European vernaculars in the Protestant Reformation need not be retold here, the fate of Arabic in Persia is much less well known:

> the knowledge of Arabic and its use amongst cultivated Persians would not disappear from Iran with the coming of the Saljuqs in the 5th/11th century and the triumphal manifestation of the ethnic genius of that people in the New Persian literature. But the 4th/10th and 5th/11th centuries did see the swan-song of Arabic belles-lettrist compositions in this sense that, henceforth, that genius had its own Islamicized tongue, Persian, at its immediate disposal. This was not a repudiation of Islam. On the contrary, the Arabic of the Qur'an would always remain sacred to the Persian Muslims; but ordinary Arabic literature was something else again.[36]

During this "swan-song" of Persians writing their literature in Arabic, a certain decadence was apparent among the Persian-speaking Arabic *literati*:

> There is sort of exaggerated skill in these Persian masters of Arabic. Their figures of speech, their ornamented rhymed prose, the very rapidity with which they can toss off a composition, even a *qaṣīda*, on the spur of the moment, all point to a perfection that is almost acrobatic, as if they were all superb jugglers.[37]

The Arabic of such Persian masters was bookish, showing an erudition not grounded in the language as spoken by native speakers.[38] In the eleventh century C.E., Persian literary culture began to reach a new stage of maturity, and the position of Arabic in Persian culture began to shift. Arabic scholar Victor Danner, in his article on "Arabic Literature in Iran," argued that "even though great masters of Arabic would appear in later centuries, by the time of al-Bīrūnī (d. 442/1050),[39] on the eve of the Saljuq reign in the Near East, the cultivated Persians no longer gave Arabic a unique place."[40] However, al-Bīrūnī himself still very much retained Arabic as the privileged language of scholarship, as demonstrated by this passage from his *Kitāb al-Ṣaidala* (also known as *Kitāb al-Ṣaidana*):

> The rope that ties us to Islam is not so frail as to snap nor its citadel such that it would be razed to the ground. All the arts of the world have been transferred to the Arabic language; it has penetrated deep in to our hearts, and its charms have crossed into the innermost reaches of our being, although to every people their own language appears to be sweet, since they use it day in, day out.
>
> When I observe my language [i.e., Persian], I find that if any art is rendered into it, it would look *de trops* [sic] and odd. On the other hand, if the same art is rendered into Arabic, it would look natural and good, even though Arabic does not happen to be my mother tongue. Arabic satire to me appears better than Persian panegyrics. Anyone who reads a Persian translation of a scholarly tract will have perforce to agree with me. This language is suited only to the tales of Khusraw and the romance of Laylá.[41]

While al-Bīrūnī denigrated Persian as a scholarly language, he at least conceded a place for his native tongue in poetry and literature. However linguistically conservative he might himself have been, he nonetheless noticed a change in the attitude of some of his contemporaries. According to Danner, al-Bīrūnī reports being asked, "What is the point in knowing the nominative and accusative declensions and all of those other things you know regarding defective formations, or rare words, in Arabic?"[42] In Danner's view, this comment exemplifies a general trend of Persians in the mid-eleventh century C.E. beginning to prefer Persian over Arabic, even for scholarly discourse.

Arabic Grammar as an Intellectual Discipline

The phrasing of this question to al-Bīrūnī about the value of knowing Arabic points to the crucial link between the cultural significance of Arabic in Qushayrī's time and the teaching of grammar. An exploration of the development of Latin and Arabic grammar as intellectual disciplines and of their respective places in the Western European and Islamic medieval education systems will broaden and deepen our understanding of Gerson's and Qushayrī's spiritual grammars.

The importance of grammar in medieval Islamic civilization was in general determined by its use for understanding the Qur'an and hadith.[43] Grammar was one of the ancillary subjects taught in the madrasa because of this usefulness to the religious sciences. While so-called "foreign sciences," such as philosophy and chemistry, were studied privately, the *awqāf* that endowed the madrasas taught and subsidized the ancillary subjects.[44] Ibn al-Anbārī (d. 577/1181), himself a professor in a madrasa, listed these as *naḥw* (grammar focusing on syntax); *lugha* (lexicology); *taṣrīf* (morphology); *ʿarūḍ* (study of poetic meter); *qawāfī* (study of poetic rhyme); *ṣanʿat al-shiʿr* (prosody); *akhbār al-ʿarab* (Arab tribal history); and *ansāb* (Arab tribal genealogy).[45]

> to these eight fields of ʿulum al-adab, the literary arts, he [Ibn al-Anbārī] added two others which he originated, namely: (1) ʿilm al-jadal fi 'n-nahw, the science of dialectic for grammar, and (2) ʿilm usul an-nahw, the science of grammatical theory and methodology, on the analogy of usul al-fiqh, legal theory and methodology, since both grammar and law are rational sciences derived from what is non-rational, that is, transmitted by tradition.

Theology, a discipline of rational reflection on and interpretation of divine revelation, is similarly a rational science derived from what is nonrational.

The way these fields of knowledge were taught in the medieval Islamic education system was principally through memorization:[46] "The advice of 'Abd al-Latif al-Baghdadi . . . was typical: 'When you read a book make every effort to learn it by heart and master its meaning. Imagine the book to have disappeared and that you can dispense with it, unaffected by its loss.' "[47] While learning by heart was essential, the significance of disputation, *munāẓara*, in the realm of grammar as in theology, demonstrates that creative and analytic thinking were not at all extrinsic to Islamic education.[48]

In terms of sequencing of knowledge, grammar came after basic literacy training, which consisted of learning to read and write primarily through copying and memorizing passages from the Qur'an: "[The Qur'an] was the schoolboy's first textbook, which he memorized from a tender age, his prayerbook as he grew up into adolescence and adulthood."[49]

This first phase of education occurred in the institution known as a *maktab* or *kuttāb*,[50] a medieval Islamic institution devoted solely to humanistic studies. The *kuttāb* was "a grammar school, a Koranic school, an elementary and secondary school, but most especially, a school where writing was taught."[51] A pupil might spend more than five years in these elementary schools.[52] Such elementary schools were apparently in existence even in the first hundred years after the Hijra and well established by the early Umayyad period—that is, the late first century A.H. / seventh century C.E.[53]

One example of an early *kuttāb* was in Kufa, founded by al-Ḍaḥḥāk b. Muzāḥim (d. 105/723). The subjects of primary education there included such things as swimming, arithmetic, how to pray, and how to perform ritual ablution. Reading and writing were instilled using the Qur'an as the textbook. Boys copied verses onto their tablets. They also studied the legends of the prophets (*qiṣaṣ al-anbiyā'*) and poetry.[54]

To advance from basic literacy to true reading proficiency in the Arabic father language, the discipline of grammar (*naḥw*) is required. Without knowing grammar, a student cannot read an Arabic text aloud correctly. Since a normal Arabic text does not include the diacritics that came to indicate short vowels, and since final vowels indicate grammatical case, a student must study Arabic grammar in order to be able to supply the vocalizations, thus "no grammar, no possibility of reading correctly."[55]

Grammar or *naḥw* was then studied after pupils left the *kuttāb*. "The maktab [that is, *kuttāb*] prepared the student for the long years of graduate work with a master humanist in *adab* studies."[56] To give a sense of how an individual could work through this system of education, consider the example of Aḥmad b. ʿAlī al-Zauwal (509–86/1115–90), who finished his studies at the *kuttāb* at fourteen, and then for the following eleven years studied grammar and lexicography under al-Jawaliqī (d. 539/1144).

At the macroscopic level, the fields of knowledge in medieval Islamic civilization can be categorized into three divisions: "the Arabic literary arts," "the Islamic religious sciences," and "the 'foreign sciences' or 'the sciences of the Ancients,' especially the Greeks."[57] Grammar was the primary element of the first of these divisions and was the most important tool necessary for studying the religious sciences. Madrasas thus typically had a grammarian on staff.[58] Within humanistic studies, grammar was likewise the foundation and prerequisite for studies in poetry, composition, epistolography, and oratory.[59]

In each field of knowledge, the curriculum comprised certain textbooks for which authorized instructors were available. For example, in the madrasa, standard books that students studied on *ḥadith* included Bukhārī's and Muslim's *Saḥīḥ*; in positive law (*furūʿ*) and legal thought (*uṣūl*), the *Risāla* of Shāfiʿī; in Qur'anic exegesis (*tafsīr*), Zamakhsharī's *al-Kashshāf*; and in Arabic language and grammar, Sībawayhi's *Kitāb* and Ibn Mālik's *Alfiyya*.[60] Authorization or certification of instructors to teach was called *ijāza*.[61] The basic mechanism of this certification system was the chain or *isnād* of oral transmission of knowledge from scholar to student. In the fourth/tenth to fifth/eleventh centuries, the written *ijāza* was apparently not very widespread; there was rather an oral *ijāza*, which in some exceptional cases was even fabricated: "A man taught what he knew, and it was upon that that he was examined for permission to teach. Occasionally, a man was certified to teach only one book."[62]

The Islamic education system in this period was not systematized or regulated outside of this certification or *ijāza* system.

> To be sure, no network or hierarchy of specialized places of learning can be pointed to. A teacher could teach in a mosque or in his home, in a shop or by the riverside. . . . Nor was there any notable systematization in the curriculum. Neither matriculation nor graduation interfered with the students' search for learning. Age restrictions and required courses were similarly absent. Travel for purposes of study was regularly indulged in, but the routes traversed varied greatly with the individual.[63]

The certification system thus had to cover whatever a man taught, wherever he taught, and to whomever he taught and "had to be an authority whose ultimate sanction was more of a moral or ethical rather than financial or institutional nature."[64]

Grammar as an Islamic Discipline of Knowledge

Besides the diglossic language situation and the place of grammar in medieval Islamic education, broad understanding of the evolution of Arabic grammar as a discipline of Islamic knowledge will help us see the significance of the grammar handbook genre in Qushayrī's world. We will focus our attention on a few highlights of this evolution—namely, grammar's link to the early study of the Qur'an, Sībawayhi's monumental

Kitāb, and the adaptations of the discipline of grammar to meet the pedagogical needs of an expanding empire and the intellectual challenges posed by the philosophical currents of the so-called *falāsifa*.

Arabic grammatical scholarship traces its origins to the codification and explication of the Qur'an. Indeed, in the era immediately following the event of revelation to Muhammad, the centerpoint of the scholarly activity of the Islamic community was the Qur'an. During the Prophet's life, the Islamic community's scripture was preserved both as an oral and a written text. The Prophet would recite Qur'an for others to hear and learn. At the same time, Muhammad had revelation secretaries, such as Zayd ibn Thābit, who wrote down records of the revealed Qur'anic verses. Once the Prophet died, the Islamic community had to undertake significant orthographic innovation, lexicographic explanation, and morphological and syntactic analysis in order to record and standardize a written Qur'anic text. Sifting the variant readings or oral realizations of the Qur'an known as the *qirā'āt* required sensitivity to the linguistic features of the Arabic language. Moreover, the corpus of pre-Islamic or "*jāhilī*" poetry, which served the Arabic grammatical and humanistic tradition thenceforth as the second model of eloquence and purity, presented lexical, morphological, and syntactic problems even more complicated than those in the Qur'an. With the Qur'an, a text-based civilization came into being. The event of the Qur'an made the Arabic language into more than a tribal language and a vehicle for great poetic artistry. From an Islamic perspective, Arabic is the very language in which God expresses Himself, and the Qur'an is that divine expression.

The earliest extant examples of Qur'anic exegesis (called *tafsīr* in Arabic), starting with Muqātil ibn Sulaymān's (d. 767), focused on the meaning and applicability of the Qur'an for daily life, as well as the linguistic forms in the scriptural text. In *Arabic Grammar and Qur'ānic Exegesis in Early Islam* (1993), scholar of Arabic Kees Versteegh explains how certain words that exegetes such as Muqātil used in nontechnical ways to explain the Qur'anic text eventually became technical terms in the grammatical tradition for specific syntactic phenomena.[65] Examples include *ṣilah* (connection), *na't* (attribute), *khabar* (account), *taqdīm* (placing first), *iḍmār* (deletion), and *istithnā'* (exception).[66]

Also in the second Islamic century came the *Urtext* of the entire tradition of Arabic grammar and Arabic linguistics—namely, *Kitāb Sībawayhi*—that is, *The Book of Sībawayhi*. 'Amr ibn 'Uthmān Sībawayhi (d. 177/798) was a native Persian speaker, born in Shiraz, who moved to

Basra in the mid-eighth century C.E. originally to study law. Allegedly because of a public grammatical error, the scholar began focusing attention on *naḥw* and never turned back. His book, one of the first books of any kind in the Arabic language, is not only the authoritative source of the Arabic linguistic and grammatical tradition, but indeed the magnum opus of that tradition. Unlike his successors in the tenth century, Sībawayhi did not write the kind of systematic grammar that explicitly names its principles and carefully categorizes linguistic features in a clear hierarchy of rules.[67] Rather, Sībawayhi was "primarily a descriptive grammarian."[68] He was a tireless collector of linguistic data, "no matter how anomalous."[69] He did attempt to create a system, but it was not a system of categorization and compartmentalization. Instead,

> Sibawayhi was clearly trying to replicate linguistic competence by putting it into words, so the challenge for us as readers is to follow a linear description of a process that is non-linear by nature, namely the infinite consultations and simultaneous cross-references that go on all the time in the mind of the speaker and, it is safe to assume, of the observer Sibawayhi as well.[70]

By this account, Sībawayhi's *Kitāb* was no pedagogical grammar. Instead, he was trying to replicate in the structure of his book the nonlinear mental system and processes in the mind of a competent Arabic speaker.

These two strands in the *Kitāb* of, on the one hand, collecting as much linguistic data as possible and, on the other, of systematizing this data, became the hallmarks of two semi-mythical schools of grammatical thought, the Basran and the Kufan. The grammatical conflict between the Basrans and the Kufans became the stuff of lore in Arabic culture. The key difference between the two was supposedly the analogical method of Basra versus the analytical method of Kufa.[71] In Basra, analogy (*qiyās*) was the principle that grammarians used to "show the harmony of the whole and of all the parts in the whole, in particular to gather up the exceptions to the rule and to show that they are merely apparent exceptions," whether on the morphological, phonetic, or syntactic level.[72] On the other hand, in Kufa, the emphasis was reportedly on laying bare the disparate linguistic data:

> The Kufan is first of all an ardent seeker, collector of poetry and vocabulary. He gathers. When explanation was necessary, he gave his opinion on each individual case. He has no concern for ordering, coordinating,

subordinating . . . properly speaking he has no system, that which one would call his system is simply the sum total of decisions.[73]

Despite the allure of the lore, the analytic "Kufan" method was typical of Arabic grammarians before the tenth century C.E.:

> The primary interest of the earlier grammarians is not (as it will be for their successors) in explicitly laying down general rules and principles in order to classify and analyse linguistic facts; it is rather in examining and discussing isolated, specific data, especially when these data exhibit some kind of deviance from the most general behaviour of the class to which they belong.[74]

Al-Mubarrad (d. 285/898) is one major Basran grammarian from this early period whose *Muqtaḍab* fits this description of what later came to be known as a Kufan approach. Ironically, al-Mubarrad and his disciples, who dominated Arabic grammar from the end of the ninth century until the end of the tenth, were the ones who first spoke of the grammarians of Basra as a "school" or *madhhab*.[75]

Then, as a dominant, canonical system of Arabic grammar emerged in the tenth century, al-Mubarrad's disciples naturally dubbed that canonical system "Basran" out of respect to their debt to their master.[76] In so doing, they attributed a much more coherent and systematized set of grammatical doctrines to the early Basran grammarians than is actually warranted. Likewise, these grammarians in the classical period after al-Mubarrad attributed to "the Kufan school" any grammatical doctrine that was not sound or that did not fit their system. By their time, the Kufan tradition had been suppressed to the point that no one was around to defend it. Thus, these classical grammarians constructed two fictional "schools" by retrojecting onto "the Basrans" a kind of rationalizing coherence based on *qiyās* and onto "the Kufans" an unsystematized reverence for all received linguistic data, a principle alluded to by the term *samāʿ*. The reality is that both *qiyās* and *samāʿ* were crucial in the theories of early grammarians, whether in Basra or in Kufa, and that in neither locale were grammarians striving for the particular kind of systematic coherence that was valued in Baghdad two centuries later.

The standard account of the origins of pedagogical Arabic grammar looks to imperial politics. The sons of Abbasid caliph Hārūn al-Rashīd (r. 170–93/786–809) did not know Arabic as their mother tongue, and so it became a priority of the caliph that a kind of grammar of Arabic be created to teach it to his sons.[77] The demise and suppression of the Kufan tradition thus resulted in part from the pedagogic needs of the Islamic state. As pedagogy became more central to the purpose of the discipline of Arabic grammar in the Islamic world, the Kufan approach of always being open to new linguistic data no matter whether it fit or contradicted the increasingly dogmatic and prescriptive rules of grammar handbooks became more and more unacceptable. In sum, "This [openness] was a position that could not survive the ideological and administrative demands of the Islamic state, and the Kufan approach was eventually forced into irrelevance."[78] A so-called Basran approach or, more accurately, the systematizing and categorizing approach of classical grammarians in the tenth century and after, fit the educational and political needs of the Islamic regimes of that period much better than a less coherent, less tidy, less prescriptive approach, which in fact was the approach of early grammarians in general, whether from Basra or Kufa.

Beyond the political and sociological demands on the discipline of Arabic grammar to teach the imperial "father language" to the citizens of an expanding Islamic state, intellectual and philosophical influences from another branch of Islamic knowledge contributed to the development of *naḥw*. During the tenth century, Arab grammarians were greatly influenced by their interactions with *falsafa*, the school of Arab philosophers who held to a number of specific doctrines, such as the eternity of the world, influenced by Hellenic thought.[79] *Falsafa* reached its peak in influencing Islamic thought during this period and offered both conceptual resources and challenges to the grammarians. For one, *falsafa* had its own endemic tool for analyzing utterances—namely, logic. Language, whether Arabic or any other, was for this philosophical tradition merely the outer form, the *lafẓ*, of a deeper meaning, *maʿnā*. One aspect of the grammarians' response to the intellectual stimulus provided by *falsafa* is epitomized in the *Kitāb al-Uṣūl* by Ibn al-Sarrāj (d. 316/928). Plural of the word *aṣl*, the *uṣūl* in the title of Ibn al-Sarrāj's book means principles, origins, or foundations. Ibn al-Sarrāj and so many other classical Arab grammarians after him attempted to systematize the Arabic language into a coherent theory founded on explicitly stated principles and codified rules. In this way, grammarians fashioned logical systems like the doctrines in the philosophical treatises of their rivals the *falāsifa*—that is, the proponents of the school of thought known as *falsafa*. This *uṣūl*-based branch of Arabic grammar, comparable to the Latin pedagogic grammatical tradition of which Donatus is the icon, is the beginning of the didactic kind of Arabic grammatical literature from which post-classical grammar textbooks would eventually develop. "If the early era was one of explicatory descriptivism, by the early fourth/tenth century Arabic grammar had moved into what may be termed an era of categorizing compartmentalization."[80]

Besides this systematization according to foundational rules, another aspect of the grammarians' response to *falsafa* was to develop a kind of speculative approach that inquired into the *ʿilal*—that is, the root causes. The more profound insights of root cause "*ʿilal*" theory originated in the perspective that the Arabic language is a truly marvelous, even mysterious, ordered whole and that grammar can explain not only how the linguistic system works but also why it is as it is. The *Khaṣāʾiṣ* of Ibn Jinnī (d. 392/1002) and the *Kitāb al-Īḍāḥ* by al-Zajjājī (d. 340/951) are the most significant extant examples of this *ʿilal* kind of grammatical writing. Zajjājī's *Īḍāḥ* also exemplifies the development of an inextricable link by the tenth century between education and grammar. While this trend began in the ninth century with such "consciously short summaries of Arabic grammar," as the *Muqaddima fī al-Naḥw* attributed to Khalaf al-Aḥmar and the *Muwaffaqī* of Ibn Kaysān, a chapter in al-Zajjājī's tenth century *Īḍāḥ* connects studying Arabic grammar with acquiring understanding of Arabic culture and Islamic religion.[81]

Latin Grammar as an Intellectual Discipline

Turning now to the place of Latin grammar in Western civilization, we find considerably more scholarly resources than those regarding Arabic grammar in Islamic civilization.[82] With the notable exception of the anecdote about Greek philosopher Crates of Mallos (fl. second century B.C.E.) breaking his leg on a sewer in Rome and lecturing about grammar during his recuperation, there seems to be generally less lore and more clarity regarding the beginnings of the Latin grammatical tradition than of the Arabic grammatical tradition.[83] Moreover, the place of grammar in Western thought was well established thanks to the construct of the medieval trivium of grammar, rhetoric, and dialectic. Tracing the development of this discipline in the West, we will see its roots in ancient Greece as well as its somewhat problematic integration into what became a Christian civilization.

Grammar was systematically treated in the West only after the death of Alexander the Great in 323 B.C.E. Though some grammatical topics were analyzed in treatments of logic or rhetoric in the preceding Hellenic Age, the first systematic Western grammar was written in the first century B.C.E. by the Stoic philosopher Crates of Mallos, who brought his grammar to Rome, perhaps due to an unexpected convalescence there, as mentioned previously.[84] It was also in this period that the eight parts of speech, or more precisely the eight parts of a sentence, were introduced, probably by a certain Tryphon. The division of words into these eight categories (noun, verb, participle, article, pronoun, preposition, adverb, and conjunction) has been "one of the most enduring characteristics of European grammar."[85]

Though grammar was certainly present as a discipline in Greek civilization before the Common Era, it became a more central area of inquiry in the Middle Ages. One scholar sees the ascendancy of the disciplines of the trivium shifting "from rhetoric in antiquity, to grammar during the early Middle Ages, to logic in the High Middle Ages."[86] This trivium itself along with the quadrivium of arithmetic, geometry, music, and astronomy comprised the dominant schematization for the disciplines of knowledge in medieval European civilization but traces its roots to the Greek academies and their legacy in Rome of the second century B.C.E.[87]

These arts of the ancients were not subsumed into Christian thought without a certain hesitancy about accepting wholesale the divisions of pagan scholarship. Such trepidation was particularly pronounced among those so-called "church fathers" of the patristic period who were themselves converts to Christian faith: "Ambivalence arose from the efforts of many individuals to integrate the segments of their lives before and after conversion, the early quest for erudition with the later quest for holiness."[88] Two striking examples of this Christian ambivalence to pagan knowledge are St. Augustine and St. Jerome, to whom Aelius Donatus himself taught Latin grammar. These Christian scholars certainly made great use of their training in the pagan literary arts, but also regarded the pagan arts as "conduits of superstition, heresy, and pride." The church fathers criticized the knowledge offered by the pagan arts as empty, in contrast to the transcendent truth knowable through Christian faith.[89] Though this strand of thought persisted in the Christian tradition, by the seventh or eighth century C.E. the seven liberal arts took on "a preeminent role" in Western culture.[90] By one account, grammar became the most important of these arts from late antiquity until the rise of universities because the Latin of intellectual discourse and scholarship was no longer anyone's native language.[91]

Two conceptions of the work of the grammarian emerged from the classical tradition: pedagogy and speculation.[92] The pedagogical grammarian produced grammar books for a teacher to use to teach correct and effective Latin to students. It is this pedagogical discipline that is symbolized on Chartres Cathedral by the schoolmaster who instilled in Europeans their father language. "With isolated exceptions, Latin was the only language so studied and taught. . . . Latin was the common language of business and commerce, science and industry, philosophy and literature, and, most importantly, of theology and religion."[93] This pedagogic tradition of grammar was more closely aligned in the trivium with rhetoric than with logic. The works of Aelius Donatus (fl. fourth century C.E.) and Priscianus Caesariensis (fl. 500 C.E.) were the centerpieces of this kind of medieval grammatical study, and, with time, extensive commentaries developed around them.[94] These foundational textbooks of Latin study initiated students into "the culture embodied by the language."[95] While the Latin of Aelius Donatus himself embodied the culture of Roman imperialism, the Latin of Gerson's *Donatus moralizatus*, or *Moralized Grammar*, embodied the culture of Christian doctrine.

One important turn in the development of this pedagogic branch of grammar in the later Middle Ages was that in the twelfth and thirteenth centuries it was swept up into a "veritable craze for versifying" such that "almost every species of literary production occasionally appeared in verse."[96] Of particular importance among these versified Latin grammars, both of which appeared around the turn of the thirteenth century, are Alexander de Villa Dei's *Doctrinale puerorum*[97] and Evrard de Béthune's *Graecismus*.[98] By this era, students were coming to the study of Latin from their own vernacular mother tongues.[99] The versified form of the *Doctrinale* and *Graecismus* aided memorization and thus made learning grammar easier than "the catechism-like, question-and-answer format of Donatus's *Ars minor*."[100] These two texts were so successful that "they came to rival Priscian's *Institutiones* as standard advanced grammars, studied in universities as well as in lower schools, and the object of continuous and sophisticated glossing through the later Middle Ages."[101]

The speculative branch of the discipline of grammar investigated philosophical questions about the nature of language and indeed the nature of the world.[102] Speculative grammar, which gained ascendancy in the thirteenth and fourteenth centuries especially, took its name from the Latin word for "mirror," *speculum*, because "it attempted to mirror the structure of the universe."[103] According to early twentieth-century medievalist Louis Paetow, it was the influence of Scholasticism that brought about this new branch of the discipline of grammar: "Instead of referring to examples from the best Latin literature to explain a doubtful point, the grammarians now preferred to solve the matter by the rules of logic."[104] In other words, speculative grammar more closely aligned with logic, while pedagogical grammar aligned with rhetoric. Precursors of fully developed speculative grammar who also combined logic and grammar include Peter of Spain (fl. 1135–ca. 1160), Peter Helias (fl. ca. 1150), and John of Garland (fl. 1214–52). Starting with these authors, "the grammarian was also to be a philosopher."[105]

Grammar in Medieval European Education

Both the pedagogic and the speculative branches of grammar were important in medieval European education. The beginning of the pedagogic branch was Donatus's *Ars minor*, which had been the "*Schulgrammatik* or 'school grammar' of the Roman Empire" and then became the primer of the medieval schoolboy.[106] Also called *De octo partibus orationis*, the *Ars minor* provided a concise introduction to the parts of speech, "the heart of the grammarian's doctrine."[107] Indeed, Donatus was the veritable icon of Latin grammar:

> During the Middle Ages, the very name Donatus, in forms like *donat* and *donet*, became synonymous with *grammar* itself in a variety of vernacular languages including Irish, Welsh, French, English, and Provençal. Even after the Middle Ages gave way to the Renaissance, the grammar's influence continued to be felt. Luther and Rabelais learned from the Donatus, the first French-language book printed (1460) was a translation of the Donatus, and a reference in Cotsgrave's *Dictionarie* [sic] *of the French and English Tongues* (1611) indicates that the Donatus was then still in use in English schools.[108]

If Muslim children in the medieval world became literate primarily by copying and memorizing the Qur'an as their first textbook before moving on in secondary education to the study of grammar, Christian children seemed to have begun their elementary education primarily with Donatus's *Ars minor.*

The speculative branch of grammar appeared in medieval European education not through the basic textbooks but through the commentaries and instructional activities of grammar masters. While the hierarchically structured organization of Donatus's *Ars gramamtica* and its abbreviated form, the *De octo partibus orationis* or *Ars minor*, seem "to presuppose a view of language as a rational, logical system, . . . the *Ars* does not articulate any philosophical principles."[109] However, in late medieval times, even "grammar masters outside the universities began to infuse their teaching with contemporary philosophical interests."[110]

Latin grammar was one of the principal subjects of elementary and secondary schools, which must have been widespread in medieval Europe, though education was neither free of charge nor obligatory.[111] In fact, preparatory schools existed in multiple institutional forms, including monastic and cathedral schools. The very existence of universities speaks to the existence of schools for children.[112] Moreover, since the usual entry requirement of the universities was that students already speak, read, and write Latin, which after late antiquity ceased being anyone's mother tongue, Latin must have been central to the curriculum of preparatory schools. "It would have been idle for students to stream to Bologna to learn Roman law, if they had had no previous training and did not understand the Latin of the *Corpus iuris*."[113]

Evidence from Italy, France, and England illustrates the nature and scope of elementary and secondary education in medieval Europe.[114] In Italy, in the *Chronicles* of the history of Florence, Giovanni Villani (d. 1348) estimated between eight and ten thousand children learning to read at the elementary level and 550 to 600 students in four different secondary schools studying grammar and logic. Genoan notarial records provide evidence of contracts that parents drew up with teachers for the education of their children. Regarding France, the autobiography of Guibert de Nogent (d. 1124) observes that there were both more and better grammar teachers in the early twelfth century than in the mid-eleventh.[115] As for England, "At Oxford between 1300 and 1347 grammar school boys 'paid a terminal fee varying from four to five pence, when the usual cost of a scholar's board for one week was eight pence, and a manuscript Donatus, containing about six thousand words, cost three pence.' "[116]

At the university level, grammar was generally not a focus of study—especially the pedagogic grammar that, as we have seen, was a centerpiece of medieval European primary and secondary schooling. Remedial grammar seems to have been available at universities for students who were not sufficiently lettered to begin the normal course of studies.[117] Given the young age of some students admitted to universities, the teaching of pedagogic grammar at universities is especially unsurprising. At one of the colleges at Toulouse "no one under eight or above twenty-five years of age could be admitted,"[118] and "scholars above ten years were obliged to take an oath of obedience to the rector."[119] After Johannes de Garlandia (ca. 1195–ca. 1272), grammar seems to disappear for over a century from the records of the University of Paris.[120] During this period, the ascendancy of dialectic over its sisters, rhetoric and grammar, is pronounced in Paris, a city whose intellectual community at the time became fixated on philosophy, logic, metaphysics, and theology. Grammar reappears at Paris only in 1366 by being mentioned in the oaths that bachelors in the arts had to swear as candidates for their license. In these oaths, it is clear that "grammar now was hardly more than an entrance requirement to the important work of the arts course which consisted of logic and philosophy."[121]

In southern France a considerably different picture is apparent. At Toulouse, in the University of Perpignan, and perhaps also at Orange, Cahors, and Avignon, "grammar flourished . . . more than it did anywhere else in Europe."[122] In the early fourteenth century, Toulouse granted degrees in grammar, including the bachelor's degree, the licentiate, and the master's degree.[123] Many of these universities in southern France even had separate faculties of grammar.[124] A 1328 statute from Toulouse reveals the lecture program that the masters in grammar undertook. The textbooks mentioned are *Priscianus maior*, the *Doctrinale, Alexander, Ebrardus, Historiae Alexandri, Hympni, and Metrificatura*. A century later, statutes from 1426 and 1489 "still mention the *Doctrinale, Ebrardus, Alexander*, and *Priscianus maior* as the grammatical books in common use at the university."[125]

In sum, the study of pedagogic grammars was one of the principal undertakings of preparatory schooling in medieval Europe. While in the fourteenth century at the University of Paris grammar was primarily a prerequisite for the arts course, at the University of Toulouse and seemingly at other universities in southern France, grammar played a more vital role in higher education and scholarly inquiry. Donatus is apparently not mentioned as part of the normal grammar at universities and thus can be clearly placed in the realm of preparatory school rather than university study.

The Discipline of Spiritual Grammar

Our investigation of the position of Latin and Arabic and the discipline of grammar in the worlds of Gerson and Qushayrī respectively has revealed some striking similarities. The diglossic sociolinguistic situations in which each author lived and wrote had come about many centuries before through the spread of empires. By the respective eras of our authors, the Arabic of Persia's Muslim conquerors and the Latin of the Roman Empire were on the cusp of being relegated primarily to religious roles. The Renaissance and Reformation in France brought the French vernacular into its own as a language of power and prestige, while an Islamicized New Persian emerged with increasing confidence into the eleventh century and gradually became the cultural language of the Islamic East. The discipline that focused on the grammar of the waning standard languages in Paris at the turn of the fifteenth century and Nishapur in the eleventh century had thus for centuries been foundational to the respectively Christian and Islamic educational systems.

As we have seen, initiation into the discipline of grammar came early to pupils in both contexts, even if it came earlier in students' education in the Christian West compared to those in the Islamic world, where the Qur'an was the starting point of schooling. At the same time, in both worlds the discipline of grammar encompassed profound intellectual and religious inquiry and extended into the most advanced levels of scholarship. Though any literate Latin or Arabic reader would know the rudiments of grammar, a small elite pursued erudite philosophical and theological questions through this fundamentally linguistic discipline.

We have also seen how the Islamic regimes of the ninth and tenth centuries suppressed Kufan grammatical thought and how Emperor Charlemagne's Christian regime instituted a new *grammatica* imposing distinctly English pronunciations onto Latin. Classical grammar, like orthodox theology, was shaped by rulers, empires, and their scholarly elites, like Alcuin of York and Rabanus Maurus working at the behest of Charlemagne. Recognition of the power of these high-register languages and of the discipline of grammar in the cultural worlds of Gerson and Qushayrī permits and demands an analysis of the power dynamics of these authors' troping of grammar. The grammatical performances of *The Grammar of Hearts* and *Moralized Grammar* reference the authoritative discourses of linguistic order in the Arabic and Latin worlds, respectively. These languages of literary, political, and religious authority are thus confirmed and reinforced in their significance by the trope of spiritual grammar. The structure of these languages that the discipline of grammar teaches to students is re-presented by *The Grammar of Hearts* and *Moralized Grammar* as spiritual reality, ultimate reality.

The prescription of classical grammar and the hegemony of orthodox theology thus worked in alliance to command and control subjects. As we shall see in the following chapters, Qushayrī and Gerson were both champions of hegemonic orthodox theologies that were implicated in and abetted by normative grammars of classical languages. As pedagogues and religious authorities, Qushayrī and Gerson devoted themselves to forming others—students, parishioners, Sufi novices, and priest apprentices, as well as scholarly readers throughout their respective worlds and religious communities. The discipline of classical grammar afforded these authors a powerful tool for exercising this office of forming others. Though Michel Foucault's study of disciplines focused on the operations and techniques of power in early modern Europe, his insights into the function of pedagogical disciplines to form subjects are not without relevance to our consideration of spiritual grammar:

> [The individual subject] is also a reality fabricated by this specific technology of power that I have called "discipline." We must cease once and for all to describe the effects of power in negative terms: it "excludes," it "represses," it "censors," it "abstracts," it "masks," it "conceals." In fact, power produces; it produces reality; it produces domains of objects and rituals of truth. The individual and the knowledge that may be gained of him belong to this production.[126]

The Grammar of Hearts and *Moralized Grammar* place the reading subject in a particular linguistic and spiritual reality. Embedded and enmeshed in the grammatically shaped structures of that reality, readers of these spiritual grammars discover their position and learn how to move within their reality.

2 Genres and Genders of Gerson

Saint Jean-en-Grève Church. Paris, around the turn of the fifteenth century. It is Mass on the Feast of the Holy Trinity, a day when the church contemplates a mystery that is as central to Christian theology as it is difficult for the faithful to comprehend. Father Jean Gerson, the presider at this liturgy, is familiar to the congregants. He comes over regularly from the University of Paris, where he has been chancellor since 1395, to preach in French to the parishioners who pray at this grand church on the Right Bank of the Seine. Indeed, in 1403 Avignon's Pope Benedict XIII gives the curacy of this church to Gerson.[1] When it comes time in the church service for the sermon, Jean Gerson takes the pulpit. From the liturgy in Latin he switches to French, his mother tongue, to address this nonscholarly congregation, though he does selectively use the "father tongue" of Latin in the first few minutes of his sermon to quote scripture, cite classical sources, and lead the congregation in reciting the "Ave Maria." After introductory comments presenting the theme of his sermon, that contemplation of the soul is the surest way to come to know God, Gerson further modulates his voice and his character. He switches genders, dramatically enacting a dialogue between two sisters:

> Not long ago I learned during contemplation that the Soul was speaking in this way to wise Reason, saying to her: "Beautiful sister Reason, you have long been away from me, by means of the doors of the five bodily senses, in order to inquire into our God and to know if any can tell you certainty about Him. What do you have to tell me? What news do you have to report to me?"
>
> "Beautiful sister, I will tell you," responds Reason. "I searched by sea and by land, in the sky and in heaven, and asked the earth if she were

my God. She said no. I asked the sea if she were my God. She said no. I asked the sky, the heaven, the sun, and the stars if any of them were my God. All of them cried back in a loud voice, 'God made us. The idolaters and pagans are mistaken. We are by no means God. Seek Him elsewhere and above us.' That is how each material and bodily thing responded to me. They all affirmed that they are not worthy to be called God, for they have many imperfections: they have in themselves large and small parts and are changeable, and we acknowledge that God is completely perfect and immutable and without parts. Why without parts? Because the whole is more perfect than its parts, and nothing could be God that does not have every perfection. This is to say that any such part would not be as perfect as the whole."

"My sister Reason, while outside of me you cannot find our God in corporal things—apart from [discovering] the fact that they are not our God—nevertheless it is the case that there is One who made them. Come back to me and consider me, for I am a spiritual entity and without parts, if by any chance you hear any news about it."[2]

Performing this dialogue between two sisters, Reason and the Soul personified, preacher Jean Gerson embodied theological reasoning that he hoped his congregation at the parish St. Jean-en-Grève would themselves adopt.[3] Vesting himself in the feminine gender of these virtuous characters, Gerson put on the guises of two profound aspects of human being. In this theatrical sketch from the pulpit of St. Jean-en-Grève, Gerson acted out in his French mother tongue the empirical investigations of human reason and the spiritual wisdom of the soul. Just before the dramatization, Gerson tells his listeners that he will play a "*personnaige*," or dramatic character, and that it should not be "wasted time," just as "the simple folk [*les simples gens*] listen profitably to the Mass in Latin, though much of it they do not understand."[4] Concern for *les simples gens* is pervasive in Gerson's writings. By this term he means illiterate and semi-literate Christians, whether ordained or lay. The feminine personages whose parts he plays exemplify ways of being Christian that Gerson as pastor suggests for the parishioners. Acting out this dialogue in the middle of this sermon, which is known to posterity as *Videmus nunc*, Gerson in drag, as it were, powerfully illustrates how good Christians might plausibly and profitably seek their God.

The central argument of this chapter is that Gerson used genre creatively to advance his pastoral goals of forming Christian subjects. He experimented and innovated with genre in an effort to prod listeners and readers to move beyond "generic" molds and models of being Christian. The multiple meanings of the French word "*genre*," which include "gender" and "genus" along with "literary genre," provide us a clue to the links between textuality and subjectivity operative in spiritual grammar. In his essay "The Law of Genre," Jacques Derrida explores these multiple meanings, which will inform our exploration of the genres of Gerson.[5]

Performing Gerson

Gerson put much more effort into vernacular French writings than most of his scholarly predecessors because he wanted to reach more souls from among the growing French-reading public of his society. Gerson's gender-bending performance in *Videmus nunc* illustrates how he used texts and genres to form subjectivities. Building on Daniel Hobbins's argument that Gerson took writing extremely seriously,[6] my argument here focuses on genre as a linchpin of Gerson's creativity and experimentation as an author.

An overview of Gerson's roles in the world will deepen our understanding of him as a writer. Jean Gerson (1363–1429) lived much of his adult life at the height of the academic institution that was the intellectual center of the Western Christian world of his time.[7] He was an erudite scholar, steeped in the classical Latin literary tradition, and a talented Latin stylist. Inheriting the Western Christian theological tradition, Gerson was a *traditor*, an expert who preserved, passed on, and interpreted that tradition. Some Catholic authorities remember him chiefly for his willingness to compromise papal power in favor of a conciliar solution to the Western Schism, in which not only Rome but also Avignon boasted sitting popes. Gerson is seen by some as an "epigone" of medieval Scholasticism[8] and by others as a forerunner of the Reformation.[9] Jean Gerson was a celebrity preacher whose sermons were heard by kings, popes, university faculty, church councils, bishops, monks and nuns, students, city-dwellers, and country folk. He also had an emotionally reserved and introverted personality and avoided friendship throughout his life.[10] He took as his personal motto Phil 3.20: "Our way of life is in heaven" (*Nostra conversatio in coelis est*).[11] No matter how much Gerson lived in the center and at the height, he considered himself always an outsider, a wandering pilgrim, a refugee in this world. Gerson was both arrogant and pious. Though exceedingly concerned with sexual purity, he wrote in an explicit and matter-of-fact manner about such topics as masturbation and nocturnal emissions. He is remembered by some as a conservative or even an unoriginal theologian, though in his theological writing he eschewed the literary forms typical for scholars of his time.

The tensions and even contradictions among these aspects of Jean Gerson not only indicate the complexity of the richly lived life of a leading Christian intellectual in late fourteenth- and early fifteenth-century France, but also reveal some of the pitfalls of the interpretive frameworks employed by modern scholars to make sense of Gerson's era. Rise-and-decline meta-narratives themselves have a long and complex history, even if we only take into account scholarly attempts at making sense of Gerson's world. The fourteenth century is left unrescued by the work of those twentieth-century scholars who worked to undermine earlier thinkers' sweeping dismissal of the Middle Ages as simply a period of darkness—a historiographical framework first conceived by humanists and reformers but reinforced by Enlightenment and indeed nineteenth-century intellectuals. One important example of a twentieth-century retriever of the so-called "Middle Ages" is American historian Charles Homer Haskins (d. 1937), who found a "Renaissance" in the twelfth century.[12] Another example is French philosopher Étienne Gilson (d. 1978), who found in Thomas Aquinas and in thirteenth-century Western Christian thought more broadly a culmination of the history of philosophy and theology.[13] More recently, some Reformation scholars have looked backward from the era of Martin Luther (1483–1546) and the other great reformers to find in the centuries of 1250–1550 an entire "age of reform."[14] While we do not aim here to solve these larger historiographical issues that problematize our understanding of Gerson's world, at the very least awareness and acknowledgment of these debates can inform our literary and theological analysis. We will pay credence neither to a decline model in which the fourteenth century is a stagnant and decadent era past the prime of some medieval highpoint, nor to a rise model in which the fourteenth century is a precursor to the Protestant Reformation. Instead, we will try to understand Gerson's writings as much as possible on their own terms, in the period of the late fourteenth and early fifteenth centuries. We may well find it helpful to recognize Gerson in turns both as a schoolman and a humanist.[15]

Due both to today's historiographical approach to Gerson's period in European history and to the great diversity of Jean Gerson's life and work, understandings of him today splinter Gerson into distinct figures—conciliarist, mystical theologian, preacher, priest, professor, characteristically French, gifted stylist of Latin, popularizer, erudite master of medieval thought, man writing for men, pastor with keen concern for the spiritual development of women and children. In his writings all of these facets of Gerson's person are evident.

Turning from how historians have seen Gerson's roles in the world to how Gerson saw himself, we note that adaptive versatility as a writer was intrinsic to Gerson's self-understanding as a theologian. Gerson compared the work of a theologian to that of a physician: "The theologian must accommodate inevitable changes in spiritual appetites, revolutions of tastes, personal differences, and shifting circumstances. As we have different faces, so we have different souls. What makes some sick makes others healthy."[16] To describe this adaptive role of the theologian in moving the passions and instilling morality in various social groups, Gerson used a metaphor that more traditionally applied to confessors: "In Gerson's vision, the professional theologian was to be much more than an expert on old texts, safely protected from the wider world inside a shell of citations. He was to be like the physician, healing the multiple and varying diseases of a Christian society."[17] Referring to handbooks for lay people that doctors of medicine created when society suffered from the plague, Gerson wrote in one of his letters that theologians should follow suit and write "on the main points of our religion, and especially on its precepts, for the instruction of uneducated people."[18]

Above all, Jean Gerson's positions in the world were those of a master of theology, a university scholar, and a teacher of sacred Christian doctrine. When writing, Gerson did so as a theologian. He crafted customized cures of religious instruction for the various moral ills of different societal groups: "We see Gerson moving between the worlds of university, court, laity, and ecclesiastical hierarchy, adapting his message to each, transferring elements from one to the next, and so enriching himself and his writings through his participation."[19]

Gerson shared in common with other university theologians of his era and of the preceding century an image of theologians as leaders in the salvific work of the church. They saw themselves as having "a particular responsibility within the church as a whole and a status comparable with the major prelates."[20] Thomas Aquinas, for example, compared bishops and masters of theology to architects, while considering normal priests to be like manual laborers in "the work of spiritual construction."[21]

It was in the context of this sense of salvific purpose that Gerson took the craft of writing so seriously. He wrote to save souls and took extraordinary steps to expand the range of his writing in order to meet the range of spiritual needs that he saw for the souls in his era. In his treatise *De modis significandi* (1426), Gerson wrote about this approach to writing theology. He emphasized the importance of rhetoric for theology and not just grammar and logic. These three disciplines, rhetoric, grammar, and logic—the trivium of Western medieval learning—are the "modes of signifying" referred to in the title of the treatise. Gerson shared with previous Scholastic theologians such as Bonaventure and Aquinas an understanding of the purpose of theology as instilling morality. Unlike many of his predecessors, Gerson quite explicitly recognized rhetoric and literary genre as crucial to achieving this purpose.[22]

Genre was one of the keys to the constant literary adaptation that Gerson performed while undertaking the work of the theologian as he envisioned it.[23] Indeed, he used an extraordinary range of genres to reach audiences in new ways and to speak to new constituencies, such as the burgeoning reading public of French-language literature.[24]

One way to understand Gerson's remarkable range of genres is to regard his texts as performances and the genres he chose as the stages for these performances. Each kind of stage allows Gerson to "perform" differently and create different possibilities for embodying holiness. At times Gerson performed in vernacular French and at times in standard Latin, thus appealing to audiences more accessibly in their mother tongue or with greater power in their "father tongue." Taking a page from gender theory, we can say that sometimes he performed in mainstream, "straight" genres and other times in transgressive, "queer" genres, thus sometimes meeting readers' expectations and other times surprising them.

Gerson showed great "creativity and experimentation" in the extent to which he used "extra-university genres"—some of which were retrievals of genres from earlier periods in classical and Christian literature and others of which were novel creations.[25] He also mixed genres creatively, such as in his use of the dialogue genre in many of his sermons. Indeed, the dialogue was among his favorite literary devices. Like the *exemplum*, the dialogue in Gerson's writings was often a dependent genre that appeared in the midst of other genres. Gerson also used dialogue as an independent genre to frame his work "*De consolatione theologiae* (1418), which purports to carry on the argument of the *De consolatione philosophiae*" of Boethius (d. 525 C.E.).[26] Creative experimentation is another facet of Gerson's writing that makes his writerly ambition apparent. Gerson hoped to create classics for posterity.[27] Epitomizing this ambition was the *Josephina* (1414–18), Gerson's epic poem that depicts St. Joseph for the purpose of promoting devotion to him.

Reacting against the rhetorical habits of the schoolmen of his time, Gerson tried to find other ways to organize his writings besides the typical Scholastic use of division and subdivision. Relevant to our study of his *Moralized Grammar*, extended analogies and metaphors provided Gerson an organizational framework in numerous works besides his spiritual grammar. For example, in *De distinctione verarum revelationum a falsis*, Gerson compares true and false revelations to genuine and counterfeit currency. In his *Trilogium astrologiae theologizatae*, the thirty propositions are like "precious necklaces." In his *Propositio facta coram Anglicis*, Gerson constructs a conceit for the four *considerationes* as "a four-cornered building." While these literary frameworks might strike us today as contrived, Gerson scholar Daniel Hobbins argues that "they are evidence of a mind striving to break free from traditional models of composition, to experiment with new structures."[28] In *Moralized Grammar*, Gerson was similarly performing a literary experiment based on metaphorical schemes. This kind of literary experimentation is not so far from the extended analogies that Gerson uses to structure other writings.

One genre played a disproportionately important role in Gerson's writings. The sermon was the central genre of religious literature in Gerson's time and epitomized his approach to writing generally. In whatever he wrote, Gerson was in some sense always preaching. Sermons have a performative dimension, which influenced Gerson's writing more generally. Before considering in detail his *Moralized Grammar*, investigation of Gerson's writing in this central genre of the sermon as well as the tract, a genre newly important in Gerson's era, will allow insights into Gerson's texts as different kinds of genre performance, meant to engender sanctity among his readers and listeners.

Gerson and the Sermon

Gerson was a famous and accomplished preacher.[29] Around sixty of his sermons are extant today.[30] Before examining two examples, a word on the sermon genre in the medieval diglossic context is in order. In the life of the French society in which Gerson lived, as in medieval Europe generally, the sermon genre played a truly pivotal role. The sermon was the bridge between the written scholarly theological tradition of the clerics and the mostly illiterate Christian believers whose salvation depended on their religious education and moral uprightness. The sermon was also a bridge between Latin and the vernacular. As a literary construct, the sermon epitomized the church's performance of its ongoing apostolic function of evangelization. Late medieval France in particular was still very much a rural society whose city-dwellers were mostly as illiterate as its rural folk.[31] Sermons delivered to French Christians aimed primarily to teach the basics of theology and to exhort believers to live out a moral life as the Church defined it.[32] Sermons were the privileged medium through which the ordained taught the laity how to be Christian.

In fact, the sermon enjoyed a centrality in medieval Western Christian religious literature rivaled by no other literary genre. In an age when no sharp boundaries existed between the secular and religious, the sermon can be considered the dominant genre of literature in the lives of medieval Europeans.[33] Though largely underestimated and underutilized by modern-day theologians in their interpretation of the Christian intellectual tradition, the sermon is by any account a formidable vestige of medieval thought. From thirteenth-century Paris alone four thousand sermons are extant.[34] Preaching manuals instructing clerics on the *artes praedicandi* were also quite numerous in the Middle Ages.[35]

By one authoritative account, the sermon genre can be defined in the following way: (1) "essentially an oral discourse, spoken in the voice of a preacher who addresses an audience, (2) to instruct and exhort them, (3) on a topic concerned with faith and morals and based on a sacred text."[36] In cases where lay people constituted that congregation, preachers translated their "clerical culture into the categories of thought and linguistic forms of the laity."[37] Rhetorically, sermons operate on multiple levels: "The preacher's intent is not only to teach, but also to proclaim the Word and to exhort: to move the audience to embrace the faith and to undertake some form of action, usually requiring them to change their behavior."[38] Like the life, death, and resurrection of Jesus Christ, sermons are events that teach and demand change of those who experience them: "while the sermon certainly is a didactic genre, it incorporates proclamation and exhortation, in order to foster belief and to intensify and activate the message taught."[39] The stakes are high and preachers' responsibility grave: "Ultimately [the sermon's] purpose is eschatological and soteriological, for it is concerned with the end of time and the listeners' salvation."[40] The topic is always one way or another faith and morals, though the function could be "catechesis, conversion to the faith, persuasion to orthodoxy, rebuke, call to conversion of heart, repentance and reform."[41]

The fluidity of the sermon genre, as explained by Beverly Kienzle, also validates our understanding of intertextuality or cross-breeding as intrinsic to genre performance generally. The sermon shares characteristics with "the letter, the treatise and the commentary (and also to the speech, the shorter *vitae* and the *principia* [inception ceremonies] of university masters)."[42] Authors often recycled textual material from one of these genres and used it in another genre.

Diglossia and the Oral Nature of Sermons

Besides its fluidity, another characteristic of the sermon whose significance can hardly be overstated is its orality. In fact, in terms of content, organization, language, and the archival vestiges of sermons, the tension between the written literary text and the actual oral performance is quite often remarkable.[43] Compounding this gap between event and text is the diglossia of medieval Europe. As explained earlier, Latin was no longer anybody's native language, though it was the normal and normative language of writing, intellectual discourse, and specifically clerical life. Regarding sermons, the relationship between Latin and the vernacular is no more straightforward than that between the oral and the written. Though a manuscript might be in Latin, the sermon may well have been delivered in a vernacular.[44] Indeed, who recorded the sermon, when, in what language, and in how refined a form are all open questions to be asked of any sermon text. The stenographic reports of actual sermon performances, called *reportationes*, present scholars today with fascinating puzzles to solve:

> That *reportationes* are themselves sometimes "macaronic," a mixture of Latin and vernacular, reminds us of another problematic presented by written texts as a window on the preached word. Outside of sermons to the clergy, medieval preaching was virtually always in the vernacular. Roberto Rusconi has highlighted the bilingualism of reporting: a preacher moved from Latin texts, the Bible and his notes, to a vernacular preached word, which the reporter took down, usually in Latin shorthand. The *reportatio* itself could then be edited into more literary Latin to provide a final version. Sermon texts masque not only a motion from oral to written, but often another from one language to another.[45]

Medieval sermons and the *reportationes* about them thus provide a privileged window into how the diglossic sociolinguistic situation that we previously explored directly impacted religious literature.

Diglossia presents important challenges to studying and interpreting French sermons, at least between the early thirteenth and early sixteenth centuries.[46] Though the basic rule is that the vernacular was used in preaching to mainly lay audiences and Latin was usually reserved for preaching to the learned in convents, synods, and universities,[47] this rule is by no means without exception. "In every case, there is no reason to believe that the sermon was delivered in Latin unless it specifically states that it was. Sometimes the preserved Latin version contains such phrases as *in vulgare* or *in gallice*, but the absence of such words is not an indication that preaching was done in Latin."[48] Moreover, this complex bilingual sociolinguistic context was not unique to late medieval times.[49]

Recognizing the importance of these issues of diglossia to the role of the theologian in medieval European societies, we will examine both a French and a Latin sermon by Gerson. Unlike his sermons extant in French,[50] the Latin sermons of Jean Gerson have not yet been studied in depth.[51] As in *Moralized Grammar*, the language in question matters a great deal for the interpretation of these religious texts. Latin sermons were directed toward clerics and others schooled in the standard language. French sermons were directed to a wider audience. All French speakers could understand their oral performance, and a growing population of French readers could understand their written form. The two examples we examine will illustrate some part of the range of Christian subjectivities that Gerson endeavored to form among his listeners and readers.

Preaching in the Vernacular: *Videmus nunc*

As noted previously, in 1408 Gerson became the pastor of St. Jean-en-Grève, where he delivered this sermon,[52] but on the Feast of the Holy Trinity when he preached *Videmus nunc*, he was not yet pastor, but rather a regular guest preacher.

Videmus nunc is remarkable for its hefty theological and philosophical content. In this sense, this sermon was typical of Gerson's use of the vernacular as a vehicle for conveying Latin learning to the laity.[53] While among Christian authors a long tradition of ambivalence toward the liberal arts exists,[54] Gerson was pleased to cite pagan luminaries in the service of spiritual rhetoric. The parishioners present for this sermon heard exposition of concepts from Augustine's *De Trinitate*, Anselm's ontological argument, Plato's *Timaeus*, Aristotle's *Nicomachean Ethics*, Pseudo-Dionysius's "*via negativa*," Boethius's *On the Consolation of Philosophy*, and from John of Damascus, Richard of St. Victor, Averroes, Cicero, Seneca, Ovid, and others.[55]

Though replete with classical and patristic learning, Gerson's sermon remains accessible thanks to being such a carefully constructed literary product. One of his principal vehicles for putting forward theological and philosophical ideas in this Sunday sermon is the set of allegorical dialogues between Sister Reason and Sister Soul with which we began this chapter. As we have seen, these dramatizations couch substantive philosophical and theological material in a lively back-and-forth between imaginary characters.[56] Composed of sections on a protheme, a theme, two imaginary dialogues between Sisters Soul and Reason, a prayer, and a "loving contemplation," *Videmus nunc* retains its rhetorical unity through a consistent use of a single image to underscore the thesis of the sermon.[57] This unifying image comes from 1 Corinthians 13:12, just after the famous hymn to love: Gerson interprets the mirror mentioned in that passage as the human soul. He reworks the scriptural verse to reach the idea that in this world the soul is that mirror through which we see God. His thesis, then, is that only through turning inward to oneself can one come to know that God exists, is one, is perfect, is omniscient, and is triune.

In the excerpt quoted at the beginning of this chapter, Gerson approaches the topic of seeking God by having Sister Soul ask Sister Reason about the findings of her empirical searches using the five senses. Sister Reason's reply echoes Book X of Augustine's *Confessions*.[58] She inquired in the sea, the earth, the sky, and asked them all whether they were God, but each responded negatively, as they are all composed of great and small parts and are all changeable, while God clearly is perfect, immutable, and not composed of parts. The Soul claims superior wisdom, taking the part of the teacher in relation to her sister Reason: "Away from me you will never be able to find our God. . . . Come back to me and observe me, if perchance you hear no news about God. For I am a spiritual thing and am not composed of parts."

Later, the Soul shifts the dialogue to address the theological mystery of the Feast of the Holy Trinity: "Is it not fitting to conclude that there are three gods?" asks the Soul.[59] In Sister Reason's response to Sister Soul's question about the threeness of God we come to a pivotal moment in both the doctrinal content and the rhetorical structure of the sermon:

> Truly, my Soul, no. We must not come to that conclusion, and you can see that from what I have told you. For the Father and the Son and the Holy Spirit can have but one and the same power, one and the same perfection, one goodness, one life, one knowledge. There is one single thing out of the three, though in other creatures it is not at all so. For, if John is one man, Peter is one man, and Martin is one man, they are three men. Why? In the name of God! For the one does not have the power of the other, nor his life, nor his knowledge.
>
> And thus it is, my Soul, that any creature whatsoever cannot completely resemble its Creator, nor the deed its doer, as the image of a person externally or in a mirror cannot completely be similar in life, in knowledge, and in power to the person that the image represents, nor the shadow its light. At the same time, some similarity can indeed be found there. By knowledge of the image, like by the image of the king, one knows the king that it represents, though obscurely and imperfectly. Similarly I say, my Soul, that through you and in you, as through an image and in a mirror, I can gaze at those things that I have previously said about our God.[60]

Ever a mindful pedagogue, Gerson does not continue overmuch his doctrinal discourse, even an allegorical one. Breaking the conceit of the conversation between the sisters Reason and Soul, Gerson addresses the congregants and confesses how this kind of intellectual meditation affects his own spirit and heart:

> Devout people, this is the way in which wise Reason and the devout Soul seemed to me to converse together of the blessed Divinity and of His highness and majesty. When I came to the end of these words, then profoundly I sighed and trembled. With great wonder, profoundly moved and almost ravished outside of myself, I cried out with St. Paul the apostle, "Oh, the depth of the riches and wisdom [and knowledge of God]!"[61]

The second dialogue is less rhetorically compelling than the first, as it is composed of two long speeches by Reason with only one response by the Soul. This form thus diminishes the conceit of a conversation and the dramatic tension achieved by the first dialogue. The most significant theological contribution made by this second dialogue is Sister Reason's recourse to Augustinian psychology and trinitarian doctrine:

> If you have in your memory the semblance or representation of something—let us say of yourself—you can then set this semblance of yourself in your understanding through clear and actual knowledge of

yourself, and since you know yourself, you will form in your will a love and delight for yourself.[62]

Reason cautions that this knowledge will not be a completely faithful representation of oneself, but it will be as faithful a representation as possible. "If this is so, the memory is thus the parent of your knowledge, and your memory and knowledge together produce your love and delight."[63] Drawing on Augustine's classic treatise *De Trinitate*, especially Books IX and X, Gerson has Sister Reason develop a theory of the human person that is an image of the Trinity:

> By some resemblance—however imperfect it might be—in the blessed Trinity, the Father has in Himself a representation of Himself and of His Divinity, and of everything that once was, or is, or will be, or can be, since He knows all and is capable of all. The Father can therefore make of this representation of Himself and of His Divinity and of everything a kind of personal knowledge, as through speaking to Himself, communicating with and pouring out Himself. Because His word and this communication would not at all be perfect, if it were not completely similar to the Father, and it would not be completely similar to Him if it were not one and the same substance and power and knowledge with Him, so it is fitting that this Word which is called the Son be one and the same substance with the Father, and thus there is but one God.[64]

This theory aims to avoid impinging on the unity and uncomposed simplicity of God as the Holy One while using models of knowing and speaking to illustrate the three persons of the Trinity as knower, the one known, and the knowing relation between them or again as speaker, the Word spoken, and the speaking relations between them. God's knowledge is not a predicated attribute, but is rather perfect and complete and thus inseparable from God as knower. Similarly, God's Word is one with God as speaker of the Word. Between God's knowledge of God's self and God as knower is the relational knowing, which too shares completely in the oneness of God. Sister Reason brings out the Augustinian explanation of the third person of the Trinity by shifting from the models of knowing and speaking to the model of loving. As the Son is the Word of God's self-communication, the Spirit is the love between the Father and the Son:

> And after the Son, mustn't he perfectly love his Father? Yes, indeed, for he has abandoned to Him all that he has, without holding anything back,

> and has given Him this gift. If the Son must through recognition and gratitude give a gift to the Father just as perfect as that which he has received—and he does just that—he gives the Holy Spirit who is perfect personal love of the Father for the Son and of the Son for the Father, from which it follows that the Holy Spirit proceeds from the Son as from the Father, against the error of the Greeks.[65]

This speech by Sister Reason is pure systematic theology, a kind of dramatized academic monologue on Augustine's doctrine on the Trinity. By this point in the sermon congregants might be intellectually primed to make sense of such weighty ideas; the device of the allegorical conversation, which Gerson had so effectively used earlier on, has clearly given way here to lengthy expositions with minimal intrusion from the allegorical characters of Sister Reason and Sister Soul.

The rhetorical effect of producing a Christian subjectivity that congregants can emulate or adopt remains operative. Gerson provides a feminine French-speaking model of how a layperson can think and talk about the Triune God, one of the most challenging and profound topics in Christian theology. The character of Sister Reason shows congregants how a nonclerical French intellectual could thoughtfully talk about the Trinity. In an era when the French language was rising as a literary and intellectual vehicle, and when a francophone public who read and wrote about weighty topics in French rather than Latin was growing, this kind of Christian subjectivity was newly relevant and important.

In the concluding section of the sermon, Gerson produces a very different mold for congregants to emulate. A third sister joins holy Soul and wise Reason. This third sister is none other than "that which we call Devotion or Contemplation, the loving and the religious."[66] Sister Devotion is a model for a different Christian subjectivity, one that was in principle within reach for the sophisticated and simple alike. She is the teacher of Sister Soul: "the Holy Spirit sent [Sister Devotion] to learn and teach more perfectly to the Soul the secrets of the Holy Trinity in the Divinity." She is more highly favored than Sister Reason: "It pleases God to reveal and show Himself and His secrets more completely to Devotion than to Reason, to love than to cognition." Gerson illustrates the superiority of Devotion over Reason by comparing one of his *simples gens* to *les philosophes* and to great theologians: "a simple person who is devout and loves God, shall have much greater and more worthy knowledge of the Divinity, of His power, wisdom, and goodness, and of His gentleness and beneficence than the philosophers had, or than many great brilliant theologians and others who lack love and devotion."[67] Though Gerson recognizes the possibility for simple folk to reach this kind of knowledge of God, Sister Devotion does not personify plain piety. Rather, she is a mystic. While the mystical path was not the way of being Christian that befitted most congregants, he did not exclude the possibility of the *simples gens* receiving the grace of mystical knowledge of God.[68]

The *Videmus nunc* sermon exemplifies how Gerson put to use his talent as a writer in combining the pastoral and pedagogical roles that he had as a master of theology. Again and again, Gerson mobilized his literary skill, whether in Latin or in French, to convey his theological knowledge to a wide audience in forms that were accessible to them. "For Gerson, . . . the faith was one. It could be expressed and discussed either in Latin or in the vernacular, and there was no need to reserve the hard questions for academics."[69] As seen in *Videmus nunc*, Gerson did not merely relate the final conclusions of theological inquiry on major topics, but rather went to great pains to relate even to lay people the process of theological reflection. Gerson unstintingly conveyed what great thinkers contributed to the theological and philosophical discussion at hand. His congregants thus received an education in the classics not dissimilar from that of Gerson's students at the University of Paris. By contriving an allegorical discourse among Reason, Soul, and Devotion as three sisters and by carefully stepping through the argument of classical theological reflection on the Trinity and the human soul, Gerson creates models of Christian subjectivity for *les simples gens* and the emerging class of lay intellectuals to emulate.

Gerson was equally willing to don the illustrious gown of the university master and exercise the prestigious power of the "father tongue" as to put on the robe of the parish priest and evangelize in the mother tongue of the simple folk. Whether staging a genre performance in powerfully charged Latin grammar or the quotidian French grammar of regular people, Gerson in all cases draws on his considerable intellectual resources to instruct, admonish, and exhort other Christians to repent and follow the way of Jesus Christ.

Moreover, just as the sermon genre epitomizes Gerson's moral agenda for writing in general, so does the dialogue epitomize how for Gerson texts were genre performances intended to engender sanctity. Sister Soul, Sister Reason, and Sister Devotion are three ontological molds for the subjectivity of certain kinds of redeemed Christians. Let us now leave the parish context and see how, in his *Sermon against Gluttony*, Gerson performs in different ways for an academic congregation of mostly clerics.

Preaching in Latin: *Sermo contra gulam*

Gerson delivered his *Sermo contra gulam*—that is, his *Sermon against Gluttony*—in Latin to students and colleagues at the University of Paris. Its form is distinctive of university sermons, since it includes a section called in Latin a *collatio*, which is an extension of a morning sermon into an afternoon academic lecture. This sermon against one of the Seven Deadly Sins was delivered during Advent, one of the two major preaching seasons of the year—Lent being the other.

Gerson adapts the well-established genre of university sermon to engender in his clerical listeners the sanctity and humility that he believed were necessary to be effective priests. The performance here, then, is that of a model preacher and humble pastor—the kind of person who would succeed in bringing lay people closer to the Lord. The Christian subjectivity that Gerson performs in the *Sermon against Gluttony* is thus not a model for lay people to emulate, as the characters in *Videmus nunc*. The "gender" that Gerson performs in the genre of this Latin sermon is closer to the person Gerson was—a preacher who was humble yet aware of the importance of his mission to save souls, who could make careful moral distinctions but avoided overscrupulosity. Indeed, a reflective and confessional mode of writing that appears often in Gerson's works is evident in the *Sermon against Gluttony* and reveals numerous aspects of his self-image.

Several of Gerson's writerly techniques that he uses in *Moralized Grammar* are also on display in this sermon. Specifically, we will find in the *Sermon against Gluttony* examples of Gerson's use of word play and extended metaphor, as well as a powerful image encapsulating his view of the moral struggle that is at the center of the human condition.

Sermons such as the *Sermon against Gluttony* played an important part in university life. There were certain sermons to which attendance was required of the entire university community. Other sermons were delivered by students as part of degree requirements. These requirements were officially promulgated in university statutes.[70] The preaching of university masters at times extended beyond the university community to the laity in the surrounding city: "Masters who were also preachers participated in the direct instruction of the surrounding community. University regulations explicitly directed that theological masters preach on certain days and in specified churches in the capital."[71]

Around the beginning of the thirteenth century a characteristic form for the sermons of university masters developed. Thomas Chabham[72] wrote a *Summa de arte praedicandi* that detailed the parts of the thematic or university-style sermon, including "the opening prayer for divine aid, the protheme (or antetheme) or introduction of the theme, the theme or statement of a scriptural quotation, division or statement of parts of the theme, the development or *prosecutio* of the members named in the division, and conclusion."[73] Some but not all of these sections are evident in the *Sermo contra gulam* and *Videmus nunc.*

As seems to be common in his sermons, Gerson begins the *Sermon against Gluttony for the First Sunday of Advent* by addressing Mary directly: "I would like to know, if you please, glorious Mother of God, whether you were in the company of your blessed Son, when he approached Jerusalem the Sabbath before his Passion—he whose Advent today's Gospel recalls as does the Gospel reading of the Day of Palms."[74] With these words Gerson begins a devout allegorical prayer to Mary, the first of several introductory sections before reaching the main theme of the sin of gluttony.

Gerson imagines that if Mary had been with Jesus as he entered Jerusalem, she would have felt both joy at the honor he would receive entering like a king, and at the same time sorrow due to his impending crucifixion. She would have seen him cry as he looked upon the city of Jerusalem. Allegorizing this dramatization of the Gospel story, Gerson brings attention to the theme at hand, that of repentance:

> What should we do? What should we do, glorious Mother of God, when God wants to come among us, and learns that we are bound to refuse him through our unjust sins and as if to crucify all over again, as St. Paul said, "Crucifying once again . . ." (Hebrews 6:6). The sinner obliges God, as far as He is concerned, once more to accept death. Undoubtedly, if God and you wept over the city of Jerusalem, so much more ought we weep over the destruction of our spiritual city, which is our soul. For Jerusalem is temporal, and our soul is eternal, as [St. John] Chrysostum says.

Through this allegory, Gerson relates the Gospel reading of the day to the general topic of sin. The human soul is Jerusalem. The Lord's sorrow at human sin is thus his sorrow at seeing Jerusalem and at knowing that he will be crucified there. In sinning the sinner re-crucifies the Lord.

Gerson thus creates a trope in which coalesce the narrative of the Gospel of the day and the personal drama of each congregant's spiritual journey. The recitation of the Hail Mary prayer marks the end of this protheme section, which was like the preface of a book.[75] Prothemes aimed to gain the goodwill of the listeners. In them preachers typically promised brevity and claimed their own unworthiness. The protheme "would be followed by a prayer, sometimes a *Pater Noster* ['Our Father'] and at other times an *Ave Maria* ['Hail Mary'], enunciated by the preacher and repeated by the audience."

In this particular sermon only after the recitation of the Hail Mary does Gerson resort to the humility topos, which he incorporates into a very personal explanation of the rhetorical purpose of the sermon: "Before I turn to my main topic, I will expound the reason why I chose this theme and I will declare my intention." Gerson here begins an extended metaphor portraying sin and virtue as two forces in a great battle:

> Previously I have considered a great deal in my personal pondering, that unfaithful sin and the damned betrayer of God, his rightful Lord, were waging harsh mortal combat against human nature. . . . Thus says Job chapter 8, verse 1:[76] "The life of man upon earth is a warfare" in which it is necessary on any day whatsoever to engage in battle.

Without the grace of an aid, human nature would have been completely spoiled, and the Enemy would have triumphed completely. Answering his own rhetorical question, Gerson creates a moment of dramatic tension regarding the outcome of the "harsh mortal combat": "Who gave us this beautiful helper of virtues? I answer, that [it was] our supreme God and Savior Jesus Christ, through whose mediating Advent onto this earth, [gave us this helper] by assuming our humanity. It is this same Advent that our Holy Mother Church remembers in this very time."[77] Playing on the root meaning of advent as "approach," Gerson thus links the appearance of the saving spiritual warrior with the liturgical season before the feast of Christmas. He goes on to put some nice detail to the classic spiritual warfare metaphor: "Then I see that the battle of sinners has many partisans, trumpeters, and songsters of choirs for exhorting to victory." The foe here is not Satan the Adversary, but rather mundane human sinners who are a bad example and who lead others astray. Gerson refers to another rhetorical question that one could ask and rejects its validity. "We should not ask who they are—they are all earthly sinners, who through deeds, through words and evil exhortations bring others to wrongdoing."

To counter the partisans of sin in this battle, Gerson places himself as preacher in the allegorical combat. "Thus, on the other side, it is appropriate that virtues should have partisans and warners so that they attract and move hearts to behaving well and living well." The traditional metaphor thus becomes a very personal reflection, as Gerson describes how he sees his own place in the battle between sin and virtue:

> These warners are the preachers of truth, who must go up and speak out in a loud voice praising virtues and blaming vices. "*Lift your voice like a raised trumpet, you who preach*" (Isaiah 40:9). And because our Emperor and King Jesus Christ wanted unworthy me among other trumpeters of this sort to be one of this office to his Church and to his people, I have wanted more often to undertake the exercise of this office, but fear of deficiency and consideration of my ignorance, inability, and perhaps sometimes weary negligence have diverted me since I have so many different preoccupations. First of all I will have to attend to myself and the onslaught which has been taking place within myself before matters outside my household. . . . Thus, with the help of our Lord Jesus Christ, I have proposed more often to go up to the seat of preaching, unless some other impediment intervenes. For raising my voice in this battle of virtues against vices, I have considered that I am unable to find anything more appropriate, or more vigorous, than this sound, which even our Emperor [Christ] himself took up in his first Preaching and before him, his commissioned Precursor, the trumpeter and proclaimer, Saint John the Baptist.[78]

The reflexive and confessional tone here is noteworthy and can help us understand Gerson's self-image as a preacher. He underscores his sense of unworthiness and admits that he has often been distracted by multifarious concerns. He even refers to what seems to have been a specific insult or onslaught (*insultus*) that attacked him, adding further reason for not doing his part against the attack of sin onto the wider community. However, recognizing the importance and efficacy of preaching, Gerson pledges more frequently to take it up as a weapon in the great spiritual war.

After a rhythmic section contrasting *peccatum* and *poenitentia*, Gerson thematizes once again the idea of "advent" in four ways, the four modes of "approach," and then reads the Gospel of Jesus's procession into Jerusalem on a donkey (Mark 11:1–10). His focus here is the comparison between Jerusalem and the soul, into both of which Jesus comes.

> Regarding the morality and the theme of the first, invisible Advent, which takes place in our souls, you would like to know that in the state of innocence, the human creature was like some beautiful city, which could have been compared to Jerusalem, which is interpreted as the vision of peace: the Soul was the Queen and the Ruler. There was a peace among all subjects, that is, among all virtues of the body and the soul—a peace of reason to the will, and a peace of the will to sensuality. A peace of the whole person to God. How fortunate was that city. But alas! Sin, that jealous traitor, came to plunder it, and committed, as a first attack, gluttony disguised under the good, in the fruit of the tree, which was called the tree of knowledge of good and evil.[79]

Here, then, in the image of the soul as city Gerson brings together all the ideas of the sermon. The sin of Adam and Eve is named "gluttony," as it involved transgressive eating. This sin, as all sin, results from the acceptance by a person of a deceitful offer by the treacherous Adversary. The peace of an uncorrupted soul is disturbed by such rebellion and is in need of a return, a repentance, made possible only in the advent, the approach, of our saving Christ. "But observe the sweetness of God the most high Lord of our Jesus Christ. He did not want to abandon the soul of the human creature to such misery, but rather he wanted to come near to this city, to free our soul."[80] This section of the sermon ends with an exhortation composed of an initial question addressed directly to the congregants as "O devout people" and then a series of imperative verbs: "Take note [*Conspicite*]! . . . Flee [*Fugite*]! . . . Resist [*Repugnate*]!" These imperatives culminate in an impassioned call to repentance: "I shout out to you: Repent!"[81]

From this emotional highpoint of the sermon, Gerson takes up more comprehensively the sin of gluttony itself: "Let us persist for a short time in speaking of the evils which gluttony brings us, so that we may better beware of it." The main idea of the long section that follows is that "from the time when Adam and Eve were expelled from earthly paradise, gluttony opens for us the gate to every misery and affliction which we feel in this world." Gerson organizes his argument around the hypothetical question that someone might ask about how it was that God would have taken such great revenge, all for a single apple. To demonstrate the validity of this thesis about gluttony as opening the gate for every misery, Gerson first presents a more nuanced interpretation of the "gluttony" of Adam and Eve: "it was not on account of the apple, but on account of the disobedience of divine precepts." Returning briefly to the image of the soul as city, Gerson creates some vivid images: "Gluttony makes the person, which is supposed to be the city and habitation of God, into some habitation of enemies and even into a den of thieves or a sty of pigs."

As mentioned previously, the *Sermon against Gluttony* includes a "*collatio*" (plural: *collationes*). This academic appendix to a university sermon was a distinctive feature of preaching at the University of Paris: "a regular alternation of sermons and *collationes* on the same theme points to the Paris university milieu, where the sermon represents the morning's teaching and the *collatio* its extension in the afternoon."[82] The *collatio* typically extends the treatment of theological issues raised by the morning sermon, but usually in a more systematic and didactic manner.

Nearly as long as the sermon itself, the *collatio* at hand deals in more detail with doctrinal aspects of gluttony. Gerson declares at the start of it that he will continue on the subject of gluttony impeding the Advent of Jesus Christ—that is, his approach into our souls—by addressing three topics: (1) the evils that gluttony creates; (2) how to beware of gluttony; and (3) three remedies against gluttony. The second of these constitutes almost all of the *collatio*. In that section, Gerson proceeds by means of what he calls "small questions and responses."[83] To give a flavor of these questions, here are some of the first several:

Is gluttony always a mortal sin? (No.)

Isn't it always a sin to become inebriated? (Yes, if the person is well aware of the evils that one typically commits through drunkenness and still knowingly becomes inebriated. No, if a person reaches a drunken state without premeditation.)

Is it a mortal sin to eat or drink so that someone is aroused to lust? (Yes, especially when it is outside of marriage.)

Is it a sin every time vomiting follows from eating too much? (Sometimes yes, sometimes no, depending on the kind of eating that preceded.)

If a priest drinks after midnight, can he celebrate Mass that day? (No, and he sins if parishioners miss Sunday Mass on account of his fault.)

Isn't it a transgression of the Precept of the Church to swallow meat from the teeth on Friday that remained from dinner on Thursday? (No.)

More than twenty other questions follow these. His determinations on these issues curb overscrupulosity, while encouraging holiness and fidelity. He takes into account what was known at his time of bodily health.

From this thematic university-style Latin sermon delivered in Advent on the sin of gluttony, we have seen how Gerson's roles as university master, priest, and theologian combine rhetorically in his writing. Two features of this sermon are especially characteristic of Gerson—namely, the quite personal notes of self-recrimination in the protheme and the measured scrupulosity evident in his analysis of the sin of overindulgence in food and drink.

Videmus nunc and *Sermo contra gulam* present a range of characters for Christians to emulate. In just these two sermons Gerson performed genders and subjects that were masculine and feminine, powerful and humble, rational and spiritual, clerical and lay, literate and uneducated. Gerson drew on various aspects of his own character and social position to create these "*personnaiges*" and to put on these performances, all for the spiritual edification of congregants.

Let us now turn from Gerson's sermons to an example of his writing precisely in his capacity as professor of theology.

Gerson Writing for the Reading Public

Throughout his scholarly career, Gerson straddled the territories of the academy and the public square. He was the dean of his faculty, and so a leader among other scholars, at the same time as he was an influential voice in politics, church governance, and intellectual discourse outside the university walls. The role of the theologian was changing in early fifteenth-century French society, and Gerson's reach beyond the academy exemplifies these changes.

Daniel Hobbins argues that Gerson's embrace of one genre of theological writing in particular, the tract (*tractatus* in Latin), epitomizes this societal repositioning of the theologian as a "public intellectual." Hobbins defines a tract as "a treatment of a single moral case with some connection to this world outside the university in a form brief enough to be easily distributed."[84] He sees Jean Gerson as the dominant force in the adoption of the tract as the most important theological genre of the fifteenth century, though it was "never explicitly recognized as such."

Gerson's scholarly production gives evidence of a new age of theological writing.[85] Unlike his predecessors in theology faculties in France, Gerson published in a great variety of other genres that hearken back to pre-Scholastic monastic writings, including not only the tract, but also poetry, allegory, sermon, epistle, and treatise. Gerson did not write in such theological genres as the *quodlibet*, the *quaestio disputata*, and the commentary—neither commentaries on scripture, Peter Lombard's Sentences, nor on Aristotle.[86]

Seen from a broad societal perspective, this dramatic shift away from Scholastic theological genres can be explained by the growth of a reading public, greater availability of books, and development of intellectual life outside of monasteries and universities. Viewed in light of the Scholastic tradition, the change of preferred genres among theologians might be explained as a maturation of the traditional genres such that scholarly production was no longer so closely linked to classroom debate. Traditional Scholastic genres, whether intended for beginning students, such as the *summa*, or for advanced scholars, such as the *quaestio disputata* and the *quodlibet*, all came directly out of structured oral exercises performed within the university. In the fourteenth and fifteenth centuries, the *quaestio*, which was originally one section dealing with a particular topic in these traditional theological genres, came of age and broke away from actual classroom exchange to become its own literary genre, the tract.[87]

Gerson's wish to address the reading public on issues of contemporary concern is one reason for his embrace of the tract genre. In the tract, Gerson wrote about these matters of contemporary concern in a style and form that was appealing and accessible outside of the academy. Though the consummate late medieval professor, Gerson in his tracts adopted a vocabulary devoid of scholarly jargon and a rhetorical structure that is much looser than the Scholastic genres and more like late twelfth-century theological writings. Like other humanists of his era and the Renaissance, Gerson valued clarity over a grand display of erudition. Theology was not merely a scientific discipline for some elite class of *illuminati*. Rather, the study of theology had vital implications pertinent to all people and their salvation.

Fulfilling the roles of a theologian as both a pastor and a scholar, Gerson adapted his tracts to be comprehensible and even compelling to nonspecialists. In fact, he critiqued his peers for obfuscating their ideas with a writing style that was obscure to all but academic creatures. In his work *On the Two Kinds of Logic*, Gerson "warns that the tendency of modern theologians to ignore differences in audience and to indulge in logical, metaphysical, and even mathematical terminology in the presence of others such as the law faculties, has given them a reputation as 'sophists,' 'windbags' (*verbosi*), and even *phantastici*, or 'imaginative fools.'"[88]

Whereas Scholastic writings were typically divided and subdivided and sub-subdivided into a complex of chapters, articles, arguments, objections, and responses to objections, the tract as fashioned by Gerson most often was organized around the *consideratio*. These "were simply ideas that occurred to him on a subject. They appear constantly in tracts, sermons, and letters." The *consideratio* played an important role in Gerson's thinking and writing. It "freed him from the duress of dialectical reasoning and allowed him to write in a more leisured and meditative fashion." The result was greater fluidity than in the texts of earlier Scholastic theologians, though Gerson's works remain very much connected to the Scholastic tradition. "Abandoning chapters and articles, [Gerson] retained some basic textual organization—enough that Erasmus (who otherwise approved of Gerson, alone among schoolmen) criticized him for excessive subdivision."[89]

The titles of Gerson's tracts were themselves clear and straightforward in that they announced the subject matter of the text. A few examples of Gerson's many tracts treated the subjects of the training of children, scribal work, the *Roman de la Rose*, assassination, rents and usury, superstition and magic, the Hussites, simony, the Immaculate Conception, indulgences, the Eucharist, clerical celibacy, excommunication, abstention from meat, mortal and venial sins, cults of saints and relics, astrology, discretion of spirits, Wyclif, nobility, and Joan of Arc.[90]

Moralizing the Priestly Body: *De pollutione nocturna*

One of Gerson's most popular and famous tracts, surviving in 160 manuscripts or more,[91] treats an issue that might seem trivial to modern sensibilities. His *De pollutione nocturna* addresses the question of whether a priest who experiences a seminal emission while sleeping should celebrate the Mass the next morning or whether he is too morally sullied to exercise his sacramental office until performing penance or even some other kind of ablution.[92] A question that some today might see as indicative of schoolboyish scrupulosity or perhaps a kind of Gnostic rejection of the body and its routine function was in Gerson's world grounded both in contemporary medical theory and in centuries of moral and theological reflection concerning cultic purity, sexual desire, moral agency, and free will.

Gerson's *De pollutione nocturna*, also known as *De preparatione ad Missam* (*On Preparation for Mass*),[93] consists of ten *considerationes*:

1. No one possesses clear certitude, apart from some special revelation of God, that he is adequately ready and worthy to celebrate the mysteries of the Mass.
2. Such certitude of evidence about the dignity of the celebrant is not required for worthily celebrating without temerity, presumption, or the imputability of a new sin.
3. Neither every scruple or doubt about mortal sin, nor every lack of devotion nor disorder nor lack of attention necessarily impedes the dignity of the celebrant.
4. It could be the case that someone could at the same time laudably celebrate Mass and could also nevertheless laudably abstain from celebrating it. In this case, the former is more laudable than the latter.
5. No pollution that began and came to completion in sleep is a mortal sin.
6. Corporal pollution in sleep can possibly be not only unrelated to any preceding mortal sin, but can even result from merit.
7. No impurity of the body in itself is an impediment for the celebrant but rather only accidentally, on account of some co-occurring or following event in the soul.
8. It is possible for someone who has experienced a nocturnal emission to celebrate the sacred mysteries without any reprehension and even with merit.[94]
9. It is through divine munificence, not through our own industry, that we are made worthy for participating in the mysteries of the sacraments.
10. It is not on account of fear of contamination of the body of Christ.

In writing this tract, Gerson produced the culmination of a centuries-old conversation encompassing patristic, monastic, and Scholastic authors. Even before Gerson's synthetic treatment of the question, the Western Christian tradition judged the voices of Augustine, John Cassian, and Gregory the Great to have been the most important in this extended debate. Their writings had been the starting point for most other treatments. Gerson's contribution was in many ways to return to the teachings of these three rather than to continue the rigorist tendency that began with monastic penitential literature and peaked in Thomas of Chobham's *Summa confessorum* in the early thirteenth century.

Two major influences on the entire conversation of seminal emissions in this literature were ancient medical theory, especially that of Galen, and Judaic ideas of ritual purity.[95] The excretion of bodily fluids, as in menstruation, seminal emission, urination, and sweating, was understood in medieval medical theory as a mechanism for correcting a superfluity of humors of one sort or another. Some of the same excretive functions, such as nocturnal emissions, were considered in the Judaic tradition to cause ritual impurity.[96] While Augustine in the *City of God* famously regarded the recalcitrance of penile erections to be a result of the Fall, in *On the Goods of Marriage* (*De bonis matrimonii*) he considered nocturnal emissions sinless, comparing them to menstruation. Cassian (ca. 360–ca. 435), for his part, devoted an entire book of his *Collationes* to the topic of seminal emissions and the dreams that caused them. Writing for monks, Cassian acknowledged both the monastic goal of perfect chastity and the bodily need to relieve the natural buildup of humors. As for Gregory the Great (540–604), he formulated church teaching on the matter as being wholly dependent on the cause of the emission. If the cause was the superfluity of humors, the emission was sinless; if the cause was sexual fantasy with the consent of the man, then the emission was indeed sinful. Surveying medieval Western European Christian theological treatments of the subject, Jacqueline Murray identifies Gerson as "one of the last medieval writers to concern himself in any detail with the problem of nocturnal and other seminal emissions."[97]

One genre that treats the issue is the penitential lists of sins with the appropriate penance for each. Called the "penitential," this genre was developed in monasteries for the spiritual guidance of monks. From the tenth to the thirteenth century, these penitentials and the moral treatises written by such authors as Robert Grosseteste, Robert of Flamborough, Thomas of Chobham, Wetheringsette, Stavensby, Odo of Cheriton, Walter of Cantilupe, and Peter of Poitiers generally exhibit an increasing tendency to emphasize the culpability of the man who experiences the seminal emission.

Gerson's place in this long conversation is to recover the balanced approach of Gregory and Augustine, who made good use of contemporary medical theory. Rejecting Thomas of Chobham's position about the exercise of free will during sleep and in dreams, Gerson compares nocturnal emissions to other flows of fluids including menstruation. On the other hand, Gerson continued the tendency to associate even what he considered sinless natural movements of the flesh with more serious sexual sins such as masturbation, to which he devoted an entire tract, the *De confessione mollitiei*.

Genre Performance, Gender Performance

Through our examination of Gerson's genre performance in three of his more than five hundred extant texts, a picture begins to emerge of a writer who balanced and blended the roles of a theologian as pastor, priest, professor, *littérateur*, and public intellectual. In all of these roles we have seen Gerson's special emphasis on teaching and preaching. Though complex and multifaceted, Jean Gerson had integrity as a writer in the sense that these varied roles that he played in society intermix into an integrated composite. Gerson did not write other than he was. The great versatility that is evident in his writings manifests the complexity of his character.

The three texts that we have studied in this chapter are three different genre performances of Gerson's. The performative nature of the sermons is especially obvious due to the historical record of Gerson actually performing some version of these texts to certain congregations in specific places and times. Donning his academic garb before a scholarly audience of men, Gerson performed the *Sermo contra gulam*, including its collation, in Latin at the University of Paris. The performance of this text was that of an academic priest and a theological expert in the setting that defined his place in society. The vernacular *Videmus nunc* is a sermon that Gerson performed away from the home institution of his university. Though he eventually became pastor at St. Jean-en-Grève parish, Gerson sermonized there as a master of theology, not a typical priest.

The Latin-language tract *De pollutione nocturna* was still a different sort of performance. Presumably not orally delivered, the tract addressed a reading public of ordained men not limited to those within academic communities. Because of the content of this tract, Gerson writes in the voice of a celibate man who has a body, specifically testicles and a penis that sometimes becomes erect and emits semen, as penises do. Gerson's voice in *De pollutione nocturna* is, however implicitly, the voice of a "sexual theologian."[98]

In lieu of other forms of printed media, tracts like this gave Gerson a platform from which to speak to the literate and semi-literate public on issues of current interest. In this genre, Gerson spoke as a theologian outside the walls of either university or church. The genres of Gerson's writings are performances of his complex subjectivity for specific social purposes. He was willing to transgress conventional boundaries for the sake of saving souls.

Placing Gerson's writings in literary history, we recognize quickly that the genres in which he wrote were culturally constructed, historically situated, and performed through recognizable "acts" of citation. He wrote within a literary tradition, and he marked his texts so that readers could understand them as a sermon, an epic poem, a letter, or some other genre. From contemporary gender theory we have learned that genders too are culturally constructed, historically situated, and performed through recognizable "acts" of citation. Though subject to much regulation and "taxonomic exuberance," genders and genres are neither natural nor pure categories.[99] Both genres and genders are frames where certain kinds of performances are staged and certain kinds of meaning become possible.

3 Gerson's "Moralized" Primer of Spiritual Grammar

Like a catechism, the *Donatus moralizatus* text, which Gerson apparently wrote in the year 1411, begins with a question.[1] (See the Appendix for full translation.) That question sets up the grammatical framework that structures the rest of the text: "How many parts of speech are there?" Beginning the text already with a specialized term from the discipline of grammar, the question fronts the idea of "parts of speech," thus emphasizing it over the number of how many parts there are. Though the word *oratio*, as not only "speech," but also "prayer," presents immediately a possible pun, Gerson passes over this possibility. His response to the initial question is a straightforward number, which indicates the tally of sections in the following text, each of which is devoted ostensibly to one of the eight parts of speech in Latin: noun, pronoun, verb, adverb, participle, conjunction, preposition, and interjection. However, after this very first question-response pair with its straightforward and expected answer, the text announces its difference from other grammatical texts, including Aelius Donatus's *Ars minor*. To the question of what are these eight parts of speech, a response comes that has no reference to nouns or verbs or anything of the sort. Rather than Donatus's typology of Latin words, the naming of the "parts of speech" situates the human person in a moral web of knowledge:

> Knowledge of substance, knowledge of the precepts of God, performance of the same, knowledge of the human being in reference to God and in reference to nature, consideration of the Judgment which is to come, consideration of the joys of the elect, and consideration of the sorrows of the damned.[2]

The thus-far unmentioned eight categories of Latin words provide the basis on which these eight religious responses must be understood, as evidenced by the immediately following question, "What is a noun?" Confident that his readers already know the list of the eight Latin parts of speech, Gerson replaces them with the theological and moral items cited previously. Like the other seven sections that follow, the noun section comprises multiple questions and responses. In the noun section, eleven grammatical questions provide opportunities for religious responses.

Confirming the expectation that eight sections of the text will align with the eight dimensions of moral being given as the parts of speech, the term "*substantia*" links the definition of a noun to the first of the eight forms of knowledge that are the "parts of speech." In the remainder of the text, this expectation is realized, with the exception of the pronoun section, whose theme of human being as sinner is not identified in the list just quoted.

The Parts of Speech in Gerson's Spiritual Grammar

Noun: Knowledge of substance
Pronoun: [Recognition of the human being as sinner]
Verb: Knowledge of the precepts of God
Adverb: Performance of the same [i.e., God's precepts]
Participle: Knowledge of the human being in reference to God and in reference to nature
Conjunction: Knowledge of the Judgment that is to come
Preposition: Consideration of the joys of the elect
Interjection: Consideration of the sorrows of the damned

Gerson thus begins his *Donatus moralizatus* or *Moralized Grammar* with theological anthropology (in the noun and pronoun sections) and the moral life (verb and adverb), and he ends with eschatology (conjunction, preposition, and interjection). The participle section appears as the thematic center of the text. It combines the material on human nature with the content of moral living, just as the participle in Latin grammar is a hybrid between noun and verb. The focus of the participle section in *Moralized Grammar* is on the fundamental decision that we as human beings have before us: whether or not to live in accordance with God's will. The consequences of this decision come to realization on the Day of Judgment. The last three sections thus treat eschatological themes. The conjunction section treats the Last Judgment in itself, the preposition section deals with the fate of the saved, and last section, on the interjection, addresses the fate of the damned.

Commentary on "Moralized" Grammar

While our exploration of the Latin grammatical tradition has made clear the meaning of *Donatus*, the first word in the Latin title,[3] the modifier, *moralizatus*, still needs explanation.[4] In Gerson's fourteenth- and early fifteenth-century French context, this Latin past participle and its French equivalent "*moralisé*" referred to a tradition of transforming pagan literature into edifying Christian lessons.[5]

Ovid's *Metamorphoses* was a particular favorite for this kind of transformation in Gerson's era.[6] For late medieval France, *l'Ovide moralisé* is a seminal work in this tradition.[7] Its 72,000 lines in octosyllabic couplets were composed in the Middle French vernacular by an anonymous Franciscan sometime between 1300 and 1330 C.E.[8] Not long after, Benedictine scholar Pierre Bersuire (Latin name "Petrus Berchorius," ca. 1290–1362) composed *Ovidius moralizatus*, using *l'Ovide moralisé* as one of his sources.[9] This Latin prose moralization of Ovid's *Metamorphoses* made part of a larger compilation entitled *Reductorium morale*.[10] The textual history of moralized adaptations of Ovid's poem is complex, especially because both of the versions we have just mentioned were widely imitated and further translated.[11]

A recent study of *l'Ovide moralisé* determines its genre to be primarily a collection of material for preachers to use in delivering sermons.[12] The erudite Franciscan who was apparently the author of this French *Moralized Ovid* adapted pagan mythology to Christian teaching for its use by his Franciscan brothers who focused on preaching.[13] The mythology of the ancient world was familiar to many in fourteenth-century France and so became useful material for preachers to gain the interest of those listening to their sermons. Fitting with this intended use as a resource for preachers, each section of *l'Ovide moralisé* is organized around a sermonic theme.[14] The vernacular language in which the work is composed is an important indicator of its generic purpose. Like vernacular sermons themselves, this *Moralized Ovid* in French is on the border between clerical Latin culture and profane vernacular culture.[15] Though in French rather than Latin, the kind of theological references that run throughout it appear to presuppose a clerical readership.[16]

As for Pierre Bersuire's *Ovidius moralizatus*, an analysis of its method "reveals that [the author] wants to convey only Ovid's matter, and only so much of the matter as he requires to provide the Christian signification he sees allegorized in the tale."[17] Bersuire takes the skeletal structure of Ovid's tale and dresses it with Christian dogma. Allegorical interpretation and moralizing exegesis find the true meaning of the structural elements of Ovid's stories to be specific Christian theological referents. This tradition "of imposing Christian allegory on Ovid's stories was so ingrained that it continued to be practiced well into the sixteenth century."[18]

The significance of the word *moralizatus*, then, in the title of Gerson's work is that it alludes to the tradition of the French *Ovide moralisé* and the slightly later *Ovidius moralizatus* of Bersuire. Like the authors of these works, Gerson transformatively reinterprets a text from the classical age that had had an important place in Latin-language schooling for centuries. *Donatus moralizatus* also shares with *l'Ovide moralisé* and *Ovidius moralizatus* rhetorical purposes that aim at the Christian edification of readers. Gerson's work, however, is not an allegory—that is, some story with a double meaning.[19] There is no narrative in Aelius Donatus's original *Ars minor* whose elements can be made to correspond to a Christian dogma. At the same time, Gerson's *Moralized Grammar* shares the evangelistic purpose of Christian allegorical readings of the Old Testament. Gerson's emphasis on the ultimate effects of moral living also resemble the anagogical way of interpreting scriptures "in terms of their eschatological fulfillment."[20] Though similar to the allegorical tradition to which *l'Ovide moralisé* and *Ovidius moralisatus* belong, *Donatus moralizatus* is not in seriousness uncovering concealed meanings but rather somewhat jokingly using etymological puns on grammatical terms in order to replace grammatical discourse with religious discourse. The playful tropes do, however, have the serious effect of constructing the metaphorical schemes described in our introductory chapter. Now we will see in detail how the tropes of Gerson's genre performance operate.

NOMEN

The noun section of *Donatus moralizatus* is a catechismal meditation on the fundamental definition of a human being. Playing throughout on the double meaning of *nomen* as both "noun" and "name," Gerson answers the first question "*Nomen quid est?*," "What is a noun/name?" by directly addressing the questioner: "*Homo, quia sic vocaris.*" Human being is your name, because that is what you are called. In this first response to a question on the noun/name, Gerson inaugurates another pun that becomes thematic for the section: *substantia* as a grammatical substantive—that is, a noun, a material substance, and a being or hypostasis in philosophical terminology. "Know your substance, that is, what you are made out of, and you will then know truly what a human being is." Referencing the Genesis account of the origins of human nature, Gerson names that material that is human substance: "Here indeed is that 'knowledge of substance' which is the first part of speech, 'You are dust and to dust you shall return' (Genesis 3:19)." This reminder of the origin and postlapsarian destiny of humankind firmly establishes a somber tone of both mortality and morality. By Gerson's era, this same verse from Genesis had already for centuries been used ritually during the imposition of ashes at the beginning of Lent.[21] Your time living on earth is limited, so you had better keep always in mind what happens after this life.

Following this first question on the noun comes the other formulaic question that will be asked of all the eight parts of speech: "*quot accidunt*?" that is, "How many attributes does it have?" (835b).[22] The verb *accidere* makes part of both philosophical and grammatical technical terminology, pertaining in Aristotelian philosophy to contingent attributes and in the grammatical tradition to inflectional parts. The numeric answer to this question in each of the eight sections of the *Moralized Grammar* text sets the number of subsections or subtopics that follow the initial, definitional question of what the part of speech is. The noun is said to have six accidents or attributes: quality, comparison, gender, number, form, and case. The rest of the noun section consists of asking the value of each of these attributes ("Of what quality?,"[23] "Of what degree of comparison?," "Of what gender?," etc.), to which brief responses are given, followed by a summary discussion at the end of the overall section.

These responses provide Gerson the opportunity to describe a number of other features of human nature. He names rationality as a quality shared by all humans. He addresses gender by stating flatly that men possess the nature of a human being exactly as women do. Our number is singular, because ultimately we stand alone at the Last Judgment. In insisting on the necessity of confessing faith in Christ and keeping to that faith in order to be saved, Gerson takes the opportunity to slur those who do not believe in Christ: "They should not be called human, but brutes, for they lack the faculty of reason" (835c).

Perhaps the most punning moment in this section is the discussion of *casus*, a word whose semantic range encompasses not only grammatical case, but also the general and figurative senses of a fall and the Fall, as well as the broader idea of destiny. The human being is of the nominative—that is, in an etymological sense, the "naming" case, and the vocative—that is, the "calling" case. Human beings are of the nominative case because we are "named" mortal, despite having been created immortal, and we are of the vocative case because we are "called" worker, despite being destined for eternal repose. The Fall from grace, that fundamental *casus*, changed our name and what we are called. Among the consequences of Adam and Eve's original sin is that we must toil on earth, although we remain destined for perpetual rest in heaven (835c–d).

After treating each of the six accidents, Gerson poses one further question before undertaking a less structured discussion to deal with all that he has said about the noun up to that point. The additional question pertains to the governance of the noun. The response depicts a clear-cut moral bifurcation: "If he lives well, he is governed by God. If badly, by the devil" (835d). Here the principal idea is the soul-body relationship, wherein the "noble" soul is placed in a "most vile body, stinking, fragile." The body is like a household, and the soul is the mistress of that household or again a sagacious guest who comes to that house. Whether the lady of the house or a wise visitor, the soul should in either case rule the house. For this reason God placed the soul in the body. In itself, the soul then wants nothing else than to please God. Whenever it effectively directs the household, the resultant activities in no way impede religious devotion or anything that leads to salvation. On the other hand, if the flesh rules in place of the soul, then the household kills its mistress or puts down its wise guest. Such is a vile affront to the mores of hospitality. To live rightly, human beings must remember that their flesh is but earth, and should be kept like earth. As earth is low, so must the flesh endure difficulties. When vexed by someone, we should humble ourselves and treat the annoying person all the better. Like thirsty soil, we should soak up sound doctrine and divine grace, while keeping dry at all times of the influx of vices, flesh, and cupidity (835d–36a).

Gerson concludes the section by declaring that the "noun" or "name" of human being has now been given and by exhorting his readers to conduct themselves nobly: "You have now what [your] name is, that is to say, what it is in conformity with your substance, namely, 'noble' in accordance with your soul. I therefore beseech you to rule yourself nobly and rationally, not sinfully or carnally" (836a).

PRONOMEN

The pronoun section considers human beings insofar as they are sinners and focuses primarily on the Genesis 3 account of Eve's and Adam's primordial sin. "Just as 'human being' is your name, so also is 'sinner' what goes in the place of your name. When you pray to God, put your pronoun in the place of your noun. Say, 'O heavenly Father, not merely as a human being do I invoke you, but rather as a sinner I seek pardon'" (836b). While the noun section treated human nature as such, the pronoun section insists on the idea that humans relate to God primarily as sinners. The sin of Eve and Adam is taken as exemplary of all sin, the stages of which Gerson elaborates.

Before focusing on the example from Eden, Gerson uses the six enumerated accidents of the pronoun to state briefly some general features of being sinners. Near the beginning of this section, he switches voice, from a didactic second person to a contrite first person, as if to mark a confessional tone as he treats the subject of the nature of human beings as sinners. Whereas at first he instructs his reader with an imperative (*pone*, "put") and a subjunctive (*ut dicas*, "so that you say"), at his definition of the first attribute of the pronoun, he stops distancing himself from the subject matter and takes on the role of sinner along with his reader: "on account of the infinite and uncertain multitude of sins that I commit, I am unable to enumerate them" (836b). Throughout the text, Gerson's switching of grammatical person allows him at times to adopt an expository tone with the third person, at times a hortative or accusatory tone with the second, and at times, such as this one with the first person, a tone that models the repentance he would have his reader undertake. This technique of shifting grammatical persons is effective rhetorically and pedagogically to keep readers' engaged attention and to elicit from us an empathetic response.

Turning to the first attribute, Gerson indicates that insofar as the term sinner is a "pronoun," meaning that which takes the place of the human name or noun, it has infinite quality, for the sheer quantity of sins that we can commit is innumerable. Through playing on the meanings of "*genus*" as both grammatical gender and more generally "kind" or "type," the gender or genus of our pronoun is "*omnis*," "every," since "by sinning I participate in every 'gender' of vice, that is, mortal ones and venial ones." The confessional voice continues in response to questions about the other attributes to make a declaration: my pronoun is singular in number, because alone am I tormented by my sins, both in my soul and my conscience. It is simple, not complex in form, because in the sacrament of confession, I must clearly and distinctly confess all sins at once, in a single, undivided admission of guilt. The human pronoun is a first-person pronoun, because I can only judge myself, not others (836c).

The sixth attribute, grammatical case, becomes the source of the rest of the discussion of the section, since the word *casus* so conveniently also means "a fall" or "calamity." The Fall of humankind, then, is a fall from innocence to guilt. Paired with the exploration of case is an exploration of declension. The order of questions on case and declension is chiastic: of which case? of which declension? how many declensions for the pronoun? how many cases for the pronoun (836c–d)? This crisscrossed x-y-y-x order allows a rhetorical development of Gerson's treatment of sin to proceed in this series from the more general to the more specific.

Following the downward motion suggestion by *casus*, Gerson first poses the question, "Of which declension?," to which the answer is, "From the hands of God, into the hands of the devil." As there are five basic paradigms for the case patterns of actual nouns in the Latin language, Gerson further plays off the meaning of "*declinatio*" as "straying" or "deviating" to name four declensions of pronoun. The first declension is to stray from obedience to God in favor of the devil's suggestion. The second is to deviate from obedience to God in favor of consenting to a woman. The third is turning away from Paradise and toward this mundane world. The fourth is a decline from this world to the edge of hell (836d). Eve followed the first declension, Adam the second; apparently the two of them together the third; and presumably all unrepentant sinners the fourth.

Having raised with these last responses the subject of Eve and Adam, Gerson expounds further by enumerating six cases on the pronoun with six steps in the process of sinning: *suggestio* (suggestion), *advertentia* (paying heed), *discussio* (discussion), *delectatio* (enticement), *consensus in mente* (acquiescence in the heart and mind), and *consensus in opere* (acquiescence in deed). Before applying these steps to Eve's sin, Gerson draws a distinction between original pronouns—that is, the original sinners Adam and Eve, and derived pronouns, meaning all other human beings. To clarify this relationship, Eve's sin is next analyzed according to the six steps, frame by frame (837a), followed by a temptation that appears plausible in Gerson's own context (837b). In the case of Eve, the *suggestio* is the devil presenting the fruit for Eve to eat. The step of her *advertentia* is when she noticed that the tree looked like it would produce tasty fruit. The *discussio* is her noting to the devil that the Lord had told Adam and her that they were prohibited from eating the fruit of that tree, lest they should die. The *delectatio* is the devil responding that eating from the tree will not cause them to die but to be as gods and know good from evil. The *consensus in mente* is Eve's thinking that there shall be no immediate danger from eating this fruit, thus internally agreeing with the diabolic voice. Finally, the *consensus in opere* is her taking and eating the fruit while burning with desire. It is worth noting that while Adam and Eve together are said to have both been the original sinners, Adam's process of temptation and sin is not here taken as the model, but rather Eve's alone.

After the frame-by-frame dissection of Eve's fateful sin, Gerson states that "in just this way, anyone is lured to sin." He then gives an example, narrated dramatically in the first person: The scene is set in a village, where a chorus or a dance troop is lined up. The mere presence of such a group is already the suggestive first step. Then, second, Gerson narrates the step of noticing by using for the first time in the text a first-person nominative singular pronoun, *ego*: "I, hearing their songs or catching sight of them, open my eyes to seeing." An internal discussion ensues and then the dirty deed itself:

> Third, I argue in myself that it is not good to look at this chorus, however, remaining, I indulge in sensual pleasure. Fourth, I am enticed not only to the look of the chorus and to the sound of the song, but also to the look of the girls. Fifth, I acquiesce internally in my heart to have sex with one of them. Sixth, I carry out in deed that acquiescence by means of the desire that was conceived of internally. And thus is my soul dead. (837b)

This dramatization of the pious preacher and teacher narrating his enticement to illicit sex with a choir girl is worth coming back to as we take stock of the overall moral and spiritual effect of *Moralized Grammar*. The original sin is Eve's eating of the forbidden fruit. The exemplary sin is man's being tempted to have sex with a girl. In fact, Gerson gives another biblical example of the same sin: "David, if he had not spied perseveringly through the window onto the balcony, he would not have fallen into having sex with Beersheba" (2 Samuel 11:2–4). Regarding this paradigmatic sin of man's lusting and having sex, Gerson says, "As I have said of this vice, the same should be understood of all others" (837b).

In Gerson's *Sermo contra gulam* we saw the same special link between illicit eating and lust. There, the "first attack" of sin was "gluttony disguised under the good, in the fruit of the tree."[24] This first and paradigmatic sin of Eve and Adam "becomes a gate and an entrance for every carnal sin." His citation of Terence is one of several authorities that he cites in support of his way of connecting food, drink, and sex: "Without Ceres and Bacchus, Venus goes frigid." In *Moralized Grammar*, the way Gerson relates Eve's sin to his dramatized first-person account of falling into lust for a choir girl brings out a highly gendered hamartiology: Eve's transgressive eating is the original sin. Man's lust for women is the typical sin.

The pronoun section closes with hortatory material in the first person plural: "Let us therefore turn ourselves aside from every carnal delight." The emphasis here is that we should begin averting our attention as soon as any carnal enticement or pleasure (*delectatio*) is presented to us. With a simile, Gerson likens the first presentation of an enticement to an unfavorable wind that comes on a mill. Like the good miller, we should take hold of our attention and turn the mill to another direction so that the unfavorable wind does not cause our internal mechanisms to grind out infelicitous deeds. "Unless we abstain from the start, without doubt we will scarcely evade falling into danger." Referring to David looking on beauteous Beersheba, Gerson ends the section with the advice that it is on *advertentia*, paying heed, the second of the six steps, where we should focus in order to avoid sinning: "the eyes should be turned away [*avertendi*] lest they see vanities" (837c).

VERBUM

Having presented a theological anthropology, Gerson turns to the moral content of a life rightly lived. The verb section is built around the central definition of the verb as the precept of God. Most of the section is devoted to a brief commentary on each of the Ten Commandments. Seeing that one of Gerson's most important contributions to moral theology was his promotion of recentering Christian ethics on the Ten Commandments rather than the Seven Deadly sins, this verb section has special significance.[25] In fact, considering how Gerson used numerous other genres to provide expositions of the commandments, as in the *ABC des Simples Gens*, *Miroir de l'âme*, and the versified "Ung seul Dieux," the emphasis here on the Decalogue sheds light on the theological design and purpose of *Moralized Grammar* overall.

Although in the text of *Moralized Grammar* Gerson never explicitly draws on the name of the Ten Commandments as the "decalogue" or "ten words," he evokes in the verb section the meanings of *verbum* as not only the grammatical term "verb" but also the more common meaning "word." In explicating the precept or teaching of God, besides the commandments of the Decalogue, Gerson also includes the commandments to love God and neighbor, which he treats as interchangeable with the ten. These two are first named as the "quality" of the verb, one of the seven attributes that the verb is said to have (837c). Here Gerson's *Donatus* varies slightly from the original *Ars minor*, which at first names this attribute *modus*. The other attributes are conjugation, gender, number, form, tense, and person. The conjugation of the verb is "complete" or "total," since no one who hates a neighbor loves God or who hates God loves a neighbor. The commandments are all of a piece and must be observed "*conjunctim*," in conjunction with one another. The gender or genus of the verb is active because human beings are meant to carry out the precepts of God by action. Hearing the law is not enough (Roman 2:13). The number of the verb (837d) is perhaps the key attribute, from which Gerson generates most of the rest of the section. The verb is plural, because the precepts are either ten in number or two in number. The form of the verb is simple, in the sense of being constituted by only one single element—namely, love, which Paul calls "the fullness of the law" (Roman 13:10). Fulfilling the precepts of God is to be undertaken with a pure heart, uncomplicated by pretenses or other designs. The tense of the verb is present, since we are to carry out these precepts in this present life. The verb is of the first, second, and third person, since all of us—myself, you, and the other—should observe divine precept.

With this short series of questions and answers around the verb and its attributes, Gerson lays special emphasis on the precept of God as the Ten Commandments by moving out of Aelius Donatus's grammatical framework. Leaving the question-answer format of the Latin primer, Gerson instead proceeds to comment on each of the Ten Commandments. He follows the order established by Augustine in which the prohibition against graven images is subsumed into the first commandment, while coveting neighbor's wife and property are separated as the ninth and tenth.[26] This entire subsection of commentary on the Decalogue Gerson connects to the grammatical form by saying that it will clarify or expound upon what has been said regarding the verb as the precept of God. The kind of comment that Gerson makes about each commandment is basically an explanation of what breaking the commandment entails.

A noteworthy feature of this commentary is its tendency to expand the scope of each of the commandments.

The first commandment is not merely believing that God exists, for even the devil does that. Rather, it is about worshipping God, a precept broken, curiously, "when you insist on sensuality or vanity" (838a). The second commandment includes perjury, swearing so often that it becomes a habit, and wavering when swearing. Through citation of Matthew 5:34 and 5:37 Gerson expands this commandment from proscription of taking the Lord's name in vain to meaning that one should never swear but rather always say merely "yes" when one means "yes" and "no" when one means "no."

In his comment on the third commandment, it would seem that Gerson means to censure wasting time in games, revelries, drunkenness, or nonspiritual conversation only on holy days, but the nature of these otiose pursuits implies a rejection of them rather on all days, not merely holidays or the Sabbath. His injunction against unnecessary manual labor does not perhaps imply the same expansion beyond keeping the feasts. Gerson's construal of the fourth commandment expands the practice of honoring parents to include eagerness in providing them help and support.

Perhaps influenced by the Deadly Sin of wrath and its significance in medieval society, Gerson greatly expands the injunction against killing in the fifth commandment to cover groundless anger against your neighbor or even just "calling him stupid" (838b). Breaking the sixth commandment is not only about taking someone else's goods by force out in the open or in secret, but also stealing someone's reputation or honor through detracting from his or her good name.

The seventh commandment encompasses not only the extreme case of an act of adultery, but also the mere instance of when a man sees a girl or woman "curiously"—that is, with excessive interest or concupiscence—in other words, with inordinate desire. This understanding of the seventh commandment seems to blur the distinction between it and the ninth, though he does limit his treatment of the ninth to concern people who are married in one way or another. On both of these commandments,

Gerson also brings up the special case of vowed religious women and men as well as ordained men. Looking upon a consecrated woman is even worse than lusting after an unconsecrated virgin. Ordained men who touch a woman wrong their "spouse," the church, and vowed religious men who touch a woman similarly wrong their religious order, to whom they are espoused.

The eighth commandment involves not only your own false testimony but also encouraging anyone else to give false witness, or even to speak with such circumspect words that you mean to deceive someone. Fulfilling the tenth commandment entails positively helping your neighbor, through the seven works of mercy, in addition to the minimum standard of not wanting or taking anyone else's advantage, honor, or property, including "slave, maidservant or daughter" (839a). The verb section ends there, unceremoniously, without any closing gesture.

Before proceeding to the adverb section, let us step back and consider the wider significance of what Gerson achieves here in the verb section. As we have just now seen, in Gerson's moralized version of grammar, it is the precept of God that identifies the verb. This part of speech has seven attributes. The quality of this verb is Jesus's answer in the synoptic Gospels to the question about the greatest commandment (Matthew 22:36ff; Mark 12:28ff; Luke 10:26–28)—namely, to love God and neighbor, which Gerson treats as interchangeable with the ten Mosaic commandments. In addition to this first attribute of quality, to this verb belong the following six other attributes: a complete conjugation, active gender, plural number, simple form, present tense, and first, second, and third person. As generally throughout *Donatus moralizatus*, the questions in this section are Aelius Donatus's original questions in the *Ars minor*, and Gerson keeps these queries in the same order that Donatus originally posed them. What are different are the responses to the questions. As with the foregoing and the following sections, to each grammatical question Gerson gives a response with religious content. This is the fundamental pedagogic technique that Gerson uses to instruct his readers' souls. Together, these seven attributes touch on various aspects of the Christian idea of the divine commandments for moral human conduct. All of us are called by God to live love in this present life by carrying out in action the whole of God's teaching, summed up by Jesus's response to the question about the greatest commandment as well as by the Mosaic Decalogue. As throughout the rest of the work, there is here in the verb section nothing particularly nuanced in the theological content. Gerson uses the seven grammatical attributes of verbs simply as opportunities to elaborate slightly on the theme of God's precepts.

However, there is one remarkable aspect of this passage, when it is considered from a broader perspective on the history of Christian moral theology. There is no mention here or indeed anywhere in *Moralized Grammar* of what most people in medieval Europe considered the centerpiece of Christian teachings on morality—namely, the Seven Deadly Sins.[27] In their typical place, which was as an elaboration of the meaning of Jesus's dictum about loving God and neighbor, Gerson puts instead the Ten Commandments. In *Moralized Grammar,* Gerson puts the Decalogue precisely where the Seven Deadly Sins were normally hooked onto more biblically founded moral doctrine. Where Western Christian moral theology, especially since Pope Gregory the Great, used the Seven Deadly Sins to explicate the two greatest commandments named in the Gospels by Jesus, Gerson in *Moralized Grammar* and elsewhere used the Decalogue for this purpose. John Bossy has studied in depth the shift that took place such that for the average Christian in 1600 the Ten Commandments were "a relative novelty," whereby after that time they became "universally taught" as the moral system of the church.[28]

> For most people, for most of the Middle Ages, the moral system which was taught in Western Christianity was constituted by the Seven Deadly or Capital Sins: Pride, Envy, Wrath, Avarice, Gluttony, Sloth, and Lechery, usually in that order. The list was not Christian, but Greek and possibly astrological in origin. In its medieval form it had been given authority by Pope Gregory the Great, and systematized as part of a larger system of septenary forms of instruction during the twelfth century. It was related to the moral teaching of the New Testament by being treated as a negative exposition of the two commandments of the Gospel, the love of God and the love of one's neighbour.[29]

By pairing the two commandments from the synoptic Gospels with the Mosaic ten and then spending nearly half of the verb section elaborating on each component of the Decalogue, Gerson explains Jesus's answer to the Pharisees in the New Testament accounts by using these basic moral teachings of the Old Testament.

Gerson was not the first to argue for a fundamental linkage between the two and the ten. Thomas Aquinas had made a natural law argument about the Decalogue, but this was not compelling enough to appeal to the laity—or many theologians, for that matter.[30] Instead, it was Ockham who convinced most theologians with his view that the Ten Commandments comprised "the only comprehensive moral code available to or authoritative for Christians, and not as a summary of what was naturally so, but as a free, ungrounded, specific expression of God's legislative will."[31] Perhaps even more importantly, it was Gerson who was most responsible for bringing the Ten Commandments to the laity in a way that was accessible and appealing:

> since, at least in northern Europe, he [Gerson] was much the most influential doctor of the Christian life during the century before the Reformation, his was a conversion [i.e., conversion from focusing on the Seven Deadly Sins to focusing on the Ten Commandments] of importance. He was not the first to write an extended commentary on the Commandments, but the general agreement that he launched a new departure in the teaching of Christianity seems well founded. He did this by treating the Commandments as the rock of Christian ethics, by establishing a tradition of effective vernacular exposition, and by integrating this into a larger theological position and into a general scheme of Catholic piety which included the practice of confession.[32]

Seen in this light, *Moralized Grammar*—whatever else it may be—is one example of Gerson's overall effort to weave the Decalogue into the fabric of the Christian vision of the moral and spiritual life. This specific effort using grammar was aimed not at theologians, but at other, less expert, literate Christians. Given its peculiar literary form, *Moralized Grammar* appears to have been intended for the schooled, for only to them would the *Ars minor* of Donatus have been familiar or meaningful. Although the theological content of this spiritual grammar is not particularly profound, by giving such prominent position and emphasis on the Decalogue as God's moral teaching to humanity, Gerson in this text makes a tremendously important adjustment to the basic narrative concerning Christian existence. He portrays the Ten Commandments as among the rudiments of Christian teaching, which he depicts here in a catechetical form that would be both fresh and familiar to anybody of his era who had gone to school. In French, Gerson wrote a simple exposition of the Decalogue in his *ABC des Simples Gens*, a more extended one in *Miroir de l'âme*, and a versified version known by its first three words, "ung seul Dieux."[33] These were all extremely popular and would have been comprehensible to a wider audience than the Latin *Moralized Grammar*, which Gerson seems to have written for a narrower subset of nontheologians, lay and ordained.

ADVERBIUM

The exhortative core of the adverb section appears in the midst of the illustrations of the various circumstances or conditions in which an action is carried out: "Thus, in all things carefully practice circumspection, as you would appropriately put an adverb with its verb" (839b). Doing the "verb" of a work of mercy, one must keep in mind such conditions as when, where, for whom, in what manner, what, how much, and in what sequence. These conditions, in which the precepts of God—that is, the "verbs"—are carried out "are the adverbs of place, quality, and order."

Most of the illustrations of this idea deal with religious observances—for example, the priority that one should give to vows and prayers: "If you wish to pray, first pray what according to the Law you are supposed to pray, and the Divine Office. If you have made a vow, first fulfill your vow, then read and pray. If you have not vowed, first recite the Our Father, which God instituted for reciting, and afterwards you can recite what you please" (839b). An illustration of ungrammatical adverb usage entails improper behavior in time:

> For if at vespers time, you still carry on eating with others, or a drinking party, or some other foolish delight, such that you prefer oversleeping to getting up in the morning to hear Mass or carry out some other good work, thus changing the night into day and vice versa, without a doubt you do not place an adverb correctly with its verb. (839b)

This sentence is one of the very few moments when either Gerson or Qushayrī makes something of the idea that grammatical violation is a moral failing. Only the first of this series of illustrations treats a work of mercy: when faced with two paupers, one of whom is lying in the mud and the other of whom is begging door to door, the one who is apparently in worse condition, lying on the ground, should receive your alms first. If you are unable to give to both of them, then refuse the entreaty of the one who is actively begging. We also see here an emphasis on the need for prioritization.

Following these illustrations, Gerson treats another attribute of the adverb—namely, "comparison," referring to the various degrees to which different individuals are able to carry out the precepts of God according to their resources and personal strengths. Comparing rich and poor, the rich should give more alms. Those with abundant knowledge can give through teaching; those with high spirits or empathy can give consolation. It is likewise with religious observances: an able-bodied person can observe every fast. Someone who is sick needs mercy and gains a dispensation from fasting (839c).

The final attribute that Gerson addresses is the "form" of the adverb, which he relates to various ways of living in the world. He differentiates here between the "simple" adverb and the "composite," referring respectively to those who live alone and those who live in society. The "simple" are the hermits, who live solitary lives apart from all human intercourse. St. Anthony, John the Baptist, and St. Benedict are famous examples of these. The "composite," who are involved in the world, are of many different kinds—lay people, vowed religious, preachers, and others. In fact, encourages Gerson, "as many as we are, and as admittedly diverse, all of us are created for the glory of God, just as pictures of various images decorate a sanctuary" (839d). With this celebration of the diversity of humankind, Gerson declares that enough has been said on the adverb.

This section on the adverb is much differently and less clearly structured than the previous sections. The only questions it contains are, "What is an adverb?" and "How many attributes does it have?" As to the initial definition of the adverb in itself, the response begins with the grammatical answer: an adverb is added to a verb and completes its meaning. Referring back to the verb as "knowledge of divine precept," Gerson explains that the adverb is putting the precepts in action (839a). The bulk of the section is supposedly a discussion of the three attributes of the adverb, which are first listed as *comparatio* (comparison), *significatio* (meaning), and *figura* (form). To this list of three, Gerson adds in apposition *habitudo* (circumstance), *similitudo* (similitude), and *distinctio* (distinction). He then declares his intention to "make these three known." The relationship between the two sets of three is, however, already unclear. Perhaps the two sets are meant to be interchangeable, or perhaps the second set is supposed to be a definition or elaboration of the first set.

Gerson mentions five of these six words describing adverbial attributes at some point in the section, though not following the order in the initial list. The result is that, in contrast to the organization of *Moralized Grammar* generally, this section is somewhat confusing. It confounds the expectations of sequence followed elsewhere in the treatment of attributes for a given part of speech. First addressing "*habitudo*," the first element in the second set of three, Gerson then writes "*Significatio*," apparently as a kind of header. *Significatio*, translated here as "meaning," is the second element in the first group of three attributes (that is, comparison, meaning, and form). Gerson thus seems to be switching without explanation from the second group of three attributes to the first. In what appears to be the "meaning" subsection, he gives the series of examples illustrating the circumstances or *habitudines* and takes up "comparison," which—again violating the initial sequence—is the first element in the first group of attributes.

Toward the end of the section on the adverb, Gerson takes up "form," "*figura*," the third element in the first set, which he immediately relates to the third element of the second set, by declaring that a "distinction" must be made. At no point, however, does Gerson reuse the term "similitude," though he does use two synonyms—namely "*imago*" and "*pictura*" in the image of "pictures of various likenesses" that "ornament a sanctuary."

This lack of order in a section where the concept of right sequence for actions is mentioned is especially surprising. This relative disorder seems to indicate that this section is not as carefully wrought as the other seven sections of *Moralized Grammar*. The conclusion of the section ("these sentences about the adverb should suffice") reads as a mild justification for the adequacy of the section and its rather nonlinear organization.

PARTICIPIUM

After treating theological anthropology as nominal and moral theology as verbal, Gerson next combines the two. The section on the fifth part of speech, the participle, involves intertextual references to these preceding noun and verb sections. Just as a grammatical participle is a blend of noun and verb, so a participle in Gerson's moralized grammar refers back to the noun—namely, *homo*, human being, and verb, the precepts of God for human beings. Thus, to the question, "What is a participle?" the reply is, "knowledge of the human being according to nature and according to God" (839d). Internal reference to the previously explained noun and verb becomes especially apparent at four points in this section. First is the question relating to *genus*, the first of the six attributes said to belong to a participle: "What gender of participle is a human being?" (840a). Citing the addressee's noun or name, *homo*, Gerson refers back to his first part of speech, where the gender of the noun is defined as "shared, since human nature fits man just as it fits woman" (835c). The participle, referring to this human nature, has a gender that is "common" or "shared," just as the noun does. Similarly, the participle's case, again playing on the nongrammatical meaning of this word as "fall," is "the case of a disobedient sinner" (840a). After the question and response regarding case, Gerson brings out explicitly what was implicit in his use of the word *homo* in the gender question: "These are the genders and cases. The participle obtains these two from the noun." However, in defining the participle's gender, Gerson adds an element beyond what is contained in the noun section regarding gender. The participle's gender is both common and three. The common or shared gender comes from the noun—that is, from the human as such, but the gender of "three" belongs to the human being as participle, since human beings, through Adam and Eve, are children of God, who is three persons. As creatures of God, human beings participate in the Trinity.

A second point where we see the duality of the participle as in some ways nominal and in other ways verbal follows the questions and answers about *tempus* (tense) and *significatio* (meaning): "These two, namely, *tempus* and *significatio*, the participle obtains in a verb, I mean, what we should be according to God" (840b). As with participles in Latin, the gender of a participle in Gerson's spiritual grammar is related to the relevant noun while its meaning and tense come from the related verb. The tense of the participle is present, since penance must be done now, though our current travails are for a future reward. The participle's *significatio* or meaning has five dimensions. First, the active meaning is in actively doing good works. Second, playing with two senses of the verb *patior*, meaning "to undergo" or "to suffer" (and the etymological source of the English word "passive"), the "passive" meaning of the participle is in "suffering hardships *patiently*." Third, the neutral meaning is in preserving suitable virtues and thoughts. Fourth, the meaning of the deponent, which in normal grammar refers to a verb whose form is passive but whose meaning and syntactic function are active, plays off of the root meaning of *deponere* as "to put aside" or "to let fall," as in letting go of all mortal sins. Fifth, the shared meaning (*significatio communis*) is in preserving divine precepts and ecclesial directions.

The third reference to this nominal-verbal duality in the participle explains that two other attributes of the participle, the number and form, come jointly from both the noun and the verb (840c). Both number and form are construed to pertain to the group to which a human being belongs in relationship to God. The participle's number is in any case plural, since human beings in right relationship to God either are on earth and thus members of the group known as the church militant or are in heaven and thus members of the church triumphant. The participle's form is both simple and composite. It is simple in that the human being should be one with the faith and with the saved. It is composite in that the human being should separate from the damned.

The fourth reference to how the participle looks both to the noun and the verb occurs in the concluding section, where Gerson ranges over what was said in the section. Like the discussion at the end of the noun section, this concluding piece resembles an exhortatory homily. The main point here is that we human beings should conform ourselves to the will of God. As a participle, which can take its attributes from the verb or the noun, human beings can conform either with the will of God or with their human nature apart from God. If we find our confidence for salvation in ourselves alone, we do so in vain. God alone supplies the vitality of our withered being:

> Quickly insisting on vanities and provoked to anger or kindled with avariciousness, as an ash, insubstantial, dry, and small, left behind after the wood has been consumed by the fire. Just so are we insubstantial, dry, and vain in the absence of the fluids of divine grace, small from faintheartedness and consumed by the fire of carnal desires. (840d)

Having vividly depicted the dry deadness of human beings apart from God, Gerson exhorts us to repent, turning inward to find God, in whose image we are created. "But as sinners let us return to the heart, considering that the participle is of the same kind of meaning as the verb [*ejusdem significationis cujus generis est verbum*]. Thus may we also conform to the will of God since we are made in His image." Taking the word *generis* here in the nongrammatical sense but rather to mean simply "kind" or "sort," I understand the idea here to be that as participles take their meaning from the verb, so human beings should conform to God. Gerson exhorts us to return to the heart, where we find the imprint of God's image.

CONJUNCTIO

Following his treatment of the terrestrial moral life, including the fundamental decision that human beings can make, either to participate in the divine or to live solely according to their carnal nature, Gerson moves to the hereafter. The sixth section of *Moralized Grammar* pertains to the conjunction. Its religious content centers on that moment when God brings together all people for the Last Judgment. Gerson thus plays on the root meaning of *coniunctio* as "joining together" or "uniting."[34] The definition of conjunction is "the consideration or knowledge of the future Judgment" (841a). Its attributes are three: power, form, and order.

The power of the conjunction is divine power. This attribute Gerson expands to narrate the steps in the Last Judgment. First, with the trumpet of angels, God will bring everyone together into one flock. Then God will divide the good from the evil. Next, by bringing the elect to heaven, He will restore the brokenness of the heavenly city, which Lucifer's fall caused. Finally, God will plead the case against the damned and for the saved according to whether or not they carried out the works of mercy as described in Matthew 25:32–46 (841b).

The second attribute, form, is taken in its simple and complex varieties to refer to categories of the judged in relation to their effects on other people. The simple variety affects only themselves. Whether good or bad, they lived their lives on earth in simple goodness or simple evil, without having beneficial or deleterious effects on others. The composite, in contrast, transmitted their ways to others. If good, they not only lived well themselves but also promoted good living among other people, through teaching their ways. If bad, they not only lost their own souls, but also corrupted others. The composite, then, reached a higher degree of whatever they were. The good composite were more completely good, thanks to the benefits they brought to other souls, while the evil composite were more completely evil, owing to the harm they brought to others' souls.

The third and last attribute of the conjunction, order, pertains to the priority with which the judged are considered (841c). Those put first are the preferred—that is, the saved, which Gerson refers to as the "*praepositivi*," a term that anticipates the preposition section that follows his treatment of the conjunction. From a grammatical point of view, this term "*praepositivus*" can refer to conjunctions that are properly placed before (*prae* meaning "before" and "*positivus*" meaning "positioned") the element that they connect, like the conjunction *et*, as opposed to its synonym -*que*, which is placed after the element that it connects.[35] In Gerson's treatment of the conjunction, the damned come next. Calling the damned the "*subjunctivi*," Gerson uses a term that, like *conjunctio*, derives from the verb *jungere*, which means "to join." Though the basic spatial meaning of the prefix "*sub-*" is "under," in a temporal context the prefix can mean "directly after." Both senses can be seen at play here. The damned are subjoined—that is, added next and in a lower, inferior position.

Gerson refers to the parable of the wise and the foolish maidens in Matthew 25:1–13, where the prudent virgins were prepared with oil in their lamps to go out and meet the bridegroom when he arrived, while the foolish virgins had not sufficiently prepared for his coming. Asleep when he came, they had to wake up and go buy oil for their own lamps. When they came back to the feast, the door was locked, they were not let in, and the bridegroom did not recognize them. Gerson thus likened the coming of the bridegroom to the Last Judgment, where the saved are those who prepared well for that fateful moment, while the damned are the careless foolish ones who did not.

Expounding on the awe that all will experience when the Lord does come for that last day, Gerson reflects on several related scriptural passages and *exempla*. "If the just will barely be saved (1 Peter 4:18), who should not be afraid?" (841c). If, in uttering the "I am" (John 18:6) with which God responded to Moses' question about God's name (Exodus 3:14), Jesus caused those who came to arrest him to lie prostrate, "how much more frightful will he be when with a terrifying trumpet sound, sharper than a sword, he rends the living and the dead and sets himself up to judge them?" (841d). What is being summoned for judgment before a human king of this world when compared to being summoned before the eternal King? Even the angels shall tremble with dread. Gerson implicitly criticizes the Apostle Paul, who was so virtuous and had so clear a conscience that he could claim not to be guilty of anything (1 Corinthians 4:4). According to Gerson, even Paul shall have cause to tremble on that day. To the apostle's claim of guiltlessness, Gerson puts the rhetorical question, "Why is it that with such false security we reassure ourselves, we who run about with a thousand defects?" (841d). He cites a similar rhetorical question in Proverbs: "For who brags that he has a pure heart?" (Proverbs 20:9). Urging uncertainty, Gerson reemphasizes that "no one can know whether 'he be fit for hate or love' (Ecclesiastes 9:1)." The conjunction section closes with exhortation to mindful preparation for the Last Day: "Let us then keep before the eyes of our heart that horrible call that the angelic trumpet will sound forth: Rise you dead, come to the Judgment, and let us now think ahead about what we will say back to the Judge" (841d–42a).

PRAEPOSITIO

The seventh section continues the eschatological theme with a focus on the saved being preferred or literally and etymologically "put before" the damned, as anticipated in the conjunction section by Gerson calling the saved the "*praepositivi.*" As in the interjection section that follows, here there are only two formal questions: "What is a preposition?" and "How many attributes belong to the preposition?" (842a). Gerson defines preposition as "the consideration of the joys of the elect." It has only one attribute—namely, case, which here does not refer to the Fall, as did *casus* in the noun, pronoun, and participle sections. In considering the joys of the elect, "case" here rather refers to humility, not the fall from grace.

Two cases are relevant to the preposition, the accusative and the ablative. The accusative case is that with which the elect accuse the worldly age in all its wickedness. Humbling themselves before God, the elect thank Him for having been converted and kept unblemished by the evil of the world. The ablative, whose literal meaning can be rendered as "carried away," is the case by which the elect humble themselves before God to thank Him for having been " 'carried off' from this wicked age and brought to that heavenly city" (842b).

Before undertaking an extended consideration of the joys of the elect and thus expounding on the meaning of preposition, Gerson compares the celestial city to the worldly realm (842c). Here there are travails, there rest; here danger, there safety; here tribulation, there peace; here sadness, there joy. Here what abound most of all are vices, tribulations, and needs; there peace, purity, and sanctity. Seeking the things of this world is to dwell in a realm where carnal vices rot us, tribulations shake us, and we are ever in need of remedies for our ailments. Focusing instead on that heavenly kingdom is to reach for grace and contemplate eternally the majesty, goodness, and glory of God.

Consideration of the joys of the elect is contrived through imagining a sumptuous court, where not only does the crowned king sit splendid in regal robes, but he is also surrounded by soldiers who salute him reverently. The senses are delighted in Gerson's image of the ideal earthly court. Precious paintings and the glittering uniforms of the honor guard delight the eye; diverse music, the ear; delicate dishes, the palate; wines and other sweet-smelling drinks, the nose. The moods too would be calmed and delighted by the spectacle and amity, for no danger, fear, worry, or annoyance would be there to trouble anyone. What more than such solace could anyone want, especially if it could last forever without getting sick of it? (842c–d).

However desirable such a sumptuous royal court in this world could be, the heavenly court must be incomparably more spectacular. There,

Christ is the King enthroned. God the Father has crowned him and enthroned Christ on His right and before all humankind. The honor guard is of nine orders of angels standing at attention and praising God and the Lamb heralded by the Book of Revelation. The ornaments of the court are not paintings, but gleaming stars, and its security, peace, and joy are truly everlasting. As Paul wrote to the Corinthians, "no eye has seen, no ear has heard, nor has it entered into the heart of a human being, those things that God has prepared for those who love him" (1 Corinthians 2:9). Closing this section, like several others, with exhortation, Gerson urges silent reflection on the felicity of the saved in the heavenly kingdom, "where everything that might be desired is found, and where delight is only in the glorious son of God and seeing the Kingdom of glory in its splendor is the only satiety of souls, forever and ever. Amen" (843a).

INTERJECTIO

The eighth and final section, on the interjection, is a reflection on the fate of the damned, in contraposition to the delightful considerations of the preceding section. Referencing the kinds of interjections emitted by vexed and sorrowful souls, Gerson explicitly compares "the grammatical interjection" and "the spiritual one." Both signify outwardly something felt internally. The interjection has only one attribute—namely, "*significatio*" or meaning. Before expounding on the pains of hell using first scripture and then an extended simile, Gerson gives four different values for the meaning of the spiritual interjection.

The first meaning is the outward signification of "the delights of the demons over the torments of just so many souls" (843a). The second is "the sorrow of the damned souls." The third is the feeling of marvel among the wicked angels as they revel in the damned decrying their own blindness and stupidity for not having heeded on earth the righteous urgings of preachers to flee the pleasures of the flesh and the delights of the world, so as not to enter into the place of torments. The fourth is the dread and fear of the damned souls as "their infernal hosts torture them with inextinguishable fire, intensely hostile words, fiercely burning eyes, puffed up face, and a deathly black aspect" (843b).

After enumerating the meanings of the spiritual interjection, Gerson further expounds on the sorrows of the damned through providing exegesis of three relevant scriptural passages. The first is the end of Matthew 8:12: "there will be wailing and gnashing of teeth." The wailing is the expression of one weighed down with great sorrow and the gnashing of the teeth the expression of one burdened with great pain. To explicate this pain further, Gerson cites Isaiah 66:24, "Their worm will not die, and their fire will not be extinguished." The worm, he explains, signifies the conscience of the guilty, which is never calmed down, since it constantly gnaws and never dies. Perpetually accusing themselves, they shall give themselves over to divine judgment and be seized up with outrage and wrath. Their contempt and hopelessness shall persist, and the kindling of their carnal yearnings from this world shall in that world be whipped up to raging flames. Quoting Psalm 11:7, Gerson then provides the third scriptural basis for a masterful extended simile: "Fire and sulphur and the breath of violent winds [is] their allotted cup" (843c), whose elements he explains as further highlights of the infernal torments.

These three scriptural citations, combined with the earlier four significations of the spiritual interjection, culminate in Gerson's exercising his own creativity and artistry to depict in an extended simile the alternative to the sumptuous court seen in the preposition section:

> So that this pain might be described more clearly, let us sum up the example in a simile. A crafty smith is accustomed to having a black face, and a grimy forge where he puts an iron so that it might grow hot. Afterwards, as he wills, he and his assistants strike it with mallets. That smith of which I speak is the devil, who is deathly black. The grimy forge is the underworld, which has no brightness whatsoever. The glowing charcoals that are put there signify that this pain will endure forever. The sacks signify the pain insofar as it never or hardly will slacken. Rather, it will only be made fiery hot. The iron is the damned soul itself which is exposed there to that fire, so as to be perpetually cremated. Never do the demons leave off vituperating with savagely fierce words. (843c–d)

This sordid portrait of the execrable figure of Satan is not the end of Gerson's interjection. The concluding exhortation not so obliquely conjures up a profanity ("shit!") exclaimed in many a vexed moment, even in medieval France.[36] Once again urging repentance, so that we might cause rejoicing for angels rather than for devils, Gerson calls for reflection on our redemption by the blood of Christ, a tremendous gift whose efficaciousness we should in no way frustrate. The purpose of our repentance Gerson expresses quite colorfully: "so that just as pieces of shit issue from a stomach that needs purging, and as shavings that have been cut from wood are thrown into a fire, we might not after this life be expelled like pieces of shit, as it were, from the bowels of the church and thrown like chaff and refuse into the fire of hell" (843d–44a). Following this dirty image, Gerson closes *Moralized Grammar* piously and formulaically: "Therefore, may our hearts be fixed to that place where there are true joys. Amen."

The graphic images of the sumptuous court, the satanic smith, and the ecclesial excrement in these last two sections create especially memorable moments in reading *Donatus moralizatus*. Indeed, such colorful concrete imagery serves the overarching salvific aims of the text. This rhetorical feature fits the tradition of *Ovide moralisé*, which "like every didactic text," according to one scholar, "seeks to present concrete images that strike the imagination and prolong the memory."[37] A reader can scarcely forget the delights of the senses in the sumptuous court—precious paintings, glittering uniforms, diverse music, delicate dishes, wines and sweet-smelling drinks—and much less the purging of the execrable excrement from the bowels of the church into the fires of hell.

Gerson's Imitation of Donatus

Throughout most of *Donatus moralizatus*, the interplay between grammatical and religious meanings is unmarked. Either Gerson follows Donatus in form while filling it with religious content or he announces a departure from the format of Donatus's *Ars minor* to undertake an extended discourse on some matter of the moral life. Most often, the stylized question comes in a straightforward, plain-sense form that appears to refer only to the terminology of Latin grammar. The responses, in contrast, are replete with wordplay that takes the question in the direction of the moral or spiritual life. Both Donatus's grammar book and Gerson's moralized imitation of it begin with the question "*Partes orationis quot sunt?*," and the number given for the parts of speech is likewise eight in both texts. Where Gerson first varies from Donatus is on the naming of those parts of speech. Although he will take the noun, pronoun, verb, adverb, participle, conjunction, preposition, and interjection to be the framework of the rest of his text, Gerson replaces this list with a list of topics that more or less line up with his moralized version of each of Donatus's parts of speech. As we have seen, "knowledge of substance" sums up Gerson's treatment of the noun. "Knowledge of the precepts of God" fits with his version of the verb. Performance of God's precepts is treated under the adverb. "Knowledge of the human being with regard to God and with regard to nature" fits the duality of the participle. "Consideration of the Judgment which is to be" is Gerson's definition of the conjunction. "Consideration of the joys of the elect" is his treatment of the preposition, and "consideration of the sorrows of the damned" is his definition of the interjection. What does not quite fit into this initial list of religious topics is the pronoun section, where Gerson explores several aspects of sin, including the stages of committing a sin, after having defined the pronoun of the human being to be "sinner."

Many of the questions and even their order come in fact directly from the *Ars minor* of Donatus. Each section in Gerson's text, as in Donatus's,[38] begins with, "What is [this part of speech]?," "How many attributes belong to [this part of speech]?," and, "What is [each of these attributes]?" In each section of Gerson's text, the responses regarding the number and names of the attributes or accidents also come directly from the *Ars minor*. So, in both Donatus Aelius's *Ars minor* and in Gerson's *Donatus moralizatus*, the noun has six qualities (*qualitas, conparatio, genus, numerus, figura, casus*), the pronoun six (*qualitas, genus, numerus, figura, persona, casus*), the verb seven (*qualitas, coniugatio, genus, numerus, figura, tempus, persona*), the adverb three (*significatio, conparatio, figura*), the participle six (*genus, casus, tempus, significatio, numerus, figura*), the conjunction three (*potestas, figura, ordo*), and both the preposition and interjection one (*casus* and *significatio*, respectively). The only very slight variance in these accidents is that in listing the accidents of the adverb, Gerson reverses Donatus's order of "meaning" and "comparison."

While the constant wordplay and religious answers diverge in content from the *Ars minor*, the most striking difference from the form of Donatus Aelius's text is Gerson's use of example and explanation. Donatus gives many discrete linguistic examples with relatively brief explanations, while Gerson makes use of a few moral or religious *exempla* to generate more extended discourse. In four sections, after following the question-response format for a time, Gerson signals explicitly that he will change modes and undertake a more extended exploration of the themes raised in the section. In the noun section, his signal is "*discutiamus iam dicta*," "let us now discuss what has been said" (835d). Before his treatment of each of the Ten Commandments, Gerson similarly announces his intention to depart from the form of Donatus's model with "*declaremus iam praedicta*," "let us now expound what has been said above" (838b). Gerson begins his exploration of the two poles of human nature in the participle section with "*discurramus iam dicta*," "let us now discuss what has been said" (840c). In the preposition section, Gerson's announcement takes a somewhat different form: "*Si ergo considerare et pensare vellimus illius supernae felicitatis quanta sint gaudia,*" "If therefore we wish to consider and think about how many the joys of that celestial happiness might be" (842b). Although the remaining four sections do not feature an explicit signal to announce a departure from the question-response format in favor of an extended discourse, several of the responses in these sections are quite extended and similar to the discursive passages just named. The adverb section, for example, treats each of the three attributes (meaning, comparison, and form) at some length and with multiple examples. The pronoun section is something of a hybrid in that it both announces an extended explanation and yet also retains the careful organization of the question-response format. Directly after identifying Adam and Eve as the original sinners and all other people as "derived" sinners, Gerson writes "*declaremus praemissa,*" "let us expound on what has been laid out above" (837a) and then returns to the previous enumeration of the six cases of the pronoun (suggestion, paying heed, discussion, taking pleasure, acquiescence in the mind, acquiescence in action). His explication of these steps in committing sin consists first in a kind of exegetical exercise of the Genesis account of Eve's and Adam's actions and then in a personal account of how these same steps could apply to a sexual sin that he himself might commit.

In sum, Gerson displays at times loyal imitation and at times explicit divergence from the form of Donatus's text. Gerson borrows directly from Donatus the question-response format, the eight parts of speech as the organizing categories, the same initial questions regarding each part of speech, and even the same number and name of the attributes of each part of speech. While Gerson's most striking divergence from Donatus is in content, his most obvious formal innovation is to create extended discussions and explanations as well as moral *exempla*, in contrast to Donatus's method of providing a large quantity of specific lexical items as examples of the concepts for which he provides relatively less explanation than Gerson.

Acknowledging the Trope

At a few points Gerson creates a different kind of relationship between the grammatical Donatus and his moralization of the original text. At these remarkable moments Gerson acknowledges the overall trope of his text by explicitly combining or juxtaposing the grammatical and the religious in the same sentence. For example, in his first treatment of an attribute of the adverb, Gerson draws an explicit comparison between the grammatical art and the moral art:

> *Sic ergo in omnibus attende circumspectionem, ut adverbium debite ponas juxta suum verbum.*
>
> Thus, in all things be circumspect, as you would appropriately put an adverb with its verb. (839b)

Unlike the many grammatical questions receiving a moral response, where the two interlocutors seem almost to speak different disciplinary languages, here the moral teacher drops the pretense and acknowledges the game of mixed discourse. Living well is like composing sentences grammatically. Be careful what works of mercy or spiritual devotions you undertake, along with when, where, in what manner, how much, and in what sequence, just as you carefully modify verbs with the correct adverbs. Gerson explicitly calls upon his students to use in their moral life the same circumspection that they have learned through studying the *Ars minor.*

In the final section of *Moralized Grammar,* while defining "interjection," Gerson is explicit about the trope of his text in a somewhat different way.

> *Respondeo: quod est tristitiae damnatorum consideratio, quia sicut interjectio grammaticalis signat mentis affectum voce incognita: ita interjectio illa spiritualis signat hominis interioris motum ex passione dolorosa.*
>
> I respond that it is consideration of the laments of the damned, since just as a grammatical interjection signifies a state of mind with an unprecedented word, so does this spiritual interjection signify an emotion of the interior human being coming out of sorrowful suffering. (843a)

In this passage the two kinds of discourse that Gerson mixes throughout his playful text are named and compared directly. Rather than the respondent apparently giving a spiritual or moral answer to a grammatical question, here the response defines both what it calls the "grammatical interjection" and the "spiritual interjection." Donatus's own definition of interjection is "*Pars orationis significans mentis affectum voce incondita*"[39]—that is, "a part of speech signifying an affect of the mind with a crude utterance." Gerson's spiritual definition takes up Donatus's idea of the interjection signifying an internal emotion, but restricts the relevant affective field only to those feelings that originate in "sorrowful suffering."

Similarly mixed moments come where Gerson includes the religious content of one of his previous answers in a subsequent question or response. In the very first treatment of an attribute of a part of speech, Gerson employs this technique, thus initiating his reader into how *Moralized Grammar* works. Donatus's familiar question format regarding an attribute is simply the genitive question word *cujus* plus the name of the attribute, so "*Cujus generis?*," "*Cujus numeri?*," "*Cujus figurae?*," etc. Gerson uses exactly these, but in the very first question in his text regarding the accidents of a part of speech—that is, the first attribute of the noun—Gerson slightly expands his question: "*Cujus qualitatis est homo?*," "Of what quality is a human being?" (835b). His inclusion of the word "*homo*" in this initial question helps teach the reader how to read the subsequent questions—that is, to keep in mind not only the familiar content of the *Ars minor* but also the religious content that Gerson provides throughout his moralized version of Donatus. Later in the text, Gerson does the same in his question regarding the quality of pronouns ("*Peccator ergo, prout est pronomen, cujus qualitatis?*"; "Sinner, as a pronoun, is of what quality?" [836b]) and the gender or genus of the participle ("*Cujus generis est homo participium?*"; "A human being is a participle of what gender?" [840a]). These exceptions to the game of answering grammatical-looking questions with religious answers that play off alternative meanings of grammatical terms have the effect of eliciting a level of integration of meaning across the various sections.

This text is about the parts of speech of the human being as a moral creature rather than as a linguistic creature. The answers found here teach students their own name (*homo*, human being) and what to put in the place of their name when approaching God (*peccator*, sinner). The verb is the *verbum dei*, the word of God, which is both what God teaches humankind and what action humankind must carry out. *Moralized Grammar* teaches its students to carry out these divine teachings in a careful way, attending to all the adverbial circumstances around their actions. As a participle, the human being need not look only to his or her own nature, but also to God, whose *verbum* or divine word gives human beings knowledge of themselves. The conjunction of human beings is the great bringing together effected by God on the Last Day. The preposition is human reflection on the possibility of being preferred and placed first at that Judgment, while the interjection is the consideration of the possibility of eternal suffering in damnation.

The Grammatical Metaphor

In writing *Moralized Grammar*, Gerson weaves together what was the standard grammatical primer of his era with key anthropological, moral, eschatological, scriptural, and theological ideas comprising his intellectual and spiritual worldview. The tool that he uses to weave Donatus's *Ars minor* together with these nongrammatical ideas is primarily a literary trope, which John Alford has called "the grammatical metaphor."[40] This trope, like the book of Donatus and the ideas and beliefs to which Gerson subscribed, had its own genealogy and even tradition within the medieval Latin world. Alford's lively article about the grammatical metaphor in medieval literature thus provides important context for making sense of *Moralized Grammar*. Alford's article also contains one of the only treatments of Gerson's odd text that can be found in scholarly literature before now.[41] Through his broad knowledge of medieval literature, Alford demonstrates that playing on the etymological root meanings of grammatical terms, particularly for sexual or religious puns, is a standard and familiar technique in Latin literature. He traces a few such puns in particular that we have seen in our reading of *Moralized Grammar*. Alford also acknowledges the lack of certainty about whether Gerson was the actual author of *Donatus moralizatus*, and his general assessment of the text is that it is a mere compilation of tried and true grammatical puns developed first by other authors over the ages.

Alford's main objectives in writing his article are "to illustrate the wide variety of uses to which the metaphor was put, and to give some explanation for its popularity."[42] The two explanations that he gives for the popularity of the grammatical metaphor are: (1) Grammatical terminology is Latin in origin, so in the Latin culture of the Middle Ages people could easily recognize and exploit the semantic possibilities of the terms; and (2) "The medieval belief that grammar was necessarily related to logic or nature encouraged the use of grammatical concepts as the metaphorical equivalents of these things." These two explanations, in turn, trace the basic types of examples that he goes on to lay out—namely, those based on the form of terms themselves[43] and those metaphors based on grammatical concepts rather than terms.[44] According to Alford, metaphors of this latter type often have a deeper or broader theoretical purpose than the first type.

Alford introduces *Moralized Grammar* as an excessive culmination and unimaginative recycling of the grammatical metaphor:

> Toward the end of the medieval period, as if to prove the strength of the metaphor in one final, extravagant gesture, someone—perhaps Jean Gerson (1363–1429)—turned the entire *Ars minor* of Donatus into a moral allegory. The *Donatus moralizatus* is, properly speaking, the natural culmination of the tradition. Most of the grammatical concepts of the *Ars minor* had already been moralized separately, and it only remained for someone of sufficient imagination—or lack of it—to bring all of these efforts together under the guise of an actual grammatical treatise.[45]

Alford's own interpretation of *Moralized Grammar* retraces a certain tried and true path among scholars—namely, by conceptualizing some unimaginative period of history between the so-called "High Middle Ages" and the rebirth of the "Renaissance" during which time thinkers were merely reworking old ideas in an uncreative and excessive way. Alford notes that most of the grammatical content learned by schoolchildren from Donatus "had already been moralized separately," and so there was an inevitable momentum toward creating a simple compilation of these moral puns. The *Ars minor* was the obvious choice of framework for such an uncreative literary compilation. After all, as the standard Latin primer for a thousand years, it was rather well known. Alford's tremendous erudition in medieval literature brings a great deal to our understanding of *Moralized Grammar* by placing it in a particular field of grammatical thought and literary artifice. Through presenting so many examples of grammatical metaphor he allows readers of *Donatus moralizatus* to familiarize themselves with a way of using grammar that has its own precedents and tradition. On the other hand, Alford's dismissal of *Moralized Grammar* as an unimaginative, final, extravagant gesture before the death of the tradition of the grammatical metaphor is an obstacle to evaluating the value of this text on both theological and literary grounds. Moreover, his evaluation of the text is a suspiciously standard, deprecatory interpretation of the cultural and intellectual production of the so-called "late medieval" period.

Let us make the most of Alford's erudite contribution by examining some of the particular examples of the grammatical metaphor that he cites and that we see in *Moralized Grammar*. The first he notes is the idea of *casus* and *declinatio* as denoting "fall": "Medieval poets . . . drew elaborate comparisons between grammar and the story of Adam and Eve: original sin is referred to as 'the first declension,' and Adam and Eve are 'oblique' nouns that fell away or 'declined' from God."[46] Another example is the usage of the duality inherent to the grammatical concept of a participle. In his *Forma praedicandi* (1322) Robert of Basevorn explains Mary Magdalene's life as a participle: "Mary was a participle in the state of sin, taking a part from the noun while, losing her proper name, she was called *peccatrix*; and a part from the verb, when in the beginning of her repentance, approaching the Word (*Verbum*), the Son of God, she heard: 'Your sins are forgiven you.' "[47]

A third example is perhaps of broader significance to our present effort to make sense of *Moralized Grammar*. In Gerson's section on adverbs, we have seen his usage of the idea of grammatical correctness or propriety, marked by the word *debite*, translated here as "appropriately": "Thus, in all things be circumspect, as you would appropriately put an adverb with its verb."[48] Gerson's idea here is the flip side of a concept in the "Christian grammar" of Augustine and even more so of Anselm and others: "If words and deeds are synonymous, then it is possible to speak of one in terms of the other. Human conduct may be regarded as a kind of rhetorical system. Thus, to obey God's law is to speak correctly; to sin is to commit a solecism."[49] Alford relates how Anselm's *De veritate* (ca. 1080) is built around the premise that truth, *veritas*, can be applied just as well to linguistic propositions as to moral deeds, since "both are true by virtue of the same principle, namely, their participation in 'rightness' or *rectitudo*, of which God is the source and supreme exemplar."[50]

Besides such examples of the grammatical trope providing a religious meaning, Alford also presents examples of grammatical metaphor providing a handy framework for religious discourse, particularly sermons. Drawing on Gerald Robert Owst's *Preaching in Medieval England: An Introduction to Sermon Manuscripts of the Period c. 1350–1450*, Alford identifies "a sermon by Robert Rypon of Durham, who 'reads his clerical congregation what sounds strangely like a lesson in grammar.' "[51] Based on the brief selection of Robert Rypon's sermon that Owst cites, Alford opines that "grammar serves primarily in this case as an organizational device—what the sermon manuals refer to as the 'dividing of the theme.' "[52] Rypon was by no means unique. "The medieval preacher found in the paradigms of grammar a wealth of ready-made structures, by means of which he was able to organize his points," an observation that

Alford backs up with citations from numerous sources, including the *Gesta Romanorum*, a popular fifteenth-century collection of moral *exempla* used by preachers. Robert of Basevorn makes a similar point in his preaching manual about grammatical distinctions being useful for organizing a sermon.[53] Thomas Waleys, in his *De modo componendi sermones*, makes a point for his reader by using Donatus's grammatical idea that a preposition has only one case:

> Thus also whoever is in a position of authority (*in praepositura*) has case, that is, a fall unless he watches himself carefully. Behold how one meaning of the word *praepositio* is joined to the other by means of similitude. And also, as part of the same idea, how one meaning of the word *casus* is joined to its other meaning; for *casus* is equivocal, as is evident, in this example.[54]

To a literate audience grammatical frameworks make the religious content of sermons or other texts hard to forget.[55] Numerous authoritative sermon manuals recommend grammar as a resource for preachers to draw upon in composing their sermons, and those manuals explain precisely how to do so.

It is worth noting that besides religious puns, Alford reveals sexual puns on grammatical terms and ideas to be among the most common: "medieval poets show the utmost ingenuity in finding a sexual interpretation for virtually every distinction known to grammar."[56] Examples include the sins of the flesh as "the genitive plural," the "active" and the "passive'" as the lover and the beloved, and the "second person" as the mistress. The "grammar of love" is in some cases elaborated as a pastoral summons to leave studies and "let the face of a maiden be the book that summons us to the lecture."[57]

One other important point from Alford's article is that he believes there to be two kinds of grammatical metaphor—those playing on grammatical terms alone and those playing on grammatical concepts. Just as Le Clerc and Renan, the authors of the *Histoire littéraire de la France au quatorzième siècle* (1864), and Charland, author of the *Artes praedicandi*, find grammatical wordplay to be "puerile,"[58] so Alford does not think much of mere puns.

> The metaphors generated by grammatical terminology, though abundant, hardly rise above the level of puns or go beyond the rather mechanical functions of rhetorical *dispositio* and *amplificatio*. The metaphors gen-

> erated by grammatical theory, on the other hand, may serve both a rhetorical and a deeper philosophical purpose. The focus is no longer on the names but on the processes of grammar, which medieval thought equates with the processes of nature.[59]

Tracing from classical antiquity through medieval thought the idea that grammar is not merely convention but also conforms to reality, Alford notes that with the introduction of dialectic to grammar, principally by Peter Helias in the twelfth century, speculative grammar took on a new precision and specificity in its claims. Once features of Latin such as three persons and two genders are ascribed not only to language but also to pertain to extralinguistic reality, the grammatical metaphor became more profoundly meaningful, according to Alford. "Grammar slips over into logic."[60] Theology slips into grammar. If grammar is a kind of applied logic, its categories are not merely convention, but describe the framework for understanding and explaining reality. The grammaticization of much Christian theological inquiry starting in the Scholastic period is a vast topic of considerable importance, well beyond the scope of our present study. However, one aspect of the historical significance of *Moralized Grammar* is that it thematizes this important tendency of medieval theology. Rather than expounding on the correlation between grammar and nature through philosophical discourse, *Moralized Grammar* transforms the entire basic grammar book into a sermonic moral catechism. This transformation indirectly but profoundly raises the question of the nature of the ontological relationship between language and reality. While the technique of constant wordplay might seem puerile to some literary tastes, the composition of a grammar book that presents a theological anthropology from our origins to our final destiny and explains how to live in between these existential poles might well deserve more consideration than simple dismissal as merely a collection of boyish puns.

Alford misses a great deal in his dismissive treatment of *Moralized Grammar*. His approach is purely literary and fails to consider the religious purposes and effects of Gerson's text. Alford treats *Moralized Grammar* as an uncreative compilation of discrete grammatical metaphors, all of which, thanks to his erudition, he had seen before in medieval literature. Alford's approach skips over the truth claims made in Gerson's *Moralized Grammar* and thus obscures for him the functions of the very metaphors on which he focuses.

Gerson's literary techniques in *Moralized Grammar* serve the religious purposes for which he composed the text. Writing in Latin, he aimed *Moralized Grammar* at a schooled readership. Like his many tracts, *Moralized Grammar* is crafted not for university masters but for Latin readers of lesser scholastic accomplishment. Through his transformative adaptation of Aelius Donatus's *Ars minor*, Gerson organized *Donatus moralizatus* around a simple yet generative citation with which his readers were intimately familiar. Unlike *De pollutione nocturna*, *Moralized Grammar* is not customized for clerics. Its theological content is basic, fundamental, and equally relevant to lay and ordained readers. Performing neither for a specifically academic audience, like *Sermo contra gulam*, nor for lay people who may have only understood French, like *Videmus nunc*, Gerson in *Moralized Grammar* aimed to have salvific effects on readers who were students, whether at the primary, secondary, or baccalaureate level. Puerile wordplay appeals to young readers. Graphic images like that of the damned defecation were likely to make lessons on the interjection forever more colorful for a pupil who had read *Moralized Grammar*. In crafting this particular text for unsophisticated readers, Gerson himself did not abandon his own theological sophistication or erudition. After our study of Qushayrī's *Grammar of Hearts*, we will return to *Moralized Grammar* to deepen our understanding of the theological meanings of its metaphorical schemes.

4 From the Names of God to the *Grammar of Hearts*

We now tack east and back in history, from Latin to Arabic, French to Persian, Christian to Islamic. While juxtaposing Gerson's *Moralized Grammar* and Qushayrī's *Grammar of Hearts* creates a new context for the two texts, they are also linked to their respective times and places of origins. Attending to these original contexts grounds the fresh literary and theological understandings that the present study constructs. To prepare for understanding *The Grammar of Hearts* in both its literary form and its religious content, we will examine in this chapter two of Qushayrī's most famous works and two of his less well-known writings.

Specifically, we will consider Qushayrī's *Risāla*, the handbook used for centuries to introduce students to Sufism; his work of Qur'anic exegisis, *Laṭā'if al-ishārāt*; his commentary on the names of God, *Sharḥ asmā' Allāh al-ḥusnā*; and a work of his on spiritual direction, *Tartīb al-sulūk fī ṭarīq Allāh*. The theme of *dhikr*, meaning the invocation of the names of God, will serve as the red thread guiding our exploration of these last two works, whose genre and content are particularly relevant to the intersection of spiritual and linguistic concerns in Qushayrī's thought.

The chapter thus makes a start at sketching a Jaussian cross-section of genres in Qushayrī's world while laying out his intellectual and religious concerns and the cultural and historical forces with which he contended. Heeding Jauss's call to situate a text within what I have called the "grammar of genres" from its literary context,[1] this study of four other works by Qushayrī in four other genres provides a provisionally adequate glimpse of the system of genres in which Qushayrī formed *The Grammar of Hearts*. However, due to a lopsidedness in the scholarly attention given to Western and Islamic civilizations, adequately sketching a synchronic cross-section of the genres of Arabic or Persian literature or Islamic religious literature in Qushayrī's time is even further from our reach than creating a similar sketch for Latin or Romance or Christian literature in Gerson's world. Nonetheless, this chapter is a start.

Moreover, the prejudices of historical periodization and Orientalism powerfully simplify and distort scholarly understandings of Islamic civilizations. By Edward Said's analysis, Orientalism makes the so-called "Orient" a foil to the so-called "West," thus enabling "the West" to see its mirror-image, "a sort of surrogate and even underground self."[2] A historiographic rise-and-fall paradigm accordingly envisages Islamic civilization as the inverse of Europe's trajectory. In the narrative of this paradigm, an Islamic golden age of the tenth, eleventh, and twelfth centuries is followed by a precipitous decline in which the fall of the great Islamic empires coincides with the end of creative cultural production, especially in the realms of religious and scientific discourse.[3] Just as some in the West may like to see themselves as more or less continuing the legacy of the Enlightenment, so have some in the West tended to see the Islamic world as still now continuing the dissipated and exhausted legacy of a late medieval demise.

Christians' gaze toward "the Orient" has for centuries been anything but innocuous. As a result of this legacy, I cannot pretend perfect parallelism between my study of Gerson and of Qushayrī. At the same time, the Western historiographical and Orientalist traditions hand down not only prejudiced paradigms and prefabricated frameworks, but also a rich legacy of understanding built from technical prowess, careful research, and insightful reading. I try to make the most of the latter, while cautious of the former. In that spirit, the present chapter will be our entryway into the world of ʿAbd al-Karīm al-Qushayrī.[4]

Situating Qushayrī Historically

Qushayrī was a multifaceted public figure in his Nishapur community. Like Gerson, he was a university master, a teacher, a spiritual director, a versatile scholar, a gifted writer, and a public intellectual who supported one faction over another in political-theological controversies. He was even arrested by his ruler on account of his Shāfiʿī positions and the ruler's Ḥanafī opposition to them. Though he came to be known primarily as a Sufi, we must recognize the many fields in which this versatile religious scholar was active, including systematic theology (*kalām*), jurisprudence (*fiqh*), and poetry.[5] Qushayrī was also "a productive *ḥadīth* scholar within his intellectual milieu, even if on a modest scale."[6] It is worth noting that in the traditional lists of appellations that mark areas of expertise in Islamic biographical dictionaries, Qushayrī typically is first called a *faqīh*, meaning that he was expert in Islamic jurisprudence.[7] His own teacher in *fiqh* was Abū Bakr al-Ṭūsī (d. 420/1029) a notable master of Shāfiʿī law in Nishapur. The greatest influences on Qushayrī overall, however, were his Sufi masters, primarily Shaykh Abū ʿAlī al-Daqqāq (d. 1015) and secondly al-Sulamī (d. 1021). Qushayrī not only studied *taṣawwuf* (Sufi science) with al-Daqqāq for many years, but also married al-Daqqāq's daughter and then, upon the shaykh's death in 1015, took over his madrasa (religious school).[8]

Nishapur, where Qushayrī flourished, was the capital of Khurasan and a center for major Islamic mystical and theological development during the ninth to eleventh centuries. As an important Sufi and member of the Ashʿarī school, Qushayrī was a major figure in both of these religious developments in Nishapur. Indeed, his recognized significance in Islamic history is to a large extent based on his achievements in using the discursive tools of *kalām* (discursive, philosophical theology) and *fiqh* (jurisprudence) to give *taṣawwuf*, the science of Sufi mystical knowledge, a firmer foundation among Sunni Muslims.

The towering figure of al-Ghazālī (d. 1111), who was born a year after Qushayrī died, to some extent has overshadowed Qushayrī. Though Ghazālī is most important as a master of theology and law, he was "a product of the same scholarly milieu as that of Qushayrī in Nishapur" and studied Sufism under Fārmadhī (d. 477/1084–85).[9] Ghazālī's *Iḥyāʾ ʿulūm al-dīn* is the work that for many Muslim readers epitomizes the integration of Sufism with other central disciplines of Islamic thought.

Situating Qushayrī within the broader development of Sufism and the theological movements in Nishapur will make possible an understanding of Qushayrī's significance in the Islamic tradition.

Sufism was the result of a coalescence of several renunciatory mystical movements that eventually coalesced under the name of *ṣūfi* or *ṣūfiyya*.[10] Over a couple of centuries, starting in the ninth century A.D./third century A.H., there appears to have been a movement from *zuhd* (asceticism) to *ʿibāda* (pietism) to *taṣawwuf* (Sufism).[11] Due to the dearth of extant documentation, much in this historical process is obscure. However, it seems clear that there were different sorts of renunciants, including some called *zāhid* (from the root *zuhd*, renunciation) and others known as *ʿābid* (connected to the root *ʿibāda*, worship) or *nāsik*, pietists.

Nishapur was a locus for all of these movements. Richard Bulliet's now classic study of medieval Islamic social history, *The Patricians of Nishapur*, focuses on the home city of Qushayrī and on a handful of elite families, including his. Bulliet identifies a clear sequential progression of these renunciatory mystical movements in Nishapur:

> At the beginning of the ninth/third century asceticism alone was known, but during the century pietism made its appearance. Around the middle of the tenth/fourth century the mystic Sufi strain became common, and by the end of the eleventh/fifth century it was clearly dominant.[12]

The generations before Qushayrī, figures such as al-Sarrāj, al-Sulamī, and al-Kalābādhī, introduced *taṣawwuf* to the cultural elites of those parts of Persia called Khorasan and Transoxiana. Qushayrī inherited this legacy through his study and Sufi practice with al-Sulamī, al-Daqqāq, and others.

In discursive theology or *kalām*, schools of theological thought were on the rise in Qushayrī's era as legal schools were consolidating. Adherents of Shāfiʿī legal thought, concentrated in Khorasan, came to support Ashʿarī theology, while adherents of Ḥanafī legal thought, mostly in Transoxiana, came to support Māturīdī theology.[13] The city of Nishapur was becoming a center of Ashʿarī thought in the tenth century, though Ashʿarism had not yet become dominant:[14]

> In the 4th/10th century when al-Qushayrī was born, Ashʿarism was still relatively new, being less than three generations old. It remained questionable for many within the wider community of the ʿulamāʾ. A particular strand of traditionalism within the Sunnī community viewed the Ashʿarīs with concerted suspicion. To the more scripturally oriented ways of certain *ḥadīth* traditionalists, the Ashʿarīs seemed far removed and even elitist. The kalām of Ashʿarism looked too much like the kalām of Muʿtazilism and the Muʿtazilīs had a difficult enough time themselves in being accepted as part of the ahl al-sunna (if they even desired such).[15]

Opposition to Ashʿarī thought led to a significant politico-religious crisis in Nishapur during Qushayrī's lifetime, coming to a head in 445/1054, when Sultan Ṭughril Beg ordered the Shīʿa and al-Ashʿarī to be cursed from the mosques of all Khurasan.[16]

> [T]he public cursing of [Ashʿarī], when it transpired in the middle of the 5th/11th century, can be understood as the culmination [of] this persis-

> tent suspicion. The attack was not just a political maneuver to marginalize a particular faction within the city of Nishapur, but also signified, macrocosmically, an attempt to sever the Ashʿarīs from the Sunnī tradition completely.[17]

Qushayrī's role in this controversy was not minor. In his work *Shikāyat ahl al-sunna*, Qushayrī was the first to call the crisis a *miḥna*, thus using a history-laden term for the persecution of certain Muslims by a Muslim ruler because of specified theological beliefs. "Qushayrī soon achieved preeminence among the Shāfiʿī-Ashʿarī faction in town, and . . . was one of the top four Ashʿarī scholars who were persecuted by the Saljūq political authorities between 445/1053 and 456/1064."[18]

This anti-Ashʿarī episode in Qushayrī's life highlights the role of "public intellectual" that he played—at least to some extent—in his own society. In comparison to Gerson, Qushayrī was less oriented toward the general public and more oriented toward his scholarly work in the field of Sufism. This *miḥna*, however, was a politicization of theological debate that brought out Qushayrī's community-oriented role as a patrician of Nishapur. Most of Qushayrī's life work seems to have been focused not in this public sphere but rather in the religious and pedagogic realm encompassing students of Sufism, including his fellow Sufi masters, other Islamic scholars, and neophytes in the field. While Gerson spent a great deal of his life work as an educator of the public and as a "public intellectual," bringing university knowledge and theological teaching to the laity and speaking to issues of the day, Qushayrī was thus generally more focused on specifically Sufi concerns.

Given the religious and theological developments that were taking place, one of the main concerns that gripped Sufi scholars in Qushayrī's era was the project of legitimating their mystical knowledge using the discursive resources of theological and legal schools. Indeed, this was a time of mutual exchange and integration between *taṣawwuf* and more well-accepted and established Islamic sciences, such as *kalām*, *fiqh*, and study of hadith. "In time, the bridge thus built between Sufis and scholars came to be crossed in both directions by an increasing number of Sufi-scholars and scholar-Sufis, leading to a cross-fertilisation that ushered a new phase in Islamic cultural history."[19] Qushayrī's contribution to this cross-fertilization was extremely important, as were the contributions of Kalābādhī, Hujwīrī, and Abū Ṭālib al-Makkī. Despite al-Ghazālī's greater fame in this and other scholarly realms, Qushayrī deserves credit as one of "the principal architects" of a form of Sufism that could be adopted more widely within mainstream Sunni Islam. What he accomplished was the aspiration of his generation of Sufi scholars, namely,

> [to] process Sufi thought with the new tools of kalām and fiqh in order to develop a theologically and legally savvy form of Sufism. . . . A generation after Sulamī, two Sufi authors, Qushayrī and Hujwīrī, rose to this challenge with such skill that the surveys [of Sufism] that they produced partly eclipsed all earlier attempts and came to assume almost canonical status for most later Sufis and observers of Sufism alike.[20]

While the Sufi masters just before Qushayrī "did not shirk away from using legal and theological yardsticks in parsing Sufism for their readers," it was our author who excelled in using more well-established Islamic disciplines such as *kalām* to make the case for Sufism as an authentic and legitimate Islamic science with roots going back to the Prophet himself.[21]

By integrating Sufism or *taṣawwuf* more firmly within the fold of the Islamic sciences and justifying its existence using the tools of *kalām* and *fiqh*, Qushayrī forged a kind of Sufism that was no longer so marginalized by the dominant powers of Islamic civilization.

> Just as the Ashʿarī and Māturīdī approaches in kalām that developed as compromises between the anti-rationalist traditionalists and the rationalist Muʿtazila came to occupy the centre in all subsequent Islamic history, the "accredited" or "well-tempered" Sufism that was forged [by Qushayrī and Hujwīrī] in Khurāsān and Transoxiana in the fifth/eleventh century as a compromise between inward-looking—at times anti-social—traditionalist trends on the one hand and antinomian and libertinist tendencies on the other hand gradually but surely assumed authoritative status throughout Islamdom.[22]

Qushayrī's achievement as a principal architect of a Sufi framework firmly planted on a solid foundation in other Islamic sciences was possible because of his polymath erudition and because of the historical currents in which he found himself. One of the principal fruits of this confluence, which to a great degree established his significance in the Islamic tradition, was his *Risāla* or treatise on Sufism.[23] This work has been used in Islamic education for centuries as an introduction to *taṣawwuf* for newcomers to the field. Its reception history saw Qushayrī's significance solidified as a mediator between Sufism and mainstream Islamic scholars of the classical age.

Qushayrī's Treatise on Sufism

Calling the text a "*risāla*" places it within the tradition of a genre with a long history of development and change in Arabic literature.[24] From its pre-Islamic meaning of "the oral transmission of a message" to a denotation beginning in Ummayyad times of written correspondence or epistle, the *risāla* genre came in Abbasid and later times to comprise not only official and personal letters but also a genre of creative and sometimes very personal intellectual exploration, akin to the essay in European literature. Thus the *risāla* of this type was a monograph or treatise that, because of its literary heritage, retained some echo of both oral delivery and epistolary form. Various works in different disciplines of the religious sciences were named "*risāla*" from quite early on in the Islamic tradition, such as those of al-Shāfiʿī and Ibn Abī Zayd (d. 386/996). What is especially interesting for our consideration of Qushayrī's *Risāla* is the phenomenon of literary culture whereby innovative texts whose literary form did not fit into other genres were called a "*risāla*."[25]

Qushayrī's *Risāla* fits well into the tradition of this genre in that it is a hybrid construction of other genres put together for the purpose of presenting *taṣawwuf* as one topic. His *Risāla* combines a hagiographic *ṭabaqāt* work, covering the generations of Sufi masters, with a pedagogic textbook or manual, which, like a dictionary, focuses on explaining terms. This literary form is perfectly suited to our author's rhetorical purpose of giving *taṣawwuf* firm standing as an authentic and original Islamic discipline of religious knowledge. Applying hadith terminology to the rhetorical structure of the *Risāla*, we can say that the text begins with the *ṭabaqāt* section serving as an *isnād*, or chain of transmission, for the *matn*, or religious content, that is contained in the handbook section that follows.[26] This claim about the structure of Qushayrī's *Risāla* warrants exploration to further our understanding of how Qushayrī used genre in creative ways for specific theological and rhetorical purposes.

To bolster this claim, we need not go into any detailed consideration here of the handbook portion of the *Risāla*. Several translations are available for the *Risāla*, and many only cover the handbook section.[27] Suffice it to say here that this handbook portion of Qushayrī's *Risāla* is designed pedagogically and organized around key technical terms of Sufi thought. For these reasons the literary form can be related to the dictionary and *mukhtaṣar* genres. The latter of these was a kind of abridgment or short textbook.[28] For its content, Qushayrī drew on both his own erudition and the earlier model of the Sufi handbook *Kitāb al-Luma*ʿ, by Abū Naṣr ʿAbd Allāh ibn ʿAlī Sarrāj (d. 988).[29] Matching Qushayrī's rhetorical purpose, as we have been emphasizing here, "the hallmark" of the *Risāla* is its "happy marriage between Sufism and legal-theological scholarship."[30] Throughout the present and following chapters, we, like many other students of Sufism over the centuries, will have recourse to the content of the *Risāla* at numerous points to explicate Sufi concepts and terms.

The overall literary form and hybrid genre of Qushayrī's *Risāla* mirrors the literary form of a hadith. To convey the significance of this claim, we will need to situate the *ṭabaqāt* genre within hadith studies and then consider Qushayrī's work in relation to other Sufi *ṭabaqāt* works.

Meaning "generations," "*ṭabaqāt*" describes hagiographic collections of biographies organized chronologically. The genre is by no means unique to Sufi literature, but rather extends to include many kinds of important figures in the Islamic tradition. In fact, the field of hadith studies shows perhaps the greatest concern for and focus on religious genealogy. Many Muslims in various cultural and historical contexts have accorded near-scriptural status and authority—second only to the Qur'an—to hadith, which are sayings of or about the Prophet and his companions.

Based on theological beliefs that valorize the Prophet Muhammad's way of life in general and particularly his way of exemplifying *islām* in its Qur'anic sense of submission to God, the collection and study of hadith serve to organize knowledge about the Prophet's customs or *sunna*. The tens of thousands of hadith that were passed down from generation to generation were evaluated for their authenticity by hadith scholars. The *isnād* of a hadith, or its chain of transmission across time, is to a large extent the basis of this evaluation. Hadith transmitters were evaluated according to their reliability, and the actual transmissions of particular hadith from one transmitter to another are evaluated according to historical possibility and likelihood, as evident from temporal and geographic coincidence of the transmitters' life paths. Based on these evaluations, the authenticity of hadith is then rated and grouped into canonical, spurious, and other levels of authenticity, by which the authority of a particular hadith is gauged.

In the introduction to the *ṭabaqāt* section of his *Risāla*, Qushayrī—who was himself accomplished in the study of hadith—presents the generations of Sufis whom he describes in the pages that follow as spiritually linked to the Prophet and his companions. He thus creates a robust and reliable *isnād* for Sufi knowledge going back to the Prophet Muhammad himself. This rhetorical move fits in with a central theological purpose of the *ṭabaqāt* genre in general—namely, to establish the legitimacy of a hagiographic genealogy stretching from the Prophet to the Muslim notables whose biographies are therein presented. Qushayrī thus starts his Sufi genealogy with the Prophet Muhammad, the Prophet's companions (*ṣaḥāba*), their followers (*tābiʿūn*), and then the followers of the companions' followers (*atbāʿ al-tābiʿīn*). To these three generations after the Prophet, Qushayrī connects the elites of those concerned with religion called the ascetics (*zuhhād*) and pietists (*ʿubbād*). From there, Qushayrī makes mention of controversy among the pietistic movements and competition for the mantle of legitimacy:

> Then innovations emerged and challenges were made between the groups, each of them claiming that the *zuhhād* were amongst their number. The elite of the traditionalists (*khawāṣṣ ahl al-sunna*), who maintained their souls with God and safeguarded their hearts from the paths of heedlessness, alone possessed the name *taṣawwuf* (Sufism). This name became well-known for these great individuals by 200 A.H.[31]

Qushayrī's narrative of religious history thus claims this legitimacy for the kind of Sufis that he will go on to describe in the *Risāla*.

The first Sufi *ṭabaqāt* work comes just a generation before Qushayrī. It is that of his second Sufi master, Abū ʿAbd al-Raḥmān Muḥammad b. al-Ḥusayn al-Sulamī (d. 412/1021). Qushayrī draws heavily on al-Sulamī's *Ṭabaqāt al-Ṣūfiyya* for the *ṭabaqāt* section of the *Risāla*, as he does on Sarrāj's *Kitāb al-Lumaʿ* for the manual section. In fact, al-Sulamī's book is well known mostly as a source for Qushayrī's.[32] Despite the heavy debt owed to al-Sulamī, Qushayrī had a significantly different objective for his own *ṭabaqāt* work. Rather than aiming to legitimize Sufism within the Sunni tradition, al-Sulamī's *Ṭabaqāt al-Ṣūfiyya* is organized by generations or *ṭabaqāt* to reflect "an overall chronological progression in a continuous pattern."[33]

Qushayrī's definition and characterization of Sufis also coincide with his rhetorical purpose of legitimizing *taṣawwuf*. He systematically downplays potentially scandalous features of Sufis' lives, such as their provocative ecstatic utterances (*shaṭḥiyyāt*), and instead highlights their piety, humility, and discipline, all noncontroversial religious virtues.[34] The conclusion of the *ṭabaqāt* section of Qushayrī's *Risāla* illustrates this technique:

> The purpose of mentioning them in this place is to indicate that they are unanimous about the veneration of the shariah (*taʿẓīm al-sharīʿa*), [that they] are characterised by travelling the paths of religious discipline (*ṭuruq al-riyāḍa*), and persist in following the *sunna* without abandoning any religious customs (*ādāb al-diyāna*); [that they] agree that whoever abandons pious deeds and striving and does not build his affair on the foundation of piety (*waraʿ*) and righteousness (*taqwā*) is being insincere to God about what he is claiming.[35]

As Qushayrī endeavors to achieve religious legitimacy for *taṣawwuf* as a whole, so does he legitimize the handbook section of the *Risāla* that follows by linking it to this genealogy of pious forebears.

Sufi *Tafsīr*—Qushayrī's Mystical Scriptural Exegesis

Besides the genres of *risāla*, pedagogic handbook, and *ṭabaqāt*, the genre of Sufi *tafsīr* or scriptural exegesis was another major literary form in which Qushayrī made a significant and well-known contribution.[36] Within Qur'anic exegesis generally, Sufi *tafsīr* in particular can be considered an important genre with its own characteristics and tradition.

Gerhard Böwering, a Jesuit scholar at Yale University, has studied Sufi *tafsīr* extensively, particularly *Tafsīr al-Qur'ān* of Sahl b. ʿAbdallāh al-Tustarī (d. 896). While Sufi exegetical methodology varies, Böwering describes that Sufi's method of Qur'an interpretation as one of fluid association between Sufi concepts and Qur'anic "keynotes."[37] These keynotes can be anything from "historical references, points of religious law, eschatological events, theological terms" to "philological puzzles, foreign or rare words, legendary figures, and obscure points." One Sufi way of generating *tafsīr* is thus to fix onto some particularity of the Qur'anic text and then to bound from that point into the world of Sufi concepts and themes. This exegetical method starts with what Böwering calls "an encounter event": "The encounter between the Qur'ānic keynotes and the mystical matrix of al-Tustarī's world of ideas leads to the event of association which finds its verbal expression and written recording in the commentary."[38]

Another point of reference in the Sufi tradition of *tafsīr* is the work of al-Sulamī, whom we noted previously as vital to the development of the Sufi *ṭabaqāt* genre. In al-Sulamī's voluminous *Ḥaqā'iq al-tafsīr* (*Truths of "Tafsīr"*), he assembled around 12,000 items of Sufi *tafsīr* and ordered them according to pertinent Qur'anic passages. This work

> holds a unique place in the history of Ṣūfī commentary on the Qur'ān and fulfils the same function with regard to classical Ṣūfī *Tafsīr* as Ṭabarī's famous *Ǧāmiʿ al-bayān* [does] with regard to the early traditional exegesis of the Qur'ān. Both works are extensive and authoritative collections of items of Qur'ānic commentary within their own school of thought and embody the development of preceding centuries of Qur'ānic interpretation.[39]

Al-Sulamī's *Ḥaqāʾiq al-tafsīr* provides an authoritative model for Sufi *tafsīr* that was highly influential on the generations of Sufi exegetes after him.[40] Böwering describes al-Sulamī's methodology as "rigorous":

> First, he excluded all edifying subject matter from his work, anecdotes and hagiography alike. Second, he explicitly refrained from including themes belonging to the traditional or legal kind of Koranic exegesis, as well as philological or technical points, that is all matters pertaining to the "exoteric sciences" (*al-ʿulūm al-ẓāhira*). Third, throughout his work, he assembled only those items of interpretation, which he regarded as genuine mystic ways of reading the Koran (*ḥurūf*) in accordance with "the understanding of the divine Discourse on the basis of the language of the People of Reality" (*fahm kitābihi ʿalā lisān ahl al-ḥaqīqa*).[41]

Al-Sulamī was a trailblazer who consolidated the Sufi *tafsīr* tradition.

In contrast, Qushayrī constructed his own *tafsīr*, *Laṭāʾif al-ishārāt*, in such a way as to legitimate that tradition within the wider context of the Sunni Islamic religious sciences.[42] Unlike al-Sulamī, who kept out of his *tafsīr* any traditional philological, technical, or legal material, Qushayrī includes both these sorts of non-Sufi exegetical material and the exclusively Sufi interpretations of the inner meaning of the Qur'an.[43] Qushayrī's exegetical method follows a progressive path from the exoteric revelation of *sharīʿa*, which literally means "the way," toward the esoteric truth called "*ḥaqīqa*," or "ultimate reality." On a given verse Qushayrī begins with the most widely held traditional comments, follows that with less well-attested readings, and then adds—in some, but not all cases—distinctively Sufi interpretations.[44]

What is more, Qushayrī in his *Laṭāʾif al-ishārāt* hardly ever cites a source, Sufi or otherwise, for the exegetical material that he passes on, whereas al-Sulamī cites a specific Sufi authority for about two-thirds of the 12,000 glosses in his *Ḥaqāʾiq al-tafsīr*.[45] Ngyuen interprets this omission as partial evidence that Qushayrī wrote *Laṭāʾif al-ishārāt* for a readership of Sufis: "As such, its emphasis is on communicating the substance of exegesis rather than to reproduce the formalities demanded by scholastic strictures."[46] In light of Qushayrī's project of legitimating *taṣawwuf* alongside the more well-established Islamic sciences, we can recognize that his omission of references to sources has the rhetorical effect of presenting Sufi insights as just as valid as those coming from other Islamic disciplines. Not naming the specific person who passed down an exegetical comment, Qushayrī represents the exegetical material as of indistinguishably valid provenance.

Through a kind of rhetorical signposting Qushayrī does, however, make explicit the distinction that some of these exegetical points pertain to the outer meaning of the Qur'an while others to its inner meaning. Qushayrī "usually makes a clear distinction between the exoteric and esoteric exegetical approaches, referring to the former with expressions such as 'in the language of [conventional] exegesis' (*bi-lisān al-tafsīr*), and to the latter as 'the allusion in it [is]' (*wal-ishāra fihī*)."[47] We will see similar rhetorical signals to distinguish between exoteric and esoteric meanings in *The Grammar of Hearts.*

Dhikr—Calling out the Names of God

From the major genres of *risāla*, manual, *ṭabaqāt*, and *tafsīr*, we now turn to Qushayrī's thought on the practice of "*dhikr*" as developed in two less prominent genres of Sufi literature in order to expand our Jaussian account of the ecosystem of genres in which Qushayrī worked. At the same time Qushayrī's writings on the theme of *dhikr* bring together a number of his spiritual and linguistic concerns that are relevant to spiritual grammar.

Dhikr is the ritual invocation of the names of God. Sufis have seen the scriptural basis for their practice of *dhikr* in the divine imperative "Remember!" of Q 28:24 and Q 33:41 (*udhkur/udhkurū*). Carrying out this divine command to remember, to do *dhikr*, developed among the Sufis into a "tireless repetition of an ejaculatory litany," in which they cry out in various ways, soft and loud, alone and in group, the most beautiful names of God.[48] This kind of physical, vocalized meditation on these single words that name the Divine is a complementary counterpart to discursive reflection, which in Arabic can be called "*fikr*."

Qushayrī's own overview of *dhikr* for students of *taṣawwuf*, which he provides in his *Risāla*, emphasizes its necessity for attaining divine intimacy:[49] "The master said: '*Dhikr* is a sturdy prop on the path [*ṭarīq*] of the True One, the Most High, may he be praised. It is even the basic support on this path [*ṭarīq*]. No one reaches God except through persisting in *dhikr*.' "[50] In categorizing kinds of *dhikr*, Qushayrī focuses on two categories:

> There are two kinds of *dhikr: dhikr* of the tongue and *dhikr* of the heart. By means of *dhikr* of the tongue, the servant arrives at perseverance in *dhikr* of the heart. The [real] effect belongs to *dhikr* of the heart. For if the servant is doing *dhikr* with his tongue and his heart, then he is complete in his attainment [*waṣfihī*] [and] in the spiritual state [*ḥāl*] of his wayfaring [*sulūkihī*].[51]

This twofold progression from tongue to heart is a model Qushayrī further explores in *The Grammar of Hearts*. Both in the *Risāla* and in *Naḥw al-qulūb*, the most important kind of spiritual speech happens with and in the heart.

In the *dhikr* chapter of the *Risāla*, Qushayrī's characteristic sources and spiritual role models appear: al-Daqqāq, al-Sulamī, Abū Bakr Dulaf b. Jaḥdar al-Shiblī (d. 945), Dhū al-Nūn al-Miṣrī (d. 861), al-Ḥasan al-Baṣrī (d. 728). As is also typical for Qushayrī, he brings into the discussion a Prophetic tradition (hadith) relevant to the theme:

> According to a well-known tradition from the Messenger of God—may God bless and greet him—he said: "When you pass by the gardens of Paradise, alight and graze there!" [His followers] asked him: "What are the gardens of Paradise?" He answered: "The gatherings at which God is remembered [*ḥilaq al-dhikr*]."[52]

This image of *dhikr* gatherings as the gardens of Paradise serves to connect the prayer practice to the concepts both of a delightful dwelling-place and of the afterlife for the righteous.

The names of God that Sufis invoke in *dhikr* have their roots in Qur'anic language used to refer to God by describing various divine characteristics.[53] The names are traditionally ninety-nine in number, as in a famous hadith traced by Sunnis to Abū Hurayra and by the Shiʿa to ʿAlī ibn Abī Ṭalib himself. In some versions of this hadith, the names are listed. Reflecting on the traditional list (of which there are four versions),[54] Islamic scholars have grouped and categorized the names in multiple fashions. "Allāh" is often but not always listed as the first of the names.

One group of names from the traditional list of ninety-nine come from Q 59:22–24: the Merciful (*al-Raḥmān*), the Compassionate (*al-Raḥīm*), the

King (*al-Malik*), the Most Holy (*al-Quddūs*), Peace (*al-Salām*), the Believer (*al-Mu'min*), the Vigilant (*al-Muhaymin*), the Precious (*al-ʿAzīz*), the Omnipotent (*al-Jabbār*), the Majestic (*al-Mutakabbir*), the Creator (*al-Khāliq*), the Producer (*al-Bāri'*), the Fashioner (*al-Muṣawwir*).

Some names are negative when applied to human beings and positive when applied to God. In the human sphere, *al-jabbār*, for example, can mean "the oppressor" or "the tyrant," and *al-mutakabbir* can mean "the haughty" or "the arrogant."[55] In discourse discussing the positive and negative aspects of these divine names and their relationship to human beings, the term "*tashbīh*" means "applying human attributes to God," while "*tanzīh*" refers to keeping God free of all human qualifications.

Another categorization lists the names of majestic power (*asmā' al-jalāl*) and the names of beauty (*asmā' al-jamāl*).[56] Many of the names are in an emphatic form, such as *al-Ṣabūr*, the most patient. Others are in a simple present participle (*al-fāʿil*) form. God is *al-Wājid*, the Present or Existing, and *al-Hādī*, the One who Guides.

Many of the names come in pairs, some of which are synonymous, such as the most famous *al-Raḥmān al-Raḥīm* (the Compassionate the Merciful), others of which are antonymous, such as *al-Qābiḍ al-Bāsiṭ* (the Seizing, the Outstretching).

They are also categorized as *ṣifāt al-fiʿl* and *ṣifāt al-dhāt*. The *ṣifāt al-dhāt* are attributes of God's very self, such as *al-wājid* or *al-raḥīm*. The attributes of God's action (*ṣifāt al-fiʿl*) relate to God's way of acting in creation. For example, God is *al-Wahhāb* and *al-Razzāq*, both of which are emphatic forms relating to God's nature as one who gives and grants to creation. The first gives more a sense of gift-giving while the second emphasizes that God gives us what we need to live. He is the Most Beneficent Donor and the Provider.

The Sufi master or shaykh played an important role in imparting *dhikr* to his students and guiding them in its practice, especially from around the year 400 A.H./1000 C.E. on.[57] Before that time, in the so-called classical age of Sufism, the shaykh was more often playing the role of a professor, which Ibn ʿAbbād al-Rundī (d. 792/1390) called a "master of instruction" (*shaykh taʿlīm*). As the student-teacher relationship developed, the master became something more of a spiritual director, for which al-Rundī uses the term "master of training" (*shaykh tarbiya*). In the earlier of these two kinds of *ṣuḥba* or attachment, the student or "*ṣāḥib*" learns from the teacher or "*maṣḥūb*" "about the self-training one had to undertake, and the deeper meaning of sacred traditions and technical terms."[58] This relationship with a "*shaykh taʿlīm*" is not exclusive, and students often seek such a relationship with many masters. In the historical development of the kinds of relationship between the shaykh and the seeker, it becomes such that the master has much more power over the student, who "undergoes with him a course of treatment so to speak, subordinates himself to his supervision and submits to his drill." This tighter relationship with a "*shaykh tarbiya*" is exclusive. In this kind of relationship, once a student chooses a master as his *maṣḥūb*, he is not supposed to leave without the master's order. Moreover, the master of training or *shaykh tarbiya* "becomes a master of spiritual exercises and also has the power to apply punishment."[59]

Pointing to Qushayrī's "last will and testament to his novices" (*bāb al-waṣiyya lil-murīdīn*) that is the appendix of the *Risāla*,[60] Fritz Meier places Qushayrī in the age of the *shaykh tarbiya:*

> [Qushayrī] mentions a trial period which the candidate must go through before the shaykh can accept him, emphasizes that the candidate must bear willingly the measures of atonement which the shaykh imposes on him for certain offenses, mentions a particular attitude which he is obliged to adopt before the shaykh, speaks about the formula for [invoking] God (*dhikr*) which the shaykh "implants" (*talqīn*) in him, about withdrawal in seclusion (*khalwa*) which he orders him to undertake, about the necessity of obeying the shaykh unreservedly and not concealing from him the least thoughts and impulses within the soul, and forbids him to leave the locality of his novitiate of his own accord or to undertake journeys prematurely.[61]

All of these features of the *shaykh tarbiya* type of relationship with the *murīd* indicate clearly to Meier how Qushayrī fits cleanly into this later historical phase in the development of the spiritual master-student relationship. Moreover, Qushayrī is "one of our first crown witnesses" of how the master supervises "the least detail of [the *murīd*'s] inner development."[62] In fact, according to Meier, "A striking feature of the new era is likewise the endeavor to transfer the occult phenomena associated with the spiritual training which the novice or mystic undergoes, to the realm of discussion and description." In a great deal of his writings, Qushayrī does just that, describing poetically and with great insight the inner movements of spiritual seekers. His book *Tartīb al-sulūk* specifically "describes the psychic effects of one of the most important means a mystic possesses for approaching what he calls God and for eliminating his I-decisions—the effects of the [invocation] of God (*dhikr*)."[63]

Fī Ṭarīq Allāh—Sufi Spiritual Direction "on the Path to God"

Tartīb al-sulūk fī ṭarīq Allāh or *Gradation in Traveling on the Path to God* covers a number of the same topics as the appendix of the *Risāla*. In both texts,

> Qushayrī passes on directly from acceptance of the novice by the shaykh to reception of the [invocation] of God, and from the novice, *mutatis mutandis*, demands the same preparations and the same commitments: knowledge and observance of the religious prescriptions, permanent ritual purity, a preference for poverty over wealth, shame over honor, God over everything else, and continuous and exclusive [invocation] of God. In both books he [also] warns against extra devotional practices and against preoccupation with the secondary mystical phenomena of the [invocation] of God.[64]

In his advice to spiritual novices or aspirants near the end of the *Risāla*, Qushayrī goes into some depth on all these topics, while only giving slight mention to the effects of *dhikr*. On the other hand, in his *Tartīb* the emphasis is the reverse. There the main concern is *dhikr*, its stages and consequences, while the general rules mentioned in the previous quotation are mentioned only as prefatory remarks on the way to his major topic.

The opening section of *Tartīb al-sulūk* begins abruptly, omitting the standard form of introduction. There Qushayrī explains how a spiritual aspirant should choose a noble shaykh so that he be like "the foal of a noble stallion" rather than of an inferior one.[65] This shaykh tells the *murīd* to say, "Allāh Allāh Allāh," and "directs him to persevere continually in reciting this [invocation] [*dhikr*] of God, not to see anything else, and not to think about anything but this."[66] This imparting of the practice of *dhikr* by the shaykh provides then the thematic focus for the rest of the text.

The following passage reveals a number of further elements that will illuminate for us important aspects of Qushayrī's intellectual and religious concerns:

> If the person [invoking] God [*al-dhākir*] [invokes] God correctly [*taḥaqqaqa*] with the tongue [*dhikr al-lisān*], his [invocation] with the tongue reverts back to being [invocation] with the heart [*dhikr al-qalb*]. Once his heart [invokes] God, during the [invocation] of God states [*aḥwāl*] come over him in which he perceives his soul or rather hears from

his heart names and designations [*asmāʾ wa-adhkār*] of God which he had never heard before nor read in any book, in various modes of expression and different languages such as no angel and no human being has ever heard.[67]

Qushayrī relates here a progression from *dhikr* of the tongue to *dhikr* of the heart. If in his linguistic invocation of God, the *murīd* is able to "*taḥaqqaqa*," then he moves on to invocation of God with his heart. This verb *taḥaqqaqa* is worth dwelling on because of its multiple connections to Sufi parlance, including the name of God, *al-Ḥaqq*, the word for ultimate reality or absolute truth, *al-ḥaqīqa*, and, in its verbal forms, the realization or grasping of something of God's Truth. Meier's translation for this verb as doing *dhikr* "correctly" anticipates the discussion of spiritual etiquette that is the theme of most of this section. Notions of the achievement and realization and coming into effect of a divine truth can fill out the understanding of what this verb denotes.

The effect, then, of a certain achievement in invocation with the tongue is invocation with the heart, whose performance entails spiritual states [*aḥwāl*] coming over the person. Description of these various states constitutes a large part of Qushayrī's famous *Treatise* or *Risāla*. A remarkable feature of these spiritual states is that the seeker "hears from his heart" (*yasmaʿu min qalbihī*) names for God and ways of calling and invoking Him (*asmāʾ wa-adhkār*). These divine designations that the spiritual seeker's heart utters to him are utterly special. They are unheard of, unwritten, and unread. No angel or human being has ever encountered their expression or even the languages in which these divine appellations are spoken by the seeker's heart. We can call these invocations (*adhkār:* plural of *dhikr*) of God mystic speech.

Most of *Tartīb al-sulūk* treats a number of other very particular and, in some cases, peculiar aspects of the "steps" or "gradations" that the Sufi aspirant takes along the course of his or her *dhikr*. Qushayrī describes how, as the servant continues his *dhikr*, different states come upon him including feelings of growth ("he imagines he is growing and becoming larger until it is as if he is bigger than everything else") and fear that "casts him down utterly," and then a vacillation between this spiritual consolation and desolation, with each height rising ever higher.[68] The spiritual states have a physical dimension and manifestation as well. At times, "the person no longer perceives anything but himself," and at times "he hears the heart's [invocation] of God so clearly in his heart that he wishes he were in a desert because it seems to him that people can hear with their ears his [invocation] of God which is in his heart."[69] The *dhikr* overtakes his bodily limbs as well, as if the servant's entire being, body and spirit, reverberate with the resonant invocation of God. Continuing the description of these bodily and sensual stages, Qushayrī also describes how the servant feels "a sweetness in his mouth and in his throat." This sweetness feels as if from the roots of the teeth and brings the servant to the verge of death, and a joy that is like pain, and a dissolution of the self that is like annihilation. This annihilation and joy are sometimes accompanied by "words which are in themselves both speech as well as reply and with which the person has nothing to do." Such words of God's that the effaced Sufi observes are known from the ecstatic utterances of such figures as al-Ḥallāj, who said, "I am God" ["*anā al-ḥaqq*"] and Abū Yazīd, who said, "Praise be to me! [*subḥānī subḥānī mā aʿẓama shānī*]."[70] All of these various steps and stages that Qushayrī describes are part of the Sufi's journey with and toward God. The *Tartīb al-sulūk fī ṭarīq Allāh* is a text that attempts to account for these graded steps that all make part of the wayfaring along the Sufi path. The word *tartīb* encompasses denotations of orderly arrangement, sequenced array, and the organized layout of a structure. Qushayrī provides a "*tartīb*" of Sufi wayfaring in all of these senses.

Two formal elements of *Tartīb al-sulūk* will allow us to deepen our understanding of Qushayrī from both a literary and religious perspective: namely, the text's oral style and pastiche structure. The appearance of a Persian word in the following passage relates to both its orality and pastiche nature. The passage centers on *dhikr* using the Persian word *khudhāy*, meaning "Lord" or "God":

> And he also said: When [invocation] of God in the heart affected me ever more strongly, Abū'l-Ḥasan said to me: "Come out into the countryside with me!" Then he took me with him on the road [*fī ṭarīq*, literally "on a road"], sat me down on a rock and ordered: "Press your lips together and say *khudhāy* (God)!" I obeyed him and while doing this endeavored not to open my mouth. My mouth became full and the [invocation] of God moved into the "secret" [*al-sirr*]. Since that time I perceive that in my "secret" I say *khudhāy*. But after the [invocation] of God passed beyond the *kh* without being able to pass beyond it, it became a "protracted [invocation] of God" [*dhikr^{an} mumtadd^{an}*]. I was immediately taken away from myself and became extinguished [*fanītu*].[71]

Qushayrī portrays himself as describing how in this episode he uttered his *dhikr* internally by speaking the word "*khudhāy*" with his lips pressed together. He seems to have swallowed his *dhikr*. It fills his mouth and moves from his heart into his "secret" (*sirr*), the inmost part of the self. The narrator in the story cannot pass beyond the *kh* sound, so he just keeps incessantly making that sole sound and then loses consciousness and becomes "extinguished," undergoing *fanāʾ*. Using the Persian "*khudhāy*" imparts a liveliness to the narration by evoking the original orality of the narrator's *dhikr*.

Not long after Meier's first publication and translation of this text of Qushrayrī, he learned by correspondence that the passages in *Tartīb al-sulūk* where Persian occurs (sections 1, 5, 8, and 9 of his 1963 edition) match passages in the hagiographic work of Farīd al-Dīn ʿAṭṭār (d. 1230) called *Tadhkirat al-awliyāʾ*.[72] In Aṭṭār's work, these passages are attributed to Abū ʿUthmān al-Maghribī (d. 983) rather than to Qushayrī. Qushayrī, presumably like his original audience for *Tartīb al-sulūk*, was a native Persian speaker, so either he or his secretary could have plausibly used Persian words in an oral performance or its transcription. However, given Meier's discovery, we recognize the Persian that occurs in the passage just quoted and elsewhere in *Tartīb al-sulūk* as indicating that this work is something of a pastiche, rather than a transcription of conversations that Qushayrī had with his disciples.

From this, we see once again Qushayrī's way of relating spiritual anecdotes and Sufi lore to his readers. Some of these traditions are hadith of Prophetic *sunna*, as in the case of Muhammad's mention of "gatherings at which God is remembered"[73] (*ḥilaq al-dhikr*), while others are personal experiences of Sufi masters, including the previously cited narration about swallowing *dhikr* at the behest of Abū l-Ḥasan. Most often, these traditions and stories appear to have been not from Qushayrī's own personal experiences, but rather passed down from other authorities.

Like the *tabaqāt*-handbook structure of Qushayrī's *Risāla*, the pastiche structure of his *Tartīb* reveals a certain affinity to the Islamic discipline of hadith study. Building on our previous discussion of the methods of studying the authenticity of hadith through attention to the *isnād* of their transmission, we can now see another way that Qushayrī followed the model of hadith studies in an effort to legitimize *taṣawwuf*.

Qushayrī treats Sufi lore like *sunna*, the holy traditions of the Prophet and his companions. While in the *Risāla* Qushayrī's placement of a *tabaqāt* work at the beginning of the work resembles the "chain of transmission" or "*isnād*" of hadith, the pastiche composition of the *Tartīb* resembles the "*matn*" or "content" of hadith. In hadith, reports of Prophetic custom (*sunna*) illuminate the way of living that embodies the revelation of the Qur'an—that is, the Prophet's example. Muslims endeavor to imitate the Prophet. They therefore transmitted, recorded, and collected their cherished communal memories of how he lived because of the devotional and spiritual value of those memories. Similarly, Sufis who journeyed far in the path toward God or *ṭarīq Allāh* can be examples to others who strive to advance in their own spiritual path toward ultimate reality. Consequently, those who witnessed firsthand the sayings and doings of these great Sufis related them in the form of reports. Generations later, Qushayrī and other scholars who cherished and preserved these communal memories interwove them into other texts to instruct the faithful. Qushayrī and other scholars thus also portray the great Sufi masters of old as a special group of followers or disciples of Muhammad. Like the *ṣaḥāba* or Companions who actually lived at the time of the Prophet and saw and knew him, those great Sufi masters have their own *faḍāʾil* or virtues, such as devoted piety, firm faith, and spiritual detachment.[74]

In weaving these stories from Sufi lore into his text, Qushayrī shows profound comprehension of the nuances of what his predecessors recounted about their journeys with and to God. As editor, Qushayrī selected and arranged the accounts to create a coherent whole, whose sequence of elements elicits in his readers an understanding of the spiritual realities to which the stories allude. As commentator, Qushayrī sometimes elaborates on the subtleties and insights conveyed by these traditions from Sufi lore by highlighting particular nuances and details of the sayings and episodes. Thus, Qushayrī's craft as a writer here is very much like that of a redactor or editor. Through his compositional choices of how to put these disparate parts together, Qushayrī writes at times like an artist composing a mosaic. Each episode or tradition brings to his composition something distinct, whether the sparkle of a gem, a hue necessary to bring out a certain nuance, or a texture that adds new dimensions.

Tartīb al-sulūk also points to the oral culture of Qushayrī's world in several other ways. The *Tartīb* begins with no praise of God and the Prophet, as is standard. There is, rather, only the most brief and formulaic initiatory dedication with a *basmala*, "in the name of God the Compassionate, the Merciful," followed by "the Master Abū Qāsim ʿAbd al-Karīm Hawāzin al-Qushayrī, may God be pleased with him, said. . . ."[75]

In addition to this lack of a proper introduction, from a structural perspective the seventh section indicates the possibility of a less formal representation of oral speech. In that section a question-and-reply format evokes a scene of a student posing a query to his master, as if the professor's lecture had been interrupted by a student's raised hand:[76]

> Then he (=Qushayrī) was politely asked: Sometimes a person is in a high inner state [*ḥāla sharīfa*] but Satan wishes to return him to a lower one [*ḥāla adnā*] and for this reason causes him to become conscious of this higher state. If the person examines this thought in connection with knowledge and the commands and prohibitions, it appears to be unobjectionable and yet it comes from Satan. How can a person recognize it? Only a few people are capable of doing so.
>
> The reply: A person recognizes that this thought has an unpleasant effect [*yūḥish*] because an unpleasant feeling [*waḥsha*] from it comes over him. When the thought occurs in the heart, it hurts it and causes it to experience unpleasantness like food which has no salt in it. Because of the unpleasantness and ugliness accompanying the thought, he knows that it is not from God but from Satan, even if it is a call to do a pious act such as, for instance, if it commands him to go on the pilgrimage to Mecca or to honor his parents.[77]

Clearly marking a student-like question and a masterly response, this passage evokes medieval scholastic and spiritual relationships and ranks. The devotee or disciple has encountered a question relating to the inner voyages of heart and mind and poses that burning question to a master who is suited to answer the question with wisdom and insight. Accounts of such questions and replies by masters are familiar not only in the medieval Arabic but also in the medieval Latin scholarly tradition. Like the format of such works as Aquinas's *Summa Theologiae*, here the portrayal of a student's question and the master's response does not necessarily mark this part of the text as a transcription of an actual conversation (though it might), but this format at least suggests such oral interchange as a familiar format for interaction between Qushayrī and his disciples. The back-and-forth between novice and master is stylized in a text such as the one at hand.

As a kind of transcription of an oral explanation by Qushayrī, *Tartīb al-sulūk* furthers our understanding of Qushayrī in at least two ways. First, stylistically, the hints at orality in this text reveal the less formal, performative dimension of Qushayrī's professorial instruction to those who studied with him. Second, the *Tartīb* illuminates the personality of Qushayrī as spiritual director. We have already seen, in his account of the steps taken by the spiritual wayfarer who practices *dhikr*, the great care that Qushayrī takes in the vivid description of spiritual realities. In *Tartīb al-sulūk* Qushayrī delves into the details of the spiritual movements of servants who are on *ṭarīq Allāh*, the path of God, as those aspirants gain in spiritual maturity. From my own Christian theological perspective, Qushayrī sounds in this text at times like Teresa of Avila describing the treasures of the "interior castle" or like St. Ignatius of Loyola explaining discernment of spirits and how to identify the voice of the Adversary in his *Spiritual Exercises*.

As Sufi shaykh, Qushayrī spans the two classifications set up in Meier's historical analysis drawn from al-Rundi. "Qushayrī in the 11th century closes the old [*shaykh taʿlīm* period] and opens the new [*shaykh tarbiya*] period."[78] We have seen already from *Tartīb al-sulūk* how Qushayrī was in some sense a professorial *shaykh taʿlīm*, a master of instruction who lectured and responded to students' theoretical queries. In this capacity, he was not unlike Gerson or some other European *magister* teaching in Paris or Bologna or Oxford. The *Risāla* was a kind of textbook that Qushayrī and others would have used in instructing novices in the spiritual path. As we have also seen from *Tartīb al-sulūk*, Qushayrī was also a *shaykh tarbiya*, a master of training who acted very much like a Christian confessor or spiritual director, guiding spiritual aspirants in discerning the movements of God (and Satan).

Qushayrī's writing style and use of literary genre illustrate the extent to which he spanned the *shaykh taʿlīm* and the *shaykh tarbiya* roles. Moreover, whether in the mode of scholarly *magister* or spiritual guide, in his writing Qushayrī often reaches an extraordinary level of poetic expression. Matching the subtlety of spiritual movements with profound nuances in his prose, Qushayrī conveys the sublime, the surprising, the majestic, and the tender—whatever the spiritual wayfarer encounters.

Let us also recall that Qushayrī was a great polymath. In his writings he draws on a wide variety of fields of knowledge in order to accomplish his authorial objectives. Besides the discipline of Sufism, Qushayrī's expertise ranged from language sciences (*ʿilm al-lugha* and *adab*) to Prophetic tradition (hadith) to discursive theology (*kalām*) to Qur'anic exegesis (*tafsīr*). In the service of deepening and expanding readers' appreciation of the matter at hand, Qushayrī often draws on technical terms and concepts from these and other scholarly fields.

Sharḥ Asmāʾ Allāh al-Ḥusnā: Explicating the Names of God

Another text of Qushayrī's focuses on *dhikr* and comes at the topic from an entirely different angle. The book of Qushayrī's is known variously as the *Embellishment on the Science of Reminding* (*Al-Taḥbīr fī ʿilm al-tadhkīr*) and the *Explication of the Beautiful Names of God* (*Sharḥ asmāʾ Allāh al-ḥusnā*).[79] Whereas in *Tartīb al-sulūk*, Qushayrī writes about how the *murīd* or neophyte receives from the shaykh the practice of *dhikr*, in *Sharḥ asmāʾ Allāh al-ḥusnā* Qushayrī focuses on the names of God themselves. After Qushayrī, Ghazālī (d. 1111) wrote a particularly influential book in this genre,[80] *Al-Maqṣid al-Asnā*, as did Fakhr al-Dīn al-Rāzī (d. 1210), *Lawāmiʿ al-bayyināt*. Qushayrī's work in this genre may have been the first Sufi work devoted specifically to the names of God.[81] However, outside of Sufi literature there was already a tradition whereby Islamic scholars reflected on the divine names in discourse encompassing philological and theological dimensions.[82]

Sufi and non-Sufi texts of this genre share some common traits, though the Sufi writings are distinguishable by how much they bridge the devotional and the discursive. Islamic writings on the divine names typically show the clear influence of three more prominent genres—namely, religious manuals, *ṭabaqāt*, and *tafsīr*. Focusing on very specific words and word types that the devotee ritually invokes in *dhikr*, Islamic writings on the divine names are also profoundly linguistic and theological by nature. The discourse of this genre cannot help but be truly "theology," in the etymological sense of discourse (*logos*) about God (*theos*). As we will see, Sufi discourse on God's names provides a privileged entryway into profound reflection on the very nature of God. Qushayrī's *Sharḥ asmāʾ Allāh al-ḥusnā* is thus *fikr* on the theological content of *dhikr*. In other words, it is a discursive and devotional investigation of these special names that in the prayer of remembering and invoking God become the focal points of meditation and the script for liturgical performance.

Beyond that, *Sharḥ asmāʾ Allāh al-ḥusnā* is akin to *The Grammar of Hearts* in important ways. By writing the first Sufi treatment of the names of God, the *Sharḥ* is another example of Qushayrī's innovation with the literary genre of his religious writing, in this case by adapting an existing genre in Islamic literature to fit within *taṣawwuf*. Moreover, like *The Grammar of Hearts*, the *Sharḥ* intertwines scholarly consideration of language with spiritual matters pertaining to religious life, moral advancement,

Sufi practice, Islamic saints (*awliyāʾ*), theological orthodoxy and error, the custom of the Prophet, and the nature of God. Like the grammatical structures in *Naḥw al-qulūb*, the linguistic material of the traditional names of God become a vehicle for Qushayrī to move readers toward a deeper understanding of these important religious and spiritual topics. We also see Qushayrī in *Sharḥ asmāʾ Allāh al-ḥusnā* mobilizing multiple kinds of expertise and bodies of knowledge, as he does in *The Grammar of Hearts*. To give just a few examples, Qushayrī acts in turns as Qur'anic exegete (*mufassir*), Sufi master (shaykh), and systematic theologian (*mutakallim*). His polymathic expertise and wide-ranging religious concerns transgress disciplinary boundaries that might otherwise keep a writer from drawing on whatever fields of knowledge come to bear on a question at hand.

Sharḥ asmāʾ Allāh al-ḥusnā begins, as was customary in classical Islamic literature, with an invocational prayer adapted to the book's content. In this invocation Qushayrī uses a number of the names of God, starting with *al-qadīm*, that which is ancient beyond having any origin: "Praise be to God the Sempiternal [*al-qadīm*] whose being has no beginning."[83] After the invocational prayers, the author describes briefly his purpose in writing the book. Although Qushayrī reports receiving many questions about *ʿilm al-tadhkīr*, the science of performing *dhikr*, he at first refused to have anything to do with answering these questions. However, as he noticed how rare true understanding and how widespread illicit innovation were in this field, he decided it was best to take on writing this book after all.[84] The first nine sections, as demarcated in al-Ḥalawānī's edition, treat Qur'anic references that thematize the names of God. The first of these is "a chapter on the meaning of the utterance of the Most High: 'God has the most beautiful Names. You should address Him in your worship by these Names' " (Q 7:180). Moving into *tafsīr* mode, Qushayrī as scriptural exegete relates the occasion for the revelation (*sabab al-nuzūl*) of this particular verse as follows:

> Know that the occasion of the revelation of this verse was that a man from among the infidels [*mushrikīn*] once heard the Prophet, peace be upon him, and the Muslims calling at one time upon "God Most High [*Allāh taʿālā*]" and at another time invoking "the Merciful, the Compassionate [*al-raḥmān al-raḥīm*]." So he [the *mushrik*] said, "What is he thinking, forbidding us from worshipping idols while he is invoking two gods? At one moment he says '*Allāh*' and at another moment he says 'the Merci-

> ful'!" So, God Most High revealed [to the Prophet Muhammad] "God has the most beautiful Names" [Q 7:180], and He meant by it that God has appellations and for that reason He said "most beautiful" [*al-ḥusnā*] which is the feminine of "most beautiful" [*al-aḥsan*].[85]

The beautiful names of God, by this account, are thus connected with the central Islamic monotheistic belief of *tawḥīd*, as well as with how rightly to address the Divine. Responding to the confusion of Arabian polytheists who were accustomed to worshipping various gods by different names, God sends down to the Prophet Muhammad this revelation to clarify that there exist for the one God multiple names that are themselves appropriately described as "most beautiful." It was these rightful names for the one God that the Prophet and the Muslims were using to call upon the Lord in their prayer.

With this account of the occasion of the revelation of this Qur'anic verse (Q 7:180),[86] Qushayrī raises the theological issue of how properly to describe God—that is, what attributes to attribute to Him, a question that was important in the Islamic tradition from early on.[87] Continuing to refer to the relevant debate in the science of *kalām* or philosophical theology, Qushayrī comments on the next part of the Qur'anic verse in question: "shun those who deviate [*yulḥidūn*] with regard to His names" (Q 7:180). The verb *yulḥid* and its noun form *ilḥād* come to be interpreted during the Abbasid period as referring to doctrinal deviation or heresy.[88] Thus Qushayrī explains later in this chapter of *Sharḥ asmāʾ Allāh al-ḥusnā* the meaning of "deviating in His names":

> Heresy [*ilḥād*] with regard to the names of God Most High is of two sorts: by adding to what is permitted in the matter or by subtracting from what is commanded in the matter. The former is anthropomorphism [*tashbīh*] and the latter is divesting God of His attributes [*taʿṭīl*]. The anthropomorphizers describe God by what is not permitted, and those who divest [God] of His attributes deny what is ascribed Him. For this reason, the People of the Truth said, "Our religious belief [*dīn*] is a path between two paths, which is to say, there is no anthropomorphism [*tashbīh*] and no divesting God of His attributes [*taʿṭīl*].[89]

Qushayrī thus names two kinds of heresy in the matter of God's names. Using terms that invoke an extraordinarily important theological debate, Qushayrī explains that Sufis or "the People of the Truth" ("*ahl al-ḥaqq*") take a middle way between the heretical extremes of *tashbīh* and *taʿṭīl*.

Qushayrī goes on to comment on a number of other Qur'anic verses relevant to his topic, including the following:[90]

ISRAELITES 17:110
Say: "Call upon Allah [God], or
Call upon Rahman:
By whatever name ye call
Upon Him, (it is well):
For to Him belong
The Most Beautiful Names.

MARY 19:65
Lord of the heavens
And of the earth,
And of all that is
Between them: so worship Him,
And be constant and patient
In His worship: knowest thou
Of any who is worthy
Of the same Name as He?"

THE MERCIFUL 55:78
Blessed be the name
Of thy Lord,
Full of Majesty,
Bounty and Honour.

THE MOST HIGH 87:1
Glorify the name
Of thy Guardian-Lord
Most High, . . .

THE CLOT 96:1
Proclaim! (or Read!)
In the name
Of thy Lord and Cherisher,
Who created—

One rhetorical effect of Qushayrī's authorial choice to treat each of these Qur'anic verses in which the name or names of God are referred to as such is that Qushayrī thus grounds quite firmly in revelation his own discourse on the names of God. As we have seen by our consideration of part of his treatment of "The Elevated Places" (Q 7:180), Qushayrī uses the opportunity of commenting on these verses to bring up other considerations that expand his treatment of the topic of these most beautiful names of God. Having treated these Qur'anic verses, Qushayrī turns to the name "*Allāh*," a name that has a most special significance as a name for God to Muslims. He begins the "Chapter on the name of the Most High '*Allāh*'" with an etymological discussion:

> The discourse in this chapter includes several topics, among which is what can be said about the derivation of this appellation: Is it derived from a meaningful word or not? And if it be derived from a meaningful word, what is that word? There are different opinions about this issue.[91]

One view on the origins of the word is that it is something like a proper name:

> There are those who say that this name is not derived from a meaningful word, but rather specifically designates God Most High. He has an absolute name [*ism khāliṣ*], as others have proper names and epithets [*asmāʾ al-aʿlām wal-alqāb*], except that no epithet or proper name [*ism al-laqab wal-ʿalam*] is applied to the description of the Most High since God has not reserved any such name for Himself [*tawqīf*]. This is one of the teachings of al-Khalīl ibn Aḥmad.[92]

The Arabic philologist al-Khalīl ibn Aḥmad (d. 175/791 or 170/786 or 160/776),[93] teacher of Sībawayhi, thus teaches, according to Qushayrī's account, that God has "an absolute name" that "specifically designates" Him alone in a similar way as human beings have proper names and nicknames or epithets that designate them individually or their attributes.

> It is told of al-Shāfiʿī, may God have mercy on him, that he went along with this teaching, and that Shaykh al-Husayn ibn al-Fuḍayl followed his example in this. There are many Sufis [*ahl al-ḥaqq*] who agreed with this teaching, professing that we have not seen the specialists in language [*ahl al-lugha*] conjugate forms from the root of this name, nor have they used it for anyone other than God.[94]

Many Sufis, along with the great jurist al-Shāfiʿī (d. 363/974), agreed with al-Khalīl's teaching about the name "Allah" being a kind of special designation for God alone. After all, experts in Arabic philology neither call anyone else by this name nor form other words by derivation from the name "Allah."

> Rather the little that the use of the word "*Allāh*" appears in their [i.e., language specialists'] discourse, it accords with revelation [*al-shar*ʿ] in its description of the Most High and not description of anyone else, for they used to write "in your name, O God" and God Most High said: "Do you know anyone who is His namesake?" (Q 19:65) In the exegesis of this verse it is rendered as "Do you know anyone named *Allāh* except *Allāh*?" This is one of the miracles of the Prophet, peace be upon him, that indicate his truthfulness in that report when he reported that He had no namesake, and God, may He be praised, constrained hearts from the insolence of applying this appellation in the description of anyone else, despite the great number of enemies of religion, plus the vehemence of their desire and the abundance of their occasions for calling the Prophet, peace be upon him, a liar in what he recounted. For this reason, some of the masters taught that taking on the attributes [*takhalluq*] of every name of God is righteous, except for this name [Allāh], which is for devotion not imitation [*takhalluq*].[95]

Referring here to a saying common among Sufis, "Assume the character traits of God" (*takhallaqū bi-akhlāq Allāh*), Qushayrī notes that one of the special characteristics of this name of God, "*Allāh*," is that humankind is not called upon to take this name as a trait of our own.[96] Meditation on any other divine name can lead eventually to an understanding that entails a transformation of the human person in conformity with that name.

Qushayrī goes on to consider other denotations for the purported roots of the word "Allāh":

> There are also those who say that the root is to lose one's head or to become enraptured [*ilah*], and *ilālah* [approximation of *allāh*] is the one in whom one becomes enraptured in the midst of needs or takes refuge in Him in vicissitudes, just as "sufficient" [*kāfi*] is the name for that with which one is satisfied, and blanket [*liḥāf*][97] is that with which one covers oneself [*yaltaḥif*]. With this meaning they recite: "I took refuge in you in the hardships that hit me / I found you completely generous and noble." Al-Ḥarith ibn Asad al-Muḥāsibī agrees with this teaching in the community of scholars and Qur'anic exegetes. Among the scholarly community this [i.e., the word *Allāh*] is not deemed a definition, in the sense that it is not the case He was a god [*ilāh*] only after being described as such.[98]

The purported lack of a productive linguistic root for the name "Allāh" becomes the grounds for Qushayrī to theologize about the nature of divinity. God is God not because of any action or merit.

> So if this is correct in its attribution, then this expression is appropriate for commentary without definition, a concept that we affirmed on account of the outcome of the consensus [*ijmāʿ*] that He has always been Divinity, even if this designation is not something He merited on account of an action that He made manifest or on account of a meaning that comes about in something eternal, such as our description for Him that He is "Creator" and "Worshipped." For back in the beginning of time there was not anyone seeking refuge in Him because He was *Allāh* and it was right to seek refuge in Him. And there are those [things] for whom it is inconceivable that they would seek refuge in Him, such as solid objects and accidental attributes. It is conceivable that the one who does not have reason or the capacity to differentiate would fly to Him in refuge, as it is conceivable for whoever accepts this argument regarding what we have shown to be correct.[99]

Qushayrī's reflection on the nature of God turns smoothly into moral reflection on humankind.

> For whoever knows that the One he worships—may He be praised—is the One to Whom to take refuge in hardships turns away from everything but Him and has not accepted anyone other than Him while dwelling in this world or the afterlife. What shows that this is true is that such a person prefers God's satisfaction to his own carnal desires. Then [that person] knows that even if he strives fervently and makes every effort, the most he can accomplish is incapability and falling short, for if Mercy envelops him, then heaven is his abode; but if he deserves punishment [and] the decree is against him, then Fire is his dwelling place. (Q 39:19)[100]

What starts as a general moral reflection then becomes specifically Sufi in nature.

> For if the servant's heart takes refuge in his Lord without being seized by his direction and inmost or being designated by his companions and friends, then [divine] succor rushes to him presently, and friendship with God is realized for him in the future. In some of the [Sufi] lore, if you have recourse to Him at the first sign of hardships, He lends assistance with all kinds of benefits, but [if] you have recourse to your peers, then He increases your troubles. Some of the masters have said: "A man's true

> belief in the Oneness of God is only known at the first jolt of the tribulation," meaning by this, that his attention to God with his heart is immediate.[101]

Qushayrī's abstract pronouncement about Sufi forebears is then made concrete by a story whose theme is taking refuge in God.

> It was recounted concerning Aḥmad ibn Abī al-Ḥawārī that he said, "I was with Abū Sulaymān al-Dārānī on the road to Mecca, and a water-skin fell from me. So I told that to Abū Sulaymān, and he said, 'O Pathfinder to the goal of our searches, O Guide from going astray, return to us the object of our search.'" He [Aḥmad ibn Abī al-Ḥawārī] said, "It was not long at all until a man approached saying, 'Who lost a water-skin?' and lo and behold, it was my water-skin," he said. "So, I took it, and Abū Sulaymān said, 'Did you reckon that He would leave us without water?' So we continued for a while, and it was bitterly cold so we had on a fur garment. We then saw a man wearing tattered rags who was sweating profusely. Abū Sulaymān said, 'We shall share with you from the favor of what we have.' And the man said, 'Heat and cold are two creatures from the creation of God. If they come upon me, or if they leave me, I have been a captive in this desert for 30 years, so I do not tremble or shake. A warm wind from His love clothes me in the cold, and the coolness of His mercy clothes me in the heat. O Dārānī, invite pious renunciation and you will find cold. O Dārānī, weep and cry out and be pleased with the refreshment [sent from God].'" [Aḥmad ibn Abī al-Ḥawārī] said, "So, Abū Sulaymān continued on, saying 'No one but he [i.e., that man captive in the desert] is superior to me in Sufism.'"[102]

Dārānī's reliance on God brings the apparent miracle of the return of the water-skin, but his faith is dwarfed by that of the mysterious desert dweller who relied on God's protection from the elements for three decades.

> [Qushayrī] said: This narrative indicates that Abū Sulaymān trusted in his taking refuge in God, may He be exalted, and that he did have recourse to him upon the loss of the water-skin, so when what was lost returned back to him God made real what the man believed would happen. Then God preserved him from the cause of conceit by showing him someone who was greater than he [*maʿnāhū*]. He diminished in his eyes the state of his ego by giving him insight into the superiority of spiritual station of

> someone else over him. This is God's way with His friends [*awliyā'ihī*], [namely] that he preserves them from heeding their deeds and diminishes in their eyes their spiritual states, to which they devote themselves wholeheartedly.[103]

Spiritual progress is infinite in potential. Elevated ranks each bring their own special temptations, such as spiritual pride, but God provides help at every step of the way, even in averting this kind of temptation.

Another chapter of *Sharḥ asmā' Allāh* where we can acquire greater familiarity with Qushayrī's way of proceeding from linguistic knowledge to theological and spiritual reflection is the chapter on the word "He."

> Know that "he" is a noun used for referring [to someone or something]. In Sufism it tells of the end of spiritual realization. For those who specialize in the exoteric, in order to be a meaningful utterance, "he" needs a connection to what it designates. For, if you said "he" and then went silent, the utterance would not be meaningful until you said, "He is standing" or "sitting" or "He is living" or "dying" or something of that sort.
>
> On the other hand, among the Sufis if you say "he," nothing else comes into their hearts but remembrance of the True One, for they are content without any announcement that follows their consumption in the truths of intimacy from being taken possession of in their inmost selves by the remembrance of God and from their effacement through their witnessing rather than their sensing anyone besides Him.[104]

Böwering's characterization of Tustarī's method of exegesis comes to mind here. The Sufi encounters the Qur'anic text, focuses on a "keynote," and then, being preoccupied with esoteric spiritual realities, bounds into the realm of *taṣawwuf.*

> Imam Abū Bakr ibn Fūrak, may God be pleased with him, said, "He [*huwa*] is two letters, the letter *hā'* and the letter *wāw*." *Hā'* is articulated in the furthest depth of the throat, indeed, the last place of articulation, and *wāw* is articulated from the lips, which is the first place of articulation. It is as if to indicate that the origin of every being that exists is from Him and the end of every being that exists is in Him. He Himself has no beginning or ending. This is the meaning of His utterance, "He is the first and the last." (Q 57:3) Saying "He is the first" bespeaks His having no beginning in time, and "the last" indicates the impossibility of His

> non-existence. He is the first in His doing favors for you from the beginning, and the last in His granting gifts for you and His perdurance with you out of never-ending kindness. The ordering of every goodness that you possess is through Him, and the completion of every such goodness is up to Him. God, may He be praised, said, "Perfectly on the one I favor." (Q 6:154)[105]

Qushayrī here mobilizes anatomical knowledge of the speech apparatus—namely, the glottis as the place of articulation for the *hāʾ* at the beginning of the Arabic word *huwa* (meaning "he") and the lips as the place of articulation for the *wāw* that is the second and last letter in that Arabic word. This anatomical knowledge turns then to theological reflection on God as the sempiternal, the first and the last, like the glottis and the lips are the beginning and the end of the parts of the human speech passage.

> It was related about one of them [i.e., the Sufis] that he said, "I saw one of the enraptured ones, and I said, 'What is your name?' He replied, 'He.' I said, 'Who are you?' He replied, 'He.' I said, 'Where did you come from?' He replied, 'He.' 'Who do you mean when you say "He"?' He replied, 'He.' No matter what I asked him about, he replied 'He.' So I said, 'Perhaps you mean God,' he said." At which [the enraptured one] let out a cry and gave up his ghost.[106]

The Sufi preoccupation with spiritual realities is epitomized in this last passage. Once again we see here a progression of linguistic to theological to spiritual Sufi material.

Qushayrī's two books on *dhikr* provide illuminating parallels to *The Grammar of Hearts*. Situated among some of the other genres in which Qushayrī wrote, including the major genres of Sufi *ṭabaqāt*, handbook, and *tafsīr*, *Sharḥ asmāʾ Allāh al-ḥusnā* and *Tartīb al-sulūk fī ṭarīq Allāh* show to differing degrees the influences of all of these prominent genres of Sufi literature. The hagiographic genealogies, explications of key concepts, and fertile associations of source texts with spiritual realities that are respectively the specialties of the *ṭabaqāt*, handbook, and *tafsīr* genres all are evident in the two less commonly known works of Qushayrī that we have examined in some depth in this chapter. We will see similar influences from these more prominent genres in the structure and content of *The Grammar of Hearts*. Moreover, the two works whose starting point is *dhikr* have already brought to our attention a number of practical, conceptual, theological, and spiritual connections between language and *taṣawwuf.* After the foregoing study, Qushayrī's nimble versatility in weaving these various strands together in his texts should now be all the more discernible in the artfully dense *Grammar of Hearts.*

5 Forming Spiritual *Fuṣaḥā*ʾ

QUSHAYRĪ'S ADVANCED *GRAMMAR OF HEARTS*

My earth and My heaven do not encompass Me,
but the heart of My servant who has faith does encompass Me.

The heart of the believer is the focus of this famous hadith, which speaks paradoxically of the presence of God in creation. The physical limits of the known world, the heaven and earth, do not delimit the divine. *Allāhu akbar*: God is greater and grander than the world. Yet somehow, the heart of the believer holds the presence of God. According to this saying, which was related by God to the Prophet Muhammad not as Qur'an but as another kind of divine utterance called by Islamic scholars a "holy saying," a *ḥadīth qudsī*, the divine is powerfully and mysteriously enthroned in the Muslim heart. While this *ḥadīth qudsī* about God's presence in the heart has been important to Sufis and other Muslims over the centuries, Qushayrī's "grammatical" exploration of the heart provides a distinctive contribution to Islamic understandings of God's work within human beings.

> There are four kinds of grammatical case: raising [*al-rafʿ*], rectification [*al-naṣb*], diminution [*al-khafḍ*], and curtailing [*al-jazm*]. Hearts likewise have these categories. . . .
>
> As for the diminishment [*al-khafḍ*] of hearts, it is through eliciting embarrassment, seeking unremitting dread, the necessity of lowliness, the preference of lassitude, perseverance in humility, and submitting the self to the sacrifices of righteous struggle.
>
> It could be the diminution of sin—denying anyone who asks you for something that is not legally permitted—without a response or a dispute, or confirmation and aversion.

In this way, the gnostic diminishes the obstacles of the masses by despising his fate and holding himself and his action in disgust now and in his future.[1]

Qushayrī's purpose in *The Grammar of Hearts* is to develop his reader into a spiritual *faṣīḥ*, eloquent in mystic speech and skillful in spiritual intercourse. He accomplishes this through providing the wayfarer with an account of a great variety of possibilities for the inner life and ways of the heart. Using grammatical topics and terms as starting points for exploring human-divine relations, Qushayrī adopts a spiritual pedagogy akin to that of the mother of all Arabic grammar books, Sībawayhi's *Kitāb*.[2]

The heart in the Sufi tradition is a special place of human-divine intimacy. The heart is where God is most present to us and where our journey to God occurs. The basis for this tradition begins with the 132 occurrences of the word *qalb* (or its plural, *qulūb*) in the Qur'an.[3] "The Qur'an repeatedly emphasizes God's extraordinary closeness and proximity to the human heart (e.g., Q 8:24 . . .) as well as the uniquely all-encompassing divine knowledge of *what is in their hearts* (4:66, 33:51, etc.)."[4] These ideas of intimacy and divine knowledge of human intentions at times go so far in the Qur'an as to speak of the heart in the stead of the entire human person, a part for the whole. By this synecdoche, the heart is "the enduring individual self or ongoing seat of our moral and spiritual responsibility."[5] One example is Q 2:225: "He will call you to account for what your hearts have earned."

Seemingly in contrast to the idea of human agency that is implicit in this synecdoche, the Qur'an also consistently stresses that God is responsible for the changing states of the heart. The heart is both "the locus of true Remembrance of God (*dhikr Allāh*, at 13:28) and [the locus of] the grace of divinely bestowed Peace and Tranquility." Much more often than either *dhikr* or grace, "the Qur'an refers instead to God's sealing, veiling, hardening, locking, binding, closing, or frightening hearts."[6]

Among the hadiths that are major influences on the great Sufi Muḥyī al-Dīn ibn ʿArabī (d. 1240) in his understanding of the heart, the hadith with which we began this chapter stands out. This *ḥadīth qudsī* also comes down to us in the Sufi tradition in a briefer formulation: "The heart of the person of faith is the Throne of the All-Merciful": "*qalb al-mu'min ʿarsh al-Rahmān*."[7] The heart (sing. *qalb*; pl. *qulūb*) of the believer is here said somehow to encompass the Lord. It is the throne on which God sits. It is the key to understanding in what sense humanity is created in the image and likeness of God. It is also an organ with special epistemological functions, as highlighted by another famous hadith that influenced Ibn ʿArabī: "(True spiritual) Knowing is a light that God projects into the heart of the Knower." Standing firmly in the same Sufi tradition, Qushayrī aims with his *Naḥw al-qulūb* to school believers' hearts.

In the passage from *The Grammar of Hearts* already cited, Qushayrī starts with the grammatical topic of case, *al-iʿrāb* in Arabic. After naming the four cases, the shaykh declares that they not only belong to Arabic, but also to hearts, the communicative organ for intercourse with God. The term *al-khafḍ*, referring to an Arabic case often associated with the Greek and Latin genitive, literally means "diminishment," "lowering," and "lessening," meanings that in Qushayrī's application to the heart take the discussion to the spiritual virtue of humility. The grammatical cases or desinences in Qushayrī's Sufi interpretation refer to motions of the heart. This particular heart motion of lowliness is found when someone turns aside from a temptation extended by another and does so without judgment. With spiritual detachment, the ones who know God also know their place in the world. They adore God, rather than some grandiose image of themselves and their impact on the world.

Qushayrī's pedagogical method is apparent in this passage. Contrary to the expectations of bossy advice that the word "grammar" may conjure up for readers of English today, Qushayrī in *The Grammar of Hearts* describes the ways of lowliness more than he prescribes norms. Considering just this single excerpt already raises the question of the author's sense of purpose in his book of *naḥw* or grammar. Students of Arabic strive through much toil and exertion to master the grammatical endings—how to form them and use them correctly. But Qushayrī writes this grammar book not as some grammar maven, but rather from his position as Sufi master. What does he hope to impart to his readers by means of his odd grammar manual? More specifically, let us take this example of applying the *iʿrāb* to the heart, which here as elsewhere in the text is the symbolic center of the human being. By this example and others like it, does Qushayrī aim to instruct readers prescriptively on how to speak with their hearts or simply to describe to readers the nature of heart-speech?

Underlying this question is an important distinction to which grammatical discourse attended carefully in the twentieth century—namely, the distinction between grammars that tell readers how they *should* use language and grammars that describe how speakers of a language actually *do* use language.[8] Indeed, looking back at grammatical writings across the centuries, both of these rhetorical purposes are evident. Viewing *The Grammar of Hearts* in the context of the Arabic grammatical tradition, we see that the way Qushayrī mixes prescriptive and descriptive turns out to be one of the striking similarities to Sībawayhi's *Kitāb*, which is the magnum opus of Arabic grammar. Indeed, briefly considering Qushayrī's text with relation to Sībawayhi will aid our understanding what kind of thing this strange "spiritual grammar" is.

Qushayrī and Sībawayhi

Modern Sībawayhi scholar Michael Carter has described the *Kitāb* as being primarily descriptive, since Sībawayhi considered as wide a field of data as possible and applied to it an inductive method in order to discover the underlying structures of the language. The fact that Sībawayhi did not exclude data that did not fit the general principles that he discovered demonstrates that intellectual honesty was a higher value for him than purporting to identify flawlessly clean and elegant rules that might better serve a prescriptive grammarian. To feed his project, Sībawayhi exhibited a keen, even surprisingly eager interest in gathering actual data from native speakers of this kind of Arabic that we call "eloquent," "*fuṣḥā*." Because of Sībawayhi's voracious appetite for actual linguistic data, "the *Kitāb* often appears to be an anthology of inconsistencies."[9] Another scholar has called Sībawayhi's approach "explicatory descriptivism" because of how the *Kitāb* gathers examples of related grammatical phenomena, describes them in detail, and provides comments that both elucidate and justify the variant forms.[10]

However, the normative demands of the state determined that eventually and perhaps inevitably the primarily descriptive approach of Sībawayhi be adapted to educational purposes that in the later so-called Basran grammatical tradition took the form of prescriptive handbooks. This "avowedly pedagogical approach to the presentation of Arabic grammar" was apparent already in the ninth century.[11] Moreover, though the *Urtext* of Arabic grammatical writings was basically descriptive in its method, it contained a prescriptive current, for even in Sībawayhi the ideal of *faṣāḥa*, meaning purity and eloquence of linguistic expression, was a key concept. Later, developing students' *faṣāḥa* became the ostensible objective of most grammars, though the descriptive legacy of Sībawayhi was not entirely abandoned.

The Grammar of Hearts is thus in this regard more like Sībawayhi's *Kitāb* than later pedagogical grammars. For example, in describing or defining the following terms on linguistic and Sufi levels, Qushayrī writes in the mode of explaining a reality, not in the mode of clearing up errors: *naḥw, kalām, ism, fiʿl, ḥarf, al-mufīd, al-muʿrab, al-mabnī, al-rafʿa, al-naṣb, al-khafḍ,* and *al-jazm*. In each case, however, underlying all of these discussions is a prescriptive aspect to the extent that Qushayrī clearly favors spiritual advancement over spiritual immaturity. Moreover, as we shall see in the first section of the text, in his very definition of *naḥw*—that is, "grammar"—the element of correctness is crucial.

Another example of Qushayrī's subtle prescriptive bent can be found in his explanation of the mystical meanings of the four desinences, one of which, *khafḍ*, we already have seen. Each linguistic desinence relates to a spiritual virtue—namely, otherworldliness, serene indifference, humility, and self-denial. In describing these meanings, and what for example *naṣb* might mean in the way of the heart, Qushayrī subtly demonstrates a clear preference and even admiration for the associated spiritual virtue. In the case of *naṣb*, Qushayrī shows a preference for serene indifference to one's own destiny, rather than spiritual attachment. In the case of *khafḍ*, Qushayrī's several descriptions of the virtue of spiritual humility show his esteem for it over against egoism and arrogance.

Like Sībawayhi in the *Kitāb*, Qushayrī meant *The Grammar of Hearts* to be edifying to his readers by teaching them about a very complex reality. Nonetheless, neither author is heavy-handed or schoolmarmish in tone or method. Exhibiting greater fascination with the beauty and richness of the realities that they describe, Sībawayhi and Qushayrī do not orient their writing toward some kind of classroom use where pupils will be evaluated on their mastery of course material presented in these books. At the same time, they do aspire for their readers to advance to new levels of mastery. Thus, the analogue of the master of Arabic, called the *faṣīḥ*, is for Qushayrī the Sufi who has advanced far along the way of the heart.

The Grammar of Hearts is like Sībawayhi's *Kitāb* in other ways as well. The distinctive marks of Sībawayhi's text, according to Carter, are its extraordinarily wide corpus of linguistic data, adaptation of the methods of legal thought to linguistics, systematic coherence in terminology, and nonlinear model of linguistic competence.[12] In a sense, all four of these characteristics apply to Qushayrī's text. To start with, the range of spiritual states and mystical phenomena that he addresses are quite wide-ranging indeed. As Sībawayhi collected linguistic data on Arabic speakers' usage across regional dialects and variations, Qushayrī cites a great variety of spiritual movements of the heart, from the quotidian to the obscure. Second, as Sībawayhi applied the methods of legal science to Arabic speakers' behavior and speech, Qushayrī creatively applies grammatical science to behavior and speech in the spiritual domain, as Sībawayhi related legal science to the linguistic domain. Third, drawing on his own introductory handbook to Sufism, the *Risāla*, Qushayrī also maintains a "systematic coherence" in his usage of Sufi terminology throughout *The Grammar of Hearts.*

The fourth of these marks of distinction—namely, Sībawayhi's nonlinear concept of linguistic competence—is particularly evocative with regard to Qushayrī's text. Given the shifting, polyvalent complexities and ambiguities of the spiritual life, could Sufi "competence" be anything but nonlinear? Carter describes Sībawayhi's view that competence in Arabic was "non-linear, a bundle of simultaneous processes that cannot be described in the linear style of scientific discourse, but must be broken down and approached from different perspectives." In content and form, *The Grammar of Hearts* displays a dazzlingly nonlinear approach to reality, as we shall also see.

Considering the ordering of Arabic grammar books, we note that Sībawayhi and many grammarians of Arabic after him began with syntax, then treated morphological issues, and finally addressed some phonological issues.[13] The first division of grammar has nine sections and is dedicated to explanation of the behavior of word endings (*majārī*) in articulation, while its second division deals with "the transformation (*taṣrīf*) of the forms (*abniyā'*) of words in themselves, in vocabulary (*lugha*)."[14] Qushayrī does not cleanly follow this typical order. One obvious deviation from the typical book of Arabic *naḥw* or grammar is that the vast majority of the topics that Qushayrī treats are all syntactic, with some morphological material intermixed. For example, sections 11 and 53 of *The Grammar of Hearts* are primarily morphological, the former dealing with regular and broken plurals and the latter with the formation of the diminutive of triliteral nouns.

As for the topics themselves, within the areas of syntax, morphology, and phonology, grammarians developed a colorful array of concepts and terms. A number of these terms and concepts that appear in *The Grammar of Hearts* are actually not present in the *Kitāb* of Sībawayhi. To mention just two examples of post-Sibawayhan grammatical terms,[15] *fā'ida* [meaning] and *ḥukm*[16] both occur in Qushayrī's *Naḥw al-qulūb*. We thus observe that the Sufi author drew on Arabic grammatical writings beyond the *Urtext* of that discipline. In selecting topics to use as conceptual starting points for novel explanations of the intercourse of Sufis with God, Qushayrī did not seem to take as a model one particular author's grammar book, as Gerson did with Donatus.

Naḥw al-Qulūb al-Ṣaghīr

There are actually two versions of *The Grammar of Hearts*, a major and a minor version, called in Arabic "*al-kabīr*" and "*al-saghīr*," "the greater" and "the lesser." The two texts are quite different. The topics taken up in the shorter *al-ṣaghīr* version are mostly different from the material in the longer *al-kabīr* version. Exceptional cases of grammatical topics taken up by Qushayrī in the shorter version that he also takes up in the longer include the grammatical cases,[17] definite and indefinite nouns,[18] and the subjects of nominal sentences (*mubtada'*).[19] Other elements, such as the conventions used for switching from the linguistic meaning to the spiritual meaning of terms, also differ between the two versions. The meaning of the sections of both versions of *The Grammar of Hearts* can be quite enigmatic. Some of the terse sections in the *saghīr* version surpass the pithy and reach the obscure. The additional material in *al-kabīr*, which is the focus of the present study, gives the reader somewhat greater opportunities to grasp the meaning.

A fuller consideration of *Naḥw al-qulūb al-ṣaghīr* and its relationship not only with the longer *Naḥw al-qulūb al-kabīr* but also with other Sufi spiritual grammatical writings, such as the Sufi commentary on the grammatical poem by Abū al-ʿAbbās Aḥmad ibn ʿAjība, would certainly be worth undertaking.[20] Did Qushayrī first write the *saghīr* and then later expand it into the *kabīr* version? Or did he first write the expanded version and then abridge it into the *saghīr*? Perhaps such questions can be answered as researchers begin to investigate the development of spiritual grammars in Arabic.

Our purpose now is to open up understanding of the content, method, and background of the longer version of Qushayrī's *Grammar of Hearts*. In the present chapter I forgo explication of every single section of Qushayrī's text. As the reader becomes initiated into the unusual ways of connecting grammatical ideas with spiritual ones, Qushayrī's text becomes gradually more comprehensible. The number of background concepts necessary to understand *The Grammar of Hearts* is finite. Indeed, Qushayrī's *Risāla* fills us in many of these concepts, while in other instances reference to a somewhat broader theological and historical context is required. Qushayrī, like Gerson, takes as his starting point an assumption of his reader's familiarity with Arabic grammar. As such, he does not dwell on linguistic niceties or details, for they are not his concern. He rather invokes grammatical terms, concepts, and phenomena familiar to his reader in order to proceed to spiritual matters, which are his focus. Accordingly, grammatical explanations will not be our focal point here, though broad explanations of the grammatical topics invoked by Qushayrī will be provided, especially for the benefit of non-specialists in Arabic language.

Commentary on Qushayrī's *Grammar of Hearts*

This chapter is thus an attempt to instruct the reader in how to make sense of Qushayrī's book through providing a close textual analysis and whatever explanations of background ideas are necessary for understanding what Qushayrī wrote. Let us now turn to the very first section of *The Grammar of Hearts*. As noted, this commentary will not cover all of *The Grammar of Hearts*. It will start from the beginning and treat the first seventeen sections before turning to a few especially difficult later sections.

Qushayrī begins by adverting to the traditional discussion of the origins of Arabic grammar as a discipline, which from early on Arabs referred to using the rather unexpected name "*naḥw*," whose literal meaning concerns "a direction, way, or manner."

> Grammar [*al-naḥw*] in language is the pursuit of correct speech. It is said, [*naḥawtu naḥwahu*] "I went in his direction," meaning, in other words, "I pursued his way." This sort of thing in Arabic is called grammar because it is the pursuit of correct speech.[21]

Qushayrī's treatment here is connected to one of the traditional stories that explain how the science of grammar received the appellation *naḥw*. The story portrays Abu ʿl-Aswad al-Duʾalī,[22] a partisan of ʿAli who allegedly founded this science, as introducing his grammar book to the people by saying, "follow this path," "*unḥū hādhā al-naḥwa*." With this initial allusion to a topos from what by his time was a discipline of Arabic grammar that was only two centuries old, Qushayrī begins immediately his transformative technique of somehow applying grammatical terms and concepts to matters of *taṣawwuf*.

Playing on the root meaning of *naḥw* as "way" or "path," Qushayrī explains "the way of the heart" by expanding upon the concept of aiming toward or following the way of correct speech:

> But grammar of the heart is the pursuit of praiseworthy speech with the heart. Praiseworthy speech is talking to God with the tongue of the heart. Such talk is divided into calling out [*al-munāda*] and secret whisperings [*al-munājā*].
>
> Calling out [*al-munāda*] is the attribute of worshippers while secret whispering is the characteristic of ecstatics. Calling out [*al-munāda*] is at the entryway, and secret conversation [*al-munājā*] is from a position of intimacy [*al-qurb*], for the position of the worshipper is at the entryways of service, while the abode of the ecstatic is at the position [*al-bisāṭ*] of the righteous deed [*al-qurba*].[23]

This initial section purports here to define the title of the work, *naḥw al-qulūb*. If Arabic grammar is about following the "way of correct speech," here is Qushayrī's explanation for the "way" of spiritual eloquence that he means to lay out. It is not the way of correct linguistic structures, but rather praiseworthy utterances of the heart, spiritual *faṣāḥa*.

Besides clarifying what path "*naḥw al-qulūb*" aims at, this first definitional sentence of *The Grammar of Hearts* explains that the heart is the communicative organ that makes the praiseworthy utterances that *naḥw al-qalb* guides. Qushayrī goes so far as to conceive of the heart as metaphorically possessing a tongue. He then clarifies this idea of "praiseworthy speech": Praiseworthy speech is addressing God, called here *al-Ḥaqq*, a divine name that in the Sufi tradition means something along the lines of "Ultimate Reality" or "the True One."

Qushayrī then divides praiseworthy speech into two sorts, each of which is a technical term from Sufi discourse. The two sorts are "*al-munāda*" and "*al-munājā*," which I have translated as "calling out" and "secret whisperings," respectively. Other forms of these same terms appear in Qushayrī's *Risāla* when he explains the terms *jamʿ* and *farq*:[24]

> When the servant of God addresses Him—may He be exalted—in his intimate conversation [*najwāhī*] with Him as a beggar, a supplicant, a lauder, a giver of thanks, a renouncer [of evil deeds], or a humble beseecher, he

> places himself in the position of separation [*farq*]. And when he listens in his inner self to what his Lord tells him [*yunājīhī*] and hears in his heart what God imparts to him by calling upon him [*nādāhū*], admonishing him [*nājāhū*], instructing him, or intimating [something] to his heart and willing to follow [this intimation], he finds himself under the sign of unification [*jamʿ*].[25]

It is clear from Qushayrī's usage of these two terms in both the *Risāla* and in *The Grammar of Hearts* that the quieter sort of mystical speech, *al-munājā*, is for the more advanced spiritual seeker, or at least for the one who is at the time of the intercourse at a closer state of intimacy with God. Qusharyrī relates *al-munājā* to a place of closeness and the state of unification with God called "*jamʿ*." The more obstreperous "calling out," "*al-munāda*," on the other hand, is associated with a state of separation from God, called "*farq*," when the servant is focusing not on God but rather on his or her own actions of obedience or disobedience. The devout worshippers, *ʿābidūn*, enjoy "calling out," while the ecstatics, *wājidūn*, enjoy "secret whisperings." These terms appear to refer to specific ascetical and mystical movements that had particular geographical and chronological relationships with each other. A number of historical studies have attempted to trace these movements and their relationships, which may exhibit a general trend from *zuhd* (renunciant asceticism) to *ʿibāda* (pious worship) to *taṣawwuf* (Sufism).[26]

In section 2, Qushayrī names the three parts of speech identified by Arab grammarians, and then he begins to describe the general categories of relationships between these parts of speech. The traditional grammatical material in this section is particularly brief. Qushayrī very quickly moves to a Sufi meaning for these elements and their relations:

> Language comprises the noun, the verb, and the particle that occurs for [expressing] a meaning:
>
> In the grammar of hearts, the noun is God; the verb is what is from God; and the particle either belongs to the noun and thus imposes upon it a [grammatical] determination, or the particle belongs to the verb and requires a relation to it.[27]

This division of the parts of speech follows the tradition of Sībawayhi, whose initial section on "Knowledge of What the Words of Arabic Are" begins with the sentence, "The words are noun, verb, and particle which brings a meaning that is neither noun nor verb."[28] In fact, Qushayrī almost uses Sībawayhi's exact first six words, with the exception of the first word, "*al-kalām*," in place of Sībawayhi's "*fa-l-kalim*."[29] Just as Donatus in his *Ars minor* provides scores of examples to illustrate the grammatical principles that he formulates, Sībawayhi elaborates his categories of words with examples of nouns, verbs from the various tenses, and then a few particles. Qushayrī, on the other hand, like Gerson in *Moralized Grammar*, chooses not to give numerous examples but rather to expound in a different manner.

It is worth noting that word "*ism*," meaning "name" or "noun," has an important association in Sufi discourse with God and His attributes, apart from Qushayrī's decision to write "the noun/name is God," "*al-ism huwa Allāhu*." ʿAbd al-Razzāq al-Qāshānī (d. between 1329 and 1335),[30] in his *Iṣṭilāḥāt al-ṣūfiyya*, a glossary of Sufi terms, presents an entry on *al-ism*:

> In Sufi technical usage it is not the utterance of the Name which matters, but rather the essence of the thing named—whether one is considering a substantial quality, such as the Knower or the Capable, or an insubstantial quality, such as the Holy or the Salvation.[31]

Al-Qāshānī's exemplification of the two different kinds of attribute or quality (*ṣifa*) with traditional names of God, all-knowing (*ʿalīm*), Holy (*quddūs*), and Peace (*salām*) resonates with what Qushayrī associates with the topic of "the Name," as we shall see. Given al-Qāshānī's writing several centuries after Qushayrī, this resonance appears as evidence of a conceptual thread running through Sufi traditions.

From his Sufi meaning of noun, verb, and particle, Qushayrī proceeds to introduce the grammatical concepts of case and mood endings by lingering on how particles in their interactions with nouns and verbs impose a grammatical determination upon them:

> Just as, if the particle is brought to bear on a noun, it imposes upon it either the accusative case or the genitive or something else, so also the attribute of, say, knowledge, imposes upon God the determination of "the Knower," and similarly with power, life and the rest of the attributes of God.
>
> Just as there are those particles which impose upon the verb the [grammatical] determination subjunctive or jussive, the occurrence of the deeds of the True One in accord with [His] attributes imposes upon Him the quality of [being] the Noun for creation.[32]

This section moves from a categorization of the parts of mystic speech to a treatment of how particles bring about certain cases and moods in nouns and verbs. This latter topic, when applied in Sufi grammar, concerns the highly significant Islamic theological topos of the attributes of God, a topic that here culminates in attributing to God a description as "the Noun" or "the Name," both of which are valid English renderings of the Arabic word that Qushayrī uses, *al-ism*. Qushayrī's own text, *Sharḥ asmāʾ Allāh al-ḥusnā*, as we discovered in the previous chapter, illuminates the significance of the attributes of God in classical Sufi discourse as well as his ascription of "the Name" to God here in *The Grammar of Hearts*.

Qushayrī considers separately the effects that particles have on nouns and on verbs. From each, he ponders the nature of God and God's attributes. From the point of view of linguistic nouns, Qushayrī considers God in Godself. Since knowledge (*ʿilm*) abides in the divine nature, the name "the Knower," (*al-ʿĀlim*) applies to God. This word "knower" is simply the active participle derived from the same verbal root, which means knowledge (*ʿ-l-m*). The name "Knower" or the superlative form, "All-Knowing," *al-ʿAlīm*, is in some sense necessarily applied to God, since God does indeed possess knowledge. By naming two other qualities that God possesses—namely, power and life—Qushayrī indicates that the same reasoning can be used for all the other names of God, such as the All-Powerful (*al-Qādir*) and the Living (*al-Ḥayy*).

From the point of view of *afʿāl*, which means both "deeds" and "verbs," Qushayrī considers God's actions. These actions occur in creation in accord with certain attributes of God, such as His mercy, love, compassion, power, life, and knowledge. In a sense, these attributes are primary, and the actions of God flow from God's inherent being. God does as God is. Consequently, it is most appropriate to understand God in relation to the created universe as the "Noun," rather than a verb or a particle. God's being is primary. God's actions, including his very act of creating creation (*al-khalq*), come from Godself. In this way, Qushayrī speculates that as certain particles necessitate for verbs the designation "subjunctive" or "jussive," the primacy of God's attributes in Himself over God's actions necessitate for Him the designation of being "the Noun for creation."

The very brief section 3 revisits the matter of the parts of mystic speech, but this time from the perspective of meaningful communication, *ifāda*, plural: *fawāʾid*, a term that outside of the field of grammar can mean "benefit" or "use":

> The noun in the grammar of the heart is what the predicate is about in the speech of God. The verb is what the predicate is in a person's talk with God. Particles are the linkages by means of which the meaningful messages [*fawā᾽id*] of the speech of the heart are completed.[33]

At the level of the sentence, the Noun or the Name—namely, God—is the subject of mystic speech. "The address of God" or "the speech of God" reveals something about this Noun. The genitive "of God" in this noun construct could be read either as a subjective or objective genitive—that is to say, the speech of God intended by the phrase could either be the speech that God utters or it could be the speech that a "servant" (*ʿabd*) utters in addressing God. The verb, which was defined previously as "what is from God," is here identified as the predicate of the sentences of this mystic speech that occurs between servants and the True One. The phrasing in this part of the sentence indicates that, in relation to the verb, the speech under consideration is speech uttered by the servant and directed to God. The part of speech called in Arabic "particles" (*ḥurūf*) Qushayrī linked in the previous sentence to the grammatical determination that they impose upon the other two categories of words. Here he links them to the notion of the meaningful messages or benefits of heart-talk, a notion that he elaborates in the following section:

> Meaningful [*mufīd*] speech is what consists of noun and noun or verb and noun. Any other divisions besides these are not meaningful.
>
> In the grammar of the heart, there is also beneficial [*mufīd*] and non-beneficial. The non-beneficial is what is not of God. The beneficial is what is heard from God or that with which God is addressed. Anything besides these is ungrammatical language.
>
> It is said: The beneficial either points to God's self or alludes to His attributes or it is an expression about what he has wrought. . . . This is the comprehensive division of all meanings, no category of [mystic] speech which is beneficial deviates from this.[34]

Exploiting multiple meanings of the Arabic root (*f-y-d*), this section starts with the technical grammatical meaning, which refers to meaningful, grammatical utterances in contrast to ungrammatical nonsense (*laghw*). Meaningful speech, then, means syntactically sound utterances as either being nominal sentences "noun and noun" or verbal sentences "verb and noun." These two standard kinds of sentence structures in classical Arabic syntax convey complete and meaningful messages. When turning to "mystic speech"—as we are calling divine-human intercourse—Qushayrī puts into play not only this meaning of *mufīd* as "meaningful" or "grammatically correct," but also the nontechnical sense of "beneficial" and "useful." For mystic speech, the factors determining whether an utterance is *mufīd* are not syntactical but rather pertain to who the participants in the communicative act are and what the communication is about. The first of these criteria concerns the origin and direction of the utterance. Meaningful or beneficial mystic speech either comes from God or is directed to God. As for the topical content of meaningful mystic speech, there are three categories: God's inner being, God's attributes, and what God has wrought, the "*maṣnūʿāt*." This term from the root *ṣ-n-ʿ* meaning "do," "make," "fabricate," and "design" is somewhat unusual in referring to the creatures that God has made. More common to refer to God as creator and to His creations is the root *kh-l-q*.

In section 5, Qushayrī progresses from a discussion of the grammatical concept of declinable and indeclinable words to another way of categorizing speech of the heart. Associated with the two new categories of mystic speech are several spiritual states—namely, expansion (*basṭ*), union (*jamʿ*), and separation (*farq*).

> Language is divided into declinable and indeclinable. The grammatical cases change the end of the word, according to the particular nature of the grammatical governor, into either vocalization or non-vocalization or elision. "Indeclinability" means that either vocalization or non-vocalization is inseparable from the end of the word.
>
> Speech of the heart is either with a word reserved for the calling of God to a halt [*tawqīf al-ḥaqq*] or it is a word in which God allows humankind to act freely [*taṣrīf al-khalq*]. The first of these is what you hear in your heart, and without any effort on your part, you halt at it. The second is what your [divine] Master whispers according to the requirement of what hint of joyful expansion [*basṭ*] you find in it. One of these two is a state of union [*jamʿ*], and the other is a state of separation [*farq*].[35]

Using the two contrasting ideas and rhyming phrases *tawqīf al-ḥaqq* and *taṣrīf al-khalq*, Qushayrī links to Sufism the two kinds of language, meaning those words whose endings change and those whose endings do not. From the point of view of the grammatical topic treated at the beginning of the section, "*tawqīf*" and "*taṣrīf*" can be construed as referring respectively to pronouncing words without their word endings and to the conjugation of verbs. *Tawqīf* always yields the same pronunciation of a word through not saying the final vowel, while *taṣrīf* means changing a word's form according to its circumstances. Outside of a technical grammatical context, *taṣrīf* means "alteration" or "change." It also conveys the sense of acting independently or without restriction. While somewhat different from the grammatical concepts of declinable and indeclinable, the grammatical meanings of these two words refer in their own way to changing and unchanging. At first this section seems to associate the "stopping" or "standing still" with the unchanging True One (*tawqīf al-ḥaqq*) and the shifting of forms with mutable humankind (*taṣrīf al-khalq*). However, as we read further, Qushayrī explains that these ideas both have to do with spiritual states that a Sufi goes through. "The first of these is what you hear in your heart and [what] you stop (*taqif*) at without exerting yourself at all." Using a verb form derived from the same root as *tawqīf*, Qushayrī begins to show that it is the person who comes to a standstill when involved in this first kind of heart-speech. God causes the person to stop, to be seized. In the second kind of heart-speech, God allows "*taṣrīf*" of the human creature. The term now entails ideas of the spiritual aspirant shifting, changing, and "conjugating" like a verb.

Qushayrī goes on to explain when and how these two kinds of mystic speech come to the Sufi. The first category of mystic speech, the analogue of indeclinable words, comes to humankind through complete receptivity. It is "what you hear in your heart, and without any effort on your part, you halt at it." This is the spiritual state of unification, *jamʿ*, which Qushayrī describes in his *Risāla* as distinct from the spiritual state of separation, *farq*. While *farq* is related to human deeds, *jamʿ* is more radically theocentric.

The Sufi acquires the state of *farq* or "separation" through worshipful servitude. Called in Arabic "*ʿubūdiyya*," this is both the quality of being a servant of God and of simply being a human being. In the state of *farq*, God "allows a person to continue to take notice of his acts of obedience and disobedience."[36] Rather than focusing on God directly, a person in this state of "separation" focuses on his or her own deeds in relation to God. Certain kinds of prayer put a person in the state of *farq*: "When the servant of God addresses Him—may He be exalted—in his intimate conversation with him as a beggar, a supplicant, a lauder, a giver of thanks, a renouncer [of evil deeds], or a humble beseecher, he places himself in the position of separation."[37] On the other hand, *jamʿ* or "unification" is "everything that comes from the Real"[38]—that is, from God. Rather than paying attention to our own deeds or misdeeds, in the state of *jamʿ* we behold only God's deeds. Centuries after Qushayrī, in his glossary of Sufi technical terms ʿAbd al-Razzāq al-Qāshānī defines *jamʿ* as "*shuhūd al-ḥaqq bi-lā khalq*"—that is, "beholding the True One to the exclusion of creation."[39] Kinds of prayer in which God takes the lead and the person is receptive bring about the state of unitive *jamʿ* in the one praying:

> And when [the spiritual aspirant] listens in his inner self [*bi-sirrihī*] to what his Lord tells him [*yunājīhī*] and hears in his heart what God imparts to him by calling upon him [*nādāhu*], admonishing him [*nājāhu*], instructing him, or intimating [something] to his heart and willing him to follow [this intimation], [the spiritual aspirant] finds himself under the sign of unification [*jamʿ*].[40]

This state of unification, then, *jamʿ*, entails the kind of mystic speech that God pours into your heart and causes you to be seized, listening, without exertion or effort. This type of mystic speech is the analogue of indeclinable words and comes from the unchanging God.

On the other hand, the mystic speech that the spiritual state of separation or *farq* entails is the analogue of declinable words, which change their form according to grammatical circumstance. Accordingly, this sort of mystic speech "God whispers [to you] according to the requirements of the indication of *basṭ* or expansion that you find in it." Like declinable words, this kind of mystic speech varies according to circumstance. In accordance with what the person's spiritual expansion requires, God "conjugates" the heart talk (*nuṭq al-qalb*) that that spiritual aspirant hears. With this second kind of mystic speech, the God who is Ultimate Reality, *al-Ḥaqq*, meets the worshipful servant where she or he is. This second kind of heart-talk thus fits with the more anthropocentric state of *farq* that Qushayrī describes in the *Risāla*. Aspirants in this state bring fully to mind their humanity, and God permits their full freedom of action. In the state of *farq*, one's intercourse with the divine heightens awareness of oneself and one's behavior and encourages active striving.

This expansive *basṭ* is a spiritual state that Qushayrī also treats in his *Risāla* in a section not long before the section on *farq* and *jamʿ*.[41] The state of *basṭ* is paired with *qabḍ*, meaning "contraction," and these two states are together related to another pair of spiritual conditions, *rajā᾿*, "hope," and *khawf*, "fear." While novice Sufis focus on the future and thus experience *rajā᾿* and *khawf*, more advanced wayfarers focus on the present moment and so instead undergo *basṭ* and *qabḍ*.

Contraction [*qabḍ*] is caused by an experience that descends upon one's heart. It may imply censure or indicate that one is liable for chastisement. As a result, contraction enters the heart and it contracts. When however, an experience is caused by closeness or by [God's] turning [to the servant] with gentleness and hospitality, then what enters the heart is expansion [*basṭ*]. In general, one's contraction corresponds to one's expansion and one's expansion to one's contraction.[42]

Putting this understanding of the spiritual state of *basṭ* together with Qushayrī's statement that this second type of mystic speech "God whispers [to you] according to the requirements of the indication of *basṭ* you find in it," we can perhaps venture a fuller interpretation of the passage: as the spiritual wayfarer performs acts of servitude, through worshipping God and attending carefully to his or her own obedience and disobedience, God speaks softly and confidentially into the wayfarer's heart this kind of mystic speech as a gesture of "gentleness and hospitality" in recognition of the pious servant's exertions.

While section 5, on the declinable and indeclinable, treats two different kinds of mystic speech, section 6, on the grammatical cases or "*al-iʿrāb*," treats motions of the heart and the four kinds of grammatical cases. We started the present chapter with an excerpt from section 6. As noted previously, the Arabic cases include something of both what the Greco-Latin grammatical tradition calls the "cases" of nouns and the "moods" of verbs.

There are four kinds of grammatical case: raising [*al-rafʿ*], rectification [*al-naṣb*], diminution [*al-khafḍ*], and curtailing [*al-jazm*]. Hearts likewise have these categories.[43]

He goes on to treat these four categories in order, with gradually shorter elaborations as he proceeds from "raising" to "curtailing." The first of these, called by the single term "*al-rafʿ*," roughly corresponds to the two categories that in the Greco-Latin grammatical tradition we call the "nominative case" and the "indicative mood." The Arabic term also carries in nongrammatical contexts the meaning of lifting and raising as well as elimination and removal. Qushayrī's mystical application of this term as "the raising of hearts" primarily concerns otherworldliness.

As for the nominative [raising] of hearts, it could be that you raise your heart above the world, which is characteristic of the ascetics [*al-zuhhād*]. It could also be that you raise your heart above following lusts and desires, which is characteristic of devotees [*al-ʿibbād*] and those who practice devotions [*al-awrād*] and pious exertion. It could be that you raise your heart above yourself, and that you are of the conviction that nothing comes from you, and this is characteristic of the contrite and the masters of humility and spiritual poverty.

> It could also be by raising the heart to God and purifying it from its attention to the created world.
>
> It could also be by raising your hand away from the forbidden, and then the lifting of whatever adherence to humankind you harbor. Next you raise your hand to God with a petition of needs, and then you do away with your needs amidst the strengthening of love, so that you may exist through God for God, wiping away whatever is not God.[44]

The idea of lifting or raising is interpreted here in two directions: up away from the world and up toward God. Lusts and earthly desires are low; prayerful devotions raise the human being up to God. This theme of renunciation of the world and focus on God occasions the mention of two pious movements, the *zuhhād*, meaning renunciants or ascetics, and the *ʿibbād*, meaning worshippers or devotees.[45] The first were known especially for their ascetic discipline and the second for their piety. As the Sufism of Baghdad spread and became known, these and other such groups of pious renunciants eventually became folded into the single category of Sufi.[46]

The Arabic grammatical term that encompasses the Greco-Latin analogues of the accusative case and the subjunctive mood, *al-naṣb*, when taken out of the grammatical context, means setting up, putting up. Another form from the same root, *al-intiṣāb*, is similarly "righting," "raising." Qushayrī plays off of this semantic range to elicit a spiritual meaning centered around the kind of spiritual discipline that leads to serene indifference:

> As for the accusative [*al-naṣb*, rectification] of hearts, it could be the righting of the body in order to bring it into line, and thereupon the righting of the heart in the place of witnessing by the goodly bowing of one's head in silence, and furthermore the righting of the inmost soul through the attribute of solitude and purification from moments of disunion.
>
> The human being is at times made right [*manṣūb*] for the course of the verdict of destiny without having any choice, or having any preference in what [fate] is before him, or any preoccupation from him about

> it, neither when a feeling of burdensomeness takes over him, nor when reception awaits him, nor when haste threatens him.
>
> These people have in themselves neither luck nor lot [*naṣīb*]. The True One makes their lot His Truth, rather than their luck, since they are the succor of creation, standing firm for the True One in the Truth.[47]

Earlier in the chapter, we considered Qushayrī's treatment of the term *khafḍ*, which corresponds to the Greco-Latin genitive. The term in Arabic literally means "diminishment," "lowering," and "lessening," and so Qushayrī connects it to humility.

The last grammatical case that Qushayrī treats is "*al-jazm*," called in English the "apocopate." This case corresponds roughly to the Greco-Latin "jussive mood" of verbs. Since in this form, Arabic verbs generally end with the silent "*sukūn*" marking rather than a vowel, the technical grammatical meaning of this term is more clearly and directly related to the general sense of the word "*al-jazm*," which is "cutting off" or "curtailment." Grammatical endings in *al-jazm* do indeed seem cut off. *Al-jazm* marks absence. Qushayrī's application of this concept to the mystic heart concerns the virtue of self-denial:

> As for the apocopate [clipping] of hearts, clipping means cutting so it could be the curtailing of attachments, as well as tranquility under the course of the ordinances of truth without transgressing any single aspect of the comportment [required by] religious law.
>
> Clipping of hearts could also be cutting them off from the dangers of desires, for desires and ultimate meaning are opponents, so it cuts the necks of demands, desires and choices with the swords of despair, then it comes to rest through God for God with God, for if it returns to striving for illicit permissions, the [Sufi] Path bears witness against it of its polytheism and apostasy.[48]

This rather long sixth section nicely represents the allegorical possibilities of Qushayrī's hybrid genre. Through his elaboration of multiple meanings for each of these grammatical categories, Qushayrī invests the grammatical concept of *al-iʿrāb* with a new dimension of meaning—namely, spiritual virtues.

While section 6 takes four grammatical cases to expound on four virtuous movements of the Sufi heart, section 7 explores four different types of people using the four possible terminal vocalizations for indeclinable words. First Qushayrī accords these four vocalizations with a spiritual meaning by playing off the nongrammatical semantic value of the names of the vocalizations:

> There are four kinds of indeclinable terminal vocalizations in grammar: /u/ vocalization [*ḍamma*, gathering], /a/ vocalization [*fatḥa*, opening], /i/ vocalization [*kasra*, brokenness], and non-vocalization [*sukūn*, silence]. The esoteric meanings on the tongue of the people of ultimate realities have the following types:
>
> Enclosing [*ḍamm*] the inmost secrets entails defending them from others. The opening [*fatḥa*] of hearts is purifying them from cares through revelations of divine secrets. The breaking [*kasra*] of hearts entails their prostrations upon unexpected visions and surprise encounters. The silence [*sukūn*] of esoteric matters is their falling silent before the True One through the quality of continual intimacy throughout the totality of various spiritual states.[49]

The meanings of these four vocalizations all have to do with positive aspects of the experience of a Sufi receiving divine revelations and encountering God. The sacred knowledge thus received may not be shared with those who are not prepared for it, thus the Sufi defends these truths from others by keeping it "wrapped up" in himself. Perhaps referring to the rounding of the lips necessary to vocalize /u/, this word *ḍamma* also means "wrap," "enclose," and "gather." As in Ibn ʿArabī's *Futūḥāt makkiyya* (a title translated in English as *The Meccan Revelations*), the word *fatḥa*, in grammar the name of the /a/ vocalization, derives from the root *f-t-ḥ* meaning "opening," a metaphoric expression common in Sufi discourse to refer to divine revelation. The name of the /i/ vocalization, "*kasra*," means "breaking," and so Qushayrī relates it to the humility with which a heart reacts when God suddenly comes upon it. Using the term "*sujūd*," from which mosques take their Arabic name, Qushayrī calls this "breaking" of hearts "prostration," as when a Muslim praying puts her or his face completely to the floor in ritual prayer. Finally, "*sukūn*," the vocalization that is nonvocalization, is the silence that is the only adequate utterance in the face of true intimacy with God across the vagaries of spiritual moods.

After this introduction to the four desinences, our Sufi master goes into greater depth, expounding on the fate and character of four types of human characters and destinies associated with words that end invariably in one of these terminal vocalizations. Before getting to these four types of person, however, Qushayrī shifts from the religious topic of aspects of encountering God to the various components of a human being's character and destiny, exploiting the grammatical distinction between words that change their endings and those that do not:

> In the declinable and the indeclinable there are other symbolic meanings.
>
> The declinable word changes its desinence through the difference of grammatical operators, while the indeclinable is what occurs with only a single mark. Just so among the attributes of servants there are those that accept change and influence. These are what are grouped together by the person's behavior and mannerism.
>
> There are also those that do not accept transformation or substitution, and they are the attributes of the person's character imposed on him by the True One, may he be praised. This is according to those graces that God has previously given the person and is also according to the portions that God has previously ordained for the person.[50]

The indelible aspects of a person comprise certain features of a person's character that God imposes on him, plus the graces that God has granted him and the portion or lot that God has given him. These are structural features of a human life, unchanging and unchangeable no matter the circumstances, like the final vocalization of indeclinable words. Happiness in life is contingent on accepting rather than resisting these fated aspects of ourselves that God has ordained for us:

> Whoever is miserable has expressed resistance to His decree. His toil did not benefit him, nor his pain. Whoever is happy accepts God's decree, and thus his sin has not excluded him from his ordained state of happiness.[51]

On the other hand, other aspects of a human being are mutable: particularly how a person chooses to act. Such behaviors can change and be influenced by other outside factors (*ʿawāmil*), like the desinence of declinable words that changes according to the grammatical operators (also called *ʿawāmil*) that act on them.

In returning to the four terminal vocalizations and considering the types of people who are "indeclinable" in their adherence to one of these vocalizations, Qushayrī begins with "*kasr*," breaking. This type of person is the most miserable of the four:

> Among the types of indeclinability are what are built upon breaking [*kasr*]. The member of this category is always broken. His brokenness

> never heals nor does his poverty ever change, nor his harm ever cease. His situation is never made right in any way. His morning is affliction, and his evening is misery. His good fortune is reversed, and his luck is little. His star is ill-fated, and his aim is turned back on him. If he enters a river to drink, its water recedes, and if he finds pearls, after just a little while he loses them.[52]

The person of the "*fatḥ*" type, on the other hand, lives a charmed life.

> There are those indeclinable ones who are built on opening [*fatḥ*]. That person's comfort does not cease, and he is permanently settled. His fragrance wafts from afar,[53] and he delights in the company of his drinking companion, and his drink does not get roiled by his absence. He does not change his Path on account of being veiled from the divine Light for a long time. The hall has an empty place for him even if he tarries in arriving. The sun is a shadow next to the gleaming of his light, and the full moon turns shy when he appears unexpectedly.[54]

Whether the openings of divine revelation shed light upon him, or whether he is veiled from the favor of such light, this type of person is steadfast in his way, steady in his spiritual path. Even a long period of spiritual desolation does not dissuade him from his spiritual commitments and convictions. Humorous touches mark these two last depictions. The ill-fated man is so unlucky that when he wades into a river to drink, it dries up, and even if he happens upon a pearl, he only loses it soon thereafter. The fortunate man, by contrast, is so bright in the light he receives from the Lord that the sun is a mere shadow by comparison to such a person, and the moon so dim that it is embarrassed if he runs into such a man.

The next type of person is, however, perhaps even closer to God.[55] A sort of holy fool, the ones built on guarding or enclosing [*ḍamm*] the divine secrets in themselves are relieved of normal responsibilities and obligations. They have completely renounced their discursive rationality and rely totally on God. Like the very young, the mentally ill, and those of very low intelligence, these holy fools are not treated in Islamic law as competent adults. The reactions they receive from the common folk, however, include blame and confusion, especially for the puzzling utterances that they sometimes make.

The final type of person is hapless and ineffectual. Whereas the word for nonvocalization, "*sukūn*," Qushayrī previously interpreted quite positively as the "silence" that a Sufi keeps when possessing continual intimacy with God, here Qushayrī takes it to mean unmoving and unable to make progress.

> Then there are those indeclinable ones built on silence [*sukūn*]. That person is planted in his place, turned away from his intent. He does not profit from his diligence, and his good fortune does not make him happy. Life seems long to him. Occurrences take place continuously to him. From his first state to his final end, he never gets past *Sūrat al-Ikhlāṣ* [Q 112]. He never gets out of a situation of impairment.[56]

Utterly passive, such a person cannot even go deep in prayer. He is interrupted even when reciting some of the shortest of Qur'anic sections, such as "Sincerity," Sūra 112. With that, the section ends with a stoic observation about human fates: "Such are the standings: different types, varied roles."

Section 8 of *The Grammar of Hearts* is comparatively simple and centers on the Arabic grammatical terms for "definite" and "indefinite" nouns and the resonance of these terms with the Sufi idea of gnosis.[57] The conceptual link here between the ideas from Arabic grammar and Islamic spirituality come primarily from the idea of knowledge, whose triliteral root "*ʿ-r-f*" refers not only to gnosis or esoteric knowledge (*ʿirfān*) but also to the grammatical quality of definiteness ("*maʿrifa*"), in the sense related to the so-called "definite article"—that is, the word "the" in English and the prefix "*al-*" in Arabic.

Qushayrī refers first to the two possible categories for nouns with regard to their definiteness, and then he proceeds to claim that in humanity there are likewise two such categories. Whether speaking of nouns or human beings, the "unknown," the "indefinite," becomes "*maʿrūf*," "known," "definite." For the noun there is no higher degree than to reach the definite, and for the human person there is no higher degree to reach than mystical knowledge, "*ʿirfān*." A cryptic saying of the wise is then given to attest to gnosis as the highest rank possible for the human creature: "The one who returned only returned from the path, but as for the one who arrived, he did not return." Remembering that the destination for the Sufi is God, we can understand the meaning of this dictum to be that the person who fully arrives at mystical union with God never leaves such a state, while if a spiritual wayfarer comes back to abide among other people, his return was merely a return from the spiritual path that he undertook, not a return from the destination for which he was aiming. Reaching God, the wayfarer has nothing to come back to.

Sections 9 and 10 are also rather straightforward. Both deal with the dual form of nouns, a form constructed by adding two letters to the end of a word. Pointing out that it is ungrammatical either to put this dual word ending onto the word "*wāḥid*," "one," or to remove the dual marker from the word "*ithnān*," "two," Qushayrī makes connections to the nature of God as ultimately One and to that of animals, which are created to be coupled.

> The symbolic expression from this is that the word "one" has no dual form, and the word "two" has no singular [i.e., non-dual form], for it is not said of "one," "two ones," or from "two," "a single two." This is absurd implicitly.
>
> Likewise, it is impossible that He who is the One in Ultimate Reality abandon His Oneness, in implication or in being. Moreover, it is absurd implicitly that the one who correctly is two turn into an individual without having a second. God the Exalted said: "We created everything in pairs, so that perhaps you may take heed." (Q 51:49)[58]

Qushayrī thus begins his spiritual treatment of the grammatical dual with the principle of the oneness of God, called in Islamic theology "*tawḥīd*." Reflected in the first half of the basic declaration of faith, the *shahāda*—"There is no God but God"—*tawḥīd* is both a rejection of polytheism and idolatry and an affirmation of God as undivided, unchanging, and eternal. Citing a section of the Qur'an where the Noah story is referenced, Qushayrī argues that what has been created to have a mate can no more become radically singular than God can cast off His Oneness.

The dual represents several changes, such as the change from the singular form to the dual form and the change from the nominative *-āni* dual ending to the oblique *-ayni* version of that ending. For Qushayrī, these morphological changes correspond to changes in spiritual states.

> At one point it is nominative with the letter *alif*, and at another it is accusative or genitive with the letter *yā'*. Likewise, the servant does not remain in his heart renunciant and unattached as when in the most celestial of his qualities, for if an attachment of close relations occurs, he falls into spiritual inconstancy [*talwīn*] again and again.[59]

When a Sufi loses focus on God and forms a worldly attachment, he falls from the stable state of being grounded in "*tamkīn*" to the inconstancy of "*talwīn*," a pair of terms that Qushayrī explains in his *Risāla*.[60] The very fact that a noun can fall into a state of change from its initial singular state to a dual state is indicative of this potential for a Sufi to lose the unattached, God-centered state:

> The singular noun does not remain singular, for its quality [of being singular] is in its letters. So, if it includes another [letter] in it such that it becomes a dual, it falls into a state of change.[61]

This spiritually dual state, brought on by worldly attachment, is always a kind of fallen state.

> As the *nūn* of the dual is always vocalized with /i/ [*maksūra*], so the one who possesses spiritual attachments is broken [*maksūr*] of wing, and utterly casts himself about.[62]

A Sufi can only undergo a single spiritual state at any one time. Naming four such states, which are also described in the *Risāla*, Qushayrī teaches that when a spiritual state overcomes someone, the opposite of that state diminishes:

> Just so, the quality of the gnostic [*al-ʿārif*]: if any characteristic of his esoteric knowledge [*maʿrifa*] is dominant in him, then the quality that is its counterpart is obscure and hidden.
>
> So, if what is dominant in him is spiritual contraction [*qabḍ*], then his spiritual expansion [*basṭ*] is concealed. But if what is dominant in him is expansion [*basṭ*], then his contraction [*qabḍ*] is hidden. And if what is dominant in him is intimacy, then so on with dread as its counterpart. If dread is dominant in him, then so on with intimacy as its counterpart. And so forth in this way with the whole lot of attributes.[63]

This spiritual reality of oppositional pairs of spiritual states Qushayrī connects to certain linguistic phenomena involving the letter *nūn*. He specifically refers to the dropping of the letter *nūn* from the dual marker when the dual-form word is the first element in a noun construct pair, called an *iḍāfa* in Arabic grammar. Claiming that this dual *nūn* is the counterpart of the phenomenon of nunnation, in which a *nūn* sound is added to certain non-dual indefinite nouns, Qushayrī explains that this nunnation substitute, the *nūn* of the dual word ending, cannot coincide with the word being the first element of a noun construct. First elements of a noun construct are by definition definite, while nunnation marks indefiniteness.

> The *nūn* of the dual is dropped in a noun construct [*iḍāfa*], because it is in the place of nunnation in the singular. The nunnation and the noun

> construct are two indications for definiteness [*maʿrifa*], so they do not occur together.[64]

A question that logically arises from Qushayrī's grammatical explanation in this passage is: if the dual *nūn* is a marker of indefiniteness, why do dual nouns still retain their *nūn* when made definite by the definite article "*al-*"? Pursuing this kind of logical question on a grammatical topic would not serve Qushayrī's rhetorical purpose, so he does not mention it. His focus is on spiritual realities, not grammatical lessons.

The next two sections move from the grammatical topic of the dual to the plural of nouns, particularly the concepts of sound plurals that are formed by merely adding a suffix to the singular and of broken plurals in which the internal structure of the singular noun form is reconfigured through various combinations of prefixes, infixes, and suffixes. The grammatical word for "plural" is the same as the Sufi term for "mystical union." This word, "*jamʿ*," is the fundamental subject of these sections. In both the grammatical and the Sufi realms, there are two types of *jamʿ*:

> There are two kinds of plural [*jamʿ*]: sound plural and broken plural, and likewise in symbolic expression: What the Sufis call mystical union [*jamʿ*] are of two sorts:
>
> There is the mystical union whose possessor is faultless. This is the one who observes the religious law in the time when mystical union has come over him.
>
> There is also the mystical union in which the possessor's soundness is broken. This is the one who does not observe the proper conduct [*ādāb*] of spiritual knowledge in line with what he is called to [do].[65]

However, whereas both types of linguistic *jamʿ* are grammatically sound, only one kind of mystical *jamʿ* is correct.

> The symbolic meaning is that just as the sound plural [*jamʿ al-salāma*] [in language] is where the linguistic form of the singular stays intact. Similarly, the sound union [*jamʿ salāma*] of this [Sufi] Path is where one's mind is unimpaired by specious doubt, and one's conduct is unimpaired by illegitimate innovation, and one's soul from carnal desire, and one's heart from heedlessness and backbiting, and one's inmost self from any veil of separation.
>
> The broken plural is where the linguistic form of the singular breaks apart. Likewise the person who has been possessed by the mystical union

of the masses is the one who has abandoned the junctions of truth and strayed from the boundaries of revealed law.[66]

In his description of the sound and unsound kinds of mystical union, we see Qushayrī's commitments to orthodoxy appear. As part of his larger objective of legitimizing Sufism as an authentic Islamic science, Qushayrī argued vociferously that Sufis were bound by the strictures of religious obligation as much as any other Muslim. Reacting against the renunciants who claimed that their spiritual accomplishments gave them license to ignore certain religious obligations, Qushayrī's spiritual vision encompassed both adherence to the outer meaning of revelation and insight into inner meanings of the same. The *ẓāhir* or outer meanings were not superseded by the inner or *bāṭin* meanings. In fact, in addition to the standards of righteous conduct operative on all Muslims, Sufis had their own *adab* (plural, *ādāb*) or rules of conduct that pertained to their own special circumstances as they moved through various aspects of the spiritual life. The distinguishing feature of those whose union with God is sound is that they observe the precepts of the revealed law, *sharīʿa*, and of Sufi *adab*, while those whose union is broken do not.

Just as in section 10 the change from singular to dual was related to "*talwīn*," "spiritual inconstancy," so here is the change from singular to plural related to the changes of spiritual condition:

The symbolic meaning is that if a noun changes to the plural state, an inconstancy and a change occur, again and again, from excess and dearth, from exchanging and endowing. Just so the standing of the possessor of mystical union [*jamʿ*] passes from his ego. At one moment, the True One appears in the valleys of intimacy. At another moment, He rectifies him in the state of distancing. It is an erasure of choice: "and he counts them awake though they are asleep." (Qur᾽ān, Sūrat al-Kahf, 18)[67]

Qushayrī then exemplifies this ebbing and flowing of human existence by relating traditions about the Sufi master al-Shiblī and about the Prophet:[68]

One day al-Shiblī came out in shabby clothes and was told as much, to which he responded:

"For one day you see us in silk that we have drawn / and one day you see us in iron morose // and one day you see us when we are kneading the sopped bread / and one day you see us eating dry bread."

And the Prophet, peace be upon him, once said:

"Indeed, I am not like one of you, for I dwelled with my Lord who gave me to eat and to drink."

And once he said: "I am the son of a woman who eats jerked meat."

At one point he pronounced judgment on ten men [that they would reach] heaven, and at another point he said: "Indeed there is a seal on my heart."[69]

Whether it is our garb or our source of nourishment or our degree of spiritual insight, human beings—even the Prophet himself—undergo changes from high to low and back again.

Qushayrī closes the section by considering the dichotomy between sound and broken plurals from a different angle. Whereas sound plurals follow a single and simple paradigm, there is a great variety among broken plurals. Similarly, among Sufi masters there are on the one hand those who even at an advanced stage of spiritual maturity retain their quality of knowledge, and on the other hand there are those who are eccentric or even idiosyncratic. Such people are persecuted and ostracized, though others cannot know how close to God these strange types in fact are.

The sound plural has a single model, and the broken plural has many types, different models, and problematic explanations.

Just so is the one who is preserved in his state of knowledge and he—in terms of his station—is the master of his time and the leader of his era. As for the one in the Sufi way who is a union of brokenness [*jamʿ taksīr*], he undergoes tribulation to which no one guides him, and is driven away to be among those who have no portion of the Sufi way, but he is hidden in the Truth itself, and he is at the very essence of nobility.

Whoever is on the side of this saying[70] is considered to be among the people charged with keeping religious obligations.

Their colors are of sundry sorts but / they are soaked with the same water from a single spring.

The person in this state is in a problematic state and a dubious moment. The general models do not fall upon his position, and penetrating appraisals do not oversee the ambiguities in his condition.[71]

This section brings to mind al-Ḥusayn al-Manṣūr al-Ḥallāj (d. 922).[72] By many accounts executed for his ecstatic utterances, most famously "I am the True One," al-Ḥallāj seems to be the kind of special type who did not fit the mold of the predictable and normative. The following section continues this line of thought regarding people who are unto their own by connecting them to a class of Arabic nouns that have a special way of declining through the grammatical cases.

> Among nouns there are some special nouns that are unique in their forms in that they form their nominative with *wāw*, their accusative with *alif*, and their genitive with *yāʾ*. They are six nouns: your father, your brother, your thing, your father-in-law, your mouth, and possessor of property.
>
> The symbolic meaning is that just so from among people there are those who are special in their types and matchless in their standings [*aḥkām*] from among those who are similar to them and who resemble them.
>
> One of them said: "Not every human being [*bashar*] is a joy [*bishr*]."
>
> In other words, his standing [*ḥukm*] is distinguished from any other standing and is distinctive from them in its meaning.[73]

With that, Qushayrī moves on from the grammatical topic of nouns to verbs, a topic on which he dwells for three sections.[74]

The concept of transitivity of verbs occasions mention of people through whom blessings from God extend beyond themselves to affect others, like so many verbal objects.

> There are two kinds of verbs: intransitive [*lāzim*] and transitive [*mutʿaddin*].
>
> In the symbolic meaning likewise there are two types of actions of the servant: obligatory [*lāzim*] and excessive [*mutʿaddin*]. The obligatory is the one whose blessings on its doer are restricted, and the excessive is the one whose benefits to the other are in excess.
>
> There are several types of transitive verb. Among them is the type that extends to a single object, the type that extends to two objects, and the type that extends to three objects.
>
> The symbolic meaning is that likewise the servant could exceed his blessings to the world of people, such that the Sufi masters said: "If one of the friends of God traverses a country then God forgives the people of that country."
>
> And immediately afterwards: "If a grief-stricken person in a community weeps, God forgives that community through that person's weeping."[75]

The following section treats a special subset of verb forms, those that end in *nūn* in their indicative and drop that *nūn* in their subjunctive and jussive forms.

> Five instances of verbs have their indicative with a letter *nūn* and their subjunctive and jussive by dropping the *nūn*: he does [*yafaʿlān*], she does [*tafaʿlān*], they do [*yafaʿlūn*], you (plural) do [*tafaʿlūn*], and you (feminine singular) do [*tafaʿlīn*].[76]

These five forms, which occur with the adherence of this additional letter, are compared to certain actions that only have a specified religious significance when some additional factor coincides with them.

> Likewise in symbolic expression: There are some actions that are special and only obtain in the presence of an additional element that occurs simultaneously with them. It is given them on the condition of a close associate that unites with them, like [the ritual of] throwing small stones at the devil, for example, is only a pious deed [*ṭāʿa*] during the *ḥajj*, just as hurrying between Ṣafā and Marwa is only a worshipful practice [*ʿibāda*] during *ḥajj* and *ʿumra*. Moreover, if someone makes a movement on account of a certain Sufi master or gnostic or saint, that person benefits from the [holy person] up until the ecstatic time of that master passes by and thereafter there is no value for the person.[77]

The pilgrimage to the holy cities of Mecca and Medina only has the status of *ḥajj* during a designated time of year, and numerous requirements must be fulfilled in order for such a voyage to have the status of either *ḥajj* or *ʿumra*. Unless these requirements are met, the component rituals to be performed do not count as a *ṭāʿa* (pious deed) or *ʿibāda* (worship).

Qushayrī's extensive consideration of various kinds of defective verbs and defective human actions is rather self-explanatory, linked as it is by the word that denotes both "verbs" and "actions": *afʿāl*.[78] The following short section on assimilation, with its religious connection to the Sufi concept of union with God, is likewise clear.[79] In fact, by this point in *The Grammar of Hearts*, Qushayrī's method begins to become clear to the reader. Many of the concepts central to the text have already appeared, and this exegesis has provided much of the background necessary to understand the world that the text opens up to us. Before leaving off exegesis, let us consider just a few more sections of the text to bring out a few other important features of Qushayrī's spiritual and theological outlook.

One such feature is the Qur'anic basis of Qushayrī's theological vocabulary and spiritual understanding. Putting aside explicit scriptural citations, let us consider the idea of following through on something good until the point of completion. Qushayrī works with this idea in sections 21–23 by linking it to the grammatical concept of the *mubtadaʾ*, the subject of a so-called nominal sentence, one of the two basic kinds of sentence structure in traditional grammatical analysis of Arabic syntax. His spiritual treatment of this grammatical concept focuses on the idea of completing a spiritual benefit. In this regard, these sections of *The Grammar of Hearts* echo such Qur'anic passages as in Sūrat Yūsuf (Q 12:6), where God tells Yūsuf (Joseph) that He will teach him the interpretation of dreams and thus "bring to completion His grace on you and on the family of Yaʿqūb [Jacob] just as He brought it to completion on your forefathers, Ibrāhīm and Isḥaq [Abraham and Isaac]." Similarly, in Sūrat al-Fatḥ (Q 48:2), God tells Muhammad that He has granted the Prophet victory in order to forgive his sins and "bring to completion His grace on you and guide you to the straight path."

Qushayrī thus begins section 21 by stating that once the subject of a nominal sentence (the *mubtadaʾ*) is announced, unless there is a predicate (a *khabr*)—that is, some "news" about that subject—the entire utterance is meaningless nonsense (*laghw*).[80] The Sufi master then ties this concept of what makes a complete sentence to the religio-ethical idea of spiritual perseverance and moral consistency.

The structure of this section is as follows:

1. First, a concise statement of the grammatical principle ("a *mubtadāʾ* without a *khabr* is nonsense") followed by a slight elaboration of the meaning of this principle, using five technical terms—namely, *mubtadāʾ/ibtidāʾ* (subject); *khabr* (predicate); *fāʾida* (meaning); *khaṭāb* (utterance); and *laghw* (nonsense).
2. Next, a religio-ethical variation of this principle, interweaving the same grammatical terms with a number of technical Sufi terms: *ʿirfān, al-ṭāʿāt, ḥāl*, rendered in my translation as gnosis, pious deeds, and state, respectively.
3. Last, three sayings regarding spiritual integrity that exemplify the religious meaning:
   a. a saying of the Prophet,
   b. a saying of "the common people"
   c. two lines of poetry.

In the grammatical version of the idea of completeness, Qushayrī uses only the verb *tamma*. In the religious variation of the idea, Qushayrī uses forms of *tamma* (*tatammu, tamām*) and two synonyms (*khawātīm, intihā᾽*). One effect of this interweaving of synonyms is that the simple and familiar grammatical terms *mubtadā᾽* (the subject of nominal sentence) and *fā᾽ida* (the meaning of a complete sentence) morph and change semantically such that from them spiritual meanings emerge. In Sufi vocabulary, *ibtidā᾽* and variations of the word can refer to the status of a Sufi novice, who has just begun his devotion to the spiritual life. Or, in a more general Sufi context, the term can refer to the less formal initiation of a spiritual practice or attitude or the onset of a spiritual state or *ḥāl*. The grammatical term *fā᾽ida*, in turn, is roughly the opposite of *laghw*, nonsense, and is thus the distinctive feature of a complete and meaningful sentence. In Sufism, Qushayrī explains that *fā᾽ida* can mean "spiritual benefit," the fruit of a God-given grace, or alternatively "spiritual utility," meaning that which helps the spiritual wayfarer advance in her journey toward God.

The three ensuing sayings each highlight a different nuance to the religio-ethical formulation of this section's central idea. The first, a Prophetic saying, emphasizes the idea of culmination. We only know the true nature of an event or phenomenon when it has come to its culmination. The second, a saying of "the common people," points out the significance of the central idea both when it pertains to the lot that God apportions each of us and when it pertains to a spiritual initiative undertaken by an individual. Steadfastness might be a word we could use to express the nuance here. In the third, the poetic lines, the emphasis is on consistency of action, specifically in interpersonal relations. Culmination, steadfastness, consistency—these are the spiritual nuances that Qushayrī brings out of the central theme of this section, which begins with the grammatical idea of what makes a complete sentence. This section, like many sections of *The Grammar of Hearts*, begins grammatically and very simply. From there as Qushayrī moves into spiritual territory, his teaching fans out to elaborate several nuanced variations on the central theme.

In section 22, Qushayrī begins with the spare grammatical assertion that several types of predicate or *khabr* exist and lead to a complete, meaningful sentence:

> The predicate of the subject of a nominal sentence [*mubtada᾽*] comes in several types, and the meaning [*fā᾽ida*] of the utterance occurs by way of any of them.
>
> Just so, if you follow a path to the True One or instigate some matter, do not set about doing what does not bring you to completion, whether

> your actions be the road of worship [*ʿibāda*] or the way of spiritual seeking [*ʾirāda*] or the way of knowledge [*ʿilm*] or the way of asceticism [*zuhd*], for the measure of a thing is in sticking to it. So if you instigate a matter, know that its benefit [*fāʾida*] is not complete except in bringing it to perfection.
>
> Divest yourself of the world, for verily you fell into the world and you were naked.[81]

Exploiting the semantic range of the word *fāʾida*, which in general refers to benefit or utility and which in the specific context of Arabic syntax refers to the meaning of a complete sentence, Qushayrī connects the various kinds of predicate that can bring a nominal sentence to completion with the various ways to God. Whether someone follows the scholarly path of knowledge, *ʿilm*, or one of the paths of pious renunciation that were prevalent during the formative age of Sufism[82]—namely, asceticism (*zuhd*), devotion (*ʿibāda*), or spiritual seeking (*irāda*)—what is important is following the path to its destination in God. Failing such perseverance, these spiritual paths bring no benefit, just as a subject without a predicate is only a sentence fragment. The section culminates with a verse that exhorts complete renunciation of the world. Taking just a few steps toward asceticism is not enough. Since we were born into the world naked and bare, detaching ourselves fully from worldly concerns is entirely in line with our human nature. Indeed, detachment is our destiny. Qushayrī's spiritual teaching in these sections thus exhorts the seeker to follow God's way, bringing to completion what goodness he has begun.

Besides his being thoroughly grounded in Qur'anic teachings, another aspect of Qushayrī's intellectual profile that comes out in *The Grammar of Hearts* but that we have not yet dwelled on is his expertise in *kalām*, the Islamic scholarly discipline of theological inquiry and discourse. Qushayrī was in particular an adherent and defender of Ashʿarī positions, which became dominant in Sunni orthodoxy. In sections 24 to 27, Qushayrī treats a famous and important theological issue that received enormous attention from Ashʿarī and other *mutakallimūn*—that is, the specialists in *kalām*. The issue in question was how to understand human agency and free will in light of the omnipotence of God.

The Ashʿarī position on this issue developed the idea of *kasb* or *iktisāb*, the "acquisition" of actions by the people who ostensibly carry them out. Ashʿarī *mutakallimūn* begin their treatment of this issue with an emphasis on God as Creator of all things, including human actions. Humans are not the ultimate creator or cause of their actions, but rather "acquire" their actions.[83] Another important term in these discussions was *fāʿil*, which is simply the active participle of one of the most basic Arabic words for "to make" or "do." *Fāʿil* in general means "doer," and in grammar it is a term that refers to the agent of a verbal action. It is therefore no surprise that Qushayrī connects his grammatical discussions of the *fāʿil* with theological treatment of the origination of actions and ultimate causality. In sections 24 to 27 Qushayrī treats these topics, also making use of the passive participle *mafʿūl*, which in everyday usage can mean the one acted upon and in grammar refers to the various kinds of grammatical object.

Section 27 is a particularly brilliant treatment of this infamously subtle and vexed theological question. Qushayrī takes as his starting point the grammatical phenomenon of passive verbs, whose subjects take the nominative case, just as true verbal subjects do.

> What has not named the agent of the action working on it [*fāʿil*] is nominative. Because it has not mentioned its verbal agent, the object of the verb settles in the place of the agent and takes on the word endings of the agent. For a verb must have some verbal agent, so we say, "Zayd was struck."[84]

Moving from the grammatical to the theological, Qushayrī makes the highly effective rhetorical move of grouping together all types of people who do not acknowledge God as the actual *fāʿil*, the Ultimate Doer or Actor or Agent.

> The symbolic meaning is that if people of heedlessness doubt the existence of the Creator, they trace actions to those who have been acted upon and they delude themselves that the object of action has reached the rank of the Actor and they ascribe entities to those people [who have been acted upon]. For the knowledge that these originated occurrences must all have an Originator [*muḥdith*] is a necessity.
>
> So then if they have not affirmed the Creator, they trace the verb back to the objects of the verb. One [of them] in his delusion puts natural disposition in the place of the Ultimate Doer, another the stars, another the celestial spheres, another fortune and luck, another the government, another destiny, another some Zayd, and still another some ʿAmr.[85]

Qushayrī thus puts theological adversaries of the Ashʿarī position on "acquisition" or "*kasb*," who attribute the causality of actions to a human being—here the proverbial Zayd or ʿAmr—into the same camp as pagans, astrologers, and polytheists who believe in the magic power of planets and stars or a divinized notion of luck.[86] Returning to the grammatical phenomenon with which he began the section, Qushayrī relates the sort of faux agency manifest in the subject of passive-voice verbs to the agency imputed to people and things who in any case are not subject but object, not *fāʿil* but *mafʿūl*.

> Just as the nominative case endings of the word that has not named its verbal agent are not in truth, so the delusion that the power of creative origination is from things [*mafʿūlāt*] and people [*mafʿūlīn*] that are acted upon has no truth to it.

This theological topic also comes up in section 44, examination of which will give some sense of the subtlety of the Ashʿarī position and how it strove to maintain something of human free will and agency. In that section, the grammatical starting point entails verbs that are known to occur in only a few specified forms.

> There are some verbs that do not conjugate fully, for example *niʿma* [which occurs only in the past singular and means "What a perfect . . . !" or "How wonderful . . . !"], *baʾisa* [which occurs only in the past tense and means "to be wretched"], *ʿasā* [which gives the sense of "perhaps" or "might" and also only occurs in the past tense]. Concerning this matter there are topics and rules in the science of grammar.[87]

Qushayrī relates these incomplete verbs to actions to which the Ashʿarī concept of acquisition (*kasb* or *iktisāb*) does not apply. Evidently, for Qushayrī, a human being is only the acquirer or *muktasab* of a given action if she or he acts freely in choosing to bring about that action. Certain actions happen to someone in such a way that Qushayrī excludes them from counting as instances of "acquisition." He gives the examples of the seeing and understanding that occur after someone chooses to open his or her eye and the understanding of what someone hears that occurs after the person chooses to listen:

> The symbolic meaning from this is that there are some actions that are not complete, in the sense that the servant does not have the power to act freely in it according to what he wants. Rather, some [actions] are by him and [others] on him.
>
> Examples of these actions are opening the eyelid and listening followed by comprehending—in other words, seeing and hearing. This is

> not the servant acquiring [*muktasab*], for if he listens and opens his eyelid, it is God who creates comprehension according to the typical course of events. So this action is lacking the nature of free action in it, since he by his power commands and prohibits, but the reward or the punishment happens to him.[88]

This nuanced discussion of a major topic from the discipline of *kalām* indicates Qushayrī's expertise in that field and highlights the presence of such systematic theological concepts in his *Grammar of Hearts*. While such academic theological topics do not often feature in this spiritual grammar, they are present enough to suggest a level of intellectual integration between the science of *taṣawwuf* (Sufism) and the science of *kalām* (discursive theology) on the part of Qushayrī.

While aporia in *The Grammar of Hearts* remain, through this reading Qushayrī's *modus operandi* in this spiritual grammar has become familiar. Though more arduous than Gerson's *Moralized Grammar*, reading *The Grammar of Hearts* with understanding is more within reach thanks to the prior experience of working through Gerson's primer.

Now that we have come to know both authors through examples of various genres and then have attended to the particular method, content, and background of their respective spiritual grammatical texts, in the final chapter of this study we will examine both spiritual grammars in more sustained and direct comparison with each other. The first fruits of this comparison will be a fuller articulation of the significance of the genre of spiritual grammar and of the theological visions imparted by the two examples at hand. Interpreting this genre and our authors' theological visions leads to the construction of a new theology of grammar for our time.

6 The Fruits of Comparison

CONSTRUCTING A THEOLOGY OF GRAMMAR

A theology of grammar is born from our reading of *The Grammar of Hearts* and *Moralized Grammar*. These queer texts violate the law of genre. They mix. They exceed expectations and traverse disciplines. Their mingling is creative and fruitful. Through their mixing a religious genre takes form. They crossbreed and generate saintly genders, molds for holy human being.

Weaving together the linguistic and the spiritual, these pedagogical texts reveal to the seeker the structures of the realities in which we abide. Ricoeur argues that "texts speak of possible worlds and of possible ways of orientating oneself in those worlds."[1] These spiritual grammars are in this sense paradigmatic.

Our retrieval of these weird works wrought by famed medieval masters assembles the scaffolding for constructing a contemporary theology of grammar for us here and now—Muslims, Christians, and others who risk reading vulnerably across religious traditions. Juxtaposing these two texts, we too are transgressing boundaries and mixing what is not to be mixed, the Islamic and the Christian. This comparative exercise bears its own fruit, a theology of grammar.

In this final chapter, our back-and-forth juxtapositions and comparisons accelerate and culminate in the fulfillment of their interpretive purpose. Appropriating one of Ricoeur's definitions of interpretation, the inquiry we have undertaken throughout this study has been "devoted to the power of [these two works] to project a world of [their] own and to initiate the hermeneutical circle between the apprehension of those projected worlds and the expansion of self-understanding in front of these novel worlds."[2] True to Ricoeur's theory, "the process of understanding a metaphor" has been "the key" for understanding the two texts in question here.[3] Ricoeur also turns this formula around: "from one other standpoint, it is the understanding of a work as a whole which gives the key to metaphor." Metaphor unlocks the whole; the whole unlocks metaphor. This study now completes the circle, revisiting and completing our understanding of the two texts and the metaphor that is key to both.

Though evoking the discipline of comparative theology throughout, the present text now begins its last theological gesture. Playing the role of a scholarly monograph—a more recent academic genre of discovery and contribution—this study makes multiple claims: to illuminate a genre previously in the shadows; to bring two odd texts from long ago into our contemporary horizon of understanding; and to begin the construction of a theology of grammar. This last chapter completes the fulfillment of these claims.

With one final act of commingling, our performance of reading these texts together brings them to life anew. Juxtaposed, their queer genre is strikingly apparent and newly comprehensible. The two texts inform each other. Spawned by this dual performance, a fuller image of the genre of spiritual grammar emerges. The theological significance of *The Grammar of Hearts* and *Moralized Grammar* is in their genre, and that genre in turn makes possible a new theology of grammar.

Comparative Textual Analysis of Excerpts

Let us consider excerpts from the two texts in juxtaposition.[4]

Jean Gerson, *Donatus moralizatus*	**ʿAbd al-Karīm al-Qushayrī, *Naḥw al-qulūb***
What is a verb? I respond: It is God's teaching [praeceptum Dei], namely, that we love each other. How many attributes belong to a verb? Seven. Which? Quality, conjugation, genus, number, form, tense, and person. [1] Of what quality? Plainly of such a quality: Love your Lord God with your whole	**The subject of a nominal sentence requires a predicate.** The predicate is that by which the meaning of an utterance becomes complete. If the instigation of a nominal sentence occurs, then what completes the meaning of the utterance must also occur, or else the utterance is nonsense. Instigation works the same way when it comes to gnosis, for there must be what completes its

heart, with your whole mind, and your whole ability, Deuteronomy 6:5, and your neighbor as yourself, Romans 13.9.

[2] Of what conjugation?

A complete one: because one part is of no value without another, for no one loves God who hates a neighbor, nor vice versa. Likewise, whoever breaks one of the teachings "becomes the guilty party with respect to all of it," as James said (James 2:10) And thus it is necessary that they all be observed in conjunction.

[3] Of what genus?

Active, because it behooves us to carry it out by action, if we would like to observe it, because "those who hear the law will not be justified before God but rather those who do it" (Romans 2:13).

[4] Of what number?

Plural, because they are ten: To believe in God; not to swear by Him in a false manner; to celebrate the holidays; to honor parents; you shall not kill; you shall not steal; you shall not commit adultery; you shall not give false testimony; you shall not commit adultery; you shall not covet something that is not your own. Or, they are two, that is, love of God and of neighbor.

[5] Of what form?

Simple, because he should be served in the unity of a pure heart, that is, in love not in pretenses. For the fullness of the law is love, as Paul says. (Romans 13:10)

[6] Of what tense?

Present, because this teaching should be carried out in the meaning—namely, its continuation to the state of culmination. If, say, someone instigates pious deeds, then he must complete them. The Prophet, peace be upon him, said: "The essence of affairs is in their completion."

The common people pass around a similar saying: If someone receives from Him the instigation of a merciful destiny, then he must also in the end and final outcome receive favor and grace. If someone in the past has instigated the friendship of God, then he will surely be graciously bestowed with the favor of preserving it up to the end. On this point, it is said:

"Indeed, if a generous person loves you tenderly, he will downplay your ugly qualities and bring to prominence your beautiful qualities

And just so someone who is fed up [with you], if he wants to break off, he conceals your pleasant qualities and tells tales about how you used to do this or that."

present, that is, everyday that we
are in this life.

[7] Of what person?
First, second, and third, because I,
you, and he—we all should keep
this teaching. The Lord said, If
you wish to enter this life, observe
the commandments (Matthew
19:17)

On the left side of the page is the verb section from Gerson's *Moralized Grammar*, where the central theme of the section is the Decalogue. On the right side of the page is the twenty-first of the sixty sections of Qushayrī's *Grammar of Hearts*. As discussed previously, this section centers on a grammatical maxim regarding the syntax of nominal sentences: "The subject of a nominal sentence requires a predicate." A *mubtadaʾ* must have a *khabar*.

In considering these excerpts together, let us first identify connections between the two texts on a literary or theological level in terms of form or meaning. How could one of the two texts raise questions about or shed light on the other? Does the language of one echo in the other? Placed next to each other, what contrasts and differences between the two texts become apparent, highlighting the distinctiveness of each? The effort of noticing and establishing links between the texts will then lead to further insights into the theological character of each text separately and deepen our understanding of the genre of spiritual grammar that the two texts enact.

Semantically, the clearest link between the two excerpts revolves around the idea of completeness. While the main idea of the verb section of *Moralized Grammar* is the content of God's teachings to humanity, a secondary point is that these teachings are all integral to God's single *verbum*, which Gerson has us construe here to mean both God's "word" to us and God's "verb" for us: to love one another. The conjugation of the verb is "complete" or "total," since no one who hates a neighbor loves God or who hates God loves a neighbor. The commandments are all of a piece and must be observed "*conjunctim*"—that is, in conjunction with one another. Gerson strengthens this argument through a scriptural citation from the Letter of James (James 2:10) that "whoever breaks one of the teachings 'becomes the guilty party with respect to all of it.'" These parts of Gerson's verb section echo the main idea of the juxtaposed section of Qushayrī's text. In fact, though Gerson leaves the multiple meanings of *verbum* unacknowledged, at play in the section are the uses of the word both in the technical grammatical sense of "verb" and in a more common sense to refer either to any word or utterance or to an action or deed. Thus, for Gerson, the verb of spiritual grammar is verbal on multiple levels. It is at once an utterance of God to humanity that teaches us what to do and at the same time the action that is the active adherence to the instructional content of that divine utterance. After taking this full sense of "verb" into account, the resonance between the cited excerpts becomes only clearer.

Qushayrī meditates on the spiritual meaning of the grammatical reality that for an utterance to be meaningful, it must be complete. All the necessary pieces must be there, otherwise the sentence is meaningless babble. If the beginning of a linguistic utterance—that is, a *mubtadaʾ*—appears, then, unless a *khabar* (predicate) also appears, the speaker's attempt at uttering something meaningful is aborted, a failure. While the grammatical analysis of a linguistic utterance in Arabic into *mubtadaʾ* and *khabar* only applies to nominal sentences, Qushayrī does not analogously restrict the figurative spiritual meaning. He instead applies it to any movement of the soul. Qushayrī develops the proposition that the same principle holds in the spiritual life. What is true for *khiṭāb* (speech) is true for *ʿirfān*, meaning esoteric Sufi knowledge. Structurally, Qushayrī indicates the parallelism between the two elements of *khiṭāb* and *ʿirfān* through the repetition of the phrase "what completes the meaning" or, more literally, "that by which the meaning becomes complete." He first uses this phrase to define the term *khabar*, approximated in my translation by the English term "predicate," which is "that by which the meaning of an utterance becomes complete." Then he repeats the phrase in articulating the rule about a *mubtadaʾ* (subject) needing a *khabar* (predicate) in order to make a complete sentence: "If the instigation of a nominal sentence occurs, then *what completes the meaning* of the utterance must also occur, or else the utterance is nonsense." Finally, Qushayrī substitutes *ʿirfān* for *khiṭāb*, gnosis for speech, and applies the principle to the spiritual life: "Instigation works the same way when it comes to gnosis [*ʿirfān*], for there must be *what completes its meaning*, namely, its continuation to the state of culmination." In this way Qushayrī transforms the idea of a predicate completing a subject into a general principle about meaningful movements or actions in the spiritual life. Such movements are consistent. They have integrity. The evidence for sincerity is steadfastness.

Turning back to the excerpt from Gerson's text, we see that this idea of completeness and consistency appears not only in the answer about the conjugation of the verb being total or complete (*totius*), but also throughout this section on the verb. The word "*perficere*" in the response about the "*genus*" of the verb being "active" carries the meaning of culmination. Living the law of God is not merely about hearing it, but also "perfecting" (an English word derived from *perficere*) the law through performing it in action. Gerson conveys this message by resorting to no less an authority than St. Paul the Apostle. The idea likewise comes out in Gerson's description of the form of the spiritual verb. That form is "simple, because he should be served in the unity of a pure heart, that is, in love not in pretenses." The phrase "*unitate puri cordis*" refers to a kind of integrity by which one's inner intentions and outer actions are unified. This kind of personal consistency is quite similar to what Qushayrī describes with these two lines of poetry:

> Indeed, if a generous person loves you tenderly, he will downplay your ugly qualities and bring to prominence your beautiful qualities.
>
> And just so someone who is fed up [with you], if he wants to break off, he conceals your pleasant qualities and tells tales about how you used to do this or that.

True intentions are revealed through word and action. The word "*satara*," repeated in the second and fourth lines here and meaning "conceal," points to how a person's ultimate desire determines how she regards the other person. Her perspective determines what she says and what she withholds. There is thus a kind of consistency even in this selectivity about what to say about the other person.

Building on this semantic connection between the two excerpts, let us consider the more detailed and formal question of how the religious content and the grammatical content intermix. Gerson's technique for intermixing is simple and straightforward, like the theological content of the religious answers that he gives to Donatus's grammatical questions. Gerson poses Donatus's grammatical question about the nature of the verb almost without alteration, and then merely responds in a religious way. To be more precise, Gerson generally begins his response to the grammatical question with a single grammatical word, but then takes the meaning of this term out of the realm of grammar. So, the "*genus*" of the spiritual verb is "active" (rather than grammatically passive or deponent), because living out God's precepts must be an activity that human beings perform as agents. The grammatical number of the spiritual verb is plural (and not singular), because the commandments are numbered either ten (as in the Decalogue) or two (as in Jesus's summary of the law).[5] The form of the verb is simple (not complex) because the human being must perform divine law with integrity and as a whole person, without being divided into parts like those words called "complex" because they are composed of roots and prefixes. Similarly, the tense of the spiritual verb is present (not past or future) because now, in this life, is the time in which we carry out God's precepts (or not). The spiritual verb has all three grammatical persons (that is, first, second, and third) because I, you, and the other person must all carry out God's teachings. These responses are all constructed by Gerson using the same trope. As readers of Gerson, we have become accustomed to the playful and predictable logic of his sermon-like answers to the catechetical questions.

Qushayrī's technique of intermixing the grammatical and the religious, like the theological content of *The Grammar of Hearts*, is more subtle. In the passage here, the word *kadhālika*, which is rendered in my translation as "the same way," but which also means "similarly" or "thus," signals the transition from the grammatical to the spiritual realm. As noted previously, Qushayrī also repeatedly uses the phrase "that by which the meaning becomes complete," both in the grammatical introduction and in the spiritual part of the section. However, to grasp fully the analogues between the two realms takes some work on the part of the reader. In fact, there is here no straightforward one-to-one correspondence between the grammatical and spiritual. For "predicate" (*khabar*), Qushayrī's spiritual lesson gives multiple analogues. That which completes an instance of "instigation" (*ibtidāʾ*) in the spiritual realm of *ʿirfān* Qushayrī first identifies rather vaguely as "its continuation [that is, the continuation of *ʿirfān*] to the state of culmination [*intihāʾ*]." This religious principle Qushayrī then illustrates with the example of pious deeds (*ṭāʿāt*): "If the instigation of pious deeds occurs, then their completion [*tamāmihā*] is necessary." After this illustration, presumably of Qushayrī's own making, there follow the three different kinds of sayings previously discussed. The first has a new synonym for completion, *khawātīm*, whose semantic range includes sealing, as when a letter has been completed, put in its envelope, and sealed with a signet. The second saying, that of the common people, twice uses *intihāʾ*, the previously mentioned synonym:

> If someone receives from Him the instigation of a merciful destiny, then he must also in the end [*intihāʾ*] and final outcome receive favor and grace. If someone in the past has instigated the friendship of God, then he will surely be graciously bestowed with the favor of preserving it up to the end [*intihāʾ*].

But in any case, "culmination" is not what a predicate is, but rather what a predicate does to a nominal sentence. The reader must ponder in each of these instances what exactly the analogue of the grammatical predicate or *khabar* might be. Qushayrī writes stimulating conundrums, not memorizable rules. While Gerson packs his meaning in playful shifts from the grammatical to the religious, Qushayrī's full meaning can only be unpacked through careful reflection on the shifts in his nuance.

In both cases—Gerson's more straightforward way of mixing grammatical and religious discourses and Qushayrī's more subtle style—the authors convey meanings that they could not have conveyed in any other genre of religious literature.

Taking a global view of the two juxtaposed excerpts, we see that they both present a structural principle about right living and the spiritual life. In addition, the excerpt from *Moralized Grammar* presents the core concept of the content of right living as seen from a Christian viewpoint. The idea common to both excerpts pertains to the "how" of the spiritual or moral life. Meaningful moral movement requires following through on beginnings. Gerson's text additionally identifies the fundamental "what" of the moral life. Love is God's word to us. It is the action to which we are called.

Reframing the Genre of Spiritual Grammar

Capped off with this last back-and-forth reading of *Moralized Grammar* and *The Grammar of Hearts*, our investigation of the genre of spiritual grammar as frame, stage, and performance approaches its end. The remaining task is to complete the delineation of this genre and the interpretive retrieval of these two texts. Completing this interpretation, with a focus on the metaphors of spiritual grammar, is the beginning of constructing a theology of grammar. Put another way, the genre performance of the two texts is the linchpin of my interpretation of them, and interpreting their genre is itself a foray into the construction of a theology of grammar.

As we have seen, both texts participate in a genre of religious literature that represents spiritual realities through an extended metaphor that relates the structures of those realities to grammatical concepts and categories. While I may claim this metaphoric scheme to be the mark of the genre, by no means do I aim to revive the taxonomic project of defining clear and distinct borders between mutually exclusive classes of writing as part of a totalizing system. In fact, I mean to sharpen and then erase some demarcations that define the genre of spiritual grammar. For example, let us recall the distinction between spiritual grammar and linguistic theology, such as Bhartṛhari's *Vākyapadīya*, the "*Treatise on Sentences and Words*."[6] *Vākyapadīya* and religious writings like it say something "serious" about linguistic matters while spiritual grammars are "playful" in their troping of grammar for religious purposes. We must recognize that metaphors haunt philosophical and theological discourse, and indeed all language, regardless of how intentionally speakers or writers trope. As such, we note how markedly metaphoric Gerson's *Moralized Grammar* and Qushayrī's *Grammar of Hearts* are, even while we connect the troping genre performance of these queer texts to the more "serious" genre performance of the *Vākyapadīya*, which appears to play it straight.

Like any genre, at least as conceptualized by Derrida and Frow, spiritual grammar too is a fluid and evolving performance of intertextual citation.[7] Citing grammatical terms and interweaving them, as metaphor, into religious discourse is a theological move that authors can perform fleetingly, as in Rahner's comment about God establishing creatures "out of nothing in their own non-divine reality as the grammar of God's possible self-expression."[8] Alternatively, beyond fleeting performances of the genre of spiritual grammar, authors can organize entire works as spiritual grammar, as Qushayrī and Gerson did.

Neither of these authors has recourse to theory to make prosaically explicit the overarching connection between language and theology as Bhartṛhari does. Neither endeavors to articulate why he chose to use grammar as a vehicle for talking about or teaching about God, destiny, or the spiritual path. Rather than explain or justify themselves with theory, Qushayrī and Gerson instead baldly performed a dual discourse. As learned scholars, they enacted a queer sort of "bilingual" or macaronic lecture, nimbly navigating and allusively adhering to the intricacies of two disciplinary languages at once, back and forth and back again. If readers or listeners are to make any sense of this queer performance, they must have a preparation in the grammatical discipline. Likewise, the understanding reader or listener must possess a degree of familiarity or maybe even commitment to the religious discourse that the master makes parallel to the linguistic. Gerson wants his readers to turn away from sin. Qushayrī, in a less heavy-handed way, anticipates the spiritual progress of his readers. Both hope for their readers to dwell in the friendship of God. These spiritual grammars thus implicitly but necessarily bring to the attention of their readers the fundamental metaphor that spiritual reality is like language. While not elaborating a self-referential theory, these two works of religious literature pose a problematic and a possibility about this resemblance.

Consummate writers, they took the literary craft of their theology quite seriously. Reenvisioning these religious scholars as humanists or even *littérateurs* may help us to recognize the literary quality and theological significance of these texts. Our examination, in chapters 2 and 4, of other religious writings by each author has already established the high ambitions, agile versatility, and rhetorical acumen of both men. Gerson broke from the dominant genres of his age, retrieved genres that were *passé*, and re-formed them for new uses. The tract is the clearest example of this kind of literary innovation for specific religious and rhetorical purposes. Qushayrī likewise was no slave to the generic conventions of his time. His work on the names of God, *Sharḥ asmāʾ Allāh al-ḥusnā*, was the first of its kind, a daring and influential experiment in a new literary genre, imitated most famously by Ghazālī.[9] Besides these achievements, additional readings, for example from Gerson's epic poem the *Josephina* and Qushayrī's Qur'an commentary *Laṭāʾif al-ishārāt*, could illustrate the poetic prowess of each scholar. Our exploration of various genres over the course of this study—the sermon, *collatio*, tract, *tafsīr*, Sufi manual, *ṭabaqāt*, and others—has indicated how each of these genres of religious literature forms "implicit realities . . . as a pre-given reference."[10] Our analysis and interpretation of *Moralized Grammar* and *The Grammar of Hearts* demonstrate the validity of John Frow's point that genre "works at a level of semiosis—that is, of meaning-making—which is deeper and more forceful than that of the explicit 'content' of the text." Our central question inquiring into the theological significance of the literary genre of *Donatus moralizatus* and *Naḥw al-qulūb* is even more crucial than we first imagined. The genre of a religious or theological text is no mere ornament. Genre is no afterthought added to a preexisting message or content. Like "a sculptor's mould," it "gives structure to its materials."[11] There is no text without a genre and no theological content without a generic frame. The genre of spiritual grammar and specifically *Moralized Grammar* and *The Grammar of Hearts* projects a world and demands that readers expand their "self-understanding in front of these novel worlds."[12]

Drawing on the conceptual resources and educational importance of the intellectual discipline of grammar in their respective cultural contexts, Qushayrī and Gerson created these hybrid texts somewhere between theological treatises and pedagogical grammars, like those by Sībawayhi and Donatus. Underlying this surprising and strange generic creation was for both scholars an implicit understanding of language itself as a model for the spiritual realities that they hoped to highlight for their readers and of grammar as the structure of those realities. However inchoate, unarticulated, and unelaborated the two theologians' general theories of language, a fundamental metaphorical scheme relates the high-register language that each author knew through study to the spiritual realities that they knew through devotion. With this metaphoric scheme, the genre provides an ontological frame for a theology of grammar.

Qushayrī comes closest to addressing explicitly the matter of these metaphors. He provides two different answers to the question that necessarily arises when opening any grammar handbook: what is the language for which this book is a grammar? In other words, if Sībawayhi's *Kitāb* is a grammar of the Arabic language, for what language is Qushayrī's *Grammar of Hearts* a grammar? In section 1, he explains that "grammar of the heart is the pursuit of praiseworthy speech with the heart. Praiseworthy speech is talking to God with the tongue of the heart."[13] The first language for which he is writing a grammar is the intercourse between God and human being, which a person speaks and hears with his or her heart. "Grammar of hearts" in this sense means grammar for the language that hearts speak. Qushayrī does not by this mean that our hearts speak Arabic when conversing with God. *The Grammar of Hearts* is not a linguistic grammar, because the grammar of hearts is only metaphorically related to the grammar of Arabic. Grammar is also, prescriptively, a quest for such intercourse, which is by definition "praiseworthy."

The second answer that Qushayrī gives regarding the language for which *The Grammar of Hearts* is a grammar is that the language in question is reality, or even the Ultimate Reality, which encompasses both creation and its Creator. Indeed, Qushayrī juxtaposes these two different answers to our question of language. Section 1 points to "talking to God" as the language in question. Section 2 defines the language in question as encompassing God and all that is from God:

> Language comprises the noun, the verb, and the particle that occurs for [expressing] a meaning: In the grammar of hearts, the noun is God; the verb is what is from God; and the particle either belongs to the noun and thus imposes upon it a [grammatical] determination, or the particle belongs to the verb and requires a relation to it.[14]

While the idea that the grammar of hearts pertains to mystic speech (meaning the intercourse between God and human being) is predominant at the start of the text (sections 1–5), this latter idea about the grammar of hearts pertaining to *all* of reality is predominant throughout most of the rest of the text.

The two interlocking metaphorical schemes relating language to spiritual realities and grammar to the structure of those realities operate similarly in *Moralized Grammar* and *The Grammar of Hearts*. Their genre creates a literary frame with ontological effects that shape theological meanings. Interpreting these metaphorical schemes as they operate in the two texts reveals the theological significance of their genre and, in a Ricoeurean sense, opens up a world for readers in which the theology of grammar is fundamental.

The grammatical metaphors convey in powerful and subtle ways both descriptive and prescriptive dimensions of religious teachings. The descriptive dimension of the grammatical metaphor for religious teachings indicates the intelligibility of the structures of spiritual reality. Scholarly effort by religious experts can and does reveal valid descriptions of these structures. The prescriptive dimension of the grammatical metaphors for religious teachings coalesces the pastoral with the pedagogical. A believer who is well trained in spiritual grammar behaves properly like a pupil who is schooled in the grammar of a standard language. Understanding spiritual reality is, by this metaphor, like understanding the intricacies of a high-register language. Through instruction from experts, students can learn the ways and patterns of the reality that encompasses human intercourse with the divine in the here and the hereafter. In coalescing the pastoral and the pedagogical, the metaphors of these spiritual grammars create an alliance between the powers of two discursive fields. The Islamic and Christian pastoral discourses and the Arabic and Latin pedagogical discourses of Qushayrī's and Gerson's worlds were each complex mixtures of the liberative and the oppressive. By combining the pastoral and the pedagogical, Qushayrī and Gerson draw upon these disciplines and their power simultaneously.

As we have noted, these metaphors also profoundly and evocatively convey human embeddedness in spiritual reality. On one level, the metaphor relating spiritual reality to language conveys a communal dimension to the religious vision of spiritual reality. Muslims share in common a vision of spiritual reality, like speakers and readers of a language share in common a cultural tradition. Like a language, that religious vision is passed on, generation to generation. On another level, the scheme of language metaphors puts spiritual reality at the heart of what it is to be human. Just as our sense of self, our understanding, and our very possibility of communicating are all profoundly linguistic, so does the spiritual reality in which we exist establish who we are, what we can know, and how we can transcend ourselves. On still another level, the scheme of linguistic metaphors depicts God as conversing with each human being in the depths of the heart and as present in a meaningful and all-encompassing reality within which all entities have their being.

Spiritual grammar depicts the human condition as embedded in a moral order as in a linguistic order. In some sense, we exist in language. It surrounds us. We are born into it. The academic disciplines of Latin and Arabic grammar teach the schoolchild descriptively and prescriptively how to operate within this world of language. There are right ways and there are wrong ways to place our adverbs, conjugate our verbs, and use our pronouns. None of us knows our language as something of our own creation. We receive it. We become members of it. We belong to it. We are given to it, as it is given to us. Existence comes as a given. *Es gibt.* Grammar constitutes the way of initiation into the world, the means of receiving it intelligibly, and the path of right conduct within it. Language is the world that we belong to and that belongs to us. Grammar structures that world.

Gerson's implication of religious content into the grammatical form of Donatus's primer has the unannounced, unacknowledged effect of expressing in a very rhetorically powerful way the idea that we as human beings are born not only into a linguistic order, but also a moral and spiritual order. The power of this expression is precisely what Gerson gains theologically from writing *Moralized Grammar* in the genre that I have dubbed "spiritual grammar." Let us then recap the vision of the spiritual order that Gerson conveys in *Moralized Grammar* with this overall interpretive conclusion in mind: as creatures, we come into this terrestrial reality as male and female, as rational, as fallen from our original destiny, and yet as fated to be judged by Jesus Christ on the Last Day. Our substance (*nomen*) is body and soul, with both primal animalistic impulses and noble God-like inclinations. We are sinners (*pronomen*) through our own individual replication of the primordial sin of our earliest ancestors. We are not, however, trapped in a moral order where there is no direction or meaning. God has revealed how we human beings are meant to live. These teachings (*verbum*) have come to humankind in many ways, not least through the precepts of the Decalogue and through the teachings of Jesus of Nazareth, exemplified by his life, death, and resurrection. There are different ways (*adverbium*) for us to live out divine precepts. These ways vary according to our place in the social order and our individual personalities and charisms. Even in carrying out divine teachings, we must use common sense and good judgment so as to respect more than merely the letter of divine law. Without choosing or creating our state of being, we human beings are finite and limited, with the ever-present option of rejecting God's will and disdaining the gracious gift of divine presence. Whether we reject God's grace or not, we are created in God's image (*participium*). Love is an ever present option, as is sin. The moral and spiritual reality in which we are situated will culminate in the resurrection of the dead and the judgment of all (*coniunctio*) on the basis of our choices and actions in life. The tribunal of Christ the King will decide for each of us whether we belong to the elect who dwell in the heavenly kingdom, where eternal delight and joy await us (*prepositio*), or to the damned who dwell in the infernal fires of hell, where torture and torment, pain and suffering will be our never-ending sorrow (*interiectio*). This is our reality as human creatures. Our being is embedded in this spiritual reality as deeply and as inescapably as in language. Grammar enables us to see and understand and operate in the reality in which we live.

Qushayrī's *Grammar of Hearts* similarly conveys our embeddedness in a moral and spiritual order of reality, though untangling the strands of the complex theory that he weaves is a more complicated undertaking. Drawing on the Sufi tradition in which he was an expert wayfarer, Qushayrī primarily emphasizes the wide range of nuanced spiritual realities that the spiritual seeker can encounter as he or she journeys through life. These topics correspond in some sense to the adverbial *how* of Gerson's spiritual grammar. Thematically, such material comprises about half of the spiritual topics raised in *The Grammar of Hearts.* Topics under this general heading include kinds of spiritual states (sections 12, 30, 31, 34, 53, 54);[15] spiritual attachment and unattachment (12, 18, 20, 28, 33); the spiritual journey (21, 22, 23, 53); spiritual advancement and regression (38, 39); spiritual serenity and inconstancy (10, 40); and observations about the reality of the spiritual life (36, 55). The second major grouping of topics in the *Grammar of Hearts* pertains to the nature of human beings, similar to the theological material in Gerson's noun, pronoun, and participle sections. Under this heading in Qushayrī's text, topics include kinds of individuals (6, 7, 27, 29, 31, 47, 48, 52, 58, 60); the nature of humankind and creation collectively (2, 9, 25, 26, 55, 56, 57); kinds of spiritual attributes (19, 35, 59); and different kinds of people with relation to the Sufi community (29, 37, 50, 51). Additionally, Qushayrī at a few points addresses the nature of God (for instance, 2, 9, 24); mystical union of a human being with God (for instance, 11, 17); and mystic speech between God and human being (1, 2, 3, 4, 5).

Spiritual grammars, then, need not address only the grand scheme, the broad strokes, the meta-narrative of creation, revelation, sin, and judgment. A spiritual grammar can also investigate and depict the variegated intricacies of human beings and their spiritual life. Getting into some of the fine details of Arabic and spiritual grammar, Qushayrī treats very particular temptations and graces, even rare personal charisms and divine gifts. He details the features of a range of human characters—some spiritually strong, others weak; some spiritually gifted, others challenged.

Through his descriptive grammar of Sufi spiritual life, Qushayrī, like Gerson in *Moralized Grammar,* reveals a theological vision of the nature of the human person, of God, and of their interactions. The heart is the focal point of this vision. The heart is the place where human-divine relations happen. It is the organ with which the *murīd*, the one who desires God, speaks to the Lord, and it is also the organ through which the All-

Merciful reveals Himself to the eager God-seeker. The heart is the mirror that, polished, reflects the Lord God. It is what catches the light of God's revelations about Himself such that the believer attains true spiritual knowing. As in the famous *ḥadīth qudsī*, the heart of the faithful servant somehow encompasses God in ways that the heavens and the earth do not. The metaphorical schemes created by the genre of the grammar manual are precisely where Qushayrī provides an answer to the question implied in this *ḥadīth* regarding how the heart of the faithful servant encompasses God in ways that the heavens and the earth do not.

The structures of spiritual reality thus include both the great arc of human destiny and the very specific details of common and unusual spiritual states. These are the elements and processes of spiritual grammar that Saussure describes as chess pieces and rules of the game.[16] Qushayrī's portrayal of different types of human beings, distinct in their attributes, actions, strengths, characters, relationships, and progress, sets these characters in a linguistic field and grammatical system. They—and God, in this metaphor—are like elements in a single language, the language of reality. The structures of this reality and theological attempts to describe those structures are the grammar of reality. This is Qushayrī's version of spiritual embeddedness. The various spiritual states, the happenings in the spiritual journeys of these human players in the game where God is both maker and participant, are like the linguistic processes that take place to and among the elements of this language. Qushayrī's observations about the realities of spiritual life are like a linguist's descriptive grammatical rules about what happens in a language.

Understanding *The Grammar of Hearts* as a grammar for the language of the intercourse between God and human beings, we can see in a new light the significance of the heart as the focal point in Qushayrī's theological vision. On the level of the individual, the heart is the organ of human-divine intercourse. It is the locus and means for a person to hear and speak with God. The heart thus uses "the grammar of hearts" to produce and to understand heart-speech. On a macrocosmic level, the heart is what characterizes and defines the human within the language of reality. In that cosmic language, the heart is the "core" (and "*coeur*") of the human person. Through these metaphors, Qushayrī illuminates just how the heart of the faithful servant somehow encompasses God in ways that the heavens and the earth do not.

Qushayrī's theology of the heart does not seem in any way at odds with Ibn ʿArabī's. As James Morris explains, Ibn ʿArabī teaches that the heart is *insān*, meaning that the heart is "the very inner reality of fully realized human being."[17] Put another way, "the Heart in itself is by its very nature nothing but the timeless 'place' of the divine Self-manifestation."[18] As Ibn ʿArabī himself puts it at one point, "For God sees nothing of the human being (*al-insān*) but the heart."[19]

As in Gerson's *Moralized Grammar*, the understanding of the human subject that Qushayrī puts forward in *The Grammar of Hearts* is profoundly linguistic. The heart of the human person, the place of God's self-manifestation, is also the organ of mystical converse. That locus of talking with the divine is the core of the human being, the most human feature of human being. With "the tongue of the heart" the human person follows the way of the heart, the grammar of hearts, *naḥw al-qulūb*. The God-seeker thus uses *naḥw* to pursue praiseworthy speech and talk to God.[20] How the heart responds to the temptations and invitations that God extends becomes definitive of the character of each human being. The utterances of the heart, those expressions of our inmost being, create our very selves. Not only that, but besides this inner dialogue that sculpts, refines, and defines the self, contextualized as a member of creation, indeed of all reality, created and uncreated, the human being is like a linguistic element of one cosmic language within which we all live and die. "In the grammar of hearts, the noun is God; the verb is what is from God."[21] We—along with all of creation—are what is from God. Your *nomen* is human being. Your pronoun is sinner. The verb is God's command for you. Though the specifics of the tropes are different, the theological visions constructed by these two spiritual grammars are not far from one another.

Spiritual grammar, then, has to do both with the great story that pertains to all of us, as in *Moralized Grammar*, and with the personalized interactions that individuals can have with God, as in *The Grammar of Hearts*. Spiritual grammar can depict not only the spiritual order into which all human beings are born but also the mystic speech that a chosen few trade with the divine. While Gerson wrote *Moralized Grammar* for Latin readers who were not theologians, Qushayrī's *Grammar of Hearts* is for an even smaller number, a special few—namely, those who devote themselves to the spiritual life. Spiritual grammar is thus not just for the neophyte memorizing the primer and its paradigms nor for just anyone who once went to school. It can also be carefully gauged for the advanced student, eager in his searches for deeper knowledge, wider wisdom. *The Grammar of Hearts* is an advanced spiritual grammar. These two instances of the genre exemplify two poles on a continuum of spiritual advancement. One can thus also imagine an intermediate spiritual grammar that is neither for the neophyte nor the spiritual elite.

For both Gerson and Qushayrī, grammar offers a description of realities. Though there are important differences between their respective views of the spiritual order, there are striking similarities between how the two use grammar as a vehicle for conveying spiritual understanding. The realities described by grammar become more or less understood by the student according to his or her assiduousness. The technical terms and conceptual categories are aids devised by those scholars who previously traversed the territory of language. Like maps with their borders and contour lines, grammatical rules measure and plot out what is otherwise a vast world in which the language speakers, hearers, writers, or readers are situated, though they may possess only a scant understanding of where exactly in that territory they themselves are, and much less of how to make sense of the movement from point A to point B.

Gerson and Qushayrī regard similarly the moral and spiritual realities that they respectively describe. As Gerson saw it, the great moral drama of sanctity and perdition, which is at once macrocosmic and microcosmic, eschatological and already now, is the reality of our human condition, whether any of us heed the call to repent and be saved or not. As a master of the university and a preacher of the church, Gerson endeavored to call the attention of his readers and to teach them the grammar of redemption and perdition. Like an actual grammar instructor, Gerson hoped to teach his students about the realities in which they were already situated.

Qushayrī likewise regards the spiritual realities that he describes as aspects of ultimate reality. They are ever present, always there. They are just for the student to discover. The *murīd* proceeds through specific ranks and levels and inner states, if he persists.[22] As a master wayfarer, Qushayrī offers his students advice—advice that they may only understand upon reaching along their journey a certain vista. He describes a progression of inner states and conditions that only become comprehensible as the journeyman approaches them or takes his leave from them.

While Gerson's objective is to sketch out the grand map of the world in which it is our destiny to make our way, Qushayrī paints pocket portraits to be kept and regarded only when reaching the right step in the journey. The mystery of language, which is at once vast and deep in our hearts and minds, provides the two masters with an abiding store of metaphors and conceptual resources. We are situated in a reality that is also situated in us. The mystery of grammar, the structure of that reality within us and within which we abide, provides our two masters with a way of explaining that reality to their pupils and a discourse for training novice wayfarers in how to conduct themselves properly in the language of reality.

The Fruits of Comparison

The work of this experiment in comparative theology is nearly complete. Before the end, a moment of reflection on the fruits that this comparison has borne will help consolidate what we have learned.

Juxtaposing and comparing *The Grammar of Hearts* and *Moralized Grammar*, we see at first look that the texts are quite different, as are their authors. Without an integrated approach to the texts, the staging of the two together might come across as a multicultural, interreligious variety show. Indeed, each text is worthy of retrieval and study in the context of its author's *oeuvre* and the linguistic, literary, and religious tradition from which it comes. Chapters 2 and 4 have afforded us just such an occasion. However, creating an intertextual link between the two texts has enhanced our study of each and has further led to a constructive literary and theological enterprise that reading neither by itself would have allowed. Gerson's elementary spiritual grammar provided us with the readerly formation necessary to make sense of the more advanced *Grammar of Hearts*. Qushayrī's more ambitious text brings a more fertile suggestivity to the reading of *Moralized Grammar* than what the Latin text would otherwise evoke. Beyond these fruits, comparative study of the two texts has made possible a reflection on their generic frames that would have been rather shortsighted if focused on just one or the other of the two. Though there was almost surely no historical connection between the two texts—that is, no influence by the eleventh-century figure Qushayrī on Gerson in the latter author's composition of *Moralized Grammar* near the turn of the fifteenth century, the two writers' performances of genre are undeniably akin. Genre is always a kind of citation. It is inherently intertextual. *Moralized Grammar* and *The Grammar of Hearts* do not cite each other, but in the service of religious goals each cites grammar manuals in a remarkably similar way. By setting the two textual performances on a common stage, we are able to make sense of these pieces of experimental theater in ways that would not have been otherwise possible.

Reading these texts together has made *The Grammar of Hearts* more comprehensible and *Moralized Grammar* more profound. The function of the various signposts that Qushayrī erected to indicate shifts from linguistic to spiritual grammar became more apparent when related to Gerson's full-scale citation of Aelius Donatus's pedagogical questions around which the familiar Latin primer was organized. Qushayrī varied his signals. At times he uses the singular or plural of "heart" (*qalb/qulūb*) to mark the turn to Sufi meanings, and other times he uses "*al-ishāra*," which literally mean "the indication," but is also a common Sufi term for "allusion" to the "inner" (*bāṭin*) sense. The nature of the back-and-forth in Qushayrī's text is now familiar to us, but before being initiated into the text and without the comparative model of Gerson's *Moralized Grammar*, how and why Qushayrī intermixed grammatical and spiritual discourses was puzzling, even disconcerting.

The wordplay in Gerson is also quite obvious, even puerile, as befits an elementary spiritual grammar. The puns of the eight headwords are not profound, but rather playful. Gerson's play with the roots of "preposition" (placed before), "interjection" (cast among), "conjunction" (bringing together), and the rest launches theological lessons. Moreover, the puns and play of words are not profoundly connected to the theological content of the lessons. The topics of Gerson's lessons are instead rather tenuously tied to the etymological puns. The technique itself, however, is obvious. Nonetheless, since what is at stake in *Moralized Grammar* is eternal life or death, salvation or damnation, the puns, though playful, never trivialize the subject matter. Qushayrī's wordplay is sometimes more thoughtful, with conceptual connections that are not mere puns but rather metaphors in which a linguistic phenomenon described by grammar is likened to a theological or religious phenomenon. The tone of *The Grammar of Hearts* is never puerile or facile. Its more solemn tone fits the aura of sanctity around Arabic grammar in Islamic civilization due to the ties between Arabic grammar and the Qur'an. Though neither author makes theological claims about the status of Latin or Arabic per se, the two grammatical traditions, as we explored in depth in

Chapter 1, provide somewhat different intertextual cultural and intellectual resonances to the spiritual grammars embedded in these two traditions.

In the process, the stage, the frame, the genre of their performances comes into the foreground, and the literary search ensues for other examples of religious texts that enact this sort of experiment. On a theological level, this theater festival of spiritual grammars elicits ontological questions about the range of reality-forming effects that this hybrid genre entails. Recognizing that any genre implicates a certain limited set of ontological possibilities, in reading this genre we wonder about the worlds it creates. It is this kind of reading and wondering that led to the theological interpretation advanced here. The vision made possible through the genre of spiritual grammar sees spiritual reality as in us and around us, like language embeds us in an inevitable web in which exists the only way to form our subjectivity.

The theological interpretation that we have put forward for these texts and the theological vision that we have found in them are from the very beginning and to the very end accounts of the theological effects of the literary genres of the text. Unlike most theological studies, in this project I have repeatedly and continually raised the question of genre and pointed to the centrality of genre. While the experimental work that Gerson and Qushayrī did with genre to create these spiritual grammars makes obvious the justification for my special emphasis on genre here, I believe that similar attention to the genres of other religious and theological writings could bring insight and precision to our interpretations of them.

Another fruit of comparison is that as the genre of spiritual grammar has emerged with greater clarity, it has illuminated the broader field of the theology of language. Indeed, we are now in a position to resituate this genre within the broader field of linguistic writings on religious topics and religious writings on linguistic topics.

Let us recall the two sets of connections between the religious and the linguistic in this broad body of literature. The first set of connections involves the two interlocking metaphorical schemes elaborated in our interpretation of *Moralized Grammar* and *The Grammar of Hearts*. The second involves straightforward theological reflection on language and on scholarly discourse about language, including grammatical discourse. These playful and serious theological uses of language sciences as mediating disciplines all contribute in various ways to a theology of language. Besides illuminating this broader field of theology of language, the present study has also marked a space for the genre of spiritual grammar and the theology of grammar within that field.

Taking language both as a focal point for theological reflection and for exploiting scholarly understandings of language for generating theological discourse, theology of language comprises two interrelated modalities. The first is a theological treatment of language, and the second is a theology constructed using academic discourses about language. We note that several of these academic discourses about language are modern-day descendants of the discipline of grammar in the classical Greco-Roman and medieval Islamic and Christian worlds. Theology of language in both senses can be found throughout history and across linguistic and religious traditions. A thorough mapping of the field of theology of language is in order, but beyond the limits of our present journey. Instead of this larger task, we will take on the more modest task of demonstrating how the discovery of the genre of spiritual grammar and the construction of a theology of grammar shed new light on the broader field of the theology of language in the Islamic and Christian traditions.

Starting with the theology of language in the Islamic tradition, the present study of *Moralized Grammar* and *The Grammar of Hearts* raises new questions about the religious significance of the Arabic language in which God revealed the Qur'an to the Prophet Muhammad. For example, Qushayrī's analogy of the heart, as the organ for mystic speech, to the tongue, as the organ for quotidian speech (as well as the worshipper's recitation of the Qur'an), provokes reflection on the contours of theology of language in Islam.

In the Introduction, we touched on scholarly discussions of how language was instituted and who instituted it (*waḍʿ al-lugha*) as one topic within Arabic and Islamic thought where religious and linguistic discourse intersects. Such discussions, as far as we know presently, started among Muʿtazilite theologians around the early to mid-ninth century.[23] Involving intense analysis of such issues as whether the one who instituted language (*wāḍiʿ al-lugha*) was God or humankind and whether the relationship between language and the physical world was arbitrary or not, these debates include a strong theological focus on language. The inimitability of the Qur'an (*iʿjāz al-qurʾān*) is another topic within Islamic and Arabic discourse, where we can find a theological focus on language. In this field of Islamic discourse, the topic of language can be a way into contemplating God's relation to humanity and the very nature of God. The history of the grammatical discipline that we examined in Chapter 1 demonstrates how Qur'anic exegesis (*tafsīr*) served as a laboratory for the development of grammatical terms and analysis.[24] Reconsidering these elements of Islamic intellectual history from our vantage point now at the end of our study of spiritual grammar, we can see even more clearly that reflection on the Qur'an is the beginning and the end of Islamic theology of language. Divine utterance, revelation, and words for the worshipper to utter in prayer, the Qur'an is central to Islamic thought and praxis generally and to an Islamic theology of language in a special way.

The fundamental Sufi distinction between the *bāṭin* and the *ẓāhir*, the inner and the outer, the esoteric and the exoteric, may be of help as we reconsider the theology of language in light of spiritual grammar. As we know, Arabic is the *ẓāhir* (exoteric) language par excellence in the Islamic tradition. It was the language of the Prophet Muhammad, to whom God chose to reveal the Qur'an. Since that time, Arabic has been the predominant language of religious discourse of Muslims the world over.

Indeed, the religious sciences and the language sciences are intimately interconnected in Islamic intellectual history, above all because the very source of the Islamic tradition is dazzlingly linguistic. Both the Islamic religious sciences (*ʿulūm al-dīn*) and language sciences (*ʿulūm al-lugha*) came into being because of the Qur'ān. From an Islamic point of view, the highpoint of the history of the Arabic language is God's revelation to the Prophet Muhammad. Consequently, grammarians' efforts from the very beginning were immensely important to Islamic civilization precisely because of their usefulness in appreciating the medium and the content of the Qur'ān, which are both inherently Arabic. As Versteegh explains, the purpose of Arabic grammars was based on religious or even theological foundations:

> Since by definition the speakers of Arabic could not make mistakes, the purpose of linguistics was not a prescriptive one. . . . Arabic linguistics was, however, not purely descriptive either: for grammarians such as Sībawayhi it was not enough simply to describe the language as it was used or spoken. Their aim was much more ambitious: since language is part of God's creation and since Arabic was the language selected by God for his final revelation to humankind, it was bound to be a perfect language without deviations or exceptions. Every single part of the Arabic lan-

> guage must exhibit this perfection and it was the self-appointed task of the grammarian to show in the tiniest detail of the linguistic structure that this was indeed a system in which every element was in its place, in which every phenomenon was explicable.[25]

Turning *al-naḥw*, "the way," back once again to the speech between God and humankind, Qushayrī walks a novel "way" along the original path of the Arabic grammatical tradition. In his *Naḥw al-qulūb*, he reveals new language-like structures in which "every element was in its place, in which every phenomenon was explicable." If Arabic is the language of revelation par excellence that Sībawayhi and so many other grammarians studied, spiritual realities comprise the language to which the grammar of hearts pertains. Sībawayhi focused his study on the *ẓāhir*, the exoteric; Qushayrī and Gerson on the *bāṭin*, the esoteric.

Qushayrī is astoundingly creative in his reading of the *ishāra*, the spiritual indications, of grammar. At once erudite and profound, Qushayrī's descriptive spiritual grammar draws on the richness of the Arabic grammatical tradition while revealing the even greater treasures of Sufi knowledge. As if flipping over the methodically constructed apparatus that had been originally created for the purposes of analyzing God's speech to the Prophet Muhammad, Qushayrī discovers on the underside of that apparatus of Arabic grammar a fantastic alternative dimension. Like the back side of a tapestry, so many threads—whose first-order purpose is a precise representation for the face of the tapestry—are found to have completely other functions within a swirling effusion of color, whose structure is perhaps less precise but more evocative and profound. Qushayrī uses *ẓāhir* grammar in the tradition of Sībawayhi to elucidate the *bāṭin* grammar of spiritual reality. Qushayrī's implicit authorial pretense is to be a mere researcher and discoverer, like Sībawayhi, who interviewed so many Bedouins to gather data from their diverse dialects. However, both Qushayrī and Sībawayhi clearly played an important role as creators of the very knowledge that they imparted to their students.

While eyes of faith see the spiritual realities that Qushayrī and Gerson studied to be in existence just as much as the linguistic realities that a competent grammarian illuminates, the discursive activities of describing and explaining phenomena are by no means neutral. Discourse creates our reality as it discloses truth.

Turning to the Christian tradition, we see that the word of God is central to the theology of language, as it is in Islamic thought. As noted previously, an obvious starting point for a Christian theology of language—in both its *ẓāhir* and *bāṭin* varieties—is the beginning of John's Gospel: "In the beginning was the Word" (John 1:1). In light of the discovery of spiritual grammar and this interpretation of *Moralized Grammar* and *The Grammar of Hearts*, the Prologue of John's Gospel looks somewhat different: this exceedingly influential Greek sentence shows itself to be an example of spiritual grammar. The Gospel of John puts the multivalent term "*logos*" where the Book of Genesis has God the Creator ("In the beginning God created the heavens and the earth" [Genesis 1:1]). John thus relates a conceptual term pertaining to language to a structural element of spiritual reality—namely, God.

As ultimate revelation of God, Jesus Christ, the Word in flesh is the focal point of Christian thought and praxis and is central to Christian theology of language. Sermons, scriptural commentaries, and theological reflection on Jesus Christ as the Word of God thus comprise part of an already existing collection of resources that are in some sense a theology of language. Our discovery of spiritual grammar draws new connections between this body of writings and other works within the field of the theology of language.

Hans-Georg Gadamer's retrievals of classical Christian thought on the Word of God, the *verbum Dei*, offer a way to consider the Western Christian theology of language more generally.[26] Gadamer's exploratory retrievals and interpretations of the theology of language that he finds in Augustine and Thomas Aquinas illustrate the kind of constructive theological work on language and grammar that needs still to be done today.

Gadamer explores how the Stoic ideas of the inner *logos* and the outer *logos* comprised a conceptual resource to church fathers like Augustine as they reflected on the mystery of the Trinity. As these early Christian scholars reflected on God the Father's utterance of the Word, they concurrently considered the nature of language itself. In Gadamer's reading of Augustine, "the 'true' word, the *verbum cordis* [literally, the word of the heart] is completely independent" of sensory appearances in whatever human language.[27] "The inner mental word is just as consubstantial with thought as is God the Son with God the Father."[28] Put another way, the inner word "is the mirror and the image of the divine Word."[29] With this understanding of the creative Word by which God the Father called creation into being, Gadamer sees Augustine as endeavoring an understanding of the unity of the Son with the Father and the Father with the Son.

By this account, the way Augustine, within his theology of language, used the Stoic idea of the inner *logos* as "consubstantial with thought" is an example of spiritual grammar operating simultaneously on the metaphorical and "serious" levels.

Gadamer also explores how Thomas Aquinas took up the issue of the *verbum Dei* in other ways in a commentary on the Gospel of John and in an opusculum called *De natura verbi intellectus*, which Thomas likely did not actually author.[30] Gadamer points out how Thomas makes important distinctions between the nature of language and the nature of the Trinity. In explaining these differences, Gadamer seizes on a fascinating image that Thomas creates to demonstrate the nature of language:

> the word is like a mirror in which the thing is seen. The curious thing about this mirror, however, is that it nowhere extends beyond the image of the thing. In it nothing is mirrored except this one thing, so that the whole mirror reflects only the image (*similitudo*).[31]

As "the perfect reflection of the thing," the word "has left behind it the path of the thought to which alone . . . it owes its existence. This does not happen with the divine mind." The Word of God, Jesus Christ, thus cannot be said to owe his existence to the Father.

Gadamer's retrievals of theology of language in Augustine and (pseudo)Aquinas constitute his own creative interpretative achievement. Gadamer's "ontological hermeneutics" builds on these retrievals and is on the verge of beginning a modern-day Christian theology of language. Whereas spiritual grammar uses as its mediating discipline the kind of grammar that describes the structures of language, Gadamer takes important steps toward building a theological ontology that uses philosophy of language as its mediating discipline.

Two further examples can illustrate the theological nature of the ontology that Gadamer builds using language science. In the first example, Gadamer echoes John 1:4 ("in [the Word] was life, and that life was the light of all mankind") while making a claim about the epistemology of language: "the word is that in which knowledge is consummated—i.e., that in which the species is fully thought . . . in this respect the word resembles light, which is what makes color visible." This comparison between word and light evokes an image of the intellect in preverbal thought as groping around in a murky, dark gray cloud of indistinct figures. When a word is found, the thought becomes lucid (John 1:5, "the light shines in the darkness") and the light of the word clarifies the color of the thing and its outline.

In the second example, Gadamer is overtly theological while theorizing about that nature of language. He notes a dialectic between the unity and the multiplicity of the Word of God. That Word who appeared in the world as Redeemer is only one, and yet this appearance was an event that is repeated in preaching:

> the proclamation of salvation, the content of the Christian gospel, is itself an event that takes place in sacrament and preaching, and yet it expresses only what took place in Christ's redemptive act. Hence it is one word that is proclaimed ever anew in preaching.

Most important here for Gadamer's purposes is that the meaning of the word has the nature of an event. In Gadamer's own writing, like that of Augustine and Aquinas that he retrieves, we can see at times a sophisticated theology of language that mixes the metaphorical with the philosophical. Because of our study of spiritual grammar these different levels of discourse are more clearly discernible.

Situated in relation to the examples of *verbum Dei* discourse that we have presented, Gerson's *Moralized Grammar* appears simple and unsophisticated. Unlike the works of Augustine and Aquinas that Gadamer retrieves, Gerson's work attempts no subtle treatment of theological intricacies. The ambitions of *Donatus moralizatus* lie elsewhere. Reaching out to an audience of non-elite readers of Latin, Gerson's spiritual grammar is subtle and sophisticated not in its philosophical or theological content, but rather in its rhetorical and literary design, which is finely shaped to achieve crucial pastoral goals. Exploiting the power dynamics of the classroom and the authority of the classroom teacher, Gerson stages a kind of pedagogical sermon in a catechetical form. The result of this performance is that *Moralized Grammar* portrays basic features of spiritual reality as being indisputably valid and unavoidably operative just like nouns and verbs and the other parts of speech. There is no escape from language, which grammar enables us to understand. Likewise, there is no escape from spiritual reality, which religious teaching enables us to understand.

Taking into account *The Grammar of Hearts* and *Moralized Grammar*, we can see that the place of spiritual grammar within the broader field of the theology of language stems from its metaphorical nature, which ignites the imagination and frees the intellect to think beyond the constricted bounds of prosaic logic. Whether a basic spiritual grammar like *Donatus moralizatus* or a more advanced spiritual grammar like *Naḥw al-qulūb*, the metaphors of this genre engage a sense of play that can be adopted to more or less sophisticated theological content.

Spiritual Grammar Today

This study of *The Grammar of Hearts* and *Moralized Grammar* has drawn on modern-day descendants of the intellectual discipline of grammar such as linguistics and philosophy of language, as well as other fields such as literary studies, philosophical hermeneutics, genre theory, post-Orientalist Islamic studies, and critical theory. The outcome has been to create a comparative theological interpretation of these two fascinating works that is at once true to the texts and meaningful in the twenty-first century. To a large extent, these spiritual grammars are meaningful in special ways today because of the so-called "linguistic turn" of the last century. Contributing to that intellectual movement, the theories of Saussure, Jauss, Ricoeur, Gadamer, Foucault, Derrida, and others make these two texts not only more comprehensible to us now but also more relevant.

Spiritual grammar makes a provocative contribution to our understandings today of textuality and subjectivity. Specifically, the metaphorical schemes that characterize the genre of spiritual grammar provide fresh and insightful ways of conceptualizing the links between text and subject, textuality and subjectivity. The spiritual grammars that we have studied "disclose a world," as any written text does. Beyond that, through their grammatical and linguistic metaphors, *The Grammar of Hearts* and *Moralized Grammar* also reveal something paradigmatic about how textuality shapes subjectivity.

It is tempting to pass over acknowledging the relevance of spiritual grammar since forgoing the risk of interpreting classics allows us to stay "unchallenged, unprovoked, untransformed by the effort and risk of entering into a conversation with the text."[32] However, even as I acknowledge this temptation, I have resolved to push beyond a position where *The Grammar of Hearts* and *Moralized Grammar* become merely "an object for our insatiable curiosity as to the strange possibilities of the human spirit."[33] Part of the reason for retrieving *The Grammar of Hearts* and *Moralized Grammar* is the sense that there is in them an "excess of meaning."[34] Comparative theologian Francis X. Clooney's call for intense attention to the local and the particular does not require that we stop with just those.

Picking up Paul Ricoeur's thought, we can see that, in adopting an ontological frame that depicts the subject as embedded in a reality that is linguistic and structured by grammar, these spiritual grammars model the relationship between textuality and subjectivity that holds for all texts. Ricoeur suggests that entering newly disclosed worlds and consequently understanding ourselves differently is intrinsic to the hermeneutic journey: "if it remains true that hermeneutics ends in self-comprehension, it is necessary to rectify the subjectivism of this proposition by saying that to self-comprehend is to self-comprehend *before* the text."[35] The subjectivity of the author and that of the reader are relativized by the text, which acquires a measure of autonomy. Thus,

> A radical way of questioning the primacy of subjectivity is to take as a guideline the theory of the text. In the measure to which the meaning of the text has become autonomous in relation to the subjective intention of its author, the essential question is not to recover, beneath the text, the lost intention, but to display before the text, the "world" which it opens and discloses.[36]

As with other texts, through our interpreting *The Grammar of Hearts* and *Moralized Grammar* and displaying the worlds that they open and disclose, we relativize our egos.

> To appropriate is to make what was strange become appropriate. What is appropriated is, then, the thing of the text. But the thing of the text only becomes my own if I disappropriate myself from myself, in order to let the thing of the text be. Then I exchange the *me, master* of myself, for the *self, disciple* of the text.[37]

We have seen how Qushayrī's and Gerson's spiritual grammars represent a world. Reading these texts transforms the self. Indeed, the authors' pastoral goals entailed forming their readers morally and spiritually. The metaphorical schemes intrinsic to spiritual grammar depict the subjectivization within structured language that Ricoeur sees as inherent to the hermeneutic journey of any subject interpreting any text. These same metaphorical schemes depict religious teachings and theology as grammatical and thereby provide fresh and insightful ways of reflexively considering the very nature of theology today. Theological writings, as texts, always "speak of possible worlds and of possible ways of orientating oneself in those worlds."[38] Through relating religious teachings to authoritative formulations of grammar, the metaphorical schemes of spiritual grammar intensify questions about the textuality of theology.

The field of the theology of language, which our discovery of spiritual grammar has newly illuminated, must continue to engage these crucial and urgent questions concerning the textual dimensions of our subjectivity, the linguistic nature of our reality, and the interrelation of these issues in theological discourse.[39] Without a theology of language, the language of theology is too easily forgotten, or regarded as transparent.

Our discovery of the genre of spiritual grammar highlights the convergence today of those previously mentioned disciplines that are modern-day descendants of grammar—namely, linguistics and philosophy of language, along with other fields such as hermeneutics, literary theory, the history of subjectivity, ontology, and theology. In the onset of this convergence, Heidegger's rethinking of Being, expressed in extremely self-conscious and creative use of the German language, represents an unforgettable new wave, verging on a tsunami. Reframing philosophy as coming out of and taking its departure from "the hermeneutic of Dasein," Heidegger stitches together philosophical inquiry with language theory, plus—using a metaphor of this hermeneutic as a "leading thread"—takes philosophy to the verge of theology.[40] One of the discoveries of this project, besides uncovering and retrieving two obscure texts and a genre of writing in which they both participate, has been that the spiritual grammars in question contribute to contemporary, postmodern inquiries into textuality, subjectivity, and language. *The Grammar of Hearts* and *Moralized Grammar* thus fruitfully mix with the monumental achievements of Heidegger, Ricoeur, Gadamer, and Derrida, who in reflecting on language collaborate in bringing philosophy to the threshold of theology.[41]

To these already substantial intersections and convergences, I add genre theory and gender theory. The queer, genre-bending performances of *The Grammar of Hearts* and *Moralized Grammar* intensify a problematic that Derrida's "*Loi du genre*" provocatively exposed. In theology, questions of genre and gender are no longer marginal and should no longer be deferred. Further attention to theological genre could lead to gendered theology that no longer represses the questions of masculinity, heteronormativity, or phallogocentrism. Gender can no longer be left to the verge. Theological investigation can no longer content itself with vestiges of the forgotten presence of the phallus.

Appendix: Translation of Jean Gerson's *Moralized Grammar*

HOW MANY PARTS OF SPEECH ARE THERE?

Eight.

What are they?

Knowledge of substance, knowledge of the precepts of God, performance of the same, knowledge of the human being with regard to God and with regard to nature, consideration of the Judgment that is to be, consideration of the joys of the elect, and consideration of the sorrows of the damned.

WHAT IS THE NOUN?

"Human being," because that is what you are called. If you know your substance, whence you are made, truly you know what a human being is.

Here is knowledge of substance that is the first part of speech: "you are made from earth and to earth you will return" (Genesis 3:19).

How many attributes does a noun have?

Six.

What are they?

Quality, comparison, gender, number, form, case.

Of what quality is the human being?

Of the appellative quality: since it is common to all human beings to be made from earth, even of quite ordinary earth or material. It is also common to all human beings to be a rational animal.

Of what degree of comparison?

None, since the human being should not be increased through presumption, nor decreased through an aggressive attitude. And for that reason the [human being's] name is substantive so that he might have to contend with no fear or presumptuous hope that is excessive.

Of what gender?

Common, since human nature befits man just as it befits woman.

Of what number?

Singular, since any person before the Tribunal of Christ gives an account for himself.

Of what form?

Simple, since [the human being] cannot be divided into multiple parts. It is necessary, if the human being should be saved, that he confess faith alone in Christ, and not be separated from it. For those who do not have this faith are not to be called human beings but brutes, since they lack reason.

Of which case?

Nominative and vocative, since [the human being] is now *named* mortal, who had been created immortal, and *called* worker who had been destined for eternal rest.

Of what declension?

Third, since to be declined, that is, to be humbled should be threefold, before God, before neighbor, and before oneself.

From what is it governed?

If he lives well, he is governed by God. If badly, by the devil.

Now let us discuss these things that have been said: O human being, if you want to consider what you are in terms of your soul, without doubt you will find yourself most noble of the animals. For your soul was made in the likeness of God, and marked by his image, having in itself the virtue of understanding, will, and memory. This soul was infused by God into your base, stinking, and fragile body, so that as a most wise mistress and as a sage host, it might rule your house. Therefore, to the extent that the soul is of its own accord, it always wants to do those things that are pleasing to its Lord, and to this end it directs its exterior senses toward exterior duties, which do not lead toward anything whatsoever that detracts from devotional reading or to gazing upon the Lord's cross, or to other salubrious things that seem useful to it. Thus, if you follow the will of the flesh, you oppress the host, you kill the mistress: this relationship of hospitality, in which such a noble guest is endangered, is clearly evil and mean. If therefore you wish to live according to the soul, not according to the flesh, consider that your flesh is earth, [and] you therefore abide by the conditions of the earth. For earth is low, carrying all hard things by virtue of patience, so the more you are bothered by someone, may you treat him well all the more. May you also strive to soak up a deluge of sound doctrine and divine grace, and may you be dry from the flow of vices, of flesh, and of earthly desire.

You now have what a noun is, that is, what it is in terms of substance, namely, it is "noble" in terms of the soul. I therefore ask that you govern yourself more nobly and rationally, not in a base and carnal way.

WHAT IS A PRONOUN?

I answer: as "human being" is your noun, so "sinner" is your pronoun. When therefore you pour out prayer before God, put your pronoun in the place of your noun, so that you say: "O heavenly Father, not as a human being do I call upon you, but as a sinner I ask pardon."

How many attributes does a pronoun have?

Six, namely, quality, gender, number, form, person, and case.

"Sinner," as a pronoun, is of what quality?

Infinite, because I cannot enumerate the infinite and uncertain multitude of faults that I commit.

Of what genus?

Every: because by sinning I participate in every genus of vice, that is, mortal ones and venial ones.

Of what number?

Singular: because singularly do my sins torment my soul and destroy my conscience.

Of what form?

Simple: because I cannot divide them into various confessions, but when I want to confess to a priest, I must declare all things clearly and distinctly in a simple and single confession, with contriteness of heart and the intention of changing my ways.

Of what person?

First person: because I am not in a position to judge others, but only myself, in saying: "I am this miserable person who am so, and thus I have lived in the sight of God and the angels."

Of what case?

From the state of innocence, to the state of guilt.

Of what declension?

From the hands of God, into the hands of the devil.

How many declensions are there for the pronoun?

Four.

First is from obedience to God to the suggestion of the devil: through this did Eve decline.

Second is from obedience of God to agreement with woman, as Adam declined through Eve.

Third is from Paradise to this world.

Fourth is from this world to the edge of hell.

How many are the cases for the pronoun?

Six. First is suggestion. Second is paying heed. Third is discussion. Fourth, taking pleasure. Fifth, acquiescence in the mind. Sixth, acquiescence in deed.

What are the original and derived pronouns?

Adam and Eve are the original ones. All other human beings are said to be derived from these two.

Let us clarify the foregoing:

First, the devil presented to Eve the fruit for eating. That is the suggestion.

Second, Eve saw that the tree looked delectable and sweet to eat. That is the paying heed.

Third, she says that the Lord prohibited them from enjoying this fruit, lest they die. This is the discussion.

Fourth, when the devil responds that they will not die but be as gods, knowing good and evil, she begins to be enticed. That is the enticement.

Fifth, thinking no danger to be imminent in the enjoyment of this fruit, she acquiesces internally to the voice of the devil. This is acquiescence in the heart.

Sixth, glowing with desire at the look of the beautiful and sweet fruit, she eats. This is the acquiescence in deed. In just this way, anyone is lured to sin.

First, a chorus is lined up in some village.

Second, hearing the songs of the chorus or seeing it, I open my eyes to seeing.

Third, I argue in myself that it is not good to look at this chorus, however, remaining, I indulge in sensual pleasure.

Fourth, I am enticed not only to the look of the chorus and to the sound of the song, but also to the look of the girls.

Fifth, I acquiesce internally in my heart to have sex with one of them.

Sixth, I carry out in deed that acquiescence by means of the desire that was conceived of internally. And thus is my soul dead. As I have said of this vice, the same should be understood of all others. Let us therefore turn ourselves aside from every carnal delight, when it is presented to us: as the miller turns the mill when he sees a wind that does not suit him. Unless we abstain from the start, without doubt we will scarcely evade falling into danger. Like David, if he had not spied perseveringly through the window onto the balcony, he would not have fallen into having sex with Beersheba [2 Samuel 11:2–4]. Hence, the eyes should be turned away lest they see vanities.

WHAT IS A VERB?

I respond: It is God's teaching [*praeceptum Dei*], namely, that we love each other.

How many attributes belong to a verb?

Seven.

Which?

Quality, conjugation, genus, number, form, tense, and person.

Of what quality?

Plainly of such a quality: Love your Lord God with your whole heart, with your whole mind, and your whole ability, Deuteronomy 6:5, and your neighbor as yourself, Romans 13:9.

Of what conjugation?

A complete one: because one part is of no value without another, for no one loves God who hates a neighbor, nor vice versa. Likewise, whoever breaks one of the teachings "becomes the guilty party with respect to all of it," as James said (James 2:10). And thus it is necessary that they all be observed in conjunction.

Of what genus?

Active, because it behooves us to carry it out by action, if we would like to observe it, because "those who hear the law will not be justified before God but rather those who do it" (Romans 2:13).

Of what number?

Plural, because they are ten: to believe in God; not to swear by Him in a false manner; to celebrate the holidays; to honor parents; you shall not kill; you shall not steal; you shall not commit adultery; you shall not give false testimony; you shall not commit adultery;[1] you shall not covet something that is not your own. Or, they are two, that is, love of God and of neighbor.

Of what form?

Simple, because he should be served in the unity of a pure heart, that is, in love, not in pretenses.

For the fullness of the law is love, as Paul says (Romans 13:10).

Of what tense?

Present, because this teaching should be carried out in the present, that is, every day that we are in this life.

Of what person?

First, second, and third, because I, you, and he—we all should keep this teaching. The Lord said, If you wish to enter this life, observe the commandments (Matthew 19:17).

Now let us clarify these things that have been said. O human being, you believe in the one God. Well, the devil also believes, and it brings him nothing. If you truly believe in him, adore him, worship, honor him! You break this precept when you insist on sensuality or vanity.

Second, you should not swear by Him in a false manner. You break this, when you perjure or swear habitually or when wavering you swear. Thus the Lord says, "You shall not swear at all . . . but let your word 'yes' be yes, and your 'no' be no" (Matthew 5:34, 37).

Third, you should celebrate the holidays, that means, by frequenting church, concentrating on prayer, devotional reading, or works of mercy. You break this when you waste your time in the leisure of games, revelries, drunkenness, or conversations that are not of a spiritual nature, or when you perform manual labor that is not at all necessary.

Fourth, you shall honor parents by obeying them, showing them reverence, and providing support as you can. You break this, when you curse them or spurn them or bother them or do them harm or when you are not eager to provide them support.

Fifth, you shall not kill. You break this when you become angry at your neighbor without reason or when you deride him or by calling him stupid or when you wish for someone's death that you either are not strong enough to carry out yourself or are afraid to do so.

Sixth, you shall not steal. This you break when you violently snatch the goods of anyone, whether secretly or openly, or when by detracting from someone else you steal reputation or honor.

Seventh, you shall not commit adultery, that is, you shall not indulge yourself in any way. If you are not able to abstain, marry and then you can indulge legitimately. This you break not only when you perform an act, but also when you look at some female with curiosity and concupiscence, and even more so when you desire a virgin or a woman who has been consecrated to God.

Eighth, you shall not declare false testimony against anyone. This you break also when you incite or exhort others to testify falsely, or when you trick others with careful words so as to deceive them.

Ninth, you shall not covet someone else's wife. You shall not commit adultery. This you break when you separate from your own wife and bring home another or you touch someone else's wife and not your own, or if you have intercourse with a women while in a religious order or if you are a secular priest and you touch a woman: you thus wrong your wife whom you have taken as your spouse, that is, the church, as an inconstant religious priest has to his religious order.

Tenth, you shall not covet something that is not your own. This you break when you get in the way of someone else's benefit by adding to your own advantage. Or if you abduct someone else's slave, maidservant, or daughter or you desire an act of respect that is paid to someone else or his dignity, pension, or anything of the like. For you should not harm but rather help out your neighbor. Therefore, pay out love to your neighbor, that is, the seven works of mercy, providing support to the one who is hungry, thirsty, naked and cold, hungry, ill, imprisoned, or troubled.

WHAT IS AN ADVERB?

What is added to a verb, and completes its meaning. If therefore a verb is knowledge of divine Precept, as has just been said, an adverb is the exhibition of the action. But still this is the case in a different way than what has been said above, as will become clear in what follows.

How many attributes belong to an adverb?

Three, namely, comparison, meaning, and form, which is to say, circumstance, similitude, and distinction.

Let us now make these three known.

Whoever wants to carry out the Precepts of God must also observe circumstance, that is, the manner of his action. So, if for example he wants to do a work of mercy, he must consider when, where, for whom, in what manner, what, how much, and in what sequence. These are the adverbs of place, quality, and order.

Meaning. You see two paupers, one lying in the mud, the other begging door to door: give alms to the first and you would send off the other if you do not have enough resources for both of them. If you wish to pray, first pray what according to the Law you are supposed to pray, and the Divine Office. If you have made a vow, first fulfill your vow, then read and pray. If you have not vowed, first recite the Our Father, which God instituted for reciting and afterwards you can recite what you please. If you wish to fast, first follow the fasts ordained by the church, and if you would like to do more, afterwards you will be able to do so.

Thus, in all things be circumspect, as you would appropriately put an adverb with its verb. For if at vespers time, you still carry on eating with others, or a drinking party, or some other foolish delight, such that you prefer oversleeping to getting up in the morning to hear Mass or carry out some other good work, thus changing the night into day and vice versa, without a doubt you do not place an adverb correctly with its verb.

The comparison of this adverb should be done in this way: The rich are more able than the poor; thus they should give alms more widely and liberally to whatever extent they are more wealthy. Thus comparison should be done among them: whoever is strong whether in power or dignity or according to whatever should do what he can—these more, those less. One person can give gold, another one cold water, one a word of consolation, another in offering support, still another in teaching. One person is strong and can observe every fast; another is infirm and needs mercy so that he might have dispensation. One person so burns with charity that he reflects insufficiently on whatever he undergoes; another is so infirm that he falls easily into sin and he rises back up easily through repentance.

The form of the adverb is thus: Let us make a distinction: Some are simple; others are composite. The simple ones are those who remain in solitude, separate from all human conversation, as Antony, John the Baptist, Benedict, and the many who at one time were hermits. The composite ones are in great diversity. Certain ones are purely secular, others religious, still others are preachers. In fact, we are as diverse as our very number, but we all were created for the glory of God, as pictures of various likenesses ornament a sanctuary.

These sentences about the adverb shall suffice.

WHAT IS A PARTICIPLE?

I reply: it is knowledge of the human being according to nature and to God, that is to say, so that any human being might know what he is in himself and how he should be according to God.

How many attributes belong to a participle?

Six, namely, gender, case, tense, meaning, number, and form.

A human being is a participle of what gender?

Common and three. We were generated from Adam and Eve, who belong to the Trinity, that is, to God, who is three in persons. But Adam in an unmediated way, as Luke said. Enoch was the son of Shem, and

Shem was the son of Adam, and Adam was the son of God [Luke 3:38]. Eve was actually mediated, because she was made from Adam's rib.

Of what case?

The case of a disobedient sinner. That is what we are in ourselves. We spring forth from sinners and we are sinners. These are the genders and cases. The participle obtains these two from the noun.

Of what tense?

Present, because penances should be done in the present time, and toiling is for a future reward.

Of what meaning?

First, active, that is, in doing good works.

Second, passive, in suffering hardships patiently.

Third, neutral, that is, in preserving appropriate virtues and thoughts.

Fourth, deponent, that is, in throwing off all mortal sins.

Fifth, common, that is, in safeguarding the Precepts of God and the prescriptions of the holy church. These two, namely, tenses and meanings, the participle obtains in a verb, I mean, what we should be according to God.

Of what number?

Plural, as in this militant church we can be counted among the just and in the triumphant church, among the Angels.

Of what form?

First, simple, as let us not be out of harmony with Faith, by living badly here, and let us not divide from those heavenly ones who are to be saved upon judgment.

Second, composite, as let us divide here from those who were to be damned infernally.

Therefore, the participle takes two, namely, number and form, from the noun and the verb.

Let us now take what has been said into several directions. For it is obvious that we descend and are generated from sinners and that every day we fall into sinning. What is our beauty or purity, by which we please God so as to be like a maiden betrothed to her noble man? And what is our strength, by which we are able to resist a devilish suggestion, if we do not know how to oppose the allurements of the flesh? Love. If we both are dust and must return to dust, what is our nobility or stature or power, by which we, vainly confident in ourselves alone, may provide for the salvation of our souls? And if the present life is brief and the hour of death uncertain, what is this fatuousness of our heart, by which we worry so much about the acquisition of false riches, resources, dignities, and the like, all of which leave us in a moment and never return?

As Job says regarding the person of any human being, "I am as mud and likened to embers and ashes" (Job 30:19), for what else are we than full of the stench of sins like mud? Quickly catching fire and provoking others to wrath, or bringing scandal or damnation unto them, like embers. Quickly insisting on vanities and provoked to anger or kindled with avariciousness, as an ash, insubstantial, dry, and small, left behind after the wood has been consumed by the fire. Just so are we insubstantial, dry, and vain in the absence of the fluids of divine grace, small from faintheartedness and consumed by the fire of carnal desires. But as sinners let us return to the heart, considering that the participle is of the same kind of meaning as the verb. Thus may we also conform to the will of God since we are made in His image, for the person who teaches rightly and lives badly is worthy of censure. Thus also should we even more strongly be censured if, though painted in the image of God, we are called similar to Him, but through an ill-fitting life do not conform with Him. Let us therefore give honor to our Potter by carrying out His will.

WHAT IS A CONJUNCTION?

I reply, it is the consideration or knowledge of the future Judgment.

How many attributes belong to a conjunction?

Three, namely, power, form, and order.

Of what power?

Divine, because God will undertake the judgment and first He will bring together, that is, He will gather all together with the trumpet of angels.

Second, He will put asunder, that is, He will separate the good from the evil.

Third, He will make whole, that is, He will complete the number of the elect and restore them in that city that was broken by the fall of Lucifer and his associates.

Fourth, He will bring a case, that is, He will accuse the reprobate, saying, "Go, you accursed, into eternal fire. For I was hungry, and you gave me nothing to eat. I was thirsty and you gave me nothing to drink. I was naked and you did not cover me." And on the other hand he will give a just account for the elect, saying, "Come you who are blessed by my Father. Take possession of the kingdom that has been prepared for you from the beginning of the world. I was hungry, thirsty, a guest, sick, and naked, and you fed me, gave me to drink, took me in, visited and covered me." Just so at whatever time are the types of this power.

Of what form?

First, simple to the degree that they are more imperfect.

Second, composite to the degree that they are more perfect, because we will all stand before the tribunal of Christ, whether simple—that is, those who have lived in good simplicity—or those who lost themselves by living in evil simplicity, although they did not greatly harm others. There are also the composite who moved themselves and others forward in living well, that is in teaching well, or who corrupted themselves and others through an evil life and evil searches.

Of what order?

First, the preferred. Second, the subordinated. Because first the saved will be judged. Second the damned will be subordinated, as it is written that after the wise maidens came the foolish ones [Matthew 25:1–13] and after those who were on the right, the Judge will come to the ones on the left. Let us therefore ponder the power of this most delightful King, to whose command all inhabitants of the earth—kings and princes, dukes and counts—are reckoned with whatever dignity here. On that last day, they will be reckoned contemptible equally along with contemptible people. Those who here build great palaces, there they would wish well to repair to a little cave in which fleeing from the face of the Lord they might then be able to hide. For if we have in the Scriptures, "the just will barely be saved" (1 Peter 4:18), who shall not be afraid? If God shall bring to naught works and thoughts, what shall we who have no works do? If at that utterance, "I am" (John 18:5) [actually John 18:6] all those who had come to capture him at the time of the Passion lay prostrate on the ground, what will take place when he can make a horrible thunderclap, which twice as sharp as a sword shall thunder, and on the verge of rendering judgment, he shall slice through all the living and the dead?

O how can anyone be afraid when a King of this age has summoned him so as to judge him? In no way whatsoever would he feel that he had forfeited himself to the King. However, he would still tremble in front of the king at the account of the verdict. How much more therefore ought we be worried since we are certain of standing before the Last Judgment at that fearful weighing where even the Angels will be trembling with fear: but even Paul, who won so many battles for Christ, and who was of such great virtue that with a free conscience he said: I am not guilty of anything (1 Corinthians 4:4) Why is it that with such false security we reassure ourselves, we who run about with a thousand defects? "For who brags that he has a pure heart?" (Proverbs 20:9). Nay, indeed no one can know whether "he be fit for hate or love" (Ecclesiastes 9:1). Let us then keep before the eyes of our heart that horrible call that the angelic trumpet will sound forth: Rise you dead, come to the Judgment, and let us now think ahead about what we will say back to the Judge.

WHAT IS A PREPOSITION?

I reply, that it is consideration of the joys of the elect, because (as has been mentioned above) they will be put before the damned.

How many attributes does a preposition have?

Just one, namely, case. Not the case of sin, but the case of humility. And for that reason the case will be twofold in them.

First is the accusative, by which they will accuse the society of this age of total wickedness, as it is written, "The whole world is in the power of the evil one," ([1] John 5:19) and because of this those people who are pure of the evil ways of this age will humble themselves before God by thanking him, for they who had been converted here in this world, will be saved [in the next].

The second case is the ablative, by which they will rejoice of that hour in which they were carried off from this wicked age and brought to that heavenly society, and in this way they will humble themselves before God, thanking him again that he brought them from travails to rest, from danger to safety, from tribulation to peace, from sadness to joy.

If therefore we wish to consider and think about how many the joys of that celestial happiness might be, first we should recognize the evils of this world and by way of contrast how many good things belong to heavenly existence. Here for the most part three things abound: vices, tribulations, and needs. In the heavenly city, on the other hand, peace, purity, and sanctity abound. Whoever turns this matter over carefully in his mind will at once be able to weigh carefully how happy he is who pants in complete desire for that heavenly city and how vile he is who only seeks those things of this world. O with how many carnal vices does the human being rot! With how many tribulations is he shaken! How many remedies does he require! On the other hand, whoever reaches heavenly grace or glory, contemplates unceasingly the majesty and goodness and glory of God. For wherever these things are, the Spirit can in no way be impeded; he rejoices in every peace, because he has with him the peaceful comfort of complete glory, peace, and concord, and his every desire is satisfied, as the prophet said, "I will be satisfied when your glory appears" (Psalms 16:15).

Let us also consider how congenial it is to be in the inner court of a king of this temporal world, where the King sits crowned and wearing regal robes, splendid in all ways, with many soldiers circling him and showing him fitting reverence. The very court glitters with the various uniforms and is ornamented with precious paintings. There all kinds of music would come forth, and an excess of delicate dishes, and there would also be wines and other sweet-smelling drinks. Whatever could add to the charm of a place would appear there. Finally, [let us consider] that in that same place all would rejoice in the great spectacle, the peaceful amity, and the immense delight, such that every danger, fear, care, or trouble would be banished. What, pray tell, would be more desirable than this solace, especially if this could last perpetually without tiring of it?

No doubt incomparably more spectacular than every royal court of the present age is the lofty heavenly Court, where the peaceful King, namely Christ, sits crowned with the diadem with which his Father crowned him, who is at His right and spectacular in form before the sons of humankind. In that Court nine orders of angels stand on either side at the height of attention and reverence and in mutual harmony, they praise God, saying, "Salvation belongs to our God who sits on the throne and to the Lamb" (Revelation 7:10). There that royal court is decorated with glowing stars, which are more gleaming than every painting; there the souls of the Saints rejoice in peace and security and gladness that are truly everlasting. So, what do I dare, by way of comparison, to strip from such glory of the heavenly homeland, when Scripture would say, that "no eye has seen, no ear has heard, nor has it entered into the heart of a human being, those things that God has prepared for those who love him" (1 Corinthians 2:9)? Therefore, let our tongue fall silent and our mind ponder how beyond all reckoning that happiness is, where everything that might be desired is found, and where delight is only in the glorious son of God and seeing the Kingdom of glory in its splendor is the only satiety of souls, forever and ever. Amen.

WHAT IS AN INTERJECTION?

I respond that it is consideration of the laments of the damned, since just as a grammatical interjection signifies a state of mind with an unprecedented word, so does this spiritual interjection signify an emotion of the interior human being coming out of sorrowful suffering.

How many attributes does it have?

One, that is, merely a meaning. For the intolerability of the pains of Gehenna will be signified outwardly. First, the delights of the demons over the torments of so very many souls. Second, the sorrow of the damned souls. Third, the unrighteous Angels' admiration of those saying to themselves, "O how great was our blindness while in the world, for we looked so stupid when the Prelates, Preachers, and other good people [told us] to flee the pleasures of the flesh and the delights of the world, so that we would not enter into this place of torments, and now here we are suffering them deservedly because we scorned to hear them." Fourth, dread and fear, because the souls of the damned will be in absolute terror when their infernal hosts torture them with inextinguishable fire, intensely hostile words, fiercely burning eyes, puffed-up face, and a deathly black aspect.

In the Gospel it is said of this pain that "there will be wailing and gnashing of teeth" (Matthew 8:12), that is, sorrows and fierce pains will abound, because no one is accustomed to wailing unless burdened with tremendous sorrow, and likewise no one gnashes teeth unless bearing tremendous pain. Isaiah also says concerning this pain, "Their worm will not die, and their fire will not be extinguished" (Isaiah 66:24), because the worm of conscience is never allayed such that it should always endure the gnawing of the conscience, on account of which they shall entrust themselves to the Judgment of God, and, while continually accusing themselves, they shall be struck motionless from indignation and wrath. Furthermore, the pain of fire shall never be extinguished. Likewise their worm shall never die, that is, their disdain and desperation shall always endure, and the fire of their carnal yearnings that they had kindled here, shall there be brought to its height. The Psalmist says on this subject, "Fire and sulphur and the breath of violent winds [is] their allotted cup" (Psalms 50:10:7) [Psalms 11:7], that is, that a part of the torments of Gehenna will be the burning of fire, the stench of sulphur, and a wind storm that begets evil.

So that this pain might be described more clearly, let us sum up the example in a simile. A crafty smith is accustomed to having a black face, and a grimy forge where he puts an iron so that it might grow hot. Afterwards, as he wills, he and his assistants strike it with mallets. That smith of which I speak is the devil, who is deathly black. The grimy forge is the underworld, which has no brightness whatsoever. The glowing charcoals that are put there signify that this pain will endure forever. The sacks signify the pain insofar as it never or hardly will slacken. Rather, it will only be made fiery hot. The iron is the damned soul itself that is exposed there to that fire, so as to be perpetually cremated. Never do the demons leave off vituperating with savagely fierce words.

Therefore, beloved, now that we know all this, as long as we occupy this world, let us take on a state of repentance so that later the devil might not take delight in us, but rather we might add to the joy of the Holy Angels, who "rejoice over one sinner who repents" (Luke 15:10). Let us be mindful of how we are redeemed by the Blood of Christ, and let so great a benefit be in no way frustrated in us, so that just as pieces of shit issue from a stomach that needs purging, and as shavings that have been cut from wood are thrown into a fire, we might not after this life be expelled like pieces of shit, as it were, from the bowels of the church and thrown like chaff and refuse into the fire of hell. Therefore, may our hearts be fixed to that place where there are true joys. Amen.

NOTES

Introduction. Genre Trouble: Queering Grammar for Spiritual Purposes

1. References to *The Grammar of Hearts* will be abbreviated as NQ plus the section number as given in ʿAbd al-Karīm al-Qushayrī, *Naḥw al-qulūb al-kabīr*, ed. Ibrāhīm Basyūnī and Aḥmad ʿAlam al-Dīn al-Jundī (al-Qāhirah [Cairo]: Maktabat ʿAlam al-Fikr, 1994); excerpt from NQ 1. See Chap. 6 for a commentary on it.
2. See Chap. 1 for more extensive treatment of the Arabic grammatical tradition.
3. For a first overview of Qushayrī, see H. Halm, "al-Ḳushayrī," in *Encyclopaedia of Islam*, ed. P. Bearman et al., 2nd ed. (Leiden: Brill, 2011; Brill Online: Harvard University, http://www.brillonline.nl/subscriber/entry?entry=islam_COM-0548; accessed 18 April 2011).
4. See Chap. 4 for a discussion of Qushayrī's *Risāla* and some of his other writings.
5. The Latin title, *Donatus moralizatus*, is a literary reference to a tradition of transforming pagan literature into edifying lessons; see Chap. 3 of this volume for further discussion. *Ovidius moralizatus, Cato moralizatus, Aesop moralizatus* all exist. ("Moralizatus" is also in some cases spelled "moralisatus.") For Ovid, see Petrus Berchorius [Pierre Bersuire], *De formis figurisque deorum: Reductorium morale, liber xv: Ovidius moralizatus, cap. i: Textus e codice Brux, Bibl. Reg.* 863–69 *critice editus*, ed. J. Engels (Utrecht: Rijksuniversiteit, Instituut voor Laat Latijn, 1966), and F. Ghisalberti, "L'*Ovidius Moralizatus* di Pierre Bersuire," *Studj romanzi* 23 (1933): 5–136. For Cato, at the Countway Library of Medicine Rare Books Collection of Harvard University, cf. Ballard 256: Robertus de Euromodio, *Catho moralisatus: Alias speculum regiminis quo ad utriusq[ue] hominis reformationem* (Lyon: Jean de Vingle, 1497/1498). There are many versions of Aesop "moralized." Just two of the examples in Houghton Library of Harvard University are Typ 525.03.124: Aesop, *Esopus constructus moralizatus & ystoriatus ad vtilitatem discipulorum* [Milan: 1503] and Ga10.42.95: Aesop, *Esopus constructus moralizatus & historiatus & optime emendatus* (Bugelle: Antonium Mondellam, 1569).
6. There are two editions of *Moralized Grammar*: Jean Gerson, *Oeuvres complètes*, ed. Palémon Glorieux (Paris: Desclée, 1960), 9:689–700; and Gerson, *Opera omnia*, vol. 4, ed. Louis Ellis Du Pin (Antwerp: 1706; repr. Hildesheim and New York: Olms, 1987), cols. 835–44. References to Gerson's original Latin text of *Moralized Grammar* will be to

the Du Pin edition and will be abbreviated DM (for *Donatus moralizatus*), followed by the column number and letter.

A French translation of Gerson's *Moralized Grammar* was rendered by Colard Mansion, Belgian calligrapher and printer, sometime between 1479 and 1484; see Maria Colombo Timelli, "Le *Donat Espirituel* de Colard Mansion: Étude et édition," *Memorie dell'Istituto lombardo-accademia di scienze e lettere, classe di lettere, scienze morali e storiche* 40, no. 5 (1997): 257–97.

In addition, there is an English translation of Gerson's text, dated to 1597, at the Houghton Library at Harvard University (Houghton STC 3.5). Entitled *A spirituall grammer: Or the eight partes of speech moralized, which by analogical allusion, may put schollers in minde of many good lessons; and recommended to their studies*, this work is unattributed, though apparently printed by Gabriel Simson in London. Apparently, Trinity College Library also has a copy of the work. This translation omits the scatological image in the last paragraph of Gerson's original.

7. For a general overview of Gerson and his work, see Brian Patrick McGuire, *Jean Gerson and the Last Medieval Reformation* (University Park: Pennsylvania State University Press, 2005). For scholarly treatments of some of the most significant specific aspects of understanding Gerson and his work, see *A Companion to Jean Gerson*, ed. Brian Patrick McGuire (Leiden: Brill, 2006).
8. See Chap. 2 for a discussion of Gerson's sermons and some of his other writings.
9. See Chap. 1 for more extensive treatment of the Latin grammatical tradition.
10. Little is known about Aelius Donatus save that he taught St. Jerome; cf. "Aelius Donatus," *Encyclopaedia Britannica* (Encyclopaedia Britannica Online, Encyclopaedia Britannica, 2011; http://www.britannica.com.ezp-prod1.hul.harvard.edu/EBchecked/topic/169021/Aelius-Donatus; accessed 6 May 2011).

    The primer was Donatus's *Ars minor*, also known as his *De octo partibus orationis*; cf. H. R. Mead, "Fifteenth-Century Schoolbooks," *Huntington Library Quarterly* 3, no.1 (Oct 1939): 37–38.
11. "*Partes orationis quot sunt? Octo. Quae?*," DM 835A. See the Appendix for my full translation of the text and Chap. 3 for commentary on it.
12. "Cognitio substantiae, cognitio Praecepti Dei, operatio eiusdem, cognitio hominis secundum Deum, et secundum naturam, consideratio futuri Iudicii, consideratio laetitiae electorum, et consideratio tristitiae damnatorum"; DM 835A.
13. See Susannah Cornwall, *Controversies in Queer Theology* (London: SCM Press, 2011), especially Chap. 1, "What Is Queer," 9–42.
14. David M. Halperin, *Saint Foucault: Towards a Gay Hagiography* (New York: Oxford University Press, 1995), 62.
15. Mark D. Jordan, "Religion Trouble," *Gay and Lesbian Quarterly* 13, no. 4 (2007): 569.
16. Cf. the discussion of Austin's claims about "parasitic uses of language" that are "not serious" and the ensuing debate on this point; J. L. Austin, "Lecture VIII," in *How to Do Things with Words* (Cambridge, Mass.: Harvard University Press, 1962), 104.
17. Cornwall, *Controversies in Queer Theology*, 36.
18. For Judith Butler's classic elaboration of Michel Foucault's work on regulatory sexual regimes, see her *Gender Trouble: Feminism and the Subversion of Identity* (New York: Routledge, 1990).

19. The Latin word "genus" is the etymological source of the English words "generic," "gender," and "genre."
20. This risk of anachronism is noted, for example, in the following places: Simon Gaunt, *Gender and Genre in Medieval French Literature* (New York: Cambridge University Press, 1995), 19; Karma Lochrie, "Mystical Acts, Queer Tendencies," in *Constructing Medieval Sexuality*, ed. Karma Lochrie, Peggy McCracken, and James A. Schultz, Medieval Cultures Series 11 (Minneapolis: University of Minnesota Press, 1997), 180; Martín Hugo Córdova Quero, "Friendship with Benefits: A Queer Reading of Aelred of Rievaulx and His Theology of Friendship," in *The Sexual Theologian: Essays on Sex, God, and Politics*, ed. Marcella Althaus-Reid and Lisa Isherwood (London and New York: T. and T. Clark, 2004), 26.
21. Gaunt, *Gender and Genre*, 286.
22. Ibid., 288.
23. *Nīshābūr*, as it is transliterated from the Persian, is located in northeastern Iran on today's map.
24. *The Oxford English Dictionary*, 2nd ed., ed. J. A. Simpson and E. S. C. Weiner (Oxford: Clarendon, 1989), 16:257.
25. Karl Rahner, *Foundation of Christian Faith: An Introduction to the Idea of Christianity*, trans. William V. Dych (1978; repr. New York: Crossroad, 1999), 222–23.
26. Cf. Austin, "Lecture VIII," 104, and Jacques Derrida, "Signature Event Context," *Glyph* 1 (1977): 172–97.
27. Ricoeur has argued convincingly for the necessary interrelation between understanding the metaphors of a text and understanding the text as a whole: "From one standpoint the process of understanding a metaphor is the key for that of understanding larger texts. . . . But, from one other standpoint, it is the understanding of a work as a whole which gives the key to metaphor"; Paul Ricoeur, "Metaphor and the Main Problem of Hermeneutics," in *A Ricoeur Reader: Reflection and Imagination*, ed. Mario J. Valdés (Toronto and Buffalo: University of Toronto Press, 1991), 308.
28. Cf. *Bhartṛhari: Language, Thought and Reality (Proceedings of the International Seminar Delhi, December 12–14, 2003)*, ed. Mithilesh Chaturvedi (Delhi: Motilal Banarsidass, 2009).
29. Natalia Isayeva, *Shankara and Indian Philosophy* (Albany, N.Y.: SUNY Press, 1993), 43–44.
30. David Carpenter, *Revelation, History, and the Dialogue of Religions: A Study of Bhartṛhari and Bonaventure* (Maryknoll, N.Y.: Orbis, 1995), 36.
31. Ibid., 24.
32. Ibid., 63.
33. As Carpenter's account makes evident, Bonaventure, in contrast to Bhartṛhari, was no grammar expert. His Christology of the threefold Word—*increatum*, *incarnatum*, and *inspiratum*—is set around the metaphor that begins John's Gospel, but Bonaventure does not explore in detail the theological significance of grammar or language. Rather, his focus is fully on theologizing about Jesus Christ.
34. Rebecca J. Manring, "Does Krsna Really Need His Own Grammar? Jīva Gosvāmī's Answer" (American Academy of Religion conference paper, 2007). Prof. Manring graciously provided me with the text of her paper in private correspondence in January 2007.

She subsequently published an expanded and revised version of that paper: "Does Krsna Really Need His Own Grammar? Jiva Gosvamin's Answer," *International Journal of Hindu Studies*, 12, no. 3 (2008): 257–86.

35. Manring, "Does Krsna Really Need His Own Grammar?," *IJHS* 12, no. 3, 268.
36. Fakhr al-Dīn al-Razi, *Al-Maḥṣūl fī ʿilm uṣūl al-fiqh*, vol. 1, pt.1, ed. Ṭāhā Jābir Fayyāḍ ʿAlwānī (Riyadh: al-Mamlaka al-ʿArabīyyah al-Saʿūdīyyah, Jāmiʿat al-Imām Muḥammad ibn Saʿūd al-Islāmīyyah, Lajnat al-Buḥūth wal-Taʾlīf wal-Tarjamah wal-Nashr, 1979-1981), 243ff.
37. Al-Ḥakīm al-Majrīṭī, *Al-Risāla al-jāmiʿa*, vol. 1, ed. Jamīl Ṣalībā (Dimashq [Damascus]: Maṭbaʿat al-Taraqqī, 1949), 699ff. The epistle is entitled, "Fī ikhtilāf al-lughāt" ("On the difference between the languages [or dialects]").
38. Francesco Chiabotti identifies a number of such commentaries in an article on Qushayrī's *The Grammar of Hearts "al-saghīr,"* which is a much shorter text (ca. 850 words) than the one that is the object of study in the present project (ca. 5,600 words); Chiabotti, "*Naḥw al-qulūb al-ṣaġīr:* La 'grammaire des coeurs' de ʿAbd al-Karīm al-Qušayrī," *Bulletin d'études orientales* (Online) 58 (Sept. 2009), published online 1 Sept. 2010, http://beo.revues.org/83. Chiabotti lists (in footnotes 19–21) *Sharḥ al-Ājurrūmiyyah* of Moroccan Sufi Aḥmad al-Zarrūq (who lived in the fifteenth century C.E.), mentioned by Ali Lahmi Khusaim in *Zarrūq the Ṣūfī: A Biographical and Critical Study of a Mystic from North Africa* (Tripoli: General Company for Publication, 1976); Aḥmad b. ʿAjība, *Tajrīd sharḥ matn al-Ājurrūmiyya* (Cairo: 1419), excerpts trans. Jean-Louis Michon, *Le soufi marocain Aḥmad ibn ʿAjība (1746–1809) et son Miʿrāj*, 2nd ed. (Paris: J. Vrin, 1990); and Ibn Maymūn's commentary, of which there is a critical edition by A. al-Ghazlani, "Présentation et édition critique de la *al-Risālat al-maymuniyya fī tawḥīd al-ājurrūmiyya* de ʿAlī b. Maymūn al-Fāsī (853–917/1450–1511)" (master's thesis, Université de Provence Aix-Marseille I, 1997–98).
39. G. Troupeau, "Ibn Ādjurrūm, Abū ʿAbd Allāh Muḥammad b. Muḥammad b. Dāwūd al-Sanhādjī," in *Encyclopaedia of Islam*, 2nd ed., ed. P. Bearman et al. (Leiden: Brill, 2011; Brill Online, Harvard University, http://www.brillonline.nl/subscriber/entry?entry=islam_SIM-3065; accessed 5 April 2011).
40. M. G. Carter, "Mystical Grammar or Grammatical Mysticism? A Ṣūfī Commentary on the ʾĀğurrūmiyya," in *Orientalistische Studien zu Sprache und Literatur: Festgabe zum 65. Geburtstag von Werner Diem*, ed. Ulrich Marzolph (Wiesbaden: Harassowitz Verlag, 2011). I acknowledge with warm gratitude Prof. Carter's providing me with a manuscript of this article by private correspondence in March 2011.
41. ʿAlī b. Maymūn b. Abī Bakr al-Idrīsī al-Maghribī al-Ḥasanī (al-Ghumārī al-Fāsī) (1450–917/1511), *Al-Risāla al-Maymūniyya fī Tawḥīd al-ʾĀğurrūmiyya*, MS Mohamed Taher Library in Timbuktu, Mali.
42. Ahlwardt MS no. 427 III.
43. Chiabotti, in "*Naḥw al-qulūb al-ṣaġīr*," 391n23, cites Aḥmad al-ʿAlāwī, *Knowledge of God: A Commentary on al-Murshid al-Mu'in of Ibn al-Ashir*, ed. ʿAbd al-Ṣabūr al-Ustādh, trans. ʿAbd al-Kabīr al-Munawarra [sic], ʿAbd al-Ṣabūr al-Ustādh, intro. Sh. ʿAbdalqādir al-Ṣūfī al-Darqawī (Norwich: Diwan Press, 1981; [n.p.]: Madinah Press, 2005).
44. Graham Ward, *Theology and Contemporary Critical Theory*, 2nd ed. (New York: St. Martin's, 2000), ix.

45. Lisa Isherwood and Marcella Althaus-Reid, "Introduction: Queering Theology, Thinking Theology, and Queer Theory," in *Sexual Theologian*, 4.
46. Gustavo Gutiérrez, *Teología de la liberación: Perspectivas* (Lima: CEP, 1971).
47. Althaus-Reid and Isherwood, "Queering Theology," 4–5. For an excellent anthology of recent queer theological work, see Gerard Loughlin, ed., *Queer Theology: Rethinking the Western Body* (Malden, Mass.: Blackwell, 2007).
48. NQ 3.
49. For discussion of the concept of "queer" in contemporary theological contexts, see Cornwall, "What Is Queer," 9–42.
50. Derrida, "The Law of Genre," trans. Avital Ronell, *Critical Inquiry* 7, no. 1 (Autumn 1980).
51. Gérard Genette has stirred a major revisionist perspective on genre, beginning with a reinterpretation of Plato and Aristotle on the subject; see Genette, *Introduction à l'architexte* (Paris: Seuil, 1979); cited by John Frow, *Genre* (London and New York: Routledge, 2006), 59ff.
52. An illuminating discussion of this genealogy is found in Chap. 3 of Frow, *Genre*, 51–71.
53. Ibid., 53, which cites Geoffrey C. Bowker and Susan Leigh Star, *Sorting Things Out: Classification and Its Consequences* (Cambridge, Mass.: MIT Press, 1999), 62.
54. Frow, *Genre*, 24.
55. Ibid.; cites Anne Freadman, "Untitled: (On Genre)," *Cultural Studies* 2, no. 1 (1988): 73.
56. Frow, building on Genette (see *Introduction à l'architexte*), traces this triad from Book III of Plato's *Republic* through Aristotle's *Poetics* and beyond, concluding that Western genre theory "has attempted to develop a systematic account of genre on the basis of a misreading of the Socratic triad"; see Frow, *Genre*, 55ff.
57. Hans Robert Jauss, *Toward an Aesthetic of Reception* (Minneapolis: University of Minnesota Press, 1982), 79.
58. Ibid., 25.
59. Ibid., 76.
60. Derrida, "Law of Genre," 63.
61. Ibid., 55.
62. Ibid., 57.
63. Robyn Ferrell, *Genres of Philosophy* (Hants, UK, and Burlington, Vt.: Ashgate, 2002), 3.
64. Frow, *Genre*, 48. Frow cites Charles L. Briggs and Richard Bauman, "Genre, Intertextuality, and Social Power," *Journal of Linguistic Anthropology* 2, no. 2 (December 1992): 131–72. "Genre is quintessentially intertextual. . . . Unlike most examples of reported speech, however, the link is not made to isolated utterances, but to generalised or abstracted models of discourse production and reception" (147).
65. We shall discuss the discipline of Latin grammar in Chap. 1.
66. We shall discuss some of these genres of Gerson's world in Chap. 2.
67. Frow, *Genre*, 9.
68. Cf. ibid., 74–76.
69. Ibid., 10.
70. Ibid., 19.
71. Ferrell, *Genres of Philosophy*, 4.

72. Jauss's work provides a cogent and insightful theoretical framework for investigating the question of literary genre, and the collection of his essays translated into English, *Toward an Aesthetic of Reception*, reveals Jauss's special interests in Romance literary studies and medieval genres, which felicitously coincide with the contours of the career of Jean Gerson.
73. Jauss, *Toward an Aesthetic of Reception*, 38.
74. Ferdinand de Saussure, *Course in General Linguistics*, ed. Charles Bally, Albert Sechehaye, and Albert Riedlinger, trans. Roy Harris (1983; repr. Chicago and La Salle: Open Court, 1986), 23 [43 in 1922 French edition], 87 [125].
75. Jauss, *Toward an Aesthetic of Reception*, 79.
76. Ibid., 19.
77. Ibid.
78. Ibid., 23.
79. Ibid., 105; cites Jurij Striedter, ed., *Texte der russischen Formalisten*, vol. 1, *Texte zur allgemeinen Literaturtheorie und zur Theorie der Prosa* (Munich: W. Fink, 1969–72), lxvi.
80. The array of genres that Jauss considers includes fairy tale [*Märchen*], novella, *chanson de geste*, courtly novel, knightly romance, romance epic, Arthur-romance, the sermon, the moral didactic or "chastising" poem, the literature of rank (*États du monde*, the mirror of princes), animal epic, verse-farce, *poesia giocosa* or the "conflict poem," polemical lyric, thirteenth-century nonsense-poetry of two kinds, *fatrasie* and *resverie*, the lying tale [*Lügenmärchen*], *fatras*, *pastourelle*, *sirventes*-song, *exemplum*, *fabliau*, legend, miracle, *lai*, *vida*, *nova*, love-casuistry, Oriental narrative literature, Apuleius and Milanese love-stories, local Florentine histories and anecdotes; Jauss, *Toward an Aesthetic of Reception*, 81–83, 89, 92.
81. Ibid., 88.
82. Ibid.
83. Ibid., 81.
84. For a rousing rant against Strunk and White's *Elements of Style*, an American classic of prescriptive grammar, see Geoffrey K. Pullum, "50 Years of Stupid Grammar Advice," *The Chronicle of Higher Education* 55, no. 32 (17 April 2009): B15, http://chronicle.com/article/50-Years-of-Stupid-Grammar/25497; accessed 17 February 2011.
85. Jauss, *Toward an Aesthetic of Reception*, 21.
86. In focusing on other works by our two authors, I've written Chap. 2 as a sketch of the system of genres in which Gerson wrote *Spiritual Grammar* and Chap. 4 as a sketch of the system in which Qushayrī wrote *The Grammar of Hearts*.
87. Ferrell, *Genres of Philosophy*, 9.
88. Frow, *Genre*, 19.
89. Ferrell, *Genres of Philosophy*, 2.
90. Ibid., 1.
91. Butler, *Gender Trouble*, 24–25; cited in Ward, *Theology and Contemporary Critical Theory*, 32.
92. For another treatment of gender and genre together, in a discussion focusing on Ovid, Virgil, and Homer, cf. Stephen Hinds, "Essential Epic: Genre and Gender from Macer

to Statius," in *Matrices of Genre: Authors, Canons, and Society*, ed. Mary Depew and Dirk Obbink (Cambridge, Mass.: Harvard University Press, 2000), 221–46.

93. David Tracy, "On Naming the Present," in *On Naming the Present: Reflections on God, Hermeneutics, and Church* (Maryknoll, N.Y.: Orbis, 1994), 15–16.
94. Sarah Coakley connects the Christian ascetic tradition to this Butlerian idea of repeating with critical difference; Coakley, *Powers and Submissions: Spirituality, Philosophy and Gender* (Oxford: Blackwell, 2002), 159. Critical assessment of Coakley's achievement appears in Elizabeth Stuart, "Queering Death," in *Sexual Theologian*, 61.

1. Arabic, Latin, and the Discipline of Grammar in the Worlds of Qushayrī and Gerson

1. Robert Kilwardby (ca. 1215–79) defines grammar in such a way that it reinforces its intrinsic rectitude: "*scientia recte scribendi et recte scripta pronuntiandi et recte pronunciata recte intelligendi*" (the science of writing correctly, of pronouncing writings correctly, and of understanding things pronounced correctly). Kilwardby studied at the University of Paris and then taught grammar and logic there before he became a Dominican and eventually the Archbishop of Canterbury; see J. Stephen Russell, *Chaucer and the Trivium: The Mindsong of the Canterbury Tales* (Gainesville: University Press of Florida, 1998), 9. For a brief background on Kilwardby, cf. Rita Copeland and Ineke Sluiter, eds., *Medieval Grammar and Rhetoric: Language Arts and Literary Theory, A.D. 300–1475* (Oxford: Oxford University Press, 2009), 724.
2. Laura Cleaver, "Grammar and Her Children: Learning to Read in Art of the Twelfth Century," http://www.marginalia.co.uk/journal/09education/cleaver.php#note4; accessed 24 May 2013.
3. Jan M. Ziolkowski, "Introduction," in *Obscenity: Social Control and Artistic Creation in the European Middle Ages*, ed. Jan M. Ziolkowski (Leiden: Brill, 1998), 9.
4. Ziolkowski, "Cultural Diglossia and the Nature of Medieval Latin Literature," in *The Ballad and Oral Literature*, ed. Joseph Harris (Cambridge, Mass.: Harvard University Press, 1991), 194–95.
5. John Frow, *Genre* (London and New York: Routledge, 2006), 14.
6. Paul Ricoeur coined this phrase, referring to Nietzsche, Marx, and Freud as "masters of suspicion"; see Ricoeur, *Freud and Philosophy: An Essay on Interpretation* (New Haven: Yale University Press, 1970). For elaboration and analysis of Ricoeur on this point, see David Stewart, "The Hermeneutics of Suspicion," *Journal of Literature and Theology* 3 (1989): 296–307.
7. "In sum, the aim of my project is to construct a genealogy of the subject. The method is an archaeology of knowledge, and the precise domain of the analysis is what I should call technologies. I mean the articulation of certain techniques and certain kinds of discourse about the subject"; Michel Foucault, "About the Beginning of the Hermeneutics of the Self (1980)," in *Religion and Culture*, ed. Jeremy R. Carrette (New York: Routledge, 1999), 161n4. This lucid and explicit articulation of Foucault's project comes in the version of this lecture, which he delivered in the Howison Lectures at Berkeley in October 1980.

8. For a recent review of one of the most famous experiments in the social psychology of power dynamics of domination and submission, see Philip G. Zimbardo's retrospective on his role as "superintendent" and principal investigator, "Revisiting the Stanford Prison Experiment: A Lesson in the Power of the Situation," *Chronicle of Higher Education* 53, no. 30 (30 March 2007): B6–B7. For a recent reflection on the theological significance of the power dynamics in BDSM (bondage, discipline / domination, sadism / submission, masochism) scenes, see Nicholas Laccetti, "Calvary and the Dungeon: Theologizing BDSM," in *Queer Christianities: Lived Religion in Transgressive Forms*, ed. Kathleen T. Talvacchia, Michael F. Pettinger, and Mark Larrimore (New York and London: New York University Press, 2015) 148–59.
9. Foucault, "About the Beginning of the Hermeneutics of the Self," 162.
10. James Bernauer, "Cry of Spirit," Foreword to Foucault, *Religion and Culture*, xiii; see also Bernauer, *Michel Foucault's Force of Flight: Toward an Ethics for Thought* (Atlantic Highlands, N.J.: Humanities Press, 1990), and James Bernauer and Jeremy Carrette, eds., *Michel Foucault and Theology: The Politics of Religious Experience* (Aldershot and Burlington, Vt.: Ashgate, 2004).
11. Talal Asad takes up Foucault's project and applies it to medieval Christian monastic practices as well as twentieth-century discourses around the Salman Rushdie affair; see Asad, *Genealogies of Religion: Discipline and Reasons of Power in Christianity and Islam* (Baltimore and London: Johns Hopkins University Press, 1993).
12. For discussion of "suspicion" and "retrieval," or what Ricouer also called "hermeneutics of faith," within a broader historical perspective, see Jean Grondin, *Introduction to Philosophical Hermeneutics* (New Haven: Yale University Press, 1994), 15.
13. Paul M. Lloyd, "On the Names of Languages (and Other Things)," in *Latin and the Romance Languages in the Early Middle Ages*, ed. Roger Wright (London and New York: Routledge, 1991), 14, which cites T. F. Mitchell, "What Is Educated Spoken Arabic?," in *Aspects of Arabic Sociolinguistics (International Journal of the Sociology of Language*, 61), ed. Björn H. Jernudd and Muhammad H. Ibrahim (Berlin: Mouton de Gruyter, 1986), 10; cf. Ziolkowski, "Cultural Diglossia," 193ff.
14. Kees Versteegh, "Latinitas, Hellenismos, 'Arabiyya," in *The History of Linguistics in the Classical Period*, ed. Daniel J. Taylor (Amsterdam and Philadelphia: John Benjamins, 1987), 251.
15. Roger Wright, "Introduction: Latin and Romance; A Thousand Years of Incertitude," in *Latin and the Romance Languages in the Early Middle Ages*, ed. Roger Wright (London and New York: Routledge, 1991), 2.
16. Versteegh, *The Arabic Language* (1997; repr. Edinburgh: Edinburgh University Press, 2001); see especially the historical overview in Chap. 7, "The Emergence of New Arabic," 93–98.
17. Joshua A. Fishman, "Bilingualism with and without Diglossia; Diglossia with and without Bilingualism," *Journal of Social Issues* 23, no. 2 (1967): 31–32. Fishman's scholarship on diglossia and multilingualism built on Charles Ferguson's groundbreaking article "Diglossia," *Word* 15 (1959): 325–40.
18. Wright, "How Latin Came to Be a Foreign Language for All," in *A Sociophilological Study of Late Latin* (Turnhout: Brepols, 2002), 10.
19. Ibid., 12–13.

20. Ibid., 14–15.
21. Also known as Hrabanus Magnentius, this politically engaged archbishop of Mainz, socially conscious Benedictine abbot of Fulda, and erudite Carolingian luminary went to Tours to study under Alcuin in 802 C.E. His writings affirmed the study of the liberal arts for Christians (*De institutione clericorum*); advanced the field of logic through a grammatical treatise (*De arte grammatica*); and explicated the scholarly and mystical meaning of some 3,150 key words (*De universo* or *De rerum naturis*).
22. Wright, "How Latin Came to Be," 15.
23. Tore Janson, "Language Change and Metalinguistic Change: Latin to Romance and Other Cases," in *Latin and the Romance Languages in the Early Middle Ages*, ed. Roger Wright (London and New York: Routledge, 1991), 23.
24. Wright, "How Latin Came to Be,"16.
25. Ziolkowski, "Cultural Diglossia," 196.
26. Ibid., 197.
27. Victor Danner, "Arabic Literature in Iran," in *The Cambridge History of Iran*, vol. 4, *The Period from the Arab Invasion to the Saljuqs*, ed. R. N. Frye (Cambridge: Cambridge University Press, 1975), 580–81.
28. ʿAbdallah ibn al-Muqaffaʿ (d. ca. 139 A.H./756 C.E.), born in Fīrūzābād, lived in Baṣra and Kūfa, was secretary to Umayyad governors, and is most famous for his translation from Pahlavi into Arabic of *Kalīla wa-Dimna* (a collection of Indian fables), by which he had tremendous influence on the development of Arabic literary prose; see F. Gabrieli, "Ibn al-Mukaffaʿ," in *Encyclopaedia of Islam*, 2nd ed., ed. P. Bearman et al. (Leiden: Brill, 2011; Brill Online, Harvard University, http://www.brillonline.nl/subscriber/entry?entry=islam_SIM-3304; accessed 19 January 2011).
29. Ibn al-Nadīm, Abū 'l-Faradj Muḥammad b. Abī Yaʿḳūb Isḥāḳ al-Warrāḳ al-Baghdādī (d. ca. 385 A.H./ 995 C.E.) lived in Baghdad, was Imāmī Shīʿī, and wrote the important *Kitāb al-Fihrist*, which he intended as an index of all Arabic books; see J. W. Fück, "Ibn al-Nadīm, Abu 'l-Faradj Muḥammad b. Abī Yaʿḳūb Isḥāḳ al-Warrāḳ al-Baghdādī," in *Encyclopaedia of Islam*, http://www.brillonline.nl/subscriber/entry?entry=islam_SIM-3317; accessed 19 January 2011.
30. Gilbert Lazard, "The Rise of the New Persian Language," in *The Cambridge History of Iran*, ed. R. N. Frye (Cambridge: Cambridge University Press) 4:598.
31. Ibid., 600.
32. Ibid., 602.
33. Ibid., 604.
34. The only extant works in Persian by Avicenna are *Dāneš-nāma-ye ʿalāʾī* (*Book of Science*) and *Andar dāneš-e rag* (*On the Science of the Pulse*). Unlike his writings in Arabic, which were intended for scholarly audiences, these two works were introductions intended for the uninitiated. They avoid terminology, treat only elementary topics, and employ a lucid nonscholarly style; see M. Achena, "Avicenna," section xi, "Persian Works," in *Encyclopaedia Iranica*, ed. Ehsan Yarshater (London and New York: Routledge and Kegan Paul, 1989), 3:66–110. General description of Persian works are on 99–100.
35. Lazard, "Rise of the New Persian Language," 631.
36. Danner, "Arabic Literature in Iran," 594.

37. Ibid., 593.
38. As noted by Qābūs b. Washmakīr (d. 1012 or 1013) and others.
39. Abū 'l-Rayḥān Muḥammad b. Aḥmad al-Bīrūnī (Bērūnī), a Persian native speaker, known as "*al-Ustādh*" ("the Professor") for his great scholarship, lived in Kāth, capital of Khwārizm, and wrote his scientific works in Arabic. These covered math, astronomy, the physical and natural sciences, geography, language, and history. Among his approximately 180 works was *Kitāb tārīkh al-hind* (*Alberuni's India: An Account of the Religion, Philosophy, Literature, Geography, Chronology, Astronomy, Customs, Laws, and Astrology of India about A.D. 1030*, ed. and trans. E. Sachau [New Delhi: Asian Educational Services, 1993]), important to comparative theology as demonstrated by Kemal Ataman's *Understanding Other Religions: Al-Biruni and Gadamer's "Fusion of Horizons"* (Washington, D.C.: Council for Research in Values and Philosophy, 2008); see D. J. Boilot, "Al-Bīrūnī (Bērūnī) Abu 'l-Rayḥān Muḥammad b. Aḥmad," in *Encyclopaedia of Islam*, http://www.brillonline.nl/subscriber/entry?entry=islam_SIM-1438; accessed 19 January 2011.
40. Danner, "Arabic Literature in Iran," 594.
41. Al-Bīrūnī, *Al-Biruni's Book on Pharmacy and Materia Medica*, ed. and trans. Hakim Mohammed Said (Karachi: Hamdard Academy, 1973), 7–8. For the original Arabic of the same, see Abū 'l-Rayhān al-Bīrūnī, *Kitāb al-Ṣaydana fi'l-Ṭibb*, ed. ʿAbbās Zaryāb (Tehran: Iran University Press, 1991), 14.
42. Danner, "Arabic Literature in Iran," 594. Danner attributes this quotation to al-Bīrūnī's *Kitāb al-ṣaidala* but gives no exact citation.
43. George Makdisi's *The Rise of Colleges: Institutions of Learning in Islam and the West* (Edinburgh: Edinburgh University Press, 1981), 76. *The Rise of Colleges* is one of the relatively few treatments of medieval Islamic education. Makdisi's focus is squarely on law and legal education, and specifically the institution of the madrasa. More recent additions to the growing literature on Islamic education in its traditional and modern forms include: Eeqbal Hassim, *Elementary Education and Motivation in Islam: Perspectives of Medieval Muslim Scholars, 750–1400 C.E.* (Amherst, N.Y.: Cambria, 2010); Wilna A. J. Meijer, *Tradition and Future of Islamic Education*, trans. Susan Rustidge (Münster: Waxmann, 2009); and Wadad Kadi, "Education in Islam—Myths and Truths," in *Islam and Education: Myths and Truths*, ed. Wadad Kadi and Victor Billeh (Chicago: University of Chicago Press, 2007), 5–18.
44. *Awqāf* is the plural of *waqf*, meaning a religious endowment for a religious, educational, or charitable cause.
45. Makdisi, *Rise of Colleges*, 79; cites Abū 'l-Barakāt ʿAbd al-Raḥmān Ibn al-Anbārī, *Nuzhat al-alibbāʾ fī ṭabaqāt al-udabāʾ*, ed. A. Amer (Stockholm: Almquist and Wiksell, 1962), 55. Ibn al-Anbārī was an Arabic philologist who was a student, then a professor at the Niẓāmiyya madrasa in Baghdad. The *Nuzha* is a biographical history of Arabic philology; see C. Brockelmann, "Al-Anbārī, Abu 'l-Barakāt ʿAbd al-Raḥmān b. Muḥ. b.ʿUbayd Allāh b. Abī Saʿīd Kamāl al-Dīn (properly Ibn al-Anbārī)," in *Encyclopaedia of Islam*, http://www.brillonline.nl/ subscriber/entry?entry=islam_SIM-0661); accessed 19 January 2011.
46. For more on the important role of memorization (*ḥifẓ*), cf. Hassim, *Elementary Education and Motivation in Islam*, 63.

47. Makdisi, *Rise of Colleges*, 103.
48. Ibid., 123–24.
49. Makdisi, *The Rise of Humanism in Classical Islam and the Christian West: With Special Reference to Scholasticism* (Edinburgh: Edinburgh University Press, 1990), 141; cf. Hassim, *Elementary Education and Motivation in Islam*, 57.
50. Hassim, *Elementary Education and Motivation in Islam* (71–72) adds to our understanding with the following clarification: "There were two types of *katātīb* in the medieval Muslim period—one specialised in teaching literacy and penmanship, and the other taught the Qur'an and other elementary subjects. By the time of Ibn Khaldūn, however, there was some form of amalgamation between the two types of *katātīb*."
51. Makdisi, *Rise of Humanism*, 141.
52. Kadi, "Education in Islam," 7.
53. Ignaz Goldziher, "Education (Muslim)," in *Encyclopaedia of Religion and Ethics*, ed. James Hastings (New York: Charles Scribner's Sons, 1961), 5:199a.
54. Ibid., 200a.
55. Makdisi, *Rise of Humanism*, 125.
56. Ibid., 49.
57. Ibid., 88.
58. Ibid., 53.
59. Ibid., 121.
60. Kadi, "Education in Islam," 11.
61. For a rich historical account of the still living tradition of Qur'anic education and the *ijāza* system, see Ingrid Mattson, Chap. 4, "The Voice and the Pen," in *The Story of the Qur'an: Its History and Place in Muslim Life* (Malden, Mass.: Blackwell, 2008), 76–136.
62. Richard Bulliet, *The Patricians of Nishapur: A Study of Medieval Islamic Social History* (Cambridge, Mass.: Harvard University Press, 1972), 54.
63. Ibid., 48.
64. Ibid., 50.
65. Versteegh, *Arabic Grammar and Qur'ānic Exegesis in Early Islam* (Leiden and New York: Brill, 1993).
66. Versteegh, "Linguistics and Exegesis: Muqatil on the Explanation of the *Qur'ān*," in *Landmarks in Linguistic Thought*, vol. 3, *The Arabic Linguistic Tradition* (London and New York: Routledge, 1997), 11–22.
67. Georges Bohas, Jean-Patrick Guillaume, and Djamel Eddin Kouloughli, *The Arabic Linguistic Tradition* (London and New York: Routledge, 1990), 33.
68. Michael G. Carter, *Sībawayhi* (London: I. B. Tauris, 2004), 1.
69. Ibid., 135.
70. Ibid., 98.
71. Henri Fleisch, *Traité de philologie arabe* (Beirut: Imprimerie Catholique, 1961), 1:2–11.
72. Ibid., 1:2.
73. Ibid., 1:9.
74. Bohas, Guillaume, and Kouloughli, *Arabic Linguistic Tradition*, 5.
75. Ibid., 8; Fleisch 1:14.
76. Bohas, Guillaume, and Kouloughli, *Arabic Linguistic Tradition*, 7.

77. Carter, "Arabic Grammar," in *The Cambridge History of Arabic Literature: Religion, Learning and Science in the 'Abbasid Period*, ed. M. J. L. Young, J. D. Latham, and R. B. Serjeant (Cambridge and New York: Cambridge University Press, 1990), 123.
78. Carter, *Sībawayhi*, 135.
79. Bohas, Guillaume, and Kouloughli, *Arabic Linguistic Tradition*, 8–14.
80. Jonathan Owens, "The Grammatical Tradition and Arabic Language Teaching: A View from Here," in *Investigating Arabic: Current Parameters in Analysis and Learning*, ed. Alaa Elgibali (Leiden: Brill, 2005), 109.
81. Owens, "Grammatical Tradition," 107; cites ʿAbd al-Raḥmān ibn Isḥāq Zajjājī, *The Explanation of Linguistic Causes: Az-Zağğāğī's Theory of Grammar*, trans. Kees Versteegh (Amsterdam and Philadelphia: J. Benjamins, 1995), 164.
82. See Copeland and Sluiter, *Medieval Grammar and Rhetoric*, and Russell, *Chaucer and the Trivium*. For an account of the Seven Liberal Arts as gateways to a spiritual world, cf. Virginia Sease and Manfred Schmidt-Brabant, "The Seven Liberal Arts as the Path of the Soul to the Spirit—The Goddess Natura and Her Retinue," in *Thinkers, Saints, Heretics: Spiritual Paths of the Middle Ages*, trans. Marguerite V. Miller and Douglas E. Miller (Forest Row, UK: Temple Lodge, 2007), 62–73. For an older general treatment of the trivium and quadrivium, cf. Paul Abelson, *The Seven Liberal Arts: A Study in Mediaeval Culture* (New York: Teachers' College, Columbia University, 1906). For essays covering a range of topics on medieval education in the West, cf. Ronald B. Begley and Joseph W. Koterski, eds., *Medieval Education* (New York: Fordham University Press, 2005).

    For a fascinating account of education in Italy just after Gerson's era, including Chap. 2, focusing on grammatical education, cf. Paul F. Gehl's book, published as a blog: Gehl, *Humanism for Sale: Making and Marketing Schoolbooks in Italy, 1450–1650*, http://www.humanismforsale.org; accessed 6 May 2011.
83. For reference to this story as "general knowledge," cf. Charlotte J. Steiner, "Crates of Mallos," *Classical Review* 54, no. 1 (2004): 48. For identification of Crates's lecturing as the beginning of grammar in Rome, cf. "Crates of Mallus," *Encyclopaedia Britannica* (Encyclopaedia Britannica Online, Encyclopaedia Britannica, 2011, http://www.britannica.com.ezpprod1.hul.harvard.edu/EBchecked/topic/141955/Crates-of-Mallus; accessed 6 May 2011).
84. David L. Wagner, "The Seven Liberal Arts and Classical Scholarship," in *The Seven Liberal Arts in the Middle Ages*, ed. David L. Wagner (Bloomington: Indiana University Press, 1983) 9, 11.
85. Jeffrey F. Huntsman, "Grammar," in *The Seven Liberal Arts in the Middle Ages*, 69–70. Note that neither Donatus nor Gerson (following Donatus) used this list (replacing the article with the interjection) or this order for presenting the parts of speech.
86. Wagner, "The Seven Liberal Arts and Classical Scholarship," 21n42, citing Charles Sears Baldwin, *Medieval Rhetoric and Poetic ȇto ấŷŷῶ: Interpreted from Representative Works* (New York: Macmillan, 1928), 90–91.
87. Marcus Terentius Varro's (116–27 B.C.) *Nine Books of Disciplines* included architecture and medicine, which later were sidelined as more practical than philosophical. Varro's *Nine Books* was lost to medieval Europe, but exerted influence via other books about the disciplines of knowledge, especially the *Marriage of Mercury and Philology* of Mar-

tianus Minneius Felix Capella (fl. 410–39). Of most direct influence on medieval European thought regarding the disciplines, however, was Anicius Manlius Severinus Boethius (ca. 480–524); Huntsman, "Grammar," 59–60.

88. Karl F. Morrison, "Incentives for Studying the Liberal Arts," in *Seven Liberal Arts in the Middle Ages*, 53.
89. Ibid., 40.
90. Wagner, "The Seven Liberal Arts and Classical Scholarship," 21.
91. Louis John Paetow, *The Arts Course at Medieval Universities with Special Reference to Grammar and Rhetoric*, University Studies 3, no. 7 (Urbana-Champaign, Ill.: University of Illinois Press, 1910), 33.
92. Cf. Robert A. Kaster, *Guardians of Language: The Grammarian and Society in Late Antiquity* (Berkeley: University of California Press, 1988). Kaster's focus is on the *grammaticus* "who has often been overshadowed in modern studies (as he was in antiquity) by his more conspicuous colleague, the rhetorician" (ix).
93. Huntsman, "Grammar," 62.
94. Ibid., 63.
95. Joseph Farrell, *Latin Language and Latin Culture: From Ancient to Modern Times* (Cambridge and New York: Cambridge University Press, 2001), 7.
96. Paetow, *Arts Course at Medieval Universities*, 34.
97. There is more clarity about the time of the composition of Alexander's *Doctrinale* (ca. 1199) than there is about the dates of his birth (between 1160 and 1170) and death (around the middle of the thirteenth century); see Alejandro de Villadei, *El doctrinal: Una gramática latina del Renacimiento del siglo XII*, trans. Marco A. Gutiérrez Galindo (Madrid: Akal, 1993), 61–64. Gutiérrez Galindo relies on the biographical material provided by Dietrich Reichling from a century before; See Reichling, ed., *Das Doctrinale des Alexander de Villa-Dei* (Berlin: A. Hofmann, 1893), xx–xxvi.
98. We apparently know even less about Evrard of Béthune's biography, save that he was born in Béthune and died around 1212; see Anne Grondeux, *"Graecismus" d'Évrard de Béthune à travers ses gloses: Entre grammaire positive et grammaire spéculative du XIIe au XVe siècle* (Turnhout: Brepols, 2000), 7. This famous Latin grammatical work is known as the *Graecismus* due to its eighth chapter, which is devoted to Latin words derived from Greek.
99. Copeland and Sluiter, *Medieval Grammar and Rhetoric*, 544–45.
100. Huntsman, "Grammar," 77.
101. Copeland and Sluiter, *Medieval Grammar and Rhetoric*, 545.
102. For a somewhat *recherché* but erudite overview of speculative grammar, cf. Louis G. Kelly, "Introduction," in *The Mirror of Grammar: Theology, Philosophy, and the Modistae* (Amsterdam and Philadelphia: J. Benjamins, 2002), 1–10.
103. Huntsman, "Grammar," 64.
104. Paetow, *Arts Course at Medieval Universities*, 35.
105. Huntsman, "Grammar," 81.
106. Copeland and Sluiter, *Medieval Grammar and Rhetoric*, 82, 83.
107. Kaster, *Guardians of Language*, 139–40.
108. Huntsman, "Grammar," 71–72.
109. Copeland and Sluiter, *Medieval Grammar and Rhetoric*, 84.

110. Ibid., 814.
111. Lynn Thorndike, "Elementary and Secondary Education in the Middle Ages," *Speculum* 15, no. 4 (October 1940): 400–8.
112. Ibid., 403.
113. Ibid.
114. Ibid., 402.
115. Guibert de Nogent, *De vita sua* I.iv; cited in Thorndike, "Elementary and Secondary Education," 402.
116. Thorndike, "Elementary and Secondary Education," 403, cites Charles G. Crump and E. F. Jacobs, eds., *The Legacy of the Middle Ages* (Oxford: Clarendon, 1926), 260.
117. Thorndike, "Elementary and Secondary Education," 403.
118. Document cited from the year 1337; Marcel Fournier, *Les statuts et privilèges des universités françaises depuis leur fondation jusqu'en ďå̉šô: Ouvrage publié sous les auspices du Ministère de l'instruction publique et du Conseil général des facultés de Caen* (Paris: L. Larose et Forcel, 1890–94), 1:553; cited in Paetow, *Arts Course at Medieval Universities*, 55n16.
119. Document cited from the year 1311; Fournier, *Statuts* 1:472; cited in Paetow, *Arts Course at Medieval Universities*, 55n16.
120. Paetow, *Arts Course at Medieval Universities*, 45. Johannes de Garlandia's major works are *Clavis compendii*, *Compendium grammatice*, and the *Accentarius*. With its accessible introductory essays and critical editions of primary sources, Copeland and Sluiter, *Medieval Grammar and Rhetoric*, is an invaluable resource in this area.
121. Paetow, *Arts Course at Medieval Universities*, 46.
122. Ibid., 49, 58.
123. Ibid., 57.
124. Ibid., 55.
125. Ibid., 50.
126. Michel Foucault, *Discipline and Punish: The Birth of the Prison*, trans. Alan Sheridan, 2nd ed. (New York: Vintage / Random House, 1995), 194.

2. *Genres and Genders of Gerson*

1. Brian Patrick McGuire, *Jean Gerson and the Last Medieval Reformation* (University Park: Pennsylvania State University Press, 2005), 163.
2. Louis Mourin, *Jean Gerson: Six sermons français inédits; Étude doctrinale et littéraire suivie de l'édition critique et de remarques linguistiques*, preface by André Combes (Paris: J. Vrin, 1946), 156.
3. Ibid., 92.
4. Ibid., 155.
5. Jacques Derrida, "The Law of Genre," trans. Avital Ronell, *Critical Inquiry* 7, no. 1 (Autumn 1980).
6. Daniel Hobbins, *Authorship and Publicity before Print: Jean Gerson and the Transformation of Late Medieval Learning* (Philadelphia: University of Pennsylvania Press, 2009).
7. This section draws on McGuire, *Jean Gerson and the Last Medieval Reformation*.

8. Franco Alessio, "Scolastique," in *Dictionnaire raisonné de l'Occident médiéval*, ed. Jacques Le Goff and Jean-Claude Schmitt (Paris: Fayard, 1999), 1053; cited in Hobbins, *Beyond the Schools: New Writings and the Social Imagination of Jean Gerson* (Ph.D. diss., Notre Dame University, 2002), 24.
9. Heiko Oberman, *Forerunners of the Reformation: The Shape of Late Medieval Thought*, trans. Paul L. Nyhus (New York: Holt, Rinehart, and Winston, 1966); cited in Hobbins, *Beyond the Schools*, 34n84.
10. McGuire, *Jean Gerson and the Last Medieval Reformation*, 28.
11. Ibid., 53.
12. Charles Homer Haskins, *The Renaissance of the Twelfth Century* (Cambridge, Mass: Harvard University Press, 1927).
13. Étienne Gilson, *History of Christian Philosophy in the Middle Ages* (London: Sheed and Ward, 1955).
14. Steven Ozment, *The Age of Reform 1250–1550: An Intellectual and Religious History of Late Medieval and Reformation Europe* (New Haven and London: Yale University Press, 1980).
15. Erika Rummel, *The Humanist-Scholastic Debate in the Renaissance and Reformation* (Cambridge, Mass.: Harvard University Press, 1995), 39; cited in Hobbins, *Beyond the Schools*, 10.
16. Gerson, *Bene actum esset*, in *Oeuvres complètes*, ed. Palémon Glorieux (Paris: Desclée, 1960), 2:43; trans. and cited in Daniel Hobbins, "The Schoolman as Public Intellectual: Jean Gerson and the Late Medieval Tract," *American Historical Review* 108 (2003): 1333.
17. See Gerson, *De contractibus*, in *Oeuvres complètes*, 9:420; trans. and cited in Hobbins, *Beyond the Schools*, 161–62.
18. Gerson, *Epistola*, in *Oeuvres complètes*, 3:28; English: *Jean Gerson: Early Works*, trans. Brian Patrick McGuire (New York: Paulist Press, 1998), 174; cited in McGuire, "Jean Gerson and Renewal of Scholastic Discourse (1400–1415)," in *Knowledge, Discipline and Power in the Middle Ages: Essays in Honour of David Luscombe*, ed. Joseph Canning, Edmund King, and Martial Staub (Leiden and Boston: Brill, 2011), 131–32n11.
19. Hobbins, *Beyond the Schools*, 45–46.
20. Ian P. Wei, "The Self-Image of the Masters of Theology at the University of Paris in the Late Thirteenth and Early Fourteenth Centuries," *Journal of Ecclesiastical History* 46, no. 3 (July 1995): 408.
21. Ibid., 409. As another example, Gerson's mentor, Pierre d'Ailly, in 1415 at the Council of Constance, asserted that masters of theology and of canon and civil law should be entitled to vote . . . : "They hold the authority to preach and teach anywhere in the world, especially theologians, and that is no small authority among Christian people. It is of much greater account than that of an ignorant bishop or abbot who is only titular" (431).
22. Hobbins, *Beyond the Schools*, 111.
23. Genre was a vexed question among late medieval schoolmen besides Gerson. Lusignan links the "confusion of genres" in the fifteenth century to institutions of the time losing their monopoly on certain kinds of literary culture; see Serge Lusignan, "Les difficultés d'une typologie des écrits du Moyen Âge tardif," in *Pratiques de la culture écrite en France au XVe siècle: Actes du colloque international du CNRS, Paris, 16–18 mai 1992, organisé en l'honneur de Gilbert Ouy par l'unité de recherche "Culture écrite du Moyen*

Âge tardif," ed. Monique Ornato and Nicole Pons (Louvain-la-Neuve: Fédération internationale des instituts d'études médiévales; Turnhout: Brepols, 1995), 560–61; cited in Hobbins, *Beyond the Schools,* 49n2.

See also Léopold Genicot, "Du genre et de quelques genres," in *Les genres littéraires dans les sources théologiques et philosophiques médiévales: Définition, critique et exploitation; Actes du Colloque international de Louvain-la-Neuve, 25–27 mai 1981* (Louvain-la-Neuve: Institut d'études médiévales de l'Université Catholique de Louvain, 1982), and Rosalie Colie, *The Resources of Kind: Genre Theory in the Renaissance,* ed. B. K. Lewalski (Berkeley: University of California Press, 1973).

24. Brian Patrick McGuire reinforces Hobbins's argument with his study of Gerson's use of the vernacular for particular audiences: "Gerson in his pastoral writings reveals how he tried to combine theological learning and moral discourse. His method was to take his audience into consideration"; McGuire, "Jean Gerson and Bilingualism in the Late Medieval University," *Pratiques de traduction au Moyen Âge: Actes du colloque de l'Université de Cophenhague 25 et 26 octobre 2002; Medieval Translation Practices: Papers from the Symposium at the University of Cophenhagen 25th and 26th October 2002,* ed. Peter Andersen (Njalsgade: University of Copenhagen, Museum Tusculanum Press, 2004), 127.
25. Hobbins, *Beyond the Schools,* 85–86.
26. Ibid., 96, 98–99.
27. Ibid., 167–78.
28. Ibid., 114–15.
29. Catherine D. Brown, *Pastor and Laity in the Theology of Jean Gerson* (New York: Cambridge University Press, 1987), 23. Another star of Paris preaching in Gerson's era was Jean Courtecuisse (1353–1423).
30. Ibid., 17.
31. Larissa Taylor, "French Sermons, 1215–1535," in *The Sermon,* ed. Beverly Kienzle, Typologie des sources du Moyen Âge occidental 81 (Turnhout: Brepols, 2000), 750.
32. Ibid., 729–30.
33. Beverly Kienzle, "Introduction," in *Sermon,* 143.
34. Nicole Bériou, *L'Avènement des maîtres de la parole: La prédication à Paris au XIIIe siècle,* Collection des études augustiniennes: Serie Moyen Âge et temps modernes 31–32 (Paris: Institut d'études augustiniennes, 1998), 1:130; cited in Augustine Thompson, "From Texts to Preaching: Retrieving the Medieval Sermon as an Event," in *Preacher, Sermon and Audience in the Middle Ages,* ed. Carolyn Muessig (Leiden: Brill, 2002), 14n5.
35. Kienzle, "Introduction," 162.
36. Ibid., 151.
37. Ibid., 154.
38. Ibid., 155.
39. Ibid.
40. Ibid.
41. Ibid.
42. Ibid., 168.
43. The sermon, since both a literary and an oral genre, offers major challenges to the interpreter who has only a preserved text to study. One of these challenges, hidden by

the text, is that the sermon is an event, an oral performance, as well as a literary artifact. The written records of a sermon left to us today can bear many possible relationships to the actual historical event of the oral performance of that sermon. The character of that relationship between the performance and the text is neither simple nor obvious; see Thompson, "From Texts to Preaching," 13–37.

44. Beverly Kienzle, "Problems of Interpreting the Sermon," in *Sermon*, 971.
45. Thompson, "From Texts to Preaching," 17.
46. Larissa Taylor's discussion drives this point home throughout her "French Sermons, 1215–1535."
47. Kienzle, "Problems of Interpreting the Sermon," 971n31; cites Jean Longère, *La prédication médiévale* (Paris: Études Augustieniennes, 1983) 164, which "enumerates the milieux in which preaching would have been done in Latin: 'La prédication en latin parît devoir être réservée à la Curie romaine, aux assemblées conciliaires, à l'Université, aux chapitres généraux, aux moines noirs, à certains ordres commes les Victorins au 12e siècle, les cicterciens, les frères Prêcheurs, à des maisons cléricales ou religieuses, tels les couvents d'études.'"
48. Taylor, "French Sermons, 1215–1535," 747.
49. "The earliest extant French sermon, a *Sermo sur Jonas* preached in 950 [C.E.], already displays many of the traits sermon scholars have remarked about the language of later medieval sermons. Macaronic, or mixed language, sermons appear as early as the twelfth century"; ibid., 745.
50. Mourin, *Jean Gerson.*
51. Hobbins, *Beyond the Schools*, 98n43, notes this lacuna in scholarly coverage.
52. McGuire, *Jean Gerson and the Last Medieval Reformation*, 358. Longère (*La Prédication medieval*, 129) gives 1409 as the year for Gerson becoming pastor of St. Jean-en-Grève.
53. "University education still took place exclusively in Latin, but accomplished theologians like Gerson had begun to imitate the mendicant preachers who long had managed to combine Latin learning with vernacular preaching"; McGuire, "Jean Gerson and Bilingualism," 121–22.
54. Karl F. Morrison, "Incentives for Studying the Liberal Arts," in *The Seven Liberal Arts in the Middle Ages*, ed. David L. Wagner (Bloomington: Indiana University Press, 1983), 32–57.
55. All citations and *exempla* in the sermon have been listed in Mourin, *Jean Gerson*, 105–11.
56. Gerson used the same *sermonicatio* technique in his earlier *Mendicité spirituelle*, in which his two characters are Man and Reason; Mourin, *Jean Gerson*, 112.
57. Mourin's analysis of this sermon has been extremely useful; see "La technique du sermon," in *Jean Gerson* (95–104, esp. 98) as well as "Le style," ibid., 112, on this point of rhetorical unity; cf. Bériou, "Les sermons latins après 1200," in *Sermon*."
58. "Et quid est hoc? interrogavi terram, et dixit: 'non sum'; et quaecumque in eadem sunt, idem confessa sunt. Interrogavi mare et abyssas et reptilla animarum vivarum, et responderunt: 'non sumus deus tuus; quaere super nos'"; Augustine, *Confessions*, Book X, section 9.
59. Mourin, *Jean Gerson*, 161.

60. Ibid.
61. Rom 11:33.
62. Mourin, *Jean Gerson*, 166–67.
63. Ibid., 167.
64. Ibid.
65. Ibid.
66. Ibid., 169–70.
67. Ibid., 170–71.
68. Cf. ibid., 128.
69. McGuire, "Jean Gerson and Bilingualism," 128.
70. Phyllis B. Roberts, "Medieval University Preaching: The Evidence in the Statutes," in *Medieval Sermons and Society: Cloister, City, University*, ed. Jacqueline Hamesse et al. (Louvain-la-neuve: Fédération Internationale des Instituts d'études médiévales, 1998), 318.
71. Ibid., 319.
72. Also known as Thomas of Salisbury, d. 1233–36.
73. Phyllis Roberts, "Sermons and Preaching in/and the Medieval University," in *Medieval Education*, ed. Ronald B. Begley and Joseph W. Koterski (New York: Fordham University, 2005), 91; cites James J. Murphy, *Rhetoric in the Middle Ages: A History of Rhetorical Theory from St. Augustine to the Renaissance* (Berkeley and Los Angeles: University of California Press, 1974), 311–26.
74. Jean Gerson, *Opera omnia*, ed. Louis Ellis du Pin (Hildesheim and New York: Olms, 1987), 3:899A; hereafter referred to as Du Pin. English translation is my own.
75. Taylor, "French Sermons, 1215–1535," 737–38.
76. Actually Job 7:1 in the Vulgate.
77. Du Pin, 900A.
78. Ibid., 900B–C.
79. Ibid., 902B.
80. Ibid., 902C.
81. Ibid., 902D.
82. Kienzle, "Problems of Interpreting the Sermon," 970, cites Nicole Bériou, "Les sermons latins après 1200," 416–20.
83. Du Pin, 905.
84. Hobbins, "Schoolman as Public Intellectual," 1318–19.
85. "It bears repeating that Gerson did not publish a single commentary—by any meaningful definition of that term—and yet made a name as the greatest schoolman of his age. He did so by entering the public arena as no university master before him, and attempting to control the terms of debate. . . . He was often resented. But this is the whole point: unlike Thomas Aquinas, he had a public presence outside the university to be resented, and rather than lament the 'vulgarization' of scholastic theology, we should recognize the historical shift that was occurring here"; Hobbins, "Schoolman as Public Intellectual," 1334.
86. Hobbins summarizes the contention of André Combes that Gerson did in fact publish a commentary of Peter Lombard's Sentences (Combes, "Études gersoniennes, II: Note sur les 'Sententiae Magistri Joannis Gerson' du manuscrit B.N. lat. 15.156," *Archives*

d'histoire doctrinale et littéraire du Moyen Âge 12 [1939]: 365–87), as well as Glorieux's identification of that commentary as belonging instead to the pen of a certain Jean Régis ("Le commentaire sur les Sentences attribué à Jean Gerson," *Recherches de théologie ancienne et médiévale* 18 [1951]: 128–39); Hobbins, "Schoolman as Public Intellectual," 1317.

87. Hobbins, "Schoolman as Public Intellectual," 1314.
88. Ibid., 1328.
89. Ibid., 1327.
90. Ibid., 1320, and Appendix.
91. "As a point of reference, we might compare what are commonly regarded as the most popular works of the Middle Ages. Dante's *Commedia*, one of the most popular works of the entire Middle Ages, survives in some six hundred to seven hundred manuscripts. Of the medieval works commonly read in undergraduate courses today, it had no rival in circulation. Boccaccio's *Decameron* survives in around a hundred manuscripts, Froissart's *Chronicles* in over a hundred, *Piers Plowman* in fifty-three. We have eighty manuscripts of *The Canterbury Tales*, just sixteen of *Troilus and Criseyde*. Except for the *Commedia*, none of these works reached the circulation of Gerson's most popular works. His tract on nocturnal emissions survives in at least 160 manuscripts, his *Opus Tripartitum—a* work of basic Christian instruction—in more than 200 (Latin and French versions) and was printed twenty-three times in five languages before 1500 (compared to four printings for *The Canterbury Tales* and one for *Troilus*)"; Hobbins, "Schoolman as Public Intellectual," 1311.
92. The classical treatment of the issue in canon law is Gratian, "Distinction Six," *The Treatise on Laws (Decretum DD. 1–20)*, trans. Augustine Thompson (Washington, D.C.: The Catholic University of America Press, 1993), 18–21.

    Some of the recent scholarly treatments of medieval Christian discourse on nocturnal emissions, especially of priests, include the following: Dyan Elliott, "Pollution, Illusion and Masculine Disarray: Nocturnal Emissions and the Sexuality of the Clergy," in *Constructing Medieval Sexuality*, ed. Karma Lochrie, Peggy McCracken, and James A. Schultz (Minneapolis: University of Minnesota Press, 1997), 1–23; repr. in Dyan Elliott, *Fallen Bodies: Pollution, Sexuality, and Demonology in the Middle Ages* (Philadelphia: University of Pennsylvania Press, 1999), 14–34; Patrick J. Nugent, "Bodily Effluvia and Liturgical Interruption in Medieval Miracle Stories," *History of Religions* 41, no. 1 (August 2001): 49–70; C. Leyser, "Masculinity in Flux: Nocturnal Emission and the Limits of Celibacy in the Early Middle Ages," in *Masculinity in Medieval Europe*, ed. D. M. Hadley (London and New York: Longman, 1999), 103–20; James Brundage, "Obscene and Lascivious: Behavioral Obscenity in Canon Law," in *Obscenity: Social Control and Artistic Creation in the European Middle Ages*, ed. Jan Ziolkowski (Leiden: Brill, 1998), 246–59 (252–59 treat nocturnal emissions); John Kitchen, "Cassian, Nocturnal Emissions, and the Sexuality of Jesus," in *The Seven Deadly Sins: From Communities to Individuals*, ed. Richard Newhauser (Leiden and Boston, Mass.: Brill, 2007), 73–94; Jacqueline Murray, "'The Law of Sin That Is in My Members': The Problem of Male Embodiment," in *Gender and Holiness: Men, Women and Saints in Late Medieval Europe* (London and New York: Routledge, 2002), 9–22; Ruth Mazo Karras, "Thomas Aquinas's Chastity Belt: Clerical Masculinity in Medieval Europe," in

Gender and Christianity in Medieval Europe: New Perspectives, ed. Lisa M. Bitel and Felice Lifshitz (Philadelphia: University of Pennsylvania Press, 2008), 52–67; David Brakke, "The Problematization of Nocturnal Emissions in the Early Christian Church," in *Men and Masculinities in Christianity and Judaism: A Critical Reader*, ed. Björn Krondorfer (London: SCM Press, 2009); and Jennifer D. Thibodeaux, ed., *Negotiating Clerical Identities: Priests, Monks and Masculinity in the Middle Ages* (Basingstoke: Palgrave Macmillan, 2010).

93. Jean Gerson, *Tractatus de praeparatione ad Missam et pollutione nocturna*, in *Opera omnia*, vol. 3, ed. Louis Ellis Du Pin (Antwerp: 1706; repr. Hildesheim: Georg Olms Verlag, 1987), col. 323–34.
94. I am unsure how to construe the verb *contingere* in this sentence.
95. Jacqueline Murray, "Men's Bodies, Men's Minds: Seminal Emissions and Sexual Anxiety in the Middle Ages," *Annual Review of Sex Research* 10532528 (1997), vol. 8, electronic document without page numbers accessed through Academic Search Premier; originally published in *Annual Review of Sex Research* 8 (1997): 1–26.
96. "If there is among you any man who is unclean because of a nocturnal emission, then he must go outside the camp; he may not reenter the camp. But it shall be when evening approaches, he shall bathe himself with water, and at sundown he may reenter the camp" (Deuteronomy 23:10–11), and "Now if a man has a seminal emission, he shall bathe all his body in water and be unclean until evening" (Leviticus 15:16–17); New American Standard Bible, http://www.usccb.org/nab/bible/leviticus/leviticus15.htm; accessed 22 February 2011.
97. Murray, "Men's Bodies, Men's Minds."
98. Cf. Lisa Isherwood and Marcella Althaus-Reid, eds., *The Sexual Theologian: Essays in Sex, God and Politics* (London and New York: T. and T. Clark, 2004).
99. Derrida, "The Law of Genre," 224.

3. *Gerson's "Moralized" Primer of Spiritual Grammar*

1. Maria Colombo Timelli, "Le donat espirituel de Colard Mansion: Étude et édition," *Instituto Lombardo (Memorie Lett.)* 40 (1996): 257–59. For debate over attribution of *Donatus moralizatus* to Gerson, see Jean Gerson, *Oeuvres complètes*, ed. Palémon Glorieux (Paris: Desclée, 1960), 1:70. Gilbert Ouy in meeting with Timelli personally said that he "sees no particular reason to deny the attribution of the *Donatus* to Gerson." Nor does Ouy see enough reason "to attribute it to him with certitude: The question thus remains open for the time being." For date of composition, see Gerson, *Oeuvres complètes*, ed. Glorieux, 10:590. Glorieux determines that *Donatus moralizatus* was composed between April and July 1411. Between 1470 and 1505, there were some nineteen editions; see ibid., 1:76–77.
2. DM 835A.
3. Grammar is also significant in Gerson's *Anagogicum de verbo et hymno gloriae*, as elucidated in Ronald Jeffrey Fisher, *Jean Gerson's Meditation on Glory: A Study in the Semiotics of Medieval Negative Theology* (Ph.D. diss., Yale University, 1997). Fisher's study focuses on Gerson's *Anagogicum*, which is an apophatic text that Fisher closely connects to the Dionysian tradition. Fisher's investigation of "mystical grammar" is

limited to Gerson's grammatical paradigm for mystical theology as exhibited in the *Anagogicum*, which entails Gerson's recourse to the positive, comparative, and superlative modes or degrees of adjectives. It would be worthwhile reconsidering Fisher's interpretation of the *Anagogicum* in light of Gerson's much more extensive exploitation of grammar in *Donatus moralizatus*.

4. "Moralizatus" is also in some cases spelled "moralisatus."
5. Allegorical and moralizing interpretations of Greek and Roman mythology, poetry, and narratives did not by any means begin in medieval times, but rather go back to antiquity.
6. Jacqueline de Weever notes that Theodulf, Bishop of Orléans (ca. 760–821) first gave an "allegorical treatment" of the *Metamorphoses*: "He wrote in his *Carmina* that although Ovid contains *frivola multa* ('much frivolity'), much truth lies under the false covering"; de Weever, *Aesop and the Imprint of Medieval Thought: A Study of Six Fables as Translated at the End of the Middle Ages* (Jefferson, N.C., and London: McFarland, 2011), 16.
7. The only edition of the text is *"Ovide moralisé": Poème du commencement du quatorzième siècle publié d'après tous les manuscrits connus*, ed. Cornelis de Boer [Martina G. de Boer et al.], vols. 1–5 (Amsterdam: J. Müller, 1915–38). Manuscript tradition, parallels, and other background are covered in G. Paris, "Chrétien Legouais et autres traducteurs ou imitateurs d'Ovide," in *Histoire littéraire de la France* (Paris: Imprimerie nationale, 1885), 29:455–525. Later scholars have not agreed to the attribution of *L'Ovide moralisé* to Chrétien Legouais. A scholarly monograph devoted to the text is Joseph Engels, *Études sur l'Ovide moralisé* (Groningen-Batavia: J. B. Wolters, 1945). A voluminous recent study is most informative: Marylène Possamaï-Pérez, *L'Ovide moralisé: Essai d'interprétation* (Paris: Champion, 2006).
8. Raymond Cormier, "Ovide moralisé," in *Approaches to Teaching the Works of Ovid and the Ovidian Tradition*, ed. Barbara Weiden Boyd and Cora Fox (New York: Modern Language Association of America, 2010), 18.
9. For a critical edition of the first part of Bersuire's text, see Petrus Berchorius, *De formis figurisque deorum: Reductorium morale, liber xv; Ovidius moralizatus, cap. i: Textus e codice Brux, Bibl. Reg. 863–9 critice editus*, ed. J. Engels (Utrecht: Rijksuniversiteit, Instituut voor Laat Latijn, 1966); see also Daniel Javitch, "Rescuing Ovid from the Allegorizers," *Comparative Literature* 30, no. 2 (Spring 1978): 97–107. Javitch identifies the following source as the most valuable study of *Ovidius moralizatus*: F. Ghisalberti, "*L'Ovidius moralizatus* di Pierre Bersuire," *Studj romanzi* 23 (1933): 5–136.
10. Paris, "Chrétien Legouais," 506; Cormier, "Ovide moralisé," 19.
11. Cormier, "Ovide moralisé" (19) identifies the following as authors of vernacular imitations of *L'Ovide moralisé*: Guillaume de Machaut, Eustache Deschamps, Geoffrey Chaucer (in the *Legend of Good Women*), John Gower, and Christine de Pisan, who was a contemporary of Jean Gerson's. Bersuire's Latin prose version was translated into English in 1480, into French prose by Colard Mansion in 1484, and summarized in French again in the fifteenth century. There is an original page of Colard Mansion's translation in the Houghton Library at Harvard University. The accompanying booklet discusses the aesthetic and some historical features of the edition: Wytze Hellinga, *Colard Mansion: An Original Leaf from the Ovide moralisé, Bruges 1484*, intro. Wytze

and Lotte Hellinga (Amsterdam: Menno Hertzberger, 1963). For the vernacular prose summary of Bersuire's text, see *Ovide moralisé en prose ȇtexte du quinzième siècle)*, ed. C. de Boer (Amsterdam: North-Holland, 1954).

12. In her *L'Ovide moralisé: Essai d'interprétation*, Possamaï-Pérez makes much use of M.-R. Jung, "Aspects de *l'Ovide moralisé*," in *Ovidius redivivus: Von Ovid zu Dante*, ed. M. Picone and B. Zimmermann (Stuttgart: M/P Verlag für Wissenschaft und Forschung, 1994), 149–72; J.-Y. Tilliette, "L'écriture et sa métaphore: Remarques sur *l'Ovide moralisé*," in *Ensi firent li ancessor: Mélanges de philologie médiévale offerts à Marc-René Jung*, ed. Luciano Rossi et al. (Alessandria: Edizioni dell'Orso, 1996), 2:543–58; M. Zink, *La prédication en langue romane avant 1300* (1976; repr. Paris: Champion, 1983).
13. Possamaï-Pérez, *L'Ovide moralisé*, 838.
14. Possamaï-Pérez identifies these themes in ibid., 804ff.
15. Ibid., 798; cites Zink, *La prédication*, 12.
16. Possamaï-Pérez, *L'Ovide moralisé*, 838; cites Zink, *La prédication*, 140.
17. Javitch, "Rescuing Ovid from the Allegorizers," 99.
18. Ibid., 101.
19. "Allegory," in *A Dictionary of Literary Terms and Literary Theory*, ed. J. A. Cuddon and C. E. Preston, 4th ed. (Oxford: Blackwell, 1998), 20–23.
20. Graham Ward, "Allegory," in *Oxford Companion to Christian Thought*, ed. Adrian Hastings, Alistair Mason, and Hugh Pyper (Oxford and New York: Oxford University Press, 2000), 13.
21. When this practice of imposing ashes originally began, it was only for public penitents, but later it was extended to all the faithful, as decided at the Council of Benevento with Pope Urban II in 1091; see Thomas J. Talley, *The Origins of the Liturgical Year* (New York: Pueblo, 1986), 224; see also Robert Lesage, "Cendres," in *Catholicisme hier, aujourd'hui, demain: Encyclopédie en sept volumes*, ed. G. Jacquemet (Paris: Letouzey et Ané, 1948), 2:790.
22. The parenthetical references here refer to column number and letter in the Du Pin edition of Gerson's *Opera omnia*; see Introduction, note 6 for full bibliographic information.
23. It is worth noting here that in contrast to Gerson's treatment of *qualitas*, in Donatus's original enumeration the first attribute is called *modus*, translated by the English grammatical term "mood," which in his grammar of Latin entailed such values as indicative, infinitive, and subjunctive.
24. DM 902B.
25. John Bossy, "Moral Arithmetic: Seven Sins into Ten Commandments," in *Conscience and Casuistry in Early Modern Europe*, ed. E. Leites (Cambridge and New York: Cambridge University Press, 1988), 214–34, is a key article in understanding both this shift in Christian ethics to focus on the Decalogue and Gerson's role in that shift. For a recent treatment of Gerson's contribution to the Seven Deadly Sins tradition, see Nancy McLoughlin, "The Deadly Sins and Contemplative Politics: Gerson's Ordering of the Personal and Political Realms," in *Sin in Medieval and Early Modern Culture: The Tradition of the Seven Deadly Sins*, ed. Richard G. Newhauser and Susan J. Ridyard (Woodbridge: York Medieval Press, 2012), 132–56.
26. Bossy, "Moral Arithmetic," 216.

27. Ibid., 215.
28. Ibid.
29. Ibid.
30. Aquinas had made such a link around two centuries earlier, as for example in an article (I-II, q. 100, a. 3) in his *Summa Theologiae* on the question, "Do we trace all the moral precepts of the Old Law to the Ten Commandments?" (I-II, q. 100, a. 3). In explaining that we do indeed trace all moral precepts of the Old Law to the Decalogue, the first objection that Thomas puts up for consideration is reference to Jesus's own interpretation of Jewish law: "As Matthew 22:37, 39 says, the first and chief precepts of the Old Law are: 'Thou shalt love the Lord thy God' and 'Thou shalt love thy neighbor.' But these two precepts are not included in the Decalogue. Therefore, not all the moral precepts of the Old Law are included in the Decalogue." Thomas's reply to this objection is that the two precepts that Jesus named are "first and general precepts of the natural law self-evident to human reason, whether by nature or by faith." Consequently, the relationship between these two commandments and the ten is that "all precepts of the Decalogue are traceable to these two precepts as conclusions to general principles"; Thomas Aquinas, *Treatise on Law*, trans. Richard J. Regan (Indianapolis: Hackett, 2000), 73–74.
31. Bossy, "Moral Arithmetic," 222.
32. Ibid.
33. Ibid., 223.
34. There is a correlation here to the Islamic vision of the Last Day and God's "gathering" (*ḥashr*) all creatures together; see *Encyclopaedia of Islam* on "*kiyāma*," under the heading "The succession of eschatological events," section (d): the gathering (*ḥashr*):

    God "shall gather" (L.44; LIX.2). He shall gather men together "as if they had stayed (in their tombs) only one hour of the day" (X.45). He will gather the believers (XIX.85). He will gather the impious (XX.102; XXV.17; etc.). He will gather men and *djinn* (VI.130), men and demons (XIX.68). He will gather the angels (XXXIV.40). This is the universal gathering. Also taking part in this, it is decided at a later stage, will be those protected from *fanāʾ* by divine mercy; and even, according to al-Nawawī, pack-animals and wild animals. This will be the "standing" (*al-mawḳif*) in waiting for judgment. Some traditions maintain that the first who will "rise" and arrive at the place of assembly (*al-mahshar*) will be the Prophet of Islam. According to the most widespread beliefs, the prophets, the angels, and the virtuous will be spared the terrors of waiting. But humanity in general "will sweat with agony"; they will be drenched in their sweat (*al-ʿaraḳ*), which will "bridle" them, as the bit bridles the horse (cf. Ghazālī, *Iḥyāʾ ʿulūm al-dīn*, Cairo 1352/1933, iv, 436–37); Louis Gardet, "Ḳiyāma," in *Encyclopaedia of Islam*, ed. P. Bearman et al., 2nd ed. (Leiden: Brill, 2010), Brill Online, Harvard University, http://www.brillonline.nl/subscriber/ entry?entry=islam_COM-0526; accessed 29 October 2010.
35. The Nicene Creed famously describes the procession of the Holy Spirit using the "post-positional" conjunction ("*qui ex Patre Filioque procedit*"), and then goes on to use the "pre-positional" conjunction in the following phrase ("*qui cum Patre et Filio simul adoratur et conglorificatur*").
36. "*Merda*" is attested in Latin as "*vox convicii*"—that is, a word of outcry, reproach, or abuse in 1338 C.E.; see *Glossarium Mediae et Infimae Latinitatis* (Paris: Libraire des

sciences et des arts, 1938), 5:352c. The French "*merde*" is also listed as an interjection by Alan Hindley, whose *Old French-English Dictionary* [(Cambridge: Cambridge University Press, 2000), 421b] covers literary and nonliterary texts up to around 1350 C.E. The modern *Dictionnaire historique de la langue française* [ed. Alain Rey (Paris: Dictionnaires le Robert, 1993), 2:1227a] claims that "the word, in its uses as an interjection, has long served to express anger, scorn, indignation, refusal."

37. Possamaï-Pérez, *L'Ovide moralisé*, 867.
38. The exception in the *Ars minor* is in the very brief interjection section, where Donatus omits the question about how many attributes and instead formulates the question as, "What attribute does an interjection have?," to which the response is, "Only a meaning."
39. Gerson's use of the participle *incognita* instead of the "*incondita*" found in Donatus could be the result of manuscript variation.
40. John A. Alford, "The Grammatical Metaphor: A Survey of Its Use in the Middle Ages," *Speculum* 57, no. 4 (1982): 728–60.
41. Another brief treatment of the *Donatus moralizatus* occurs in Joseph Victor Le Clerc and Ernest Renan, *Histoire littéraire de la France au quatorzième siècle: Discours sur l'état des lettres* (Paris: Michel Lévy frères, 1864), 421–22.
42. Alford, "Grammatical Metaphor," 729.
43. Ibid., 729–36.
44. Ibid., 736–50.
45. Ibid., 749.
46. Ibid., 728; cites Paul Lehmann, *Die Parodie im Mittelalter* (Stuttgart: A. Hiersemann, 1963), 53, 108.
47. Cited in Alford, "Grammatical Metaphor," 735.
48. DM 839B.
49. Alford, "Grammatical Metaphor," 744–45.
50. Ibid., 746.
51. Ibid., 733; cites Gerald R. Owst, *Preaching in Medieval England: An Introduction to Sermon Manuscripts of the Period c. 1350–1450* (1926, 1965; repr. Cambridge and New York: Cambridge University Press, 2010), 329.
52. Alford, "Grammatical Metaphor," 734.
53. Ibid., 735.
54. In Thomas Marie Charland, *Artes praedicandi: Contribution à l'histoire de la rhétorique au moyen âge* (Paris: J. Vrin and Ottawa: Institut d'études médiévales, 1936), 395; cited in Alford, "Grammatical Metaphor," 735.
55. A point reiterated by Alford, "Grammatical Metaphor," 736.
56. Ibid., 731. For much more on the sexual moralization of grammar, see Jan Ziolkowski, *Alan of Lille's Grammar of Sex: The Meaning of Grammar to a Twelfth-Century Intellectual* (Cambridge, Mass.: Medieval Academy of America, 1985).
57. Alford, "Grammatical Metaphor," 733; cites "Erotischer Grammatikbetrieb," thirteenth-century Latin manuscript printed in Lehmann, *Parodie im Mittelalter*, 223.
58. Le Clerc and Renan, *Histoire littéraire de la France au quatorzième siècle*, 422; Charland, *Artes praedicandi*, cited in Alford, "Grammatical Metaphor," 736.
59. Alford, "Grammatical Metaphor," 736.
60. Ibid., 740.

4. *From the Names of God to the* Grammar of Hearts

1. See my Introduction for a discussion of Jauss and this concept of the "grammar of genre."
2. Edward W. Said, *Orientalism* (New York: Vintage/Random House, 1978), 3.
3. In this paradigm, the fall of the Abbasids in 1250 is a convenient starting point for a decline into decadence and decay, until the invasion of Egypt by Napoleon in 1798 brings "civilization" and modernization to the Islamic Middle East. A few examples here will point to a vigorous movement among historians to revise this decline view of Islamic history.

   For a challenge to standard models of gender relations in medieval Muslim societies, see Yossef Rapoport, *Marriage, Money and Divorce in Medieval Islamic Society* (Cambridge and New York: Cambridge University Press, 2005).

   For a fresh look at the legal treatment and status of women in Ottoman Egypt (sixteenth–eighteenth c.) as being "the 'slaves' of men," see Abdal-Rehim Abdal-Rahman Abdal-Rehim, "The Family and Gender Laws in Egypt During the Ottoman Period," in *Women, the Family, and Divorce Laws in Islamic History*, ed. Amira El Azhary Sonbol (Syracuse: Syracuse University Press, 1996), 96–111.

   For a critique of the idea of eighteenth-century social and economic decline, see Roger Owen, "The Middle East in the Eighteenth Century: An 'Islamic Society in Decline?' A Critique of Gibb and Bowen's Islamic Society and the West," *Review of Middle East Studies* 1 (1975): 101–12.

   For an attack on the standard Orientalist view that *ijtihād* ended around 900 C.E., see Wael Hallaq, "Was the Gate of Ijtihad Closed?" *International Journal of Middle East Studies* 16 (1984): 3–41.
4. Of invaluable help here are the historical works of Martin Tran Nguyen, *The Confluence and Construction of Traditions: Al-Qushayrī (d. 465/1072) and the Intersection of Qur'ānic Exegesis, Theology, and Sufism* (Ph.D. diss., Harvard University, 2009), and Ahmet T. Karamustafa, *Sufism: The Formative Period* (Berkeley: University of California Press, 2007). Nguyen's global look at Qushayrī in his time gives the kind of perspicacious perspective that we need more of in a field full of fragments of knowledge. The monograph version of this research has also come out: *Sufi Master and Qur'an Scholar: Abu'l-Qasim al-Qushayri and the Lata'if al-isharat* (London: Oxford University Press and The Institute of Ismaili Studies, 2012). Ahmet Karamustafa's book lends insightful analysis of the various religious, theological, cultural, and polemical currents at play in the development of Sufism around Qushayrī's time.
5. Nguyen notes that in the "adulatory introduction" in al-Fārisī's *Kitāb al-siyāq*, Qushayrī is named *imām, faqīh, mutakallim, uṣūlī, mufassir, adīb, naḥwī, kātib*, and *shā'ir*. "He brought together knowledge of the divine law with knowledge of true reality (*jama'a bayna 'ilm al-sharī'a wa-'ilm al-ḥaqīqa*)"; Nguyen, *Confluence and Construction*, 40–41.
6. Ibid., 54. *Ḥadīth* refers to the sayings and traditions of the Prophet Muhammad.
7. Ibid., 100.
8. Ibid., 36–39.
9. Karamustafa, *Sufism*, 106.
10. Ibid., Chap. 1, "The Sufis of Baghdad," 1ff. For general overviews of Sufism, see Alexander Knysh, *Islamic Mysticism: A Short History* (Leiden: Brill, 2000); Carl Ernst, *The*

Shambhala Guide to Sufism (Boston: Shambhala, 1997); Annemarie Schimmel, *Mystical Dimensions of Islam* (Chapel Hill: University of North Carolina Press, 1975).

11. *Zuhd* has two primary senses in Islamic discourse: (1) renunciation—that is, spiritual detachment from the things of this world; and (2) bodily mortification or deprivation. For fuller discussion, see "Zuhd (a.)," in *Encyclopaedia of Islam*, ed P. Bearman et al., 2nd ed. (Leiden: Brill 2011), Brill Online, Harvard University, http://www.brillonline.nl/subscriber/ entry?entry=islam_SIM-8201; accessed 4 April 2011.
12. Richard W. Bulliet, *The Patricians of Nishapur: A Study of Medieval Islamic Social History* (Cambridge, Mass.: Harvard University Press, 1972), 41–42; cited in Nguyen, *Confluence and Construction*, 65–66.
13. Karamustafa, *Sufism*, 96–97.
14. Nguyen, *Confluence and Construction*, 122.
15. Ibid., 173.
16. Ibid., 144.
17. Ibid., 173–74.
18. Karamustafa, *Sufism*, 97.
19. Ibid., 106.
20. Ibid.
21. Ibid., 96–97.
22. Ibid., 106.
23. ʿAbd al-Karīm al-Qushayrī, *Al-Risāla al-Qushayrīyah fī ʿilm al-taṣawwuf*, ed. Muḥammad ʿAbd al-Raḥmān al-Marʿashlī (Beirut: Dār Iḥyā al-Turāth al-ʿArabī: Muʿassasat al-Tarīkh al-ʿArabī, 1998). I will hereafter refer to this edition of the Arabic text as *Risāla*.
24. "Risāla," in *Encyclopaedia of Islam*, http://referenceworks.brillonline.com/entries/encyclopaedia-of-islam-2/risala-COM_0926; accessed 22 February 2012.
25. A. Arazi and H. Ben-Shammay, the authors of the *Encyclopaedia of Islam* article, give an example of this phenomenon: "Thus the original title of the *riḥla* of Ibn Faḍlān is nothing other than *Risālat ibn Faḍlān* (ed. Sāmī Dahān [Damascus: 1379/1959]), no doubt on account of its unedited nature and the impossibility of integrating it into one of the conventional literary categories"; "Risāla," in *Encyclopaedia of Islam* (2012).
26. Jawid A. Mojaddedi, *The Biographical Tradition in Sufism: The "Ṭabaqāt" Genre from al-Sulamī to Jāmī* (Richmond, UK: Curzon, 2001), 107.
27. Abū l-Qāsim ʿAbd al-Karim ibn Hawāzin al-Qushayrī, *Al-Qushayrī's Epistle on Sufism: Al-Risala al-Qushayrīyya fi ʿilm al-tasawwuf*, trans. Alexander D. Knysh (Reading: Garnet, 2007); al-Qushayrī, *Principles of Sufism*, trans. B. R. von Schlegell (Berkeley: Mizan, 1992); al-Qushayrī, *Sufi Book of Spiritual Ascent (al-Risala al-Qushayrīyya)*, trans. Rabia Harris, ed. Laleh Bakhtiar (Chicago: ABC Group International, 1997); al-Qushayrī, *Das Sendschreiben al-Qušayrīs über das Sufitum*, trans. Richard Gramlich (Stuttgart: F. Steiner Verlag Wiesbaden, 1989); al-Qushayrī, *Kuşeyrî risalesi*, trans. Süleyman Uludağ (Istanbul: Dergâh yayınları, 1978). I will hereafter give references only to the English translation of Knysh (and to al-Marʿashlī's Arabic edition, cited previously).
28. See "Mukhṭaṣar," in *Encyclopaedia of Islam*, http://referenceworks.brillonline.com/entries/encyclopaedia-of-islam-2/mukhtasar-COM_0792; accessed 22 February 2012.
29. Mojaddedi, *Biographical Tradition*, 101.

30. Karamustafa, *Sufism*, 98.
31. Mojaddedi, *Biographical Tradition*, 105.
32. Ibid., 101.
33. Mojaddedi, "Legitimizing Sufism in al-Qushayri's 'Risala,'" *Studia Islamica* 90 (2000): 39.
34. Mojaddedi, *Biographical Tradition*, 117 and 122.
35. Ibid., 122–23. The term *wara*ʿ might better be translated as "religious scrupulousness."
36. Andrew Rippin, "Tafsīr (a.)," in *Encyclopaedia of Islam*, http://www.brillonline.nl/ subscriber/entry?entry=islam_SIM-7294; accessed 7 April 2011. Though not covering the last thirty years of scholarship, Rippin's overview of the burgeoning field of *tafsīr* studies is still valuable: Rippin, "The Present Status of Tafsir Studies," *Muslim World* 72 (1982): 224–38.
37. Gerhard Böwering, *The Mystical Vision of Existence in Classical Islam: The Qur'ānic Hermeneutics of the Ṣūfī Sahl at-Tustarī (d. 283/896)* (Berlin: Walter de Gruyter, 1980), 136.
38. Ibid., 137.
39. Ibid., 110.
40. Böwering, *Sufi Hermeneutics in Medieval Islam* (Tokyo: Sophia University, 1987), 2–4.
41. Ibid., 8.
42. Cf. Nguyen, *Sufi Master and Qur'an Scholar: Abu'l-Qasim al-Qushayri and the* Lataʾif al-isharat (London: Oxford University Press and Institute of Ismaili Studies, 2012).
43. Böwering, "The Qur'ān Commentary of Al-Sulamī," *Islamic Studies Presented to Charles J. Adams*, ed. Wael B. Hallaq and Donald P. Little (Leiden: Brill, 1991), 50; cited in Nguyen, *Confluence and Construction*, 267–68.
44. Nguyen, *Confluence and Construction*, 269–70.
45. Böwering, *Sufi Hermeneutics*, 8.
46. Nguyen, *Confluence and Construction*, 327.
47. Annabel Keeler, "Sufi Tafsir as a Mirror: Al-Qushayrī the *Murshid* in his *Lata'if al-isharat*," *Journal of Quranic Studies* 8, no. 1 (2006): 4.
48. Louis Gardet, "*Dhikr*," in *Encyclopaedia of Islam*, http://www.brillonline.nl/ subscriber/ entry?entry=islam_COM-0162; accessed 23 April 2010.
49. *Risāla* 295–30; Knysh, *Islamic Mysticism*, 232–36.
50. *Risāla* 296.
51. Ibid.
52. Ibid.; Knysh, *Islamic Mysticism*, 233; the translation is Knysh's.
53. Gardet, "Al-Asmāʾ al- Ḥusnā," in *Encyclopaedia of Islam*, http://www.brillonline.nl/ subscriber/entry?entry=islam_COM-0070; accessed 23 April 2010.
54. Gerhard Böwering names the sources of those lists in "Daniel Gimaret: *Les noms divins en Islam; Exégèse lexicographique et théologique*," *International Journal of Middle East Studies* 22, no. 2 (May 1990): 247–49. Gimaret discusses them at length in *Les noms divins en Islam: Exégèse lexicographique et théologique* (Paris: Editions du Cerf, 1988), 55–68. The sources of the Divine names are: "(1) Walid (b. Muslim al-Dimashqi, d. 810); (2) ʿAbd al-ʿAzīz (b. al-Ḥusayn b. al-Tarjamān, a contemporary); (3) Zuhayr (b. Muhammad al-Tamimi, d. 779)—all three traced back to Abu Hurayra; and (4) al-Aʿmash (Sulayman b. Mihran, d. 765), which goes back to ʿAli"; Böwering, "Daniel Gimaret," 248. Qushayrī

follows Walīd's order with the exception of substituting Allāh and *huwa* for *al-raḥmān* and *al-raḥīm*; Gimaret, *Les noms divins en Islam*, 25.

55. John A. Morrow and Luis Alberto Vittor, "The Most Beautiful Names: The Philosophical Foundation of the Allāh Lexicon," in *Arabic, Islām, and the Allāh Lexicon: How Language Shapes Our Conception of God*, ed. John A. Morrow (Lewiston, N.Y.: Edwin Mellen Press, 2006), 254.
56. Ibid., 256–57.
57. Fritz Meier, "Qushayrī's *Tartīb al-sulūk*," in *Essays on Islamic Piety and Mysticism*, trans. John O'Kane (Leiden: Brill, 1999), 93–134; originally published as "Qušayrīs *Tartīb al-sulūk*," *Oriens* 16 (1963): 1–39.
58. Ibid., 93.
59. Ibid., 94.
60. *Risāla* 476–84; Knysh, *Islamic Mysticism*, 403–10. Knysh translates the section title as "Spiritual advice for Sufi novices" and notes that *waṣiyya* here could also be translated as "instruction," "bequest," and "counsel"; Knysh, *Islamic Mysticism*, 403n824.
61. Meier, "Qushayrī's *Tartīb al-sulūk*," 96. Wherever Meier translated *dhikr* as "recollection" or a derivative thereof, I have substituted "invocation" or a derivative thereof.
62. Ibid., 97.
63. Meier clarifies that the *Tartīb* is not really a book and is not necessarily Qushayrī's. A number of linguistic features indicate that the work is rather a transcription of oral instruction. Moreover, Meier mentions a number of arguments for and against the attribution of the *Tartīb* to Qushayrī ("Qushayrī's *Tartīb al-sulūk*," 99–102) and concludes that "in order to form a final judgement on this question [of the linguistic peculiarities of the *Tartīb*] and the question of authenticity, the other writings of Qushayrī besides the *Risāla* would have to be consulted, all of which [as of 1999] unfortunately remain unedited" (102). For our purposes, we presume Qushayrī to be in some sense author of this text, which in any case is helpful to our understanding of significant features of his religious world.
64. Ibid., 101.
65. Meier, "Qushayrī's *Tartīb al-sulūk*," 122 (English); 108 (Arabic).
66. Ibid., 123 (English); 109 (Arabic).
67. Ibid., 124 (English); 111 (Arabic).
68. Ibid., 125 (English); 112 (Arabic).
69. Ibid., 126 (English); 112 (Arabic).
70. Ibid., 127 (English); 115 (Arabic). As discussed previously, this word *ḥaqq* and its derivatives refer to truth and ultimate reality. *Al-Ḥaqq* is, however, a name of God, which we might render as "the True One" or "the Ultimate Reality."
71. Ibid., 132 (English); 120 (Arabic).
72. Meier, "Khurasan and the End of Classical Sufism," in *Essays on Islamic Piety and Mysticism*, 190n1; originally published as "Ḫurāsān und das Ende der klassischen ṣūfik," in *Atti del convegno internazionale sul tema: La Persia nel Medioevo (Roma, 31 marzo-5 aprile 1970)* (Rome: Academia Nazionale dei Lincei, 1971), 545–70.
73. *Risāla* 297; Knysh, *Islamic Mysticism*, 233.
74. See M. Muranyi, "Ṣaḥāba," in *Encyclopaedia of Islam*, http://www.brillonline.nl/ subscriber/entry?entry=islam_SIM-6459; accessed 5 June 2010.

75. Meier, "Qushayrī's *Tartīb al-sulūk*," 108; my rendering from the Arabic.
76. The entire discussion evokes the discernment of spirits that St. Ignatius of Loyola (d. 1556) develops in the Spiritual Exercises; cf. Timothy M. Gallagher, *Spiritual Consolation: An Ignatian Guide for the Greater Discernment of Spirits* (New York: Crossroad, 2007).
77. Meier, "Qushayrī's *Tartīb al-sulūk*," 128 (English); 115–16 (Arabic).
78. Meier, "Khurasan and the End of Classical Sufism," 217.
79. Daniel Gimaret makes a persuasive argument that these titles refer to the same work. Despite Gimaret calling al-Ḥalawānī's 1969 edition "misérable" and "non critique," it is that edition, plus al-Ḥalawānī's 1986 edition, that I have been able to access in the course of this research. Gimaret's book begins to fill a lacuna in scholarly attention to the subject of the ninety-nine names of God. He notes that, when writing the *Encyclopaedia of Islam* article on the topic, Gardet did not have access to a good number of relevant texts, the most important being Fakhr al-Dīn al-Rāzī's *Lawāmiʿ al-bayyināt*.
80. Abū Ḥamīd al-Ghazālī, *Al-Maqṣid al-asnā fī sharḥ maʿānī asmāʾ Allāh al-ḥusnā*, ed. Faḍluh Shahādah (Beirut: Dār al-Mashriq, 1971); al-Ghazālī, *The Ninety-Nine Beautiful Names of God*, trans. David B. Burrell and Nazih Daher (Cambridge: Islamic Texts Society, 1992).
81. So suggests Daniel Gimaret in *Les noms divins*, 24. Gimaret bases this suggestion on what works are covered in the two essential reference works, Carl Brockelmann, *Geschichte der arabischen Litteratur* (Leiden: Brill, 1943@-49) and Fuat Sezgin, *Geschichte des arabischen Schriftums* (Leiden: Brill, 1967@-2015).
82. Böwering, in "Daniel Gimaret," 248, names a number of these, which Gimaret treats in more detail: "the early philological treatises of al-Zajjaj [al-Zajjāj] (d. 923) and al-Zajjaji [al-Zajjājī] (d. 949)," "the lost treatises of al-Mubarrad (d. 898), Abu ʿAli al-Jubbaʾi [Abū ʿAlī al-Jubbāʾī] (d. 915), and Abu Zayd al-Balkhi [Abū Zayd al-Balkhī] (d. 934)," and "great treatises influenced by Ashʿari [Ashʿarī] thought, such as the *Tafsīr asmāʾ Allāh al-ḥusnā* of Abu Mansur al-Baghdadi [Abū Manṣūr al-Baghdādī] (d. 1037), the *Kitāb al-asmāʾ wa-al-ṣifāt* of Abu Bakr al-Bayhaqi [Abū Bakr al-Bayhaqī] (d. 1066, and [Qushayrī's treatise]."
83. Abū l-Qāsim ʿAbd al-Karīm al-Qushayrī, *Sharḥ ʾasmāʾ Allāh al-ḥusnā*, ed. Aḥmad ʿAbd al-Munʿim ʿAbd al-Salām al-Ḥalawānī (al-Qāhirah [Cairo]: Maṭbaʿāt al-Amānah, 1969), 21; al-Qushayrī, *Sharḥ ʾasmāʾ Allāh al-ḥusnā*, 2nd ed., ed. Aḥmad ʿAbd al-Munʿim ʿAbd al-Salām al-Ḥalawānī (Beirut: Dār Āzal, 1986), 18; al-Qushayrī, *Sharḥ ʾasmāʾ Allāh al-ḥusnā*, ed. Ṭāhā ʿAbd al-Raʾūf Saʿd and Saʿd Ḥasan Muḥammad ʿAlī (al-Qāhirah [Cairo]: Dār al-Ḥaram lil-Turāth, 2001). All subsequent references will be to al-Ḥalawānī's 1986 edition.
84. Qushayrī, *Sharḥ*, 19.
85. Ibid., 20.
86. "The most beautiful names belong to Allah: so call on him by them; but shun such men as use profanity in his names: for what they do, they will soon be requited."
87. J. van Ess, "Tashbīh wa-Tanzīh," in *Encyclopaedia of Islam*, http://www.brillonline.nl/subscriber/entry?entry=islam_COM-1190; accessed 24 May 2010.
88. W. Madelung, "Mulḥid," in *Encyclopaedia of Islam*, http://www.brillonline.nl/subscriber/entry?entry=islam_SIM-5487; accessed 24 May 2010.

89. Qushayrī, *Sharḥ*, 21.
90. Yusuf Ali's translation; Yusuf Abdullah Ali, *The Meaning of the Holy Qur'ān* (Beltsville, Md.: Amana, 1999).
91. Qushayrī, *Sharḥ*, 56.
92. Ibid.
93. R. Sellheim, "Al-Khalīl b. Aḥmad b. ʿAmr b. Tamīm al-Farāhīdī al-Azdī al-Yaḥmadī al-Baṣrī Abū ʿAbd al-Raḥmān," *Encyclopaedia of Islam*, http://www.brillonline.nl/subscriber/entry?entry=islam_SIM-4161; accessed 5 June 2010.
94. Qushayrī, *Sharḥ*, 56–57.
95. Ibid., 57.
96. William C. Chittick, *The Sufi Path of Knowledge: Ibn al-ʿArabi's Metaphysics of Imagination* (Albany, N.Y.: SUNY Press, 1989), 283; Chittick, *Imaginal Worlds: Ibn al-ʿArabī and the Problem of Religious Diversity* (Albany, N.Y.: SUNY Press, 1994), 45; see also Gimaret, *Les noms divins en islam: Exégèse lexicographique et théologique* (Paris: Editions du Cerf, 1988), 24–27. According to Gimaret (24), Massignon attributed this idea principally to Abū Bakr al-Wāsiṭī (d. 331/942).
97. Following Ḥalawānī's reading, which has *liḥāf* here rather than that of Saʿd and ʿAlī's reading, which has *ilḥāf*.
98. Qushayrī, *Sharḥ*, 57.
99. Ibid.
100. Qushayrī, *Sharḥ*, 57–58.
101. Ibid., 58.
102. Ibid.
103. Ibid.
104. Qushayrī, *Sharḥ*, 71.
105. Ibid., 72.
106. Ibid.

5. *Forming Spiritual* Fuṣaḥāʾ: *Qushayrī's Advanced* Grammar of Hearts

1. ʿAbd al-Karīm al-Qushayrī, *Naḥw al-qulūb al-kabīr*, ed. Ibrāhīm Basyūnī and Aḥmad ʿAlam al-Dīn al-Jundī (al-Qāhirah [Cairo]: Maktabat ʿAlam al-Fikr, 1994) 41–43; hereafter, this primary text will be referred to in these notes as "NQ." For the sake of convenience, in addition to page numbers, the section numbers assigned by editors Basyūnī and al-Jundī will also be given throughout the main text and in these footnotes. For example, this quotation is of section 6 on pages 41–43, so it will be cited as NQ 6, 41–43.
2. ʿAmr ibn ʿUthmān ibn Qanbar Sībawayhi, *Al-Kitāb*, ed. Imīl Badīʾ Yaʿqūb (Beirut: Dar al-Kotob al-Ilmiyah, 1999).
3. James Winston Morris, *The Reflective Heart: Discovering Spiritual Intelligence in Ibn ʿArabī's "Meccan Illuminations"* (Louisville: Fons Vitae, 2005), 45–100.
4. Ibid., 48.
5. Ibid., 49.
6. Ibid., 50.
7. Ibid., 52–53.

8. Geoffrey Pullum has written a number of highly lucid and humorous pieces that treat this binary, especially as it relates to Strunk and White's (in)famous *Elements of Style* and contemporary debates on "Ebonics"; see, for example, his "Ideology, Power, and Linguistic Theory," the unpublished revised text of his talk at the 2004 Modern Language Association conference: https://people.ucsc.edu/~pullum/MLA2004.pdf; accessed 6 December 2010.
9. M. G. Carter, *Sībawayhi* (London: I. B. Tauris, 2004), 135.
10. Jonathan Owens, "The Grammatical Tradition and Arabic Language Teaching: A View from Here," in *Investigating Arabic: Current Parameters in Analysis and Learning*, ed. Alaa Elgibali (Leiden: Brill, 2005), 105.
11. Ibid., 106.
12. Carter, *Sībawayhi*, 145.
13. Troupeau's *Encyclopaedia of Islam* article on "*Naḥw*" provides a lengthier outline of the subtopics within a traditional Arabic grammar; Gérard Troupeau, "Naḥw," in *Encyclopaedia of Islam*, 2nd ed., ed. P. Bearman et al. (Leiden: Brill, 2011); Brill Online, Harvard University, http://www.brillonline.nl/subscriber/entry?entry=islam_COM-0838; accessed 4 April 2011.
14. Ibid.
15. Carter, "Sībawayhi," in *Encyclopedia of Islam*, http://www.brillonline.nl/ subscriber/entry?entry=islam_COM-1068; accessed 15 May 2007.
16. The term *ḥukm* is notoriously difficult to translate. One suggestion is "part played or to be played." Others are "activity" and "standing"; cf. A. M. Goichon and H. Fleisch, "Ḥukm," in *Encyclopaedia of Islam*, http://www.brillonline.nl/subscriber/entry?entry=islam_COM-0298; accessed 7 May 2011.
17. ʿAbd al-Karīm al-Qushayrī, *Naḥw al-qulūb al-ṣaghīr*, ed. Ahmad ʿAlam al-Dīn al-Jundī (Libya: Al-Dār al-ʿArabiyah lil-Kitāb, 1977), 127–30.
18. Ibid., 130.
19. Ibid., 131.
20. Francesco Chiabotti has made the greatest contribution to date on this text; see his "*Naḥw al-qulūb al-ṣaġīr:* La 'grammaire des coeurs' de ʿAbd al-Karīm al-Qušayrī," *Bulletin d'études orientales* 58 (September 2009), published online 1 September 2010, http://beo.revues.org/83. The editor of the printed version of *Naḥw al-qulūb al-ṣaghīr*, Ahmad ʿAlam al-Dīn al-Jundī, also made a significant contribution to understanding the relationship of Ibn ʿAjība's text and Qushayrī's *Naḥw al-qulūb al-ṣaghīr* in the scholarly apparatus accompanying his edition of Qushayrī's text.
21. NQ 1, 37.
22. J. W. Fück, "Abu 'l- Aswad al- Du'alī," in *Encyclopaedia of Islam*, http://www.brillonline.nl/ subscriber/entry?entry=islam_SIM-0159; accessed 26 March 2010.
23. NQ 1, 37.
24. Qushayrī, *Al-Risāla al-Qushayrīyya fī ʿilm al-taṣawwuf*, ed. Muḥammad ʿAbd al-Raḥmān al-Marʿashlī (Beirut: Dār Iḥyā al-Turāth al-ʿArabī: Muʾassasat al-Tarīkh al-ʿArabī, 1998), 126–28. A complete English translation has been provided by Alexander D. Knysh, *Al-Qushyari's Epistle on Sufism* (Reading: Garnet, 2007). Barbara R. von Schlegell has also produced a partial translation, *Principles of Sufism* (Berkeley: Mizan, 1992).

25. Knysh, *Al-Qushyari's Epistle on Sufism*, 87. The Arabic of this passage appears in al-Marʿashlī's edition (127).
26. On these groups and their relationships, see Ahmet Karamustafa, *Sufism: The Formative Period* (Edinburgh: Edinburgh University Press, 2007). For direct discussion of the pre-history of the Sufis, see especially 1–7. He references as the most comprehensive recent source for this topic Christopher Melchert, "Baṣran Origins of Classical Sufism," *Der Islam* 82 (2005): 221–40; see also Jacqueline Chabbi, "Remarques sur le développement historique des mouvements ascétiques et mystiques au Khurasan: IIIe/IXe siècle—IVe/Xe siècle," *Studia Islamica* 46 (1977): 5–72; Wilfred Madelung, *Religious Trends in Early Islamic Iran* (Albany, N.Y.: Bibliotheca Persica, 1988), 39–53; and Richard Bulliet, *The Patricians of Nishapur: A Study of Medieval Islamic Social History* (Cambridge, Mass.: Harvard University Press, 1972), 41–42.
27. NQ 2, 38.
28. Sībawayhi's *Kitab* translated in Kees Versteegh, *Landmarks in Linguistic Thought*, vol. 3, *The Arabic Linguistic Tradition* (London: Routledge, 1997), 27.
29. Sībawayhi, *Al-Kitāb*, 1:40.
30. Pierre Lory, "ʿAbd al-Razzāq al-Kāshānī," in *Encyclopaedia of Islam*, http://www.brillonline.nl/subscriber/entry?entry=ei3_COM-22929; accessed 20 February 2010.
31. ʿAbd al-Razzāq al-Qāshāni, *A Glossary of Sufi Technical Terms*, trans. Nabil Safwat, ed. David Pendlebury (London: Octagon, 1991), 5.
32. NQ 2, 38.
33. NQ 3, 39.
34. NQ 4, 39.
35. NQ 5, 40.
36. Knysh, *Al-Qushyari's Epistle on Sufism*, 87.
37. Ibid.
38. Ibid.
39. Al-Qāshānī, *A Glossary of Sufi Technical Terms*, 58.
40. Ibid.
41. Knysh, *Al-Qushyari's Epistle on Sufism*, 79–81; Qushayrī, *Al-Risāla*, ed. Marʿashlī, 118–20.
42. Knysh, *Al-Qushyari's Epistle on Sufism*, 80; Qushayrī, *Al-Risāla*, ed. Marʿashlī, 120.
43. NQ 6, 41.
44. Ibid.
45. See note 24.
46. *Zuhd* is apparently a term that can be applied generally to the renunciatory movements in the second/eighth to fourth/tenth centuries; see Karamustafa, *Sufism*, 1.
47. NQ 6, 42.
48. NQ 6, 43.
49. NQ 7, 44.
50. NQ 7, 44–45.
51. NQ 7, 45.
52. Ibid.
53. I read the text here as *yasṭaʿ*, not *yasṭaḥ*.
54. NQ 7, 45.

55. NQ 7, 46.
56. Ibid.
57. NQ 8, 47.
58. NQ 9, 48.
59. NQ 10, 49.
60. Al-Qushayrī, *Al-Risāla*, ed. Marʿashlī, 143–45; Knysh, *Al-Qushyari's Epistle on Sufism*, 100–102.
61. NQ 10, 49.
62. Ibid.
63. Ibid.
64. Ibid.
65. NQ 11, 50.
66. Ibid.
67. NQ 12, 51.
68. Al-Shiblī, ʾAbū Bakr Dulaf b. Jaḥdar (d. 945); see F. Sobieroj, "al-Shiblī, Abu Bakr Dulaf b. Djaḥdar," in *Encyclopaedia of Islam*, http://www.brillonline.nl/ subscriber/ entry?entry=islam_SIM-6926; accessed 26 March 2010.
69. NQ 12, 51.
70. Basyūnī and al-Jundī read this as referring to anyone "who has a connection with this science, the science of Sufism"; NQ 52n12.
71. NQ 12, 52–53.
72. The life's work of Louis Massignon was devoted to this notable character from early Sufism; Massignon, *La assion de Husyan Ibn Mansūr Hallāj: Martyr mystique de l'Islam, exécuté à Bagdad le d́b mars ôd́d́: Étude d'histoire religieuse*, vols. 1–4 (Paris: Gallimard, 1975).
73. NQ 13, 54.
74. NQ14–16.
75. NQ 14, 55. Basyūni and al-Jundī (n. 4) note that in the *Risāla*, Qushayrī attributes this saying to hadith scholar Sufyān ibn ʿUyayna (d. 811); see Knysh, *Al-Qushyari's Epistle on Sufism*, 156; al-Qushayrī, *Al-Risāla*, ed. Marʿashlī, 209. There appears to be a typographical problem with this line as printed on p. 55 of NQ, while the version on p. 245 (followed here) is unproblematic. On Sufyān ibn ʿUyayna, see Susan A. Spectorsky, "Sufyān b. ʿUyayna b. Maymūn al-Hilālī," in *Encyclopaedia of Islam*, http://www.brillonline.nl/subscriber/ entry?entry=islam_SIM-7131; accessed, 26 March 2010.
76. NQ 15, 56.
77. Ibid.
78. NQ 16, 57–58.
79. NQ 17, 59.
80. NQ 21, 63.
81. NQ 22, 64.
82. See note 24.
83. For the beginning of a bibliography on this tremendously important topic in *kalām*, see Claude Cahen, "Kasb," in *Encyclopaedia of Islam*, http://www.brillonline.nl/ subscriber/ entry?entry=islam_COM-0457; accessed 17 March 2010.
84. NQ 27, 69.

85. Ibid.
86. "Zayd" and "ʿAmr" are men's names that Arabic grammarians often use in example sentences.
87. NQ 44, 87.
88. Ibid.

6. The Fruits of Comparison: Constructing a Theology of Grammar

1. Paul Ricoeur, "Metaphor and the Main Problem of Hermeneutics," in *A Ricoeur Reader: Reflection and Imagination*, ed. Mario J. Valdés (Toronto and Buffalo: University of Toronto Press, 1991), 314.
2. Ibid., 309.
3. Ibid., 308.
4. Du Pin 837C–838A; NQ 21, 63.
5. Matthew 22:34–40; Luke 10:25–28; Mark 12:28–34.
6. As noted in the Introduction, Bonaventure, whom Carpenter compares with Bhartṛhari, is not so profoundly linguistic or at all grammatical in his theology of the threefold Word. Though Bonaventure's starting point is the *verbum Dei* revealed in the Prologue to John's Gospel, he does not—at least by Carpenter's account—profoundly engage the philosophy of language or other language sciences as do other examples of Christian reflection on the *verbum Dei*, some of which we will see later in this chapter. There is, then, in this regard a greater parallel between Gerson and Qushayrī than between Bonaventure and Bhartṛhari; see David Carpenter, *Revelation, History, and the Dialogue of Religions: A Study of Bhartṛhari and Bonaventure* (Maryknoll, N.Y.: Orbis, 1995).
7. See a fuller discussion in the Introduction; John Frow, *Genre* (London and New York: Routledge, 2006); cf. Jacques Derrida, "The Law of Genre," trans. Avital Ronell, *Critical Inquiry* 7, no. 1 (Autumn 1980).
8. Karl Rahner, *Foundation of Christian Faith: An Introduction to the Idea of Christianity*, trans. William V. Dych (1978; repr. New York: Crossroad, 1999), 222–23; cited in the Introduction of this volume.
9. Abū Ḥamīd al-Ghazālī, *Al-Maqṣad al-asnā fī sharḥ maʿānī asmāʾ Allāh al-ḥusnā*, ed. Faḍlah Shahādah (Beirut: Dār al-Mashriq, 1971); al-Ghazzālī, *The Ninety-Nine Beautiful Names of God*, trans. David B. Burrell and Nazih Daher (Cambridge: Islamic Texts Society, 1992).
10. Frow, *Genre*, 19.
11. Ibid., 10.
12. Ricoeur, "Metaphor and the Main Problem of Hermeneutics," 309.
13. NQ 37.
14. NQ 38.
15. Some sections of the text treat multiple spiritual topics and thus are accounted for under multiple headings or subheadings in my enumeration.
16. See Ferdinand de Saussure, *Course in General Linguistics*, ed. C. Bally, A. Sechehaye, and A. Riedlinger, trans. Roy Harris (Chicago: Open Court), 88.
17. James Winston Morris, *The Reflective Heart: Discovering Spiritual Intelligence in Ibn ʿArabī's "Meccan Illuminations"* (Louisville: Fons Vitae, 2005), 54.

18. Ibid., 63.
19. Cited in ibid., 99.
20. NQ 1, 37.
21. NQ 38.
22. As noted previously, *murīd* literally means "the ardent desirer" and is a common term used to describe the Sufi novice, who is eager to gain the esoteric knowledge of the spiritual wayfarer.
23. Kees Versteegh, *The Arabic Linguistic Tradition* (London: Routledge, 1997), 107.
24. Versteegh, *Arabic Grammar and Qur'ānic Exegesis in Early Islam* (Leiden and New York: Brill, 1993).
25. Versteegh, *Landmarks in Linguistic Thought*, vol.3, *The Arabic Linguistic Tradition* (London: Routledge, 1997), 42.
26. Hans-Georg Gadamer, *Truth and Method*, trans. Joel Weinsheimer and Donald G. Marshall (Continuum: New York, 2004); see especially Part 3, "The Ontological Shift of Hermeneutics Guided by Language," 383ff.
27. Ibid., 420.
28. Ibid., 421.
29. Ibid., 420.
30. Ibid., 423. For classification of *De natura verbi intellectus* as wrongly attributed to Thomas, see Jean-Pierre Torrell, *Saint Thomas Aquinas*, vol. 1, *The Person and His Work*, trans. Robert Royal (1996; repr. Washington, D.C.: The Catholic University of America Press, 2005), 360.
31. Gadamer, *Truth and Method*, 425.
32. David Tracy, *The Analogical Imagination* (New York: Crossroad, 1981) 105.
33. Ibid.
34. Ibid., 102; cites Gadamer, *Truth and Method*, 253–58.
35. Ricoeur, "Phenomenology and Hermeneutics," in *Essays in Hermeneutics*, vol. 2, *From Text to Action*, trans. Kathleen Blarney and John B. Thompson (Evanston, Ill.: Northwestern University Press, 1991), 95.
36. Ibid., 2:93.
37. Ibid., 2:95.
38. Ricoeur, "Metaphor and the Main Problem of Hermeneutics," in *A Ricoeur Reader: Reflection and Imagination*, ed. Mario J. Valdés (Toronto and Buffalo: University of Toronto Press, 1991), 314; originally published translation by David Pellauer in *New Literary History* 6, no. 1 (Autumn 1974): 95–110. Ricoeur's French original: "La Métaphore et le problème central de l'herméneutique (Résumé et summary), special issue *On Metaphor, Revue philosophique de Louvain* 70 (February 1972): 93–112, 115.
39. Graham Ward's book *Barth, Derrida and the Language of Theology* (Cambridge: Cambridge University Press, 1995) is an important contribution to such a project. Ward's book is exemplary in its detailed engagement with philosophy of language (especially *Sprachphilosophie* and *Redephilosophie*), postmodern theory (especially Derrida's and Levinas's), and theological classics (most notably Karl Barth's *Church Dogmatics*). His interdisciplinary approach draws special attention to how the language of theology discloses the necessity of a renewed theology of language for today. Both Barth and Derrida point to how the tropes of religious and theological texts raise

questions with a special urgency regarding the very nature of the theological enterprise and the inevitability of theology reflexively critiquing its own discourse.

40. Martin Heidegger, *Being and Time*, trans. John Macquarrie and Edward Robinson (New York: Harper and Row, 1962), 62. Ward is among the most important heralds announcing this convergence and welcoming its arrival to contemporary theology and cultural studies. I join him in this announcement and welcome.
41. Ward's two books that I have cited in this chapter make this point astoundingly clear. Besides *Barth, Derrida and the Language of Theology*, his *Theology and Contemporary Critical Theory* (2nd ed. [New York: St. Martin's, 2000]) is especially perspicacious in drawing out the theological implications of contemporary theory.

Appendix. Translation of Jean Gerson's Moralized Grammar

This translation of Jean Gerson's *Donatus moralizatus* is based on the Latin text *Opera omnia*, vol. 4, ed. Louis Ellis Du Pin (Antwerp: 1706; repr. Hildesheim and New York: Olms, 1987), cols. 835–44; see also Glorieux's edition in Jean Gerson, *Oeuvres complètes*, ed. Palémon Glorieux (Paris: Desclée, 1960), 9:689–700.

1. Gerson uses two different verbs, *moechari* and *adulterare*, that are synonymous with the meaning of committing adultery. The Vulgate has these as "*non moechaberis*" and "*non concupisces domum proximi tui nec desiderabis uxorem eius*."

INDEX

Comparative Theology: Thinking Across Traditions / *Loye Ashton and John Thatamanil, series editors*

Hyo-Dong Lee, *Spirit, Qi, and the Multitude: A Comparative Theology for the Democracy of Creation*

Michelle Voss Roberts, *Tastes of the Divine: Hindu and Christian Theologies of Emotion*

Michelle Voss Roberts (ed.), *Comparing Faithfully: Insights for Systematic Theological Reflection*

F. Dominic Longo, *Spiritual Grammar: Genre and the Saintly Subject in Islam and Christianity*

CPSIA information can be obtained
at www.ICGtesting.com
Printed in the USA
FFHW021605240419
51986735-57389FF

9 780823 283699